Contents

MR/CJK/071100
7th November 2000

The Royal
Liverpool
Children's
Inquiry

3rd Floor
Norwich House
Water Street
Liverpool
L2 8TA

Chairman   Michael Redfern QC
Secretary   Keith Smith

Rt Hon Alan Milburn MP
Secretary of State for Health

Dear Secretary of State

Royal Liverpool Children's Inquiry

We have pleasure in presenting our Report. It faithfully follows our Terms of Reference. We have endeavoured to produce a detailed narrative which speaks for itself.

We set ourselves the standard of leaving no stone unturned in our search for the truth and will leave it to the reader to determine whether or not we have succeeded.

Yours sincerely

Michael Redfern QC
Chairman

Dr Jean W Keeling
Consultant Paediatric
Pathologist

Mrs Elizabeth Powell
Chief Officer – Liverpool (Central &
Southern) Community Health Council

Return to an Address of the Honourable the House of Commons
dated 30 January 2001 for

The Royal Liverpool

Children's Inquiry

Report

ordered by The House of Commons *to be printed 30 January 2001*

HC12–II

£40

Chapter 1. Introduction & Terms of Reference

Contents

1.   Background to the Inquiry

1.1   The need for this Inquiry arose from the evidence to the Bristol Royal Infirmary Inquiry of Professor R H Anderson, Professor of Morphology at Great Ormond Street Hospital for Sick Children, on 7 September 1999. He spoke of the benefits of retaining hearts for the purpose of study and teaching referring to collections at various hospitals around the country. He identified the largest collection at Royal Liverpool Children's NHS Trust (Alder Hey Children's Hospital).

1.2   On 25 March 1999 Ms Donna Covey, Director of the Association of Community Health Councils for England and Wales, had written to the then Secretary of State for Health The Rt Hon Frank Dobson MP. She informed him that some hospitals routinely retained human organs and tissue following post mortem examination without having obtained the proper consent of relatives. She believed the practice to be unlawful and contrary to the provisions of the Human Tissue Act 1961. In his reply of 27 May 1999 Mr Dobson shared the concerns expressed by Ms Covey about the distress felt by relatives who were not informed about the process of post mortem examination, especially when organs were retained without their knowledge. He stated that he had written to several parents explaining what was being done to make sure that the practice did not continue.

1.3   The practice of removing and retaining organs following post mortem examination has been widespread in hospitals around the country and is of long-standing. The medical profession justifies retention for the purpose of medical education and research. Their approach has been paternalistic in the belief that parents or relatives would not wish to know about retention of organs and the uses to which they are put. In some cases consent has not been obtained at all, in others consent forms have been signed but without the relatives fully understanding what was involved. In the current climate of frankness and openness it should no longer be possible for organs to be retained without the knowledge or consent of the parents or relatives.

1.4   At Alder Hey the systematic full-scale removal of organs in the period 1988–1995, which we describe as 'the van Velzen years', compounded the problem. Preliminary post mortem reports were often left incomplete. The large majority of retained organs were not subjected to histological examination. Rarely do they appear to have been used for medical education or research purposes. The organs were largely ignored, with the consequence that there was a remorseless increase in the number of organs stored in containers. There was some limited use of the organs for research purposes. However, the large majority of organs remained untouched throughout the period.

2.   Announcement of Inquiry

2.1   On 3 December 1999 Lord Hunt, Parliamentary Under Secretary of State (Lords), established this Independent Confidential Inquiry under the provisions of Section 2 National Health Service Act 1977. The purpose was to investigate the removal, retention and disposal of human organs and tissues following post mortem examination at Alder Hey.

3.   Constitution of Inquiry Panel

3.1   The Inquiry Panel was appointed on 17 December 1999. The Chairman, Mr Michael Redfern QC, was assisted by Panel Members, Dr Jean Keeling, Consultant Paediatric Pathologist, Royal Hospital for Sick Children, Edinburgh and Mrs Elizabeth Powell, Chief Officer, Liverpool (Central & Southern) Community Health Council.

3.2   The Panel convened on 22 December 1999.

4.   Terms of Reference

4.1   The Terms of Reference were widely drawn. Essentially ours was a fact-finding Inquiry to establish what happened, to draw conclusions and thereafter to make recommendations. The following are our Terms of Reference.

- To inquire into the circumstances leading to the removal, retention and disposal of human tissue, including organs of the body, from children at the Royal Liverpool Children's NHS Trust (and its predecessor NHS organisations) who have undergone post mortem.

- To inquire into the extent to which the Human Tissue Act 1961 has been complied with.

- To examine professional practice and management action and systems, including what information, and in what form was given to the children's parents, or where relevant, other family members, in respect of the removal, retention and disposal of tissue.

- To examine the role of the NHS and other persons or bodies involved.

- To consider such other issues relating to the above matters as necessary.

- To report to Secretary of State by end of March 2000 and make such recommendations as are appropriate.

Note: *These terms of reference exclude tissue and organs removed with consent for transplant purposes.*

The reporting deadline was extended by Secretary of State in the light of early findings and the need for further detailed investigation.

4.2   We considered the removal and retention of organs prior to 1962. We concentrated on events from 1962 using the Human Tissue Act 1961 as the primary statutory provision relevant to the Inquiry. We also considered the Coroner's Act 1988 and the Coroner's Rules 1984.

5.   Opening

5.1   The Inquiry formally opened on 9 February 2000 at Norwich House, Water Street, Liverpool. The Chairman gave an opening statement and published Draft Procedures and Management Arrangements. The representatives of the parties appearing at the Inquiry had agreed the Draft Procedures by 18 February 2000.

6.   Inquiry Procedure

6.1   Secretary of State had determined that the Inquiry should be confidential and the process inquisitorial. This had the advantage of speed and efficiency and encouraged witnesses to be frank in their evidence.

6.2   All witnesses provided a signed written statement prior to giving evidence. A list of witnesses and a timetable was published and regularly updated.

6.3   Our duty was 'to make and direct all necessary searching investigations and to produce the witnesses in order to arrive at the truth' in accordance with The Royal Commission on Tribunals of Inquiry (CMMD 3121 1966 paragraph 28).

6.4   From the outset we strove to remain impartial and to afford a fair hearing to all concerned. We have been aware of the need to maintain balance and to avoid the pitfalls of hindsight and retrospect. We have positively encouraged freedom of speech. There has been neither witch-hunt nor whitewash.

7. Confidentiality of Witness Evidence

7.1 At the opening of the Inquiry on 9 February 2000 all parties were invited to give an undertaking of confidentiality in respect of all oral evidence and documents produced or referred to in the course of the Inquiry. This extended to witness statements which were not circulated to any other party. The undertaking required that all confidential material be returned to the Inquiry at its conclusion.

7.2 All witnesses appearing at the Inquiry were asked whether they understood the importance of their evidence even though they were not giving evidence on oath. The answer in all cases was affirmative. Upon completion of their evidence each witness was made aware that they remained bound by the confidentiality of the Inquiry.

7.3 Whilst the evidence was confidential it was always intended that our report would be public. For this reason we have had to summarise evidence in order to justify our conclusions and in order to clarify important findings we have on occasions quoted witnesses directly.

8. Issues

8.1 Counsel to the Inquiry, after consultation with other interested parties, drew up a detailed 17-page Issues Document which formed the backbone of the Inquiry (Appendix 2). It formed the basic structure for analysis of the evidence and the issues throughout our proceedings.

9. Gathering of Evidence

9.1 In January 2000 we began collecting relevant documentation from all witnesses, Alder Hey, the NHS Executive North West Regional Office, the University of Liverpool and HM Coroner of Liverpool. All parties undertook to co-operate with the Inquiry, particularly with regard to the production of documents. We scrutinised in excess of 50,000 documents.

10. Salmon Letters

10.1   We ensured that before witnesses were called to give evidence they were informed of any general allegations to be made and the substance of the evidence in support. This information was contained in an initial letter known as a Salmon letter (a requirement of The Royal Commission on Tribunals of Inquiry) which was served on each witness. A written statement was then provided. The Solicitor to the Inquiry took the statements. Witnesses had the lawyer of their choice present at the interview. They had the opportunity to alter, add to or amend their statements before signing. Where appropriate a more detailed Salmon letter was then served with details of relevant allegations and documents likely to be referred to at the hearing. In Appendix 5 we enclose examples of both an initial and a more detailed Salmon letter.

10.2   The purpose of the Salmon letters was to assist witnesses who faced possible criticism to understand the issues which were likely to be raised at the hearing. They were not designed to prejudge issues but merely to give witnesses a full opportunity to consider all matters to be dealt with in evidence. Matters set out in the Salmon letter, but not referred to at the hearing, were not used as the basis for criticism in the Report.

11. Witness Representation

11.1   Witnesses from Alder Hey, other Trusts, the University and NHS Executive North West Regional Office had legal representation provided by their employers. Some witnesses had separate legal representation when potential conflict with their employers arose. The former HM Coroner of Liverpool Mr Roy Barter and Professor van Velzen chose not to have legal representation. Legal representatives were in attendance when their client gave evidence to the Inquiry. A full list of legal representation is attached at Appendix 1.

11.2   The parents, including those who were members of the group 'Parents who Inter Their Young Twice' (PITY II), were represented by one of two lead firms of solicitors. The parents had their lawyer present when giving evidence. All parents who gave evidence before the Inquiry provided a written statement in advance to supplement their completed preliminary evidence questionnaire.

11.3   Lawyers for all interested parties were afforded the facility of submitting written questions to Counsel or Solicitor to the Inquiry who, at their discretion, could put any relevant matter to any witness who was giving evidence.

12. Counselling

12.1　The nature of the Inquiry meant that there was every possibility that witnesses might need counselling during or following the conclusion of their evidence. Counselling facilities were made available by the Inquiry throughout the hearings. Thereafter counselling was available by appointment. This facility is still available to parents upon demand. We are indebted to Barnardos who made counsellors available on a daily basis and continue to meet that need. Any parent in need of counselling can be accommodated either by direct approach to the Inquiry or through their solicitor or the Community Health Council.

13. Parents' Evidence

13.1　The large majority of parents who contacted the Inquiry completed a preliminary evidence questionnaire (Appendix 3). A total of 402 parents responded to the Inquiry and we received 342 completed questionnaires and statements. Great care was taken in drafting the questionnaire. It was designed to encourage parents to say in their own words what they felt about events following the death of their child. They were asked about consent to post mortem examination, what they were told of the process, whether they were aware of the distinction between a Coroner's and a hospital post mortem examination and they were invited to describe the circumstances of the funeral. They were asked to express their views about the way that they had been told of organ retention in their particular case.

13.2　The parents' solicitors, PITY II and the Liverpool Eastern Community Health Council were consulted about the content of the questionnaire. It was amended in response to their concerns and suggestions. Dr George Hay, Consultant Psychiatrist, and Dr Alice Huddy, Consultant Neuropsychologist, confirmed the suitability of the preliminary evidence questionnaire.

13.3　Parents had the option of seeking advice from solicitors in completing questionnaires. Some submitted lists of questions they wanted answering. We selected 43 parents who completed questionnaires and statements to give evidence before us as a representative sample. We carefully considered all parents' written evidence.

13.4　The hearings commenced on 11 May 2000 and were due to conclude on 30 June 2000. However, because of ill health or unavoidable professional commitments, several hearings had to be rescheduled with the result that the oral evidence was not concluded until 14 July 2000. In consequence, on one or two occasions the Panel was only able to sit with the Chairman and one member because of previously arranged commitments.

The absent Panel Member received transcripts of evidence on the same day. All hearings took place in a dedicated hearing room complete with LiveNote recording technology.

13.5   We received oral and written opening and closing submissions from all parties.

14.   Expert Evidence

14.1   Eileen Goddard from the Office of National Statistics Social Survey Division was asked to review the parents' evidence and compare the evidence given at oral hearings with that provided in writing. She said 'the experiences of parents giving oral evidence are remarkably similar to other parents who came forward as a result of the Inquiry.'

14.2   We had the benefit of expert seminars on issues including Medical Ethics and University Medical School teaching. We heard of the need to incorporate within the teaching curriculum matters relating to death, bereavement, grief and the taking of consent for post mortem examination. The distinction between Coroner's and hospital post mortem examinations must be made clear as should the need for lack of objection or consent to organ retention.

14.3   We also had a seminar on Human Rights and obtained expert medical opinions from a psychiatrist, a neuropsychologist and a psychologist. They commented on how Alder Hey should have dealt with the parents in September 1999. We dealt specifically with the issue of bereavement advice and counselling. We also received evidence from a consultant forensic pathologist and a consultant in public health medicine.

14.4   We considered evidence on religious issues but operated to the highest common denominator, namely those religions which require burial within 24 hours of death, as the yardstick against which to measure post mortem procedures.

14.5   We considered legal studies by CMS Cameron McKenna entitled 'Removal, retention and use of human tissue following post mortem examination' dated November 1999 (Bristol Inquiry 23) and the Legal Study by the Bristol Heart Action Group for the Bristol Inquiry (Bristol Inquiry SUB 1/1-40 19.9.99).

15.   The Coroner

15.1   The former HM Coroner of Liverpool, Mr Roy Barter, received an initial Salmon letter and provided a signed written statement. Shortly before he was due to give evidence he received a detailed Salmon letter. He was asked about his relationship with parents, clinicians and pathologists. He was also questioned about the Coroner's procedures and the function of the Coroner's Officer. He was asked about incomplete post mortem reports in the absence of histological examination.

15.2   We concentrated our attention upon Mr Barter because the defects in the Coroner's process were readily apparent at Liverpool. Many of our findings would, however, have national implications.

16.   Professor van Velzen

16.1   We paid particular regard to the evidence of Professor van Velzen and his documents. The Solicitor to the Inquiry spent two days in The Netherlands interviewing Professor van Velzen. The interview was taped and the full transcript was put into evidence rather than a formal statement. Professor van Velzen also gave oral evidence to the Inquiry over the course of a full day. We considerably exceeded our normal sitting times to ensure we heard everything he had to say. We examined all the documents he produced.

17.   Clinicians' Seminar

17.1   A Clinicians' Seminar was held at Alder Hey on 23 May 2000. The purpose was to outline the issues and encourage the clinicians to be fearless, frank and open when giving evidence. We came away with the view that the majority of clinicians would deny knowledge as to the extent of the organ retention in the period 1988 to 1995. However, they were well aware of the long accepted and established practice of removing and retaining some organs following post mortem examination for medical education and research purposes. One of the more senior clinicians present accepted that in hindsight it had been wrong to retain organs without consent.

18.   Myrtle Street

18.1   We have used the name Myrtle Street for the premises where Professor van Velzen stored the organs accumulated between 1988 and 1995. The premises are well known locally by this name although the formal address is 98–99 Mulberry Street, Liverpool.

The Myrtle Street buildings

18.2   We include photographs of Myrtle Street in order to give some idea of the nature of the building. Construction began in September 1900 and was completed in 1902. The building was then used as the Liverpool Children's Dispensing Infirmary on behalf of the Trustees of the Liverpool Children's Infirmary. In 1975 Liverpool City Council acquired the freehold and granted a three-year lease to Liverpool Area Health Authority. In 1978 a five-year lease was granted to Mersey Regional Health Authority and this was renewed for a further five years in 1983. In 1988 a five-year lease was granted to the Secretary of State for Social Services. From 1975–1995 the premises were occupied by Alder Hey and its predecessors. In 1995 Liverpool City Council granted a tenancy terminable on six months' notice to Liverpool University. It would appear that in the period 1975–1995 Alder Hey shared their clinical use of Myrtle Street with the University who carried out academic and research work. The reason for this was that in Professor van Velzen's case he provided 6/11ths of his contracted time to Alder Hey and the remainder to his formal employer, Liverpool University. He enjoyed the seclusion Myrtle Street afforded him.

19.   Alder Hey

19.1   Alder Hey is the term we use to describe the Royal Liverpool Children's Hospital NHS Trust and its predecessors in title. It is well known locally by this name. The hospital was founded in 1914 and is probably the largest children's hospital in North Western Europe. It has a first class reputation for saving the lives of sick children and a proud history of medical achievement and clinical innovation. It is an international centre of excellence treating more than 200,000 children a year from 17 North West Health Authorities, two Health Authorities in North Wales and Shropshire. It also provides significant paediatric support to the Isle of Man.

19.2   Alder Hey is a tertiary referral hospital for many conditions. Specialist areas include bone marrow transplant, burns, cleft lip and palate, cancer, renal replacement, spinal injuries, cardiology and cranio facial surgery. It is a leader in the field of medical research into respiratory disease, paediatric surgery and infectious diseases. It is a respected research establishment in the field of oncology, neurology, radiology, rheumatology and ophthalmology.

19.3   The reputation of Alder Hey has been adversely affected by the revelation of organ retention, particularly that resulting from Professor van Velzen's practices. Parental reaction both to the organ retention and the handling of the situation which developed as a result in 1999 has adversely affected morale at Alder Hey and the influx of funds. Nevertheless, Alder Hey still attracts clinicians of the highest calibre in its specialist fields.

20.   University Institute of Child Health

20.1   The University Institute of Child Health (ICH) is a purpose built unit on the Alder Hey site. It is under the management and control of University of Liverpool. It houses the well known and respected heart collection spoken of by Professor Anderson at the Bristol Inquiry. Clinicians at Alder Hey have access to the collection for educational and surgical purposes. The collection has been of great value in the development of cardiac treatment and surgery, and has been instrumental in reducing the mortality rate in cardiac surgery.

21. Alder Centre

21.1 The Alder Centre is based at the Royal Liverpool Children's NHS Trust on the Alder Hey site and was established 11 years ago. Its purpose is to provide bereavement counselling and support. The basic running costs have been met by Alder Hey, but the cost of various projects has been met from fundraising activities. The centre was established by a small group of healthcare professionals in partnership with bereaved parents. The centre provides counselling and support for anyone affected by the death of a child whether the death has occurred in hospital, at home or in the community.

22. Site Visits

22.1 The Panel visited Alder Hey, the ICH and Myrtle Street and viewed all the collections.

22.2 Visits to Myrtle Street included close inspection of the basement areas where many of the containers were stored between 1993 and 1999. We saw a representative sample of the containers and their contents. The Chairman and Mrs Powell also visited the University of Liverpool Pathology Department in the Duncan Building at the Royal Liverpool University Hospital (RLUH). The Solicitor to the Inquiry, Stephen Jones, visited the Unit of Ophthalmology at the RLUH to view the eye collection. He also inspected a number of files at the Office of HM Coroner for Liverpool. We are grateful to the present Coroner, Mr Andre Rebello, for his assistance.

23. Technology

23.1 From the outset we used a LiveNote computer system which provided a real time transcript of oral hearings. A hard copy transcript of each day's evidence was available shortly after each day's evidence and copied to solicitors representing the particular witnesses heard that day. The friendly expertise of Claire Stanley, LiveNote Accredited Reporter, and Jacqueline Gleghorn, Specialist Editor, was much appreciated.

23.2 The documents obtained were scanned onto a computerised document management system. Witnesses were referred to relevant documents immediately on screen as required. They had been put on notice in their Salmon letters of those documents.

23.3 Immediately witnesses concluded their evidence they were reminded of the confidential nature of the Inquiry and instructed not to reveal any evidence or document relating to their examination.

24. Main Objective

24.1   Our main objective was to examine the long history of organ retention following post mortem examination. We received evidence of the practice from about 1948. We have, however, already indicated that our major concern was to look at the practice following the introduction of the relevant provisions of the Human Tissue Act 1961. The Act provided that the person in lawful possession of the body must 'having made such reasonable enquiry as may be practicable' have 'no reason to believe' that 'any surviving relative of the deceased objects to the body being used in particular for … medical education and research purposes'.

24.2   We considered the position following a Coroner's post mortem examination, which does not require consent, but is ordered by the Coroner based on information from the clinician reporting the death. We studied the obligation to establish 'lack of objection' in the event of a request to retain organs and tissue taken at Coroner's post mortem examination for medical education and research.

24.3   In relation to post mortem examination and research involving fetus we looked at the Code of Practice set out in the 'Review of the Guidance on the Research use of Fetuses and Fetal Material' published in July 1989 and commonly referred to as the Polkinghorne Report.

24.4   In particular we considered the heart collection and the huge store of body parts which accumulated in Professor van Velzen's time between 1988 and 1995. We also identified a number of other collections including fetal and eye collections and a store of children's body parts.

24.5   We examined management procedures in an attempt to resolve how organ retention had remained undisclosed for so many years and how it increased unchecked between 1988 and 1995.

25. Conclusions and Recommendations

25.1   We heard oral evidence from 43 parents who had already provided preliminary written evidence. The written evidence of all the parents was given equally careful consideration. We took evidence from 77 other witnesses, 40 of whom attended to give oral evidence. In conjunction with the detailed evidence, document management system and the LiveNote transcript, we were well placed to make our findings and recommendations.

25.2   The process we adopted was to look for confirmation in the documents and generally, where there was a conflict between oral evidence and contemporaneous documents, we preferred the document, in the absence of satisfactory explanation.

26.   Acknowledgements

26.1   We extend our thanks to those who gave of their time and appeared before us. Similarly we extend our thanks to those who provided written evidence to us but did not appear.

26.2   It was remarkable that our Secretary Keith Smith and the Assistant Secretary Gill Crouch were able to find premises and equip them in such a short space of time. They also ensured the smooth running of the Inquiry throughout its duration despite hindrances and distractions.

26.3   We are grateful to the administrative staff and security personnel for their loyal support and dedication to duty, particularly in the latter stages of our process.

26.4   Finally we can only describe the contributions from Stephen Jones, Solicitor to the Inquiry, and James Rowley, Counsel to the Inquiry, as outstanding. The quality and extent of their work enabled us to have a far deeper insight into the oral evidence and documents than we could possibly have anticipated.

Chapter 2. The Parents

Contents

1.   Introduction

1.1   We spent considerable time assessing the written and oral evidence of the parents. The content is powerful and should be highlighted. The following quotations are indicative of the emotional force generated by organ retention and its subsequent revelation.

1.2   We can do no better than to let the parents describe their feelings in their own words.

On the death of their child and the issue of consenting to post mortem examination

1.3   'I just couldn't think... I felt so empty and helpless... they shouldn't be so quick... it's rude and they catch you at your most vulnerable moment.'

'Not a lot that was said actually went in ... I was told it had to be done to check on the surgeon ... I signed the paper through tears and just wanted to grieve at home. I feel I was rushed into signing ... I feel that I should have been there to protect her ... I do understand that these things need to be done but only with full permission and a full explanation.'

'When they ask you to sign the form you are in so much turmoil you could sign your life away and would not know it.'

'I wish they had explained things to us.'

Parents' reaction to learning of organ retention

1.4 'It feels like body snatching. The hospital stole something from me. They have taken us back 11 years in our healing process.'

'They gave me skin and bone back.'

'Alder Hey stole 90% of my child.'

'I feel devastated ... I am wondering how much of her body was left.'

'I have learnt to live with my daughter's death and now I have found out that they removed her heart. It is like losing her all over again.'

'Studying her brain would help explain why her brain did not form properly and it might help treat the next child born with a similar condition. Unfortunately her brain has not been studied. Instead it sits in a jar in a storeroom somewhere.'

Handling the news of organ retention

1.5 'We are left feeling that full details are being withheld.'

'Alder Hey gave the impression that as parents we had little or no right to know what happened to our children after death.'

'Alder Hey could not cope.'

'On a personal basis I have found the representatives of Alder Hey to be very helpful, available, open and honest when dealing with our individual situation.'

'They have been helpful and regretful.'

'We are suspicious of everything Alder Hey says.'

'They have been cold and it is all telephone calls.'

'I have not spoken to anybody face to face.'

'Inept and inconsiderate.'

'Staff... have been as courteous and helpful as they can in the circumstances.'

'We were surrounded by good people at Alder Hey and wish to extend our support for them.'

'There has been a huge lack of accuracy and secrecy.'

'These poor people who have had to deal with us over the telephone... should be given sympathy and counselling themselves.'

'There has been a catalogue of public relations disasters that have only upset parents more.'

On completing the preliminary evidence questionnaire

1.6   'I am remembering things from 10 years ago that my mind put into a little black box.'

Our Inquiry looked back over a period of more than 40 years. Parents said:

1.7   'The death of a child is traumatic enough without having to relive it ten years later.'

'Try to imagine having a second funeral 34 years after the first.'

'We cremated our son in two separate boxes 31 years apart.'

1.8   We considered whether the passage of time has impaired the quality of the parents' evidence. We also considered the distress and loneliness which many parents have experienced over the years. It is possible that some parents will have suffered an adverse psychological reaction because of the death of their child.

1.9   Even taking these matters into account each parent was recalling one of life's major events, namely the death of their child. It was a unique event for them and is liable to remain imprinted upon their minds forever. We are concerned with their perception of how their child was treated at death, how the issue of post mortem examination was dealt with, how they reacted to the news of organ retention, how they reacted on learning that they had not buried their child whole and of the need for a second or more funerals. We are aware that we have only heard from those parents who have responded to the Inquiry and to that extent they are self-selected. We are left to speculate about the reaction of those who have not responded to the Inquiry. We were recently informed of one parent who received a full list of retained organs relating to their deceased child despite their stated preference not to know. These matters are analysed in Chapter 3.

1.10   We have asked Alder Hey to devise and implement an effective handling strategy, to include psychological input, for additional parents who are likely to come forward following publication of our Report. These matters are again dealt with in Chapter 3.

1.11   We have subjected the parents' evidence to critical examination. There are likely to be areas where inaccuracy prevails, particularly in respect of detail which they cannot or subconsciously do not wish to remember. This might relate to the issue of whether or not they signed a consent form or the full detail of conversations they had with clinicians following the death. However, because of the unique circumstances of the death of their child and the events of September 1999, when the issue of organ retention became public, their evidence is entitled to respect and is worthy of very careful consideration. More particularly, those who have had second and third funerals have had no difficulty recalling such recent events.

1.12   Our overall impression of the evidence from parents is that the issues which confront us are no respecter of socio-economic group or manner of life. There has been a huge consistency of response with clearly recurring themes throughout. The love parents showed for their children both in life and in death was plain to see. The care they lavished upon them in life and as far as they were allowed in death was apparent. The extent of their grief and distress was reflected in the eloquence and dignity with which they gave their evidence. On many occasions we were deeply moved. It was our privilege to share their evidence and in particular, photograph albums and baby books whenever produced. The age of the child was of no consequence to the parents. Whether stillborn or teenage, their children were deeply loved and valued as unique individuals and family members.

1.13   Each parent has posed individual questions for which they seek answers. We explained to those who gave evidence that it would be impossible to answer all questions individually but our Report should help them understand how the situation developed and how it should be prevented from recurring in the future.

1.14   The strength of the parents' evidence is such that the only way to do it justice is to include in a separate chapter (Chapter 14) faithful summaries of representative evidence. Wherever possible we have endeavoured to use the parents' own language in the narrative. We have adopted the simple strategy of marking each summary with the child's first name, age and year of death. We do this as a mark of respect and also as a permanent memory of their involvement in and contribution to the Inquiry, while preserving the anonymity of their family. We commend the summaries to all who read them for their compelling content, understandable and reasonable expression of emotion, consistency of response and identification of recurrent concerns.

2.   Death of Child

2.1   Many of the deaths occurred around the time of birth. Later deaths usually resulted from malformation, disease, infection or accidents. Sometimes deaths occurred during surgery or shortly thereafter. There were cases of older children dying from Hodgkin's disease and leukaemia.

2.2   Whatever the circumstances, the universal consequence of death has been grief. Some parents were referred to a social worker but the majority spoke of a lack of bereavement advice or counselling. They identified a great need for such a service. Their evidence should lead to a better understanding of the consequences of death including the issue of lack of objection or, as we prefer, fully informed consent to post mortem examination.

2.3   Immediately following the death of their child many parents offered to donate organs to save the life of another child in immediate need. The majority of offers were refused on the basis that the organs had been damaged in the disease process which caused death. There were several parents who carried organ donor cards with them. We were told that one or two teenagers involved in the organ retention issue had requested organ donor cards themselves when they were alive. Several parents destroyed their cards when they were told about organ retention and how it affected their child.

2.4   Parents described difficulty in understanding what was said to them by clinicians or hospital staff because of their grief. From the sample questionnaires commenting on hospital post mortems looked at by the Office of National Statistics, just 37 per cent of parents could remember reading the consent form, whilst 44 per cent said they had not read it. In the few cases where a pamphlet or booklet was made available to parents, they had found it hard to understand because of their grief and distress. Too many parents, 46 per cent, were asked for consent to a post mortem within minutes of the death of their child. There was little time for reflection, advice and counselling as appropriate.

3.   Post Mortem Examination

3.1   The vast majority of parents were told that a post mortem examination was to be carried out. Surprisingly, few were told when or where it was to be carried out. Generally, parents were not told what was involved in a post mortem examination.

3.2   Parents were given little information when a Coroner's post mortem examination was to be performed. A Coroner's post mortem is demanded by law in certain circumstances and for which consent is not required (see Chapter 9). When the Coroner's process was complete they were not asked for consent to the retention of organs for medical education or research purposes.

3.3   When a hospital post mortem examination was to be performed, some 81 per cent of parents (sample as above) said they were not told specifically that they could object. A hospital post mortem requires consent or more properly 'lack of objection'. When they did consent almost all the parents thought it was to the taking of tissue sufficient for microscopic examination and not the retention of organs. Indeed, no parent could recall being advised that they could object to the retention of organs. There was no consistency as to who dealt with establishing consent or lack of objection with parents. It was sometimes the clinician, but more usually a junior doctor or even a member of the nursing staff who dealt with establishing consent or lack of objection.

3.4   Many parents described being placed under pressure to consent to a hospital post mortem. In several cases parents spoke of the prospect of a Coroner's post mortem being used to obtain consent to a hospital post mortem examination. There were instances where clinicians allowed one parent to sign the consent form although aware that the other parent's wishes were not known.

3.5   Following Coroner's post mortem examination there was little evidence of contact or discussion between the Coroner, parents, clinician or pathologist. Only a minority of parents were informed of the contents of the post mortem report. Few parents were referred for genetic counselling even if the need was established. Some parents had further children before the results of post mortem examination were made known to them. One family lost two children close together from the same congenital heart condition. They had never seen the post mortem report on their first child.

4.   Retention

4.1   Many parents did not realise and were not told that the organs would be removed from the body, weighed and subjected to naked eye examination in the post mortem process. Those who were aware that organs were removed for this purpose were always reassured that they would be restored to the body prior to the funeral. It was rare for any parent to be told that an organ or organs would be retained.

5.   Funeral

5.1   The parents described the first funeral as dignified and respectful. Each parent believed that they were laying their child to rest intact. In some cases, particularly with regard to stillbirths, parents were told that their child would be buried in a dignified and respectful manner within the hospital grounds. They were not told where or when.

6.   News of Organ Retention

6.1   The realisation that many children had been buried without their organs caused their parents shock and distress. The parents' summaries in Chapter 14 contain accounts of personal reaction to the news.

6.2   Many parents were drip-fed information about what had or had not been retained. There was unacceptable delay between initial contact and the subsequent disclosure of what had been retained. There were too many instances of the initial information being inaccurate. Neither Alder Hey nor the University had an individual record of organs retained from each child following post mortem examination, nor did they have an individual record of organs used for research. They should have done.

6.3   Accordingly there were unnecessary delays, confusion and inaccuracies, the cumulative effect of which greatly added to the distress suffered by parents.

6.4   There was neither a proper system nor a uniform approach as to how to deal with parents. There does not appear to have been any handling strategy based upon psychological advice. Under these circumstances the telephone and correspondence were unsatisfactory means of communication. There should have been face to face meetings.

6.5   The attitude of Alder Hey has been described as insensitive and arrogant. Some parents who described Alder Hey's treatment of their children in life as 'outstanding' have changed their view because of organ retention and the handling issues. What is described is evidence of a system based upon poor crisis management.

6.6   Some parents have had to have three funerals, particularly those involved in the very recent revelation of the cerebellum *(part of the brain)* collection in August 2000. Some have had the further indignity of samples being taken from retained organs without consent immediately prior to their return. Parents wondered how such a situation could arise. They asked why organs were retained following Coroner's or hospital post mortem examinations without their consent or a record being kept of organs retained. They also asked why there was no record of organs used for research, and no regular stock-take or audit. In particular they could not understand why there was no current list of retained organs compiled before news of organ retention becoming public. This would have avoided the unacceptable delay between initial contact being established with Alder Hey and the later provision of details of organ retention, some of which were still inaccurate. Even this process was fraught with error.

7.   Overview

7.1   Parents contrasted the very full information they received about the treatment of their children in life with the absence of information in death. Had the circumstances of death received equal attention then they would have understood the intended purpose of post mortem examination, as well as the benefits to society of retaining organs or tissue for medical education and research purposes. They would then have been more inclined to give proper informed consent.

7.2   Openness and transparency requires robust organisational procedures. The most important function of post mortem examination is diagnostic. All processes where tissues are examined are aimed at identifying underlying disease. The other functions of post mortem examination, including medical education, research and audit, are desirable for the purpose of improving the health of future generations.

7.3   There will always be parents who, for personal reasons, will refuse a request for post mortem examination. Nevertheless, if the death is within the parameters of the Coroner's jurisdiction, then post mortem examination will be carried out to establish the cause of death. On the evidence we feel that many more parents would be willing to consider consenting to their children's organs or tissue being retained for the purpose of medical education and research, if the matter were dealt with openly and respectfully.

7.4   There is clearly a social need for more post mortem examinations to encourage and assist improvements in the health of future generations. The majority of parents recognise this. The major impediment to its achievement has been the unnecessarily paternalistic attitude of the medical profession based on restricting information about post mortem procedure, organ retention, medical education and research. The parents have been systematically deprived of information which they had a right to know.

8.   Summary of Parents' Criticisms and Suggestions

8.1   This is a summary of the concerns we heard from parents, together with some of their suggestions about how to address them. Parents feel they have the right to information about their child and his or her treatment in both life and death. They want to see systems in place which can help them make sense of their child's death and feel confident that they have the relevant information. They want the confidence to be able to put their children to rest.

8.2   **Concern:**

That undue pressure was brought on parents to sign the consent form.

Suggestions:

- Allow time for parents to reflect after death before discussing the issue of post mortem consent.

- Ask a psychologist to help develop a sensitive approach to giving parents the news about the death of their child, and then move on to the issue of consent.

8.3   **Concern:**

Parents would like advice and support.

Suggestions:

- Offer bereavement advice and counselling following a child's death, addressing feelings such as guilt.

- Provide formal advice and support not only to parents but also to brothers, sisters and perhaps other close relatives.

8.4   **Concern:**

Parents need to know that when they give consent their wishes will be followed.

Suggestions:

- Parents will be told if there is need for retention of organs or tissue for microscopy.

- Organs will be reunited with the body after post mortem and before funeral.

- There are legal restrictions to prevent undisclosed retention without parental consent.

- Full details of organs and tissue retained will be recorded and put on a database.

- Parents are told what will be the purpose for retaining organs or tissue.

8.5   **Concern:**

Parents need to know that a checking procedure is in place, and to be confident that swift action will be taken to correct mistakes.

Suggestions:

- Clear systems should be set up to deal with this type of issue (avoiding the hospital being defensive and unco-operative, and over-concerned with damage limitation).

- Prevent delays in supply of information by putting in place a proper management structure and database.

- Train hospital personnel to deal with parents in this kind of crisis.

- Audit the post mortem examination procedure regularly.

- Keep careful control over research on human organs and tissue.

- Establish a clear line of responsibility for issues like this, and discipline individuals if necessary.

8.6   **Concern:**

Parents did not know their rights to refuse hospital post mortem examination.

Suggestions:

- Parents need to know of their right to limit post mortem examination and of their right to object/consent.

- Information given to parents should be in non-medical language and clearly state options and possible outcomes after the post mortem examination.

- There should be clear guidelines of post mortem examination and procedure, including the different types of post mortem examination and the process.

- Parents' instructions should be obtained and followed.

- Explain the meaning of tissue and organ.

8.7   **Concern:**

No system or procedure for informing parents of post mortem examination results.

Suggestions:

- Post mortem examination and reports should be part of the individual's medical record.

- If parents wish they should be kept informed at every stage.

- GPs should have responsibility to follow up a child's death with the parents.

8.8   Parents would like to be dealt with sensitively.

8.9   Parents want to know why the practice of organ retention has gone on for so long, without their knowledge.

8.10   We have paid particular regard to the parents' suggestions in considering our recommendations, particularly relating to the handling issues at the end of Chapter 3.

Chapter 3. Handling of the Organ Retention Issue September 1999 to date

Contents

1.   Organ Retention is Revealed

1.1   On 7 September 1999 Professor R H Anderson, Professor of Morphology at the Hospital for Sick Children in London (Great Ormond St Hospital), described to the Bristol Inquiry the benefits of heart retention for the purpose of study and teaching. He identified heart collections around the country and made particular mention of the excellence of the collection at Alder Hey which dated from 1948. His evidence brought the issue of organ retention at Alder Hey into the public domain.

1.2   At Alder Hey, however, organ retention had not been limited to hearts and lungs. Between 1988 and 1995 (which we describe as 'the van Velzen years'), there had been systematic full-scale removal of organs. The organs were retained from Coroner's and hospital post mortem examinations carried out in the mortuary at Alder Hey. They were stored in the pathology department at Alder Hey until late 1989 when Professor van Velzen's department moved to virtual sole occupancy of Myrtle Street. The organs continued to accumulate within Myrtle Street until 1995.

1.3   In 1995 Alder Hey and the University had considered how to deal with this accumulated
       material. This matter is more fully analysed in Chapter 8. On 24 April 1995 Professor
       Helen Carty, Clinical Director of Support Services at Alder Hey, circulated a
       memorandum to a number of clinicians enclosing a list of post mortem examinations
       where histology had not been completed on retained 'organs'. The following day she
       also wrote to the Chief Executive at Alder Hey, Ms Hilary Rowland, about delay in
       carrying out histology on retained 'organs'. The memorandum was circulated on three
       or four occasions. Clinicians marked those cases in which they wanted the organs
       retained for histology. These organs were then transferred to Alder Hey. The hearts and
       lungs in some cases were sent to the Institute of Child Health (ICH) at Alder Hey. The
       large majority of organs remained at Myrtle Street to be used for research purposes as
       and when required. These arrangements were confirmed at a meeting in the Department
       of Pathology at Alder Hey on 21 November 1995. An opportunity was therefore missed
       by the University and Alder Hey to list and catalogue all the organs which had
       accumulated at Myrtle Street until April 1995. This was the background against which
       the revelation of the heart collection was made in September 1999.

1.4   The revelation generated some local media interest and on 18 September 1999 the
       issue of organ retention was reported on the BBC North West Regional News. On
       20 September Ms Rowland gave an assurance that the practice of organ retention
       at Alder Hey had not differed from that at other hospitals. The collection of organs
       at Myrtle Street was such that this assurance was inaccurate.

1.5   Following the revelation many parents telephoned Alder Hey to find out whether their
       child's heart had been retained. On the second day of receiving calls Ms Rowland asked
       Mrs Karen England, Acting Director of Operational Services, to manage the incident.
       Mrs England was chosen because of her background and experience of having worked
       in the histology laboratory. For the first few days management arrangements were
       informal but soon a team of senior staff, managerial and clinical, was convened. The
       purpose of the team was to agree the strategy for managing the incident and to make
       decisions which would be carried out by those individuals with delegated responsibility.

1.6   Later in the first week parents began to query whether, if hearts had been retained,
       other organs had also been kept. It was at this point that Mrs England told Ms Rowland
       that multiple organs had been taken at post mortem examinations and had remained at
       Myrtle Street when the histology department had left the building in 1995. Ms Rowland
       gave evidence to the Inquiry that until this point she had no knowledge of the full extent
       of the organ retention. However, the documentary evidence discussed in Chapter 8
       Part 8 of 'the van Velzen years' suggests that in 1995 Ms Rowland should have known
       of the existence of a substantial collection at Myrtle Street.

1.7   Mr Paul Dearlove, a senior Medical Laboratory Scientific Officer (MLSO), was
       instructed to go to Myrtle Street to establish the position. Multiple organs had been
       retained from approximately 850 post mortem examinations carried out between

September 1988 and December 1995. There were between one and three containers for each child. In total there were approximately 2,000 containers holding multiple organs and many pieces and fragments of tissue.

1.8 The Myrtle Street building (see photographs at page 12) consisted of two floors and a basement, with many rooms off the main ground floor area and the first floor. The basement had two rooms and a series of cellars at the rear (see photographs on page 32). All had low lighting and low ceilings and it was not possible to stand up straight in all the areas. The majority of the containers were stored in the cellars in the basement, with others in the 'cut-up' room and two storerooms off it on the ground floor.

1.9 The containers in the basement were dirty and covered with thick black dust. The area has now been cleaned and is illustrated in the photographs at page 32. The cleaned containers are now stored at Alder Hey in the pathology department as illustrated at page 33. Identification of some was difficult due to the conditions in which they had been kept. Some of the labels were damp and had come off. The writing on some of the containers had faded over time. On closer inspection some of the organs were poorly preserved because adequate levels of formalin had not been maintained.

1.10 Mr Dearlove explained to Mrs England that at the time the histology department had left the building in 1995 all the containers were filed in chronological order with multiple containers on the same case stored together. It was obvious that the containers had been accessed since then. Some were out of sequence and multiple containers on the same case had not been kept together. Many other containers were spread around the building, some containing animal tissue, some human tissue taken from the organs stored following post mortem examination, presumably for research work undertaken by University staff. It was therefore clear from the outset that there could be no guarantee that organs which remained in the containers were those originally taken at post mortem examination.

1.11 Between 1988 and 1999 there was no proper record of retained organs, or of access to them for research purposes at Myrtle Street. This factor alone has prevented the University or Alder Hey from providing information to parents about organ retention which was completely accurate and reliable.

1.12 On 27 September 1999 Ms Rowland briefed Professor Robert Tinston, Regional Director at NHS Executive North West (Regional Office), and warned that this constituted a major issue. He assured her that additional resources could be made available if required.

1.13 As the number of queries from parents grew Ms Rowland decided to write to all families whose child had died at Alder Hey, where the post mortem examination had been performed at the hospital and where they had the addresses. She did not write to the wider group of parents affected by the retention of hearts generally because the age of the collection made the addresses unreliable. The letter was sent to parents affected by deaths between 1988 and 1995. They were invited to contact Alder Hey to be told whether their child's organs had been retained.

1.14   Over the weekend of 2–3 October 1999 Alder Hey attempted to catalogue the organs in Myrtle Street. The containers were removed from the basement and other areas to the ground floor and sorted in order of post mortem number and year. Twelve members of staff worked a total of 151 hours and completed cases from 1988 to 1990. For the full classification process two people worked together, one identifying the organs and the other recording the data. Post mortem number, year and the name of the child were verified by both individuals prior to identification of the organs. The organs were then listed on an 'histology record sheet'. Containers which could not be clearly identified were kept to one side. If on further checking it was agreed that identification was impossible they disposed of the specimens.

1.15   On 4 October 1999 the exercise continued but instead of individual organs being listed they were classified into four groups: the brain, the heart, thoracic and abdominal organs. The histology sheet was revised to reflect this. In her witness statement to the Inquiry Ms Rowland explained,

> We felt that generally that would be as much information as parents would want or could emotionally cope with and the limitation of four groups would speed the process up.'

Eleven members of staff worked a total of 123 hours over 4–5 October and completed the outstanding cases from 1991 to 1995. When the later data was subsequently entered into the computer the earlier data was amended to reflect the revised categories.

1.16   The following weekend, 9–10 October 1999, the hearts and lungs in the ICH were catalogued. Eight pathology staff worked a total of 71 hours. The organs were classified as 'hearts' or 'hearts and lungs' and whether they were 'whole' or 'part'. This information was recorded on the 'ICH record sheet' together with the unique alphanumeric identification code from the container. The record sheets were then cross-checked against the ICH heart books so that the code could be linked to a name and post mortem number.

1.17   Over both weekends Alder Hey asked the University for their help. Their request was declined.

1.18   The cataloguing exercise was a priority and should have been carried out under the direction of senior management with an experienced paediatric pathologist in day-to-day control. The necessary staff should have been deployed to ensure that all organs at Myrtle Street and the ICH were properly identified, listed and catalogued in relation to the name of the baby or child and the relevant post mortem number. Even at this early stage, the exercise identified the difficulties with existing records of organ retention particularly at the ICH (see Chapter 7 Collections).

The basement cellars at Myrtle Street (where containers were stored)

Containers holding organs – now stored in accommodation at Alder Hey

2.   Press Release Denies Knowledge at Alder Hey

2.1   In the interim Ms Rowland had issued a press release on 6 October 1999 saying that,

> 'The hospital is devastated to learn that so many organs have been retained for research without the knowledge of the hospital, its doctors or the parents.'

2.2   Dr Campbell Davidson, the Medical Director at Alder Hey, was present at the meeting that sanctioned the press release. There is no evidence that he took instructions from the clinical directors as to the contents of the press release before it was issued. Neither did he check the accuracy of the statement for himself.

3.   The Early Enquiries

3.1   In the first month of enquiries Alder Hey received 618 calls from parents. All parents affected by organ retention were sent a letter of apology and offered three options:

- return of the organs to the family for a second funeral;

- retention of the organs for further research;

- retention of the organs at Alder Hey pending the family's decision.

3.2   Consideration was also given to a communal cremation for those who would find it too distressing to organise a second funeral. Alder Hey offered to pay for the second funeral providing the parents used a nominated funeral director.

3.3   When organs were returned to families they were firstly rechecked and a full list made on a second histology record form. This replaced the first list (of four categories) in the file as it contained more detail. A further list was completed when organs were put into caskets in preparation for funeral. More tissue was lost in the casketing process. Some parents came to witness the preparation. To avoid distress Alder Hey had disposed of any messy or liquefied fragments and pieces of faecal matter. On one occasion a tongue was deliberately disposed of in such circumstances.

3.4   In early October Dr Davidson asked the Royal College of Pathologists for assistance with an internal inquiry into the practice of organ retention. The College nominated Dr Stephen Gould, a respected consultant paediatric pathologist at the John Radcliffe Hospital, Oxford. He undertook an enormous amount of work to provide an early provisional report on 20 December 1999. His efforts were overtaken by the appointment of this Inquiry and so his report is incomplete. We have obtained great assistance from his expert professional involvement.

3.5   Meanwhile, some parents began to express concern about the broad description of organs they had received and requested more detail. Alder Hey's response was that any request for a full list of organs would be held for 48 hours to allow parents time to reflect on whether they really wanted the information. In the meantime the list was prepared. The intention was to save parents from further distress. The policy was questioned by Mrs Wendy Natale from the Liverpool Eastern Community Health Council (CHC) who said that waiting 48 hours for a list was likely to aggravate distress and not save it. A further complaint was that communication with parents was by telephone or in writing rather than face to face. Alder Hey was by now overwhelmed at the extent of the crisis.

3.6   At a meeting of parents on 1 November 1999 they discussed their difficulties in obtaining information from Alder Hey, calls not being returned and long delays in securing the return of organs. All these difficulties should have been apparent to Alder Hey. Despite assurances that parents would receive complete lists of retained organs promptly, delays in excess of two weeks were common. The CHC told Ms Rowland that she had a disaster on her hands which required a different strategy if the situation were to be retrieved. It was described to her as 'a juggernaut rolling down a hill out of control'. Ms Rowland declined to attend a meeting with parents on the basis that she had not been formally invited and it was inappropriate for her to attend.

3.7   Parents only received information if they asked for it and many did not know what to ask for in the first place. They began to describe the attitude of Alder Hey as deliberately obstructive and quite simply they did not trust Alder Hey. A support group for parents called 'Parents who Inter Their Young Twice' was set up. It became known as PITY II. This group was to represent and support parents and did so with resolve. The group was instrumental in obtaining a change in the law to allow organs to be cremated when a body has previously been buried (Statutory Instrument 2000 No 58).

3.8   In late November 1999 Alder Hey management offered to meet with PITY II when the Gould report was completed to discuss its findings. However, on 3 December 1999 the new HM Coroner for Liverpool, Mr Andre Rebello, suggested that organ retention was unlawful and the Alder Hey situation became national news again, creating a media scrimmage. Parents' anxieties and concerns heightened. The Government responded immediately by announcing that there would be an independent Inquiry.

4.   Counselling

4.1   Facilities for counselling were urgently required. The Alder Centre had been offered but was unsuitable to many parents. They did not wish to visit the site of their grief and distress and they trusted Alder Hey even less by this stage.

4.2   Before Christmas 1999 the CHC had compiled a list of local counselling services which it passed on request to one of the social workers on the Alder Hey help line. Only then did Alder Hey have a list. It is surprising that they had not obtained one from the outset.

5.   Unauthorised Sampling of Retained Organs

5.1   In January 2000 it became public knowledge that Alder Hey had been taking small samples of organs before their return without obtaining any further consent, or indeed even telling the parents. It was justified by management as being necessary to complete histology and to preserve the opportunity of advising parents as to any genetic consequences following the death of their child. In most cases this would involve histology on organs preserved in formalin for many years, rendering examination difficult if not impossible. Alder Hey claimed that they had consent to sample organs before return, based upon the consent given for the purpose of the original post mortem examination. Witnesses from Alder Hey were later to concede to the Inquiry that the original 'consent' was invalidly obtained. It was also insensitive not to ask the parents if they objected to the proposal to sample. This was accepted by Alder Hey when they ceased taking further samples without specific consent. We have seen no evidence to demonstrate that histology has yet been attempted in those cases.

5.2   Alder Hey continued to underestimate the effect of organ retention upon parents. Following the publication of the Gould report Ms Rowland compounded her earlier refusal to meet parents, indicating that it would now be inappropriate to discuss the report due to the setting up of this Inquiry. Instead she suggested parental involvement in revising the post mortem consent form.

5.3   Ms Therese Harvey, the Director of Human Resources, took over management of organ retention in February 2000. Some parents found her to be helpful and approachable. There were some improvements with the help line. Better information was made available and administration improved.

5.4   This improvement was not maintained, with increasing complaints of delay, misinformation, missing post mortem reports and discrepancy between post mortem reports and medical records. Parents continued to complain about delays in second funerals and enquire whether organs had been used in research. Alder Hey's attitude was regarded as defensive and unco-operative. There was still a lack of trust. Although some parents felt that Alder Hey was helpful, attentive and considerate, they were a minority.

5.5   A natural consequence of providing more detailed information to parents was that more questions were generated. For example, they wanted to know why organs had been stockpiled, why in some instances their child had been taken from the hospital where death occurred to Alder Hey for post mortem examination without their knowledge or consent and why the bodies of stillborn children had been stored for many years. It was impossible to provide complete answers in the absence of proper records relating to the source and usage of organs from each child.

5.6   On 23 March 2000 the Chair of the Trust, Mr Frank Taylor, resigned. The trigger was the Stephen White case, the full facts of which are reported in Chapter 4. Firstly Stephen's mother had been told that his heart had been retained. Later she was told that the heart and other organs had been retained. These were subsequently identified as brain and lung. A second funeral was arranged for 17 March 2000. On 15 March Ms Rowland visited Mrs White and told her that Stephen's organs had been mistakenly destroyed. This led to the Parliamentary Under Secretary of State (Lords), Lord Hunt, demanding a report on the incident within 24 hours from the Chief Executive. Ms Rowland provided the first report. There was insufficient detail in it and Lord Hunt asked for a second report which was prepared by the Regional Office. Lord Hunt remained concerned about the level of detail in the second report. However, there was an overriding priority to respond to the parents. He asked officials to inform them and the media, in that order, as a matter of urgency.

5.7   Lord Hunt's reaction to both reports was in our view correct and justified. The explanation of what had happened was publicised together with the announcement of a new Chair of the Trust and new interim guidance from the Chief Medical Officer to the NHS on how to deal with bereaved parents and post mortem examinations. Lord Hunt asked this Inquiry to investigate the circumstances of Stephen's case. He had every reason to act as he did and we confirm his action.

5.8   The case of Stephen White also raised an issue about fragments of organs. The report prepared for Lord Hunt suggested that the hospital had a policy of destroying fragments, which were not considered 'organs'. If this was so then until 21 February 2000, when an instruction from Secretary of State was received to the effect that no further tissue should be destroyed, fragments of organs were destroyed without reference to parents.

5.9   In her evidence to the Inquiry Mrs England explained the reason for the policy. A decision was taken at the outset to inform parents of the retention of either whole organs or substantial parts of organs, but not the many small pieces of fragments, some of which were unidentifiable. Small fragments would have been present in most of the containers. The stated justification was to avoid misleading parents into thinking whole organs had been retained when they had not. The real significance of the concealment of the fragments lies in the inherent disrespect shown to the children's organs. As information unfolded the parents' reaction resulted in them seeking everything belonging to their child including wax blocks, slides, X-rays and photographs.

5.10   As a result of the Stephen White case Ms Rowland ordered a further visual check of all organs retained to prevent further errors. She gave assurances that errors of this kind would not be repeated. However, as the cataloguing of the organs in July 2000 by Dr Gordan Vujanic, Consultant Paediatric Pathologist from Cardiff, shows (see below), these assurances could not be supported.

5.11   In succession to Mr Frank Taylor, the Secretary of State appointed Mrs Judith Greensmith as Chair of the Trust. She surveyed her inheritance and in her evidence to the Inquiry confirmed her initial view that the issue of organ retention had been 'handled on the hoof and people had reacted to crises as they arose'. She gained no sense of any 'audit trail' over what had been decided and why. Ms Rowland stood down and a new Acting Chief Executive, Mr Anthony Bell, was appointed. Mrs Greensmith, with assistance from Regional Office, recruited Mrs Kate Jackson, Director of Primary Care at Morecambe Bay Health Authority, as Project Director to handle the organ issue. She was to manage return of organs and liaison with families.

5.12   A Serious Incident Project Board (SIPB) was set up with a wide group of people represented. In addition to Mrs Greensmith there was Mr Bell, Mrs Jackson, Ms Harvey, Mr Colin Brown from Regional Office, Mr Allan Mowat (the solicitor representing the Trust), representatives from the University, Liverpool Women's Hospital, Liverpool Health Authority, the CHC and two family representatives. Mrs Greensmith also decided to establish a Family Liaison Group comprising ten representatives of affected families with the intention of looking at policy issues and how best to deal with family sensitivities. It was intended that the work would be closely monitored by Regional Office who were to receive fortnightly reports coinciding with the fortnightly Project Board meetings.

5.13   Mrs Greensmith knew that information had dribbled out to parents in two, three or four letters over a period of eight months and she regretted it. Information had had to be gathered from different locations. Mrs Greensmith intended to pull everything together. Following her appointment the atmosphere was said to be optimistic. The policies of openness, better relationships with parents and resolution of long-standing problems were the stated aim. Alder Hey apologised for past handling errors and expressed a willingness to resolve the situation.

5.14   In a press release of 23 March 2000 announcing the appointment of the new Chair, Lord Hunt confirmed that he had instructed the Regional Office to establish robust monitoring procedures to ensure that Alder Hey carried out its responsibilities in dealing with the return of organs effectively and appropriately. Professor Tinston was to take personal responsibility for ensuring arrangements were in place. As a further step, at the instigation of Lord Hunt, Alder Hey retained the services of Professor James Underwood, a respected paediatric pathologist from Sheffield, to advise on the future structuring of pathology services.

5.15   The task for the new regime was daunting. They inherited continuing problems related to sloppy mistakes, poor preparation, incomplete and incorrect information and staff working under excessive pressure. Mrs England and Mrs Waring should have been asked what the protocol was for organ retention following post mortem examination carried out by Professor van Velzen and his team (see Part 2 of 'The van Velzen Years', paragraphs 10.3 and 10.4). The practice, followed in nearly every case, was to retain every organ. The high incidence of containers lacking a full set of organs, coupled with the relatively low level of documented research, leads to the irresistible inference that organs have been lost. There is evidence of disposal as this section illustrates but none of commercial use. Alder Hey should have told the parents from the outset that what remained at Myrtle Street, unless all the organs were present, was simply what was left following research, the records of which were virtually non-existent.

5.16   Alder Hey still did not appear to fully appreciate or understand the parents' concerns. They sent out badly copied and illegible case notes. They promised information that did not arrive or arrived late. Link workers were re-allocated without the knowledge of parents involved. As the number and seriousness of problems increased they did not have any heightened sense of concern or urgency. They sought no additional resource despite the adverse handling outcomes with all the regrettable implications for parents.

5.17   The parents' representatives and the CHC described most of these problems in detail to Mrs Greensmith. They told her how Alder Hey had mishandled the situation so far. Mrs Greensmith could not have been in any doubt about the problems which she had inherited and which persisted.

5.18   In line with the stated policy of openness, the new management team now decided to send a definitive list of all organs retained to the parents. For some parents this was the third of its kind. The first communication with some parents had simply been information as to whether the heart (possibly with lungs) had been retained. The second described four groups of organs retained. In many cases there was a third more detailed list. Now there was this 'definitive' list. The list specified organs from brain to reproductive organs, skin, bone and muscle.

5.19   The content of the letter and the comprehensive nature of the list revealing that all internal organs had been retained shocked many parents. They questioned how and why it differed from previous lists they had received. Questions relating to organs missing from the earlier lists remained unanswered and parents could not trust the information received. Alder Hey should have informed parents that the only information they could provide related to what remained and not to what was taken.

5.20   Finally Alder Hey declared a 'moratorium' in June 2000 under which they would refrain from further disclosure for six weeks in an effort to catalogue precisely what remained. Dr Vujanic, the independent paediatric pathologist from Cardiff, was retained to carry out the exercise. For the first time Alder Hey seemed to have recognised that this was the starting point for answering the parents' questions. However, even this exercise was doomed to failure because of past mistakes and the lack of records.

5.21 The 'moratorium' prompted a further deterioration in the relationship between parents and Alder Hey in July and August 2000. The parents commented that the situation had reverted to the way it had been before March 2000. They called into question the independence of the SIPB.

6. University Perspective

6.1 At this stage it is necessary to put the position of the University into perspective.

6.2 Between 1989 and 1995 Professor van Velzen worked at Myrtle Street on clinical duties for Alder Hey and on research for the University. He favoured the research work as will appear in 'The van Velzen Years'. The organs removed at post mortem examination at Alder Hey were collected at Myrtle Street where they were regarded as invaluable research material. Research records, the responsibility generally of the University, were unreliable throughout. The collection grew unmonitored and unchecked.

6.3 In 1995 Alder Hey and the University negotiated over the future of the organs. As discussion in Chapter 8 Part 8 of 'The van Velzen Years' will show, most of the organs were left to the University at Myrtle Street where they remained until 1999. During this period the University had sole occupancy of Myrtle Street and still made no attempt to catalogue either the organs or their use. They failed to assist Alder Hey in recent months and in fact have never fully catalogued the organs.

7. University and Alder Hey Relationship

7.1 By July 2000 the parents' representatives were also well aware from attending the SIPB of the poor relationship between Alder Hey and the University. The University was difficult about providing and sharing information. Invited to join the SIPB, they had attended only 4 out of the first 11 meetings, claiming that they were merely observers. The University has consistently failed to acknowledge its proper responsibility on the issue of organ retention.

7.2 One week after the 'moratorium' was lifted in August 2000 a special meeting of the SIPB was convened. The purpose of the meeting was threefold:

- to confirm that the new detailed lists were complete and revealed that organs had been retained from 62 children whose parents Alder Hey had previously told were not affected;

- to reveal the existence of a previously overlooked cerebellum collection;

- to reveal that many hearts at the ICH could not be identified.

7.3 Alder Hey issued a press release referring to the first two issues but omitting reference to the third. Parents on the SIPB had argued for and obtained a 24-hour embargo on the press release to give them the opportunity of warning parents of the impending revelations. There was insufficient time to complete this exercise. Further distress for parents was the inevitable consequence.

7.4 Alder Hey chose to inform parents of this latest 'definitive' list by telephone. They did not check if they were alone, or had support before telling them about the list of organs. It was another example of lessons not having been learned from September 1999. Link workers were described as caring in the way in which they passed on the news, but this did not reduce the impact of receiving over the telephone yet another version of what organs had been retained.

8. Cerebellum Collection

8.1 The cerebellum collection was gathered from brains retained by Professor van Velzen and used for research from 1995 onwards. In August 2000 Alder Hey revealed that 146 families were affected and in particular 58 sets of parents who had already had second funerals had to be told that there were cerebella yet to be buried. Examination of the brains before their return for burial would have revealed the absence of the cerebellum. The University surely held back the existence of the collection in late 1999 for a reason rather than inadvertently. The only reason that occurs to the Inquiry is in order to complete research. They retained the collection despite public knowledge of return of organs for second funerals and the inevitability of third funerals or else concealment.

8.2 The consequence of the announcement of the collection was that parents were yet again dismayed, disillusioned and distressed. Parents were telephoned at home with the news and were told that the cerebellum belonging to their deceased child had been retained. One parent was told that their child's cerebellum had been retained and was later told that it had not. Alder Hey thought they were in a position to give parents clear answers to all the outstanding issues and resolve past errors. They still have not told the parents that the general practice was to remove every organ from every child between September 1988 and the end of 1995.

8.3   Another issue emerged. Some parents became aware that Alder Hey was still retaining blocks and slides taken from organs and requested their return. Alder Hey's response has been inconsistent, depending upon how they perceived the likely reactions of parents. Sometimes they have denied the existence of blocks and slides. On occasions they have returned them. Sometimes they have claimed that they cannot be returned as they constitute a medical record, on other occasions they have claimed that the blocks and slides constitute a medical record which may not be returned until ten years have elapsed. The policy of openness and honesty was compromised.

8.4   The case of Christopher, who died in 1988, aptly summarises general feeling among parents. On 5 September 2000 Christopher's father wrote to the Inquiry complaining that he had asked the SIPB what had happened to the remainder of his son's organs. At the outset he had been told that his son's heart, lungs and brain had been retained. Later he received a comprehensive list of other organs which had been removed at post mortem examination. He asked where these organs were, but the response was inconclusive. Karen England misrepresented that Professor van Velzen's practice was to return organs to the body before burial. Christopher's father contacted Professor van Velzen directly and he correctly denied the practice. The organs remain unaccounted for even by the end of October 2000. Christopher's father was also told that blocks and slides taken at post mortem examination were part of the medical record and could not be returned, despite the fact that Christopher had died more than ten years earlier. The pious hope was expressed that explanations given would help to put his father's mind at rest. The central concern remains unanswered.

9.   Conclusions

9.1   We have come to the following conclusions:

- The University and Alder Hey missed many opportunities to rein in and control Professor van Velzen in the period 1988 to 1995.

- The University and Alder Hey failed regularly to record access to the containers for whatever purpose.

- The University and Alder Hey failed to investigate post mortem practice in the period 1988 to 1995 which would have indicated that all organs were to be retained in every case.

- The University and Alder Hey should have retained a paediatric pathologist to head a team to catalogue the retained organs and fragments in September 1999.

- The catalogue would have revealed that it was impossible to account accurately for all the organs retained.

- The University and Alder Hey will never be able accurately to tell parents what has happened to every organ of every child who died between 1988 to 1995.

- The University has never accepted its responsibility in the matter and has left Alder Hey to make a sequence of mistakes.

- Alder Hey have made four or five separate attempts to provide parents with accurate information relating to organ retention, not learning from and compounding mistakes made in each previous attempt.

- The cerebellum collection should have been identified and revealed earlier by both the University and Alder Hey.

- Alder Hey failed to make provision for face to face communication of the news to parents.

- Alder Hey failed to make appropriate provision for advice, counselling and support to affected families.

9.2 We appreciate that in September 1999 Alder Hey was faced with a unique situation in terms of the amount and condition of organs at Myrtle Street. They had no control over the timing of the revelation at Bristol relating to the heart collection at the ICH. This was followed by an unprecedented number of parents requiring detailed information about organs retained from their children over an extensive period of time.

10. Recommendations

10.1 To prevent mishandling of this kind in the future we make the following recommendations:

- Serious Incident Procedures should be developed and put in place.

- In the event of a serious incident the Chief Executive and Trust Board shall devise a suitable Serious Incident Procedure similar to those already in place for major disasters and review it from time to time making any necessary alterations.

- When the procedure has been devised and prior to implementation the NHS Executive Regional Office shall assess its suitability and thereafter manage its performance, devising and instigating any necessary alterations from time to time.

- In devising a Serious Incident Procedure the Chief Executive and Trust Board shall consider the need for a serious incident team independent of the hospital.

- In devising a Serious Incident Procedure the Chief Executive and Trust Board shall consider the need for urgent professional counselling:

- A proportion of individuals within any group is always likely to require psychological support in the aftermath of disaster.

- An individual within the serious incident team shall be nominated to take responsibility for the arrangements and the identification of all those in need.

- Suitably trained practitioners shall provide the counselling.

- In devising a Serious Incident Procedure the Chief Executive and Trust Board shall take advice from and where necessary include within the serious incident team appropriate experts in bereavement, pathological reactions to bereavement and therapy.

- The Chief Executive and Trust Board shall make available suitably trained staff for implementing the Serious Incident Procedure.

- The Chief Executive and Trust Board shall inform all staff when a Serious Incident Procedure is in force.

- The Chief Executive and Trust Board shall ensure the proper debriefing and support of all staff associated with a serious incident.

- Universities and other public bodies shall adopt compatible procedures when acting in conjunction with an NHS serious incident.

10.2   Records should be reviewed and updated and an audit trail should be developed and put in place.

- The Chief Executive and the Trust Board shall review and update medical and pathology records to include, preferably on computer and cross-referenced, the following information:

  - name, medical record reference number and date of birth;

  - date, place of death and death certificate;

  - name and address of next of kin;

  - whether Coroner's or hospital post mortem examination;

  - date of consent for hospital post mortem examination;

  - names of pathologist and those in attendance;

  - post mortem examination reference number;

  - date of examination;

  - date of preliminary/final post mortem reports;

- date histology completed;

- record of specific instructions from the Coroner or clinicians;

- record of retained organs, samples, wax blocks, slides, photographs, X-rays, date and method of dispersal or disposal;

- case notes;

- signed consent form;

- copy of any other relevant correspondence or notes;

- name and address of general practitioner;

- date post mortem report sent to general practitioner;

- record of communication of findings to the next of kin.

- University records shall provide a confidential audit trail back to the clinical record.

- University records shall identify receipt, use, dispersal and ultimate disposal of any organ or sample.

Chapter 4. Special Cases for Investigation

Following reference to the Inquiry of Stephen White
by Lord Hunt, Parliamentary Under Secretary of State (Lords),
on 16 March 2000

Contents

1.   Introduction

1.1   On 16 March 2000 Lord Hunt requested that we investigate the circumstances of the case of Stephen White. During the course of the Inquiry we came across a number of similar serious cases, upon which we also focus in this chapter. We have carefully analysed all the evidence of each case individually. We begin with Stephen White.

Stephen White – 2 Weeks

2.   Background

2.1   Stephen James White was born on 12 May 1992 with congenital heart disease. He died during cardiac surgery on 26 May 1992. A Coroner's post mortem examination was carried out.

2.2   His mother was told in late 1999 by Alder Hey that her son's heart had been retained. Later she received a letter saying that the heart and other organs had been retained. She telephoned to clarify what was meant by 'other organs' and was told that the lungs and brain had also been retained. On 9 February 2000 she confirmed that she wished to make funeral arrangements. On 14 March 2000 she advised Alder Hey that a second funeral had been arranged for 17 March 2000 and a pathology technician was asked to locate the organs. At this point it was realised that the containers relating to Stephen White were empty. On 15 March 2000, two days before the funeral, the Chief Executive, Ms Hilary Rowland, visited Mrs White at home and told her that Stephen's organs had been mistakenly destroyed. She apologised for the distress that this caused.

3.   Reaction

3.1   Ms Rowland reported to the NHS Executive North West Regional Office on 14 March 2000. On 15 and 16 March 2000 they advised Lord Hunt, Parliamentary Under Secretary of State (Lords), of what had happened. He instructed the Regional Office to keep Mrs White fully informed of developments.

3.2   On 16 March 2000 Lord Hunt issued a press release recording his shock and anger. His reaction reflected that of parents involved in the organ retention issue. He immediately called for the resignation of the Trust Chairman, Mr Frank Taylor. He referred the Stephen White case to this Inquiry and stated that any disciplinary action, if appropriate, would be taken following publication of our findings. On the same day Lord Hunt confirmed in a media interview that the results of the report which he had requisitioned would be made public.

3.3   On 17 March 2000 the Trust, through Ms Rowland, provided Regional Office with the report which was sent on to Lord Hunt. He was unhappy with the lack of detail in the report and was disturbed by a number of aspects, highlighting both the lack of apparent accountability within Alder Hey and the failure to include a proper action plan. He demanded further information which Alder Hey provided to Regional Office the following day. However, Regional Office felt that the information provided remained inadequate and it was decided that Regional Office would now take responsibility for drafting the report.

3.4   After Regional Office had met with Ms Rowland and the Acting Director of Operations, Mrs Karen England, to clarify outstanding points, the report was redrafted and submitted to Lord Hunt on 22 March 2000. In essence the report concluded that the initial cataloguing of Stephen White's organs had listed retention of the heart, brain, lungs and abdominal organs. Mrs White had never been informed of the retention of abdominal organs. However, a routine second check of the organs, undertaken for the purpose of compiling a more detailed list, had revealed that the containers held only the heart, lung, part brain and only 'fragments' of abdominal organs. As there was a discrepancy between the two detailed visual checks the matter had been referred to Mrs England. She had given instructions for a Medical Laboratory Scientific Officer (MLSO) to dispose of the 'fragments' in accordance with an earlier decision made by

Alder Hey that fragments, which were not considered organs, should be disposed of to 'avoid any confusion'. In error the entire contents of the containers had then been disposed of with the fragments.

3.5 The report did not confirm the nature of the fragments, the date and place of destruction or the identity of the person responsible for disposing of the organs. However, Lord Hunt was under considerable pressure to act quickly in view of the problems since September 1999 in returning retained organs to parents. As the report reached a valid conclusion about the basic circumstances in which the organs had been disposed of the decision was rightly taken to publish the full report without further delay. Arrangements were made for the report to be released into the public domain at 7.00 am on 23 March 2000.

4. Publication of the Report

4.1 Lord Hunt appeared on the BBC Today programme at 7.00 am on 23 March 2000. In a press release embargoed until that time he announced the appointment of Mrs Judith Greensmith as the new Chair of Alder Hey and stated that one of her first tasks would be to review the liaison with families and to ensure that they had the support they needed. Mrs Greensmith was also to review management procedures and ensure that appropriate arrangements were in place for the return of the remaining organs to families. A new Project Board, reporting directly to the new Chair, was established to handle liaison with parents. The Regional Director, Professor Robert Tinston, was to take personal responsibility for ensuring that robust monitoring procedures were in place dealing with the return of organs effectively and appropriately.

4.2 On 15 March 2000 Lord Hunt had instructed Regional Office to keep Mrs White fully informed of developments. Despite those instructions Mrs White did not see Regional Office's report before its contents were disseminated to the media. Professor Tinston telephoned Hugh Lamont, Head of Communications at Regional Office, between 8.00 am and 9.00 am on 23 March 2000 to obtain confirmation that Mrs White had been told about the press release and the report. She had not, nor had she seen the report. Mr Lamont tried to contact Mrs White on the morning of 23 March 2000, but only managed to speak to her later that afternoon. He apologised for the fact that the report was in the public domain before she had seen it and offered to drive to her home later that day to deliver it. Mrs White said it would not be necessary and it was agreed that Mr Lamont would post the report.

4.3 Mr Lamont described Mrs White's attitude in conversation as reasonable and amicable. He drafted a letter of apology to her which he posted on 27 March 2000 enclosing a copy of the report. By this time, Mrs White had already seen the report, which had been sent to her by her solicitor to whom Mr Lamont had faxed a copy on 23 March 2000.

5. Inquiry's Findings

5.1 We accept the basic conclusion reached in the report prepared at Lord Hunt's request. The second visual check of the retained organs concluded that the fragments of tissue could not be identified as specific abdominal organs. Stephen was only 14 days old when he died, so any retained organs would have been small. Alder Hey had previously decided that fragments would be disposed of to avoid unnecessary upset to parents as in their view fragments did not constitute organs. This decision was taken without consultation with the parents and is another example of paternalism. Because of the initial decision to dispose of fragments of tissue there will be some families who sought the return of organs from Alder Hey and who have not had those fragments returned, because they have been disposed of as clinical waste. In discussions with Regional Office at the time of completion of the report for Lord Hunt, Ms Rowland accepted this inevitability.

5.2 In accordance with the predetermined policy and to avoid confusion arising from the discrepancies in the two visual checks Mrs England took the decision in Stephen White's case to dispose of the fragments. The histology record sheet was amended. In error the entire contents of the containers were then disposed of. There is no record as to the date, time, place or method of disposal. Even a proper system for reuniting retained organs would be undermined by this kind of slackness and lack of integrity.

5.3 Mrs England told us that her instruction was specific. It related to fragments and not Stephen's other organs. She had never seen the fragments for herself but relied upon information from Mrs Jackie Waring who had taken over her job as Chief MLSO in 1993. Mrs England was unable to put a date on the disposal of the organs, nor was it possible to identify which of the laboratory technicians had actually disposed of them. Mrs Waring herself observed that she could only speculate as to whether the organs had been thrown away in error or deliberately and she could not honestly comment.

5.4 Stephen's mother should have been told of the fragments from the outset. The problem in identification should not have been kept from her. Mrs England appears to have decided what was best for Mrs White to know.

6. What Did Happen to Stephen White's Organs?

6.1 We have tried to establish when disposal of the organs occurred. On 23 February 2000 the Inquiry's Paediatric Pathologist, Dr Jean Keeling, visited Alder Hey. She had asked that 200 containers be made available to her for inspection. Stephen White's containers could not be traced at the time of her visit. On 8 March 2000 Mrs England signed the organ release form in preparation for the forthcoming funeral even though she did not know where the organs were. Despite the indications of a potential problem on 23 February 2000, it was not acknowledged that the containers and the contents were missing until 14 March 2000. Had the contents of the containers been checked immediately before the release form was signed it might have avoided compounding the problem.

6.2 The question of when the organs were disposed of is highly relevant, as the Secretary of State had instructed Alder Hey in a letter that no further tissue should be disposed of in any case. This instruction was received and circulated, according to management, by Alder Hey on 21 February 2000. Regional Office's conclusion when preparing the reports requested by Lord Hunt was that the organs were disposed of 'between October 1999 to late January 2000' but procedures were not in place to be more precise than this.

6.3 Regional Office did not consider that the organs could have been disposed of after the Secretary of State's instruction was received. They noted that Ms Rowland had confirmed that no tissue had been disposed of in any case since 21 February and all staff had been made aware of the content of the letter from the Secretary of State. However, we heard specific evidence from staff at Alder Hey that the directive from the Secretary of State had not been circulated to them, so they were unaware of the express instruction not to destroy tissue. Further, in Simone's case (see paragraphs 12–24 below), it is clear that tissue was disposed of after 21 February 2000. Regional Office's assertion that the organs could not have been disposed of after Secretary of State's instruction does not therefore necessarily follow. However, we would agree that on balance it is likely that disposal did take place before the express instruction issued by Secretary of State. We are unable to date precisely the disposal of Stephen's organs due to the complete absence of proper paperwork but the date of the second visual check (between October 1999 and January 2000) identifying the discrepancy suggests disposal took place before the directive.

6.4 Mrs White should have been told of the contents of the report before it was published on 23 March 2000. Mr Lamont's explanation for failing to contact Mrs White is that he was so busy preparing the ground for the announcement of Judith Greensmith as the new Chair and dealing with other matters associated with the press release that he forgot to tell her. He also relied on the fact that the press release was only completed relatively late on 22 March 2000. Nevertheless Lord Hunt's instruction that Mrs White should be kept informed was not complied with. Someone should have been delegated to inform her of what was going on and provide her personally with a copy of the report.

7. Conclusions

7.1 The Stephen White case reveals errors and incompetence.

- In late 1999 Alder Hey sent a letter to Mrs White informing her that Stephen might be involved in the organ retention issue. Stephen's name was mis-spelt and the surname given was Little, not White.

- Mrs White telephoned Alder Hey and was told that his heart had been retained.

- Later she was told that the heart and 'other organs' had been retained.

- She was subsequently told that these other organs were the brain and lungs.

- She had thought she had buried all of Stephen at the original funeral.

- On 15 March 2000, two days before the second funeral, Mrs White was told that the organs had been mistakenly destroyed. The funeral had to be cancelled.

- On the evening of 22 March 2000 she should have received a copy of Regional Office's report explaining the loss of the organs and the reasons why the funeral had to be cancelled before it became public knowledge.

- The letter of apology from Mr Lamont was posted five days after the event, on 27 March 2000. She received a copy of the report from her solicitor, faxed to him on 23 March 2000 by Mr Lamont.

We are disappointed that no explanation has been forthcoming as to the circumstances in which the organs were destroyed. The report to Lord Hunt refers to laboratory staff being frightened to come forward. This does not reflect good personnel management. Any future reuniting of organs must prevent even fragments of organs being destroyed without parental consent. The policy adopted by Alder Hey was paternalistic and inappropriate. Mrs White had a right to know the details of everything retained from Stephen's organs.

7.2 We respectfully recommend that:

- every hospital keep proper records (preferably computerised) as to the source, consent to retain, usage and disposal of organs and tissue;

- every authorisation for release of organs for burial or cremation must not be completed until the content of the container is confirmed and the form counter-signed;

- a moratorium must be declared if records of organ retention are inadequate during which there should be an immediate cataloguing of organs retained;

- parents must never again be drip-fed information but should be kept fully informed.

Christopher and Kathryn

8.1   A fundamental prerequisite for the performance of a hospital post mortem examination is the consent of the surviving relatives. It is important that the various options open to relatives are fully explained and discussed. One option is to consent to a limited post mortem examination only. In such cases the pathologist must limit his post mortem examination to the organ(s) specified on the consent form. However, we found clear evidence that on occasions Professor van Velzen simply ignored parents' wishes and did not limit his post mortem examination as specified on the consent form or in any way. Remarkable examples of this are the cases of Christopher and Kathryn. In Christopher's case Professor van Velzen's actions came to the attention of senior management and yet no disciplinary action was taken.

Christopher – 15 Years 3 Months

9.1   In April 1993 Christopher was diagnosed as suffering from Hodgkin's disease. Later that year he was admitted to the Intensive Care Unit at Alder Hey. He died two weeks later. The death was not reportable to the Coroner but his treating consultant wanted to know whether there had been an infection which the medical staff had not been able to isolate.

9.2   Christopher's parents were asked if they would consent to a hospital post mortem examination and after discussion consented to a limited examination only. They agreed that a small chest incision could be made so that a biopsy of the lung could be taken. They specifically did not want a full post mortem examination to be performed. Their wishes were confirmed on no fewer than three separate documents prepared by the medical staff: the form sent to the mortuary attendant requesting a 'limited post mortem'; the mortuary registration form which recorded 'parents have agreed to biopsy through small chest incision'; the post mortem consent form which was said to be 'limited to a chest incision to biopsy of the lung'. Professor van Velzen, who performed the post mortem examination, had all three documents.

9.3   Professor van Velzen exceeded that authority in performing the post mortem examination. The report refers to 'opening' of the heart, trachea, bronchus, stomach, bowel and bladder and to the findings 'on section' of the lungs, pancreas, spleen and liver. The report also records the weights of both lungs, the heart, liver, spleen, pancreas and both adrenal glands and kidneys. Clearly the weight of those organs could only be accurately recorded if they had been removed from the body and weighed separately. The post mortem report was not sent to Christopher's parents.

9.4 Christopher's mother had a number of questions about her son's death and pursued those with the hospital. She learned that a post mortem examination had been performed when she had given consent only for a lung biopsy. In May 1994 she wrote to Ms Rowland requesting a meeting to discuss her concerns, writing 'a post mortem was done when I clearly stated that I did not want one'. Ms Rowland did meet her but was unable to answer all her queries. She sent a memo to the treating consultant and to her Medical Director, Dr Martin. There is no record of any written response from Dr Martin and in oral evidence he was unable to recall the case. However, the treating consultant made it very clear to Ms Rowland that what Professor van Velzen had done was unacceptable. She wrote,

> 'Professor van Velzen who performed the post mortem took it upon himself to look at various other organs through the incision he made to do the biopsy. Mr and Mrs X did not give permission for this and this has caused them extreme distress. I actually showed Mrs X the written request I had made for the biopsy and the documentation in the notes. I can understand that she feels her wishes were not taken into account.'

The consultant suggested it might be easier for Ms Rowland to discuss the case with her.

9.5 Ms Rowland did not take up that offer but instead sought Professor van Velzen's comments. His response was a tissue of lies. He wrote to Ms Rowland claiming that he had made an incision of 'no more than 7cms, just enough to allow my right hand to pass into the body cavity'. He enclosed a letter addressed to the parents purporting to explain the position. That letter claimed that he was able to assess many organs by gently touching them and feeling for abnormalities including general assessment of size; tissue samples taken would not have exceeded 1 x 1 x 1 mm; no post mortem was carried out 'in the classic sense'; he had not interfered with Christopher's skull or damaged his body; he had not removed organs from the body to be only partially replaced, but Christopher had been buried with all his organs in exactly the same position as in life. He claimed that wherever he had quoted organ weights in his report these were based on his assessment by hand, a technique he had learnt through years of practice and in which he was usually accurate to about 10 per cent – 15 per cent.

9.6 Any reasonable assessment of Professor van Velzen's response would have led Ms Rowland to conclude that that letter was nonsense. Indeed, in giving oral evidence to us Ms Rowland subsequently described it as 'pure fantasy'. However, she did not reach that conclusion at the time, and instead a letter was prepared in her name to the parents. This repeated Professor van Velzen's lies, stating that a small incision only had been made, that there had not been a full post mortem examination but only a very limited investigative procedure through that incision, and that all the internal organs had been left in place. She said that there had been no damage to the body save for the incision necessary to take lung tissue. Her assistant drafted the letter but in her oral evidence Ms Rowland accepted full personal responsibility for the letter.

9.7   Ironically, that letter, which was based on wholly inaccurate information provided by Professor van Velzen, did not actually reach the parents who, hearing nothing and feeling that they were being fobbed off, elected to leave matters due to the stress the whole process was causing.

9.8   In March 2000 the parents discovered that Christopher's organs had been retained. Their distress on being told that their son's heart, lungs, spleen and stomach had been retained, after the assurances given when the consent to the lung biopsy was obtained, can only be imagined. In her questionnaire Christopher's mother said that she felt she had buried 'an empty body' and 'felt that I had been raped because I said no'. In discussions with her link worker at Alder Hey, Sue McQueen (whom she describes as 'marvellous'), Christopher's mother became aware of Ms Rowland's 1994 letter which she had never received, which distressed her further. The denial in the letter that there had been a full post mortem examination and the statement that the organs had been returned to Christopher's body in the correct place seemed contradictory. The parents naturally began to wonder whether the letter was accurate. They wondered whether they had buried organs belonging to another child. They had endured a second funeral in June 2000. A meeting was arranged with the treating consultant to clarify the position. She explained that the letter was inaccurate.

9.9   Christopher's case is remarkable. Professor van Velzen acted without authority. The parents' wishes were flouted. In oral evidence to the Inquiry, Christopher's treating consultant described Professor van Velzen's actions as 'outrageous' and a 'total travesty of what had been agreed'. She felt that he had 'betrayed the medical trust of all people caring for Christopher'.

9.10   Dr Keeling, the Inquiry's clinical expert, confirmed that it was impossible for Professor van Velzen to have come to his conclusions about the state of Christopher's organs by carrying out an examination through a 7cm upper abdominal incision. On inspection of the containers prior to the return of Christopher's organs she found substantial tissue including five large and two smaller pieces of lung, amounting to the major part of two lung lobes. There was a slice through the heart which involved the full circumference of both ventricles. She was able to state that the organs retained were consistent with those of a child of Christopher's age.

9.11   Professor van Velzen's behaviour was unacceptable and justified disciplinary procedures. Ms Rowland failed to deal with the parents' complaint despite the clear advice of the treating consultant who exposed Professor van Velzen's actions. In oral evidence Professor van Velzen admitted that he had not acted in accordance with the instructions on the consent form, agreed that his letter to Ms Rowland/the parents was 'rubbish' and accepted that he should have been severely disciplined. The Medical Director, Dr Martin, confirmed that Professor van Velzen's letter was 'nonsense', and agreed that a final warning at least, and possibly dismissal, was merited in the light of his actions. Proper assessment of the parents' complaint at the time should have led to disciplinary action and referral of Professor van Velzen to the General Medical Council. Ms Rowland and Dr Martin, who had been asked for his comments on the case, must take responsibility for their failure to take appropriate action at the time.

Kathryn – 15 Years

10.1   Christopher's case was not the only one where Professor van Velzen exceeded the consent given by parents when performing post mortem examination. Kathryn's parents gave consent to a limited post mortem examination and were told that small tissue samples only would be taken through a restricted incision of the lung, liver and kidney. The consent form actually signed by the parents was somewhat broader. Permission was given 'for the removal of tissue for diagnostic and other purposes other than transplantation' but the agreement to limit post mortem examination was clear and accepted by the treating consultant in a report annexed to the post mortem report. Indeed, Professor van Velzen's post mortem report itself referred to a small mid-sternal incision having been made which enabled 'only the upper organs and the lower aspects of the chest organs' to be brought into view for inspection, the rest of the post mortem assessment being 'done on palpation'.

10.2   As in Christopher's case, however, the post mortem report itself belies Professor van Velzen's claim. There is reference to the 'opening' of the heart and bowel and to findings 'on section' of the lungs, pancreas, spleen, liver, kidney, thymus and adrenal glands.

10.3   In December 1999 Kathryn's parents received a letter from Ms Rowland confirming that her heart, lungs, liver, spleen and kidneys had been retained, clear evidence that Professor van Velzen had exceeded his authority.

10.4   We are also aware of another case involving the same clinical team where consent was given to a limited post mortem examination of the lungs only. In the post mortem report, however, Professor van Velzen clearly described that the organs of the chest and abdomen were removed from the body in order that the examination could be done. Histology was reported on the heart, aorta, lung, thymus, spleen, liver, pancreas, kidney and adrenal glands. The examination exceeded, by a considerable margin, the consent given by the parents.

10.5   There can be no justification for Professor van Velzen's actions in these cases. His behaviour exemplified his lack of respect for the parents and their children.

Stephen – 2 Years 1 Month

11.1   Stephen died at Alder Hey Hospital shortly after admission in October 1994. The clinician in the Intensive Care Unit asked his parents to consent to a hospital post mortem. She told them that a small sample of tissue was required for microscopic examination.

11.2   They were eventually persuaded to sign a consent form and Professor van Velzen carried out a post mortem examination. They would have liked more information about post mortem examination and now feel that the consent form should have been read out and explained to them.

11.3   In September 1999 they were told that Stephen's heart and brain had been retained and sampled following post mortem examination. The way in which they were told of the retention lacked dignity or sympathy. They have never received an apology.

11.4   A second funeral was arranged to take place in November 1999. Shortly before the funeral, they received the organ release form from the undertaker and realised that the casket included organs other than the heart and brain. This caused great anxiety.

11.5   In January 2000 Stephen's parents received a letter from Alder Hey stating that not all the organs had been returned. They were devastated, asked for their immediate return and began arrangements for a third funeral. A week later they received another letter explaining that all of Stephen's organs had been returned in November and the information contained in the January letter was just an administrative error. This left his parents in a state of uncertainty and they decided that the only way they could secure peace of mind as to precisely what they had buried was to exhume Stephen's casket from the second funeral and check its contents.

11.6   Initially Alder Hey were resistant, but after involvement of the family solicitor and the Solicitor to the Inquiry they agreed to fund the exhumation. Dr Keeling examined the contents of the casket. Stephen's parents had originally been told that the organs returned included the kidneys and liver, but these organs were not to be found. There was no spleen, an organ which, judging by the post mortem report, had been removed at the post mortem examination.

11.7   After two funerals and an exhumation the parents are still left with the following questions:

● Why were they informed in a letter in January 2000 by Alder Hey that the liver and kidneys had in fact been returned when they had not?

● Where are Stephen's liver and kidneys?

● Where is Stephen's spleen?

Stephen's parents feel that they will never be able to put their son to rest, or free themselves of the turmoil consuming their family until they have answers to these questions.

11.8   The parents complain that throughout Alder Hey have treated them arrogantly and insensitively. The information they have received has been misleading and inconsistent. They feel that in the circumstances Alder Hey should have sent someone to visit them and explain what was going on.

11.9   Stephen's is one of the most unsatisfactory and distressing cases it is possible to imagine. Alder Hey has still not provided a proper answer to any of the questions raised by his parents. The parents also feel that because Stephen died so soon after admission to hospital the death should have been reported to the Coroner. They have now reported the death to the Coroner who is to make further enquiries.

Simone – 3 Years 4 Months

12.   Background

12.1   Simone was born in 1989. She suffered from transposition of the great arteries, enlargement of ventricular septal defect and hypoplastic left ventricle. She underwent surgical intervention in 1990 and 1993. Before the first operation, undertaken by Miss Roxanne McKay, Consultant Paediatric Cardiac Surgeon, her mother was told that Simone had an even chance of surviving. Before the second operation she states that Mr Roger Franks, Consultant Cardiothoracic Surgeon, told her that the prospects of survival were as high as 75 per cent. Simone deteriorated following surgery and died in 1993.

13.   Involvement of the Coroner

13.1   Simone died three days after the operation from which a successful outcome had been expected. The present HM Coroner for Liverpool, Mr Andre Rebello, states that any death occurring within 48 hours of an operative procedure should be reported to the Coroner, as should any case where the death might be related to a medical procedure or treatment. This was clearly the case here, although Regulation 41 of the Registration of Births and Deaths Regulations 1987 is not quite so specific. In all the circumstances it would have been sensible to report the death to the Coroner. Mr Rebello has confirmed to the Inquiry that the death was not reported at the time, but it has been now and he is investigating formally.

14. Consent to Hospital Post Mortem Examination

14.1 Simone's mother gave evidence that the possibility of a Coroner's post mortem examination was used as a threat to induce her to give consent to a hospital post mortem examination. She says Mr Franks made it clear that if she did not sign the post mortem consent form then he would ask the Coroner to order a post mortem examination. She did give her consent, although she rang the cardiac department later that day to say that she wanted an independent pathologist to carry out the examination. She was told her wishes would be respected. However, correspondence shows that those wishes were treated as a request for a second opinion, but no steps were taken to arrange any such second opinion.

14.2 Mr Franks gave evidence that in his view Simone's death was not reportable to the Coroner. He denied that he would have made any reference to a Coroner's post mortem examination. However, he also told us of other deaths reported to the Coroner where a hospital post mortem examination was not just discussed with parents but on occasions actually performed. In these circumstances we prefer the mother's recollection and conclude that the nature of the discussion was inappropriate.

15. Independent Pathologist?

15.1 A hospital post mortem examination was performed by Professor van Velzen. Simone's mother's request for an independent pathologist was ignored. Mr Franks says it was Professor van Velzen's responsibility to organise the independent post mortem but the correspondence does not confirm that he was asked to make appropriate arrangements. Had Simone's death been reported to the Coroner then, under Rule 6 (1)(c)(iii) of the Coroner's Rules 1984, her mother would have been entitled to ask that the examination be performed by a pathologist not associated with Alder Hey. After the post mortem examination the findings were not disclosed to her.

15.2 Simone's mother queried whether there had been a 'cover up'. We have no evidence of this, but the lack of transparency surrounding the post mortem procedure is a matter for concern. General issues surrounding the Coroner's process are addressed in Chapter 9.

16. Initial Enquiries Regarding Organ Retention

16.1 Simone's mother was one of the first parents to make enquiries of Alder Hey after the news of organ retention became public. She telephoned in September 1999 asking if Simone's heart had been retained and was told that it had not. Some time later she made a further enquiry asking whether any of Simone's organs had been retained. She was told that someone would ring her back, but she became tired of waiting and went to the hospital demanding an answer. She was told that no organs had been retained. This was confirmed in writing a few weeks later.

16.2 Simone's organs had in fact been retained. The initial information given to Simone's mother was inaccurate. Ms Valerie Mandelson, who co-ordinated the Family Support Team from October to December 1999, was told within a few days that inaccurate information had been given. She surmises, probably correctly, that the initial check had been made under an incorrect name. Ms Mandelson's initial reaction was that Simone's mother could not be told of the error because of the distress it would cause. She says she acted out of a wish to protect her. She knew how devastating parents found it to be told about organ retention, so receiving such information, in the light of the assurances previously given, would be dreadful. However, Simone's mother had made it clear she wanted to have the information and she should have been told. Ms Mandelson now accepts that and admits that she was misguided in her actions. She was open and apologetic in her evidence to us.

17.   Amendment of the Database

17.1 Ms Mandelson then removed Simone's name from the paper printout detailing the children whose organs had been retained. The printout was the first port of call for other administrative staff to check organ retention in any particular case. She also ensured that the enquiry database on the computer indicated that the mother had been told 'no' in relation to her query regarding organ retention. She stuck a post-it on the computer in the Incident Room saying '(Mother's name): do not allocate'. Ms Mandelson says, quite frankly, that she took this action of her own accord and not as a result of any instruction.

17.2 Ms Mandelson then spoke to her line manager, Ms Sally Ferguson, the acting Director of Nursing. The two have slightly different recollections of the discussion. Ms Ferguson recalls advising Ms Mandelson to inform Ms Rowland and Mrs England of what had happened, so there could be further discussion about what should be done. Ms Mandelson believes it was 'understood' that Simone's mother 'could not' be told what had happened and the need to speak to Ms Rowland and Mrs England was purely to keep them informed.

17.3 Ms Mandelson met with Ms Rowland and Mrs England and told them what had happened. She accepts she did not ask what should be done and that no instruction was given not to tell Simone's mother the truth. However, it was understood by the three of them that unless a specific instruction was given at this point to tell the mother then there would be no further contact with her.

17.4   Ms Rowland and/or Mrs England had the opportunity to ensure Simone's mother was told immediately but did not do so. The position in early November 1999 was therefore that Simone's mother, despite having made two specific enquiries to establish whether Simone's heart and/or other organs had been retained, remained under the misapprehension that there had been no retention. Alder Hey knew this to be inaccurate. The database and printout had been amended to reflect what Simone's mother had been told, rather than what was actually the case.

18.   Identification of the Organs

18.1   In December 1999 Simone's retained organs were routinely examined and listed as part of Alder Hey's general cataloguing process. Mr Liam Nolan, a locum Medical Laboratory Scientific Officer (MLSO) employed by Alder Hey, prepared a 'full details list'. Organs were transferred from Myrtle Street to Alder Hey and afterwards were returned to the pathology stores in Alder Hey. Mr Nolan did not know that Simone's mother had not been informed of the retention.

19.   Further Enquiries Regarding Organ Retention

19.1   After Professor van Velzen's appearance on the BBC programme 'Close Up North', in February 2000, Simone's mother contacted Alder Hey again. She requested a copy of the post mortem report and saw that Professor van Velzen had performed the post mortem. She asked more questions, which came to the attention of Ms Russell, a member of the Incident Team responsible to Ms Therese Harvey, the Director of Human Resources. Ms Russell recalled the post-it on the computer, and recognised the writing. On 21 February 2000 she spoke to Ms Mandelson who explained the sequence of events. Ms Russell then went to see Ms Harvey. She explained that Simone's mother had been given inaccurate information previously and a decision had been made not to go back and tell the truth. Ms Harvey made it clear that the mother would have to be told but demanded a physical check of the organs be undertaken. This check confirmed that Simone's organs remained in the pathology department. Ms Harvey informed Ms Rowland who agreed with the decision to tell Simone's mother the truth.

19.2   Ms Sue McQueen, a help line worker, spoke to Simone's mother. She told her that part of Simone's brain, liver, spleen, kidney, reproductive organs and intestine had been retained. Subsequent correspondence confirmed that the pancreas had also been retained but there was no mention of retention of Simone's heart and lungs. The information coincided with the 'full details list' completed by Mr Nolan. Simone's mother told Ms McQueen that the organs should not be disposed of and said that she had been in touch with the Coroner, to bring Simone's case to his attention. In the interim, on 18 February 2000, Secretary of State had issued a written directive to Alder Hey making it clear that no organs should be disposed of without further instruction. We were told that Alder Hey circulated this instruction on 21 February 2000.

20. Disposal of the Organs

20.1   Despite this instruction, and unknown to Simone's mother at the time, Mr Dearlove, one of the MLSOs, disposed of Simone's organs on or around 23 February 2000. Prior to the disposal, Mr Nolan had seen the two containers holding the organs near Mr Dearlove's work area in the laboratory and had wondered why they were there. He did not pursue the issue, assuming there was a valid reason why the organs had been taken out of storage.

20.2   Mr Dearlove said that he disposed of the organs quite deliberately because he had been instructed to do so by Mrs England 'because of discrepancies in the database system'. He said that Mrs England had explained to him that 'the parents had not been told about these organs, they had been told no (organs had been retained) on several occasions and that she thought it better, rather than cause them any more distress, would I dispose of the organs'. Mr Dearlove said that he was unaware of Secretary of State's directive that organs should not be destroyed.

20.3   Mrs England denies that any such instruction was given stating that there was no reason to dispose of the organs as Simone's mother had been told of the retention. However, she accepted in oral evidence that she found Mr Dearlove 'utterly trustworthy' and that he would never have taken it upon himself to deliberately destroy organs. One of Mr Dearlove's fellow MLSOs, Ms Elizabeth Clapham, recalls Mr Dearlove returning from a meeting with Mrs England and informing her that he had been requested to dispose of the organs. This gives support to Mr Dearlove's contentions.

21. Why was an Instruction to Dispose Given?

21.1   Mr Nolan's duties included production of detailed lists to families, returning organs and casketing arrangements for families. In early/mid February 2000 he reviewed the contents of approximately 400 containers at Mrs England's request. At the conclusion of that process he advised Mrs England of a number of queries. In particular he had recognised that Simone's name was not on the histology database, but organs had been retained. At the very least, therefore, Mrs England knew that there was a discrepancy on the database, which again supports Mr Dearlove's evidence. She may even have recalled that Simone's mother had been told previously that no organs had been retained as she had been present at the meeting in October with Ms Mandelson and Ms Rowland when this had been discussed and the enquiry database also reflected this. An instruction to dispose of the organs might have been an attempt to extricate Alder Hey from an embarrassing situation.

21.2 If Mrs England knew, however, that Simone's mother was to be told the truth about the retention of organs, then clearly an instruction to dispose of organs to protect Alder Hey would have been illogical. Mrs England gave evidence that she, Ms Russell, Ms Harvey and Ms Rowland all knew that the organs had been located and that Simone's mother was to be told. She says Ms Russell told her this was to be done. She says there was therefore no motive for her to instruct Mr Dearlove to dispose of the organs.

21.3 However, Ms Russell was clear in her evidence that she did not communicate such information to Mrs England and had no cause to do so as she was directly responsible to Ms Harvey. She did not recall Mrs England being present when she told Ms Harvey of the position. The evidence therefore does not confirm Mrs England's involvement in that loop of information. We accept Mr Dearlove's evidence that Mrs England instructed him to dispose of the organs because of the database discrepancy. We are satisfied that Mr Dearlove would not have disposed of the organs without receiving specific instruction to do so.

22. What Organs were Disposed of?

22.1 The 'full details list' of retained organs given to Simone's mother did not include Simone's heart and lungs. Simone's mother telephoned Professor van Velzen who told her that his practice was to retain all the organs including heart and lungs. He said he would have sent the heart and lungs to the Institute of Child Health (ICH). Mr Dearlove gave evidence that 'one pot was in the ICH and the rest had been down at Myrtle Street and somebody removed them to Alder Hey'. This would suggest that the heart and lungs had been retained. However, the two containers which Mr Nolan observed in Mr Dearlove's work area were Myrtle Street containers, neither being a glass container of the type which he had seen in the ICH. His expectation was that one of the containers would have held the brain, and the second the other organs. If the heart and lungs were retained, they have never been successfully located by Alder Hey.

23.   The Disposal Revealed

23.1   In early May 2000 Simone's mother made a further enquiry of the help line. The list of retained organs had included 'partial brain' and she wanted to know exactly what part and what had happened to the rest of the brain. The enquiry was passed by Ms McQueen to Mr Nolan who was unable to locate the containers. It was at this stage that the previous disposal of the organs came to light. On 11 May Mrs Kate Jackson, the Serious Incident Project Board Director, spoke to Simone's mother and asked to see her at home. She agreed and Mrs Jackson broke the news of the disposal of Simone's organs. On 12 May Alder Hey issued a press statement pledging a full investigation. The press statement made public Simone's name. This was contrary to her mother's wishes and further distress was caused. Mrs Judith Greensmith, Chair of Alder Hey, whilst of the view that there was public interest in the incident, accepted that Alder Hey should have been more aware of the sensitive nature of the situation.

24.   Conclusions

24.1   The story of Simone's case is extremely disturbing from start to finish.

- Pressure was exerted on the mother to consent to a hospital post mortem examination.

- A hospital post mortem examination was performed when a Coroner's post mortem examination was more appropriate.

- Simone's mother was denied the independent pathologist she specifically requested.

- The findings of the post mortem report were not communicated to Simone's mother and her understanding of Simone's death was incomplete.

- Organs were retained without the mother's knowledge.

- When Simone's mother enquired about organ retention she was given inaccurate information.

- When it was discovered that Simone's mother had been given inaccurate information she was still not told the truth, at best because a paternalistic attitude prevailed, at worst because there was a cover up. Ms Rowland and Mrs England should have instructed Ms Mandelson to tell Simone's mother what had happened.

- Simone's mother had requested specific information about organ retention on many occasions and it should have been provided at the earliest opportunity.

- It was wrong to amend the database to cover Alder Hey's tracks and turn misinformation about organ retention into a lie.

- The mother's persistence forced Alder Hey to reveal that Simone's organs had been retained. She is still unaware as to the whereabouts of her child's heart and lungs.

- Retained organs were disposed of contrary to Simone's mother's instructions, Secretary of State's instruction and despite the involvement of HM Coroner.

- Disposal was carried out to Mrs England's instruction.

- The press release contravened the mother's right to confidentiality.

- Alder Hey has failed to explain properly to Simone's mother the circumstances of disposal of the organs.

24.2   This sorry sequence of events has incrementally increased the grief and distress of Simone's mother. There was a concerted attempt to conceal the fact of organ retention from her. There is a high incidence of suspicion that there has been a cover up. The treatment of Simone's family has been tardy, disrespectful, insensitive and totally lacking in understanding or compassion.

Chapter 5. Guide to Post Mortem Examination

Contents

1. Introduction

1.1 A post mortem examination, sometimes referred to as an autopsy, is a careful examination of a body after death by a pathologist. A pathologist, who works in hospitals and medical schools, is a qualified doctor specialising in the study of disease. The pathologist investigates the changes in body tissues and organs that cause, or are caused by, disease. Pathologists who specialise in the examination of fetus, babies and children are called paediatric or perinatal pathologists. They usually work in children's hospitals, maternity hospitals or large pathology departments in teaching hospitals.

2. Reasons for Post Mortem Examination

2.1 The post mortem examination is performed primarily for the parents to help them to understand better the reasons for their baby or child's death. The post mortem may find a medical condition that caused or contributed to death. In some cases, it will provide important information about an underlying abnormality or condition that might recur in a future baby in that family and enable appropriate genetic counselling.

2.2   Sometimes the post mortem examination does not identify the cause of death and some questions may remain. This can be distressing but may provide reassurance that death did not result from any treatable disease or birth defect.

2.3   Post mortems also have wider functions. Clinicians learn from post mortems. In many cases, the examination will confirm clinicians' diagnoses. In others there may be unsuspected findings. The availability of this information is critical in the process of audit, when clinicians constantly evaluate their own performance with the aim of improvement. Parents should derive reassurance that they are being seen or their child is being treated by doctors who are engaged in the process of critical appraisal of their own work. Post mortem information has an important contribution to make in this process.

2.4   Post mortems also contribute to research and play a role in changing methods of investigation and treatment of infants and children. For instance they offer an opportunity to compare the results of different types of scanning with the actual structure of the abnormalities found. This process has been particularly important in the development of scanning for birth defects during pregnancy and the investigation of congenital heart disease. It has resulted in the diagnosis of more complex defects, greater accuracy and diagnosis earlier in pregnancy. Some of these developments have come about over a relatively short space of time. Obstetricians and radiologists have become more confident about diagnosis, allowing them to plan the future management of pregnancy with parents. Post mortems can assist in the evaluation of new treatment protocols, or the results of surgery, and be instrumental in improving infant mortality rates, particularly from conditions such as congenital heart disease.

2.5   In an even wider context, accurate information about the cause of death makes an important contribution to epidemiology and national statistics. This and the investigation of the cause of disease is relevant in determining how best to spend health service resources.

2.6   Sometimes tissue samples in wax blocks (see paragraph 4.6 below) and slides that remain once the diagnostic microscopy (see paragraph 4.5 below) has been completed, can be used for important research into the cause of disease. These tissues can be re-examined many years later and the pathology can be better understood in the light of newer discoveries and developments.

3. Types of Post Mortem Examination

3.1 There are two types of post mortem examination.

3.2 A Coroner's post mortem examination is carried out according to the provisions of the Coroner's Act 1988 and the Coroner's Rules 1984. Parental consent is not required but parents should be informed as to when, where and by whom the examination is to be performed. This matter is considered in detail in Chapter 9.

3.3 A hospital post mortem examination is carried out according to the provisions of the Human Tissue Act 1961. Lack of objection or informed consent on the part of the parents is required. Consent needs to be fully informed and the many options available to parents need to be discussed and explained (see Chapter 11 Consent).

4. Post Mortem Examination

4.1 The most benefit can be gained from post mortem examination if it is done as soon as possible after death. Increasingly, post mortems on babies and children are performed by perinatal or paediatric pathologists. As they may not work in the hospital where the baby died, the baby may have to be transferred to another hospital for the post mortem examination to be conducted. Parents should be informed before any transfer of their baby or child is to occur and this should be part of the information provided when consent for post mortem is obtained.

4.2 In the case of fetus, babies or children, it is usual for X-rays to be taken before the post mortem. Photographs might also be taken, particularly in the presence of abnormality or trauma.

4.3 A post mortem examination will be carried out with great care and respect for the body, as if the baby or child is having an operation. Two openings are made in order to remove those organs necessary to establish the cause of death, one down the front of the body and another across the back of the head. The major organs within the body, which will be removed, examined and weighed as part of the examination include the brain, heart, lung, liver, kidneys, spleen, thymus and adrenals.

4.4 The placenta is also an important part of the post mortem examination of fetus, stillbirths and deaths of newborns. The condition of the placenta should be considered in the process of reaching a conclusion about the cause of death.

4.5 A wide range of organs and tissues are examined microscopically, especially in babies and children. Microscopy is more likely to produce new information in perinatal or paediatric post mortem examination than in adult post mortem examinations. Firstly, this is to ensure that no unsuspected disease process has been missed, even in tissues that are not obviously the site of disease. Confirmation that these tissues are normal can be helpful. Secondly, even when the naked eye inspection of organs shows an abnormality, it may not be specific for a particular disease process. For example, the lungs of newborn babies affected by pneumonia, lack of oxygen, or by hyaline membrane disease (a lung disorder affecting premature babies) look very similar on naked eye examination.

4.6   To examine tissues microscopically, small samples are taken and then passed through a process whereby they are embedded in wax blocks. Very thin sections (approximately five thousandths of a millimetre) are then cut off these blocks and placed on a glass slide for examination through a microscope.

4.7   Sometimes samples are taken for culture to look for bacteria or viruses. It may be important to take a tissue sample for chromosome analysis.

4.8   In order to obtain as much information as possible it may be important to remove and retain an organ for detailed investigation. In babies and children in particular, the brain is very soft and it may not be possible to examine it in sufficient detail until it has hardened in fixative. This can take a number of weeks. Further, it is often important for a specialist, with particular expertise, to examine the brain to ensure any pathology is fully recognised and understood. The heart may also need to be retained. This is usually in cases of a complicated heart defect.

4.9   Organs should not be retained without specific consent. Parents, properly informed, might express a willingness to delay the funeral to allow for full examination of an organ after which it can be reunited with the body, in time for the funeral to take place.

4.10   Unless the parents have consented to retention, once the post mortem examination is completed, all the organs will be returned to the body. The body is then carefully restored, usually by the mortuary technician. The baby or child can then be seen and held by family members and dressed in his or her own clothes.

5.   The Limited Post Mortem Examination

5.1   Most information is gained from a full post mortem examination, which involves examination of all the major organs of the body including the brain. However, the examination can be limited, for example to a body cavity such as the chest or abdomen. Particular organs might be specified and, in a death resulting from congenital heart disease, examination could be limited to the heart and lung. Another type of limitation might be to restrict access to a previous surgical incision or removal of small samples of tissue through a tiny incision or biopsy needle for microscopic examination. A restricted or partial examination will often provide useful information, but there is always a risk that important pathology will be missed. Because of this risk, when a more limited examination is being contemplated, discussion with the pathologist is advisable before consent is obtained.

6.   The Post Mortem Report

6.1   Most pathologists dictate their reports on the day the examination is carried out, or the following day at the latest. Delay in dictation can result in loss of important detail. The report should be produced promptly. The report should contain an accurate description and interpretation of the post mortem finding.

6.2   The pathologist should report all the findings in a way that ensures their significance is understood by the clinician. The clinician is then able to provide full and correct information to the parents.

6.3   A preliminary report to the clinician should be available within days of the post mortem, either in the form of a letter or as a provisional report. Often initial communication will be by telephone, the content of which should be recorded. A final report, however, will usually take three to six weeks to be completed, as the results of the microscopic examination and sometimes other investigations become available and are incorporated in the report and conclusions. Some investigations may occasionally lead to a final report taking even longer to complete. Such investigations might include cytogenetics or retention of the brain for detailed study.

6.4   Clinicians should be aware of the timescale for reports. It is important that the post mortem report is available following perinatal death when the mother returns for her postnatal appointment. Scheduling appointments for parents with clinicians following death is far easier when completion of the report can be confidently anticipated. This avoids parental disappointment and frustration. It encourages full information, openness and fosters the parent/clinician relationship.

7.   Communication

7.1   Good communication between clinicians, pathologists, parents and Coroner is essential. It helps to reduce the incidence of misunderstanding and should result in parents receiving the information to which they are entitled. We regard this as so important that it is fully developed in Chapters 10 and 11.

7.2   There are a number of points in the process of the post mortem at which good communication can be encouraged. The pathologist can obtain a considerable amount of information from case notes, and access to these is important for the pathologist. Direct discussion between the pathologist and clinician before the post mortem can help to clarify particular questions, especially in a complex case.

7.3   There may even be advantages, in some cases, for the discussions between clinician and pathologist to occur before the clinician discusses consent for post mortem with the parents. For instance, the pathologist may recognise the importance of retention of an organ, or other special investigation, and the clinician will be more informed to discuss this with parents.

7.4   In some cases, it may be appropriate for the pathologist to assist the clinician in discussing the post mortem with the parents. Not only is the pathologist better able to answer parents' questions about the procedure than anyone else, but it may provide parents with greater confidence about the post mortem once they have spoken directly with the person who will undertake the procedure.

7.5   It is good practice for clinicians who have been looking after the baby or child in life to attend the post mortem examination. Clinicians should have the opportunity of seeing for themselves the true extent of disease. Attendance during post mortem examination will assist in ensuring that the clinicians' expectation of the examination is realistic. A post mortem examination cannot answer every question but good communication assists the process.

7.6   Pathologists recognise that it is not always possible for clinicians to attend post mortem examination. While prior warning and flexibility in timing of the examination will increase the window of opportunity for clinicians to attend it is inevitable there will be difficulties if babies or children are transferred to other hospitals for a post mortem examination, perhaps by a specialist paediatric pathologist.

7.7   The pathologist's report will provide an accurate description of the post mortem findings and will include an interpretation of those findings in the context of the clinical history. A clinician's presence during an examination will not change the substance of the report. When a condition is missed in life it will be recorded. The results of an operation will be fully described including any associated pathology. However, while the information provided by the post mortem will assist an understanding of the causes of a baby's or child's death, in isolation the post mortem cannot constitute a complete investigation into the correctness or otherwise of complex medical management.

7.8   Once the cause of death is established, the results must be explained sensitively to the parents by the clinician or their general practitioner. The pathologist should also be available for the parents and it may sometimes be appropriate for both clinician and pathologist to be involved with explanation of the post mortem results. A copy of the post mortem report should be made available to parents. The parents' interests in the results of post mortem examination are paramount.

7.9 It is good practice for the pathologist to attend clinical meetings when cases of the babies or children they have examined are being discussed. This includes perinatal mortality meetings, prenatal diagnosis/fetal anomaly meetings and unit audit meetings. These are excellent opportunities for communication between clinician and pathologist and permit exchange of both specific and general information between other consultants in the specialty, junior staff, nursing and midwifery staff and other professionals. They are important opportunities for discussion of changes to inpatient management and improvement of interdepartmental communication.

8. The Way Forward

8.1 The most important role of the post mortem is to help parents understand why their baby or child died and it may sometimes help them make decisions about the future. It also improves the body of medical knowledge, contributing to audit, medical education and research. Parental confidence in the post mortem will only occur if the procedure is discussed by clinicians who are fully aware of the procedure and possible outcomes. This will be facilitated by good communications with their pathologist.

8.2 It is important for individual units within the hospital to maintain a high post mortem rate. The number of children who die is small. It is important to find out as much as possible from each death. Units should look critically at their post mortem rates. Current medical practice means that many children with illnesses of long duration do not die in hospital. This should not, however, preclude post mortem examination.

8.3 Fully informed consent to hospital post mortem examinations must always be obtained and we explore this in detail in Chapters 10 and 11.

Chapter 6. Accountability Structure

Contents

1.   Introduction

1.1   Readers are now aware of the aftermath of what has happened in Liverpool namely the human suffering caused by organ retention. We will now move on to explain the origin and development of the various collections of organs discovered by the Inquiry in Liverpool. A detailed analysis of what occurred between 1986 and 1995 is given in Chapter 8, the period when Professor van Velzen was appointed and worked in Liverpool.

1.2   It is useful to consider the nature of NHS and University management to help understand how events unfolded. A glossary of medical terms with which the general reader will soon become familiar is also to be found on page 521.

1.3   The National Health Service (NHS) is a complex organisation, dependent upon collaborative inter-organisational relationships. This chapter simplifies the history and explains the varied changes in structure that the NHS in England has undergone, especially in relation to Alder Hey and the North West. It provides an introduction to the duty of accountability and responsibility to which the NHS in England must adhere. For the purposes of this report, only acute hospital services and those bodies to whom they report are included. In addition to the provision and management of health services, the close relationship that exists between the NHS and Universities for teaching and research purposes is explained as well as the role of the Ethics Committees who are responsible for the formal approval of clinical research.

2. The Establishment of the NHS

2.1 The National Health Services Act 1946 made the Minister of Health responsible for the constitution of Regional Hospital Boards, Hospital Management Committees and Boards of Governors of teaching hospitals.

2.2 A Statutory Instrument entitled National Health Service (Designation of Teaching Hospitals) designated the Royal Liverpool Children's Hospital as a teaching hospital. Sections 12, 13 and 14 of the Act set out the legal status, duties and responsibilities of the Hospital's Board of Governors,

> 'It shall be the duty of the Board of Governors of every Teaching Hospital, as from the appointed day, in accordance with Regulations and such directions as may be given to the Minister, generally to manage and control the hospital on behalf of the Minister, and in particular:
>
> (a) To provide for the University with which the Hospital is associated such facilities as appear to the Minister to be required for clinical teaching and research.'

The Board of Governors of the Hospital and the University of Liverpool were jointly responsible for appointments of senior management of the Hospital.

2.3 The Health Services and Public Health Act 1968 Section 6(1) extended these powers to administer specialist patient services outside the hospital, such as at a health centre or clinic. This was the only addition to the responsibilities of the Board of Governors until wholesale NHS reorganisation in 1974.

3. National Health Service Reorganisation 1974

3.1 The National Health Service Reorganisation Act 1973 abolished the Board of Governors from 1 April 1974. Responsibility for the Hospital passed formally to the Liverpool Area Health Authority (Teaching), which was associated with the University of Liverpool and came into operation on 24 August 1973. A Chairman ran the Authority with 19 members drawn from nominations by the University of Liverpool, appointments by Mersey Regional Authority and by Liverpool District Council. As it was a Teaching Authority there was provision for three additional members to be appointed.

3.2   Further guidance in December 1976 provided for 26 members (excluding the Chairman) to include additional local authority members to be appointed from 1 August 1977. A further circular in April 1979 changed the constitution of membership of the Authority to include general members, nominations from the City Council with reserved staff and University places.

3.3   In February 1982 new District Health Authorities were introduced. Membership was reduced to 18 with two additional members if the organisation was a Teaching Authority. Liverpool was listed as a District Health Authority designated for Teaching Purposes and this Authority took charge of the Royal Liverpool Children's Hospital on 1 April 1982. The Liverpool Health Authority (Teaching) had a membership of 18 members, three appointed on nomination of the University of Liverpool, nine appointed by the Regional Health Authority and two appointed by the Local Authority. As it was a Teaching Authority, there were a further two members appointed.

4.   National Health Service Reorganisation 1990 – The Establishment of NHS Trusts

4.1   The National Health Service and Community Care Act 1990 led to the establishment of a Health Service Trust, The Royal Liverpool Children's Hospital and Community Services National Health Service Trust, from 1 April 1991. This Trust was to own and manage accommodation and services at Alder Hey and associated hospitals such as Myrtle Street, including management of teaching and research facilities. Accountability was through the Trust Board of a chairman, five non-executive directors and five executive directors. The University appointed one of the non-executive directors because of the significant teaching and research commitment. Liverpool Health Authority gave assistance to the Trust before the Operational Date.

4.2   In 1996 the Trust changed its name to The Royal Liverpool Children's National Health Service Trust. This is the Trust accountable at present for Alder Hey Hospital.

5.   The Role of Management

5.1   The role of NHS managers has evolved through the decades, starting with the Hospital Management Committee and sub-committee structure in the 1950s and 1960s. The management task was largely administrative. The 'chief executive' role was confined to that of hospital administrator, more of a facilitator and person 'who got things done' rather than someone with wide ranging managerial and executive powers. Professional staff, in the main consultants, had responsibility for the clinical service provided and how it was provided. In this respect they were unfettered by any managerial influence.

5.2   It was not until the 1960s and 1970s that a serious look was taken at the roles and responsibilities of managers and the role of clinicians in management. In the latter case, doctors became involved in management through Executive Committees of clinical divisions. Chairmen of these committees could often have a very effective and powerful say in service delivery.

5.3   NHS reorganisation in 1974 prompted change at local hospital level through establishment of multi-disciplinary management teams who managed on a consensus basis. The hospital administrator, working with functional heads of departments and senior nursing staff, made day-to-day decisions on running the hospital. This was supported and managed at a higher level through a new structure made up of district managers reporting to Area Health Authorities who in turn were accountable to new Regional Health Authorities.

5.4   A fundamental overhaul of management resulted from the Griffiths Report published in 1983. It revealed a lack of management at all levels of the NHS, the need for monitoring of performance of NHS organisations and for greater accountability of use of resources. It questioned clinical autonomy, called for a simplified management structure and aimed to strengthen management in terms of leadership, effectiveness and professionalism. Reorganisation in 1982 had already witnessed the formation of new District Health Authorities replacing old districts and areas.

5.5   Performance measures were now possible through the introduction of statistical data of hospital activity. Griffiths recommended annual performance reviews of regions, districts and hospitals. General managers were appointed at regional, district and unit (hospital) levels. They were given wide ranging responsibilities to improve performance of the NHS through leadership, change, cost improvement and the inclusion of professional staff into the overall aims and objectives of the organisation. It was anticipated that this fundamental shift in culture and responsibility of management would take up to ten years to achieve. Management training thus became a vitally important issue and General Management Training Schemes were introduced.

5.6   At this time, it was recognised that clinicians should be more involved in the management of hospitals. This was put into effect through a gradual process of developing clinical directorates. Clinical services were organised into directorates with the clinical director assuming a leadership and management role. In the early days, the unit general manager could only negotiate with and influence clinical directors, who in turn negotiated with and influenced colleagues, rather than managing through clear lines of accountability. In effect, the clinical director's managerial responsibilities were added on to clinical responsibilities.

5.7   The major reorganisation of 1990/91 included the establishment of the NHS Executive as the operational arm of the Department of Health. Its role was primarily to oversee performance of the NHS through Regional Health Authorities down to Health Authorities, newly established hospital Trusts and hospitals remaining as District Managed Units (DMUs). The reorganisation prompted a more prominent role for professionals in management and greater accountability of the clinicians themselves for their clinical work. This was through the introduction of medical audit in which all doctors were required to participate. Clinical directors were generally organised under a medical director who was also an executive director on the Trust Board, in turn accountable to the chief executive and Board.

5.8   Chief executives replaced unit general managers (UGMs) who had to compete for the posts. Some UGMs, as in the case of the Royal Liverpool Children's NHS Trust, were not appointed as chief executive. These were a 'new breed' expected to deliver a much higher profile executive role and were accountable directly to Secretary of State via the NHS Executive. With the new role came substantial increases in salary commensurate with the additional responsibilities.

5.9   Hospitals wishing to become NHS Trusts in 1991 had to demonstrate a high degree of managerial competence and control. For example, they had to provide evidence of financial and organisational fitness including effective information systems. Management had to demonstrate the necessary skills and prove that doctors and nurses were actively involved in management. The Regional Health Authority scrutinised applications for Trust status to ensure these conditions were met before submission to the NHS Executive and finally Ministers for approval.

5.10   By 1991, with the establishment of Trusts, the greater involvement of clinicians in management through the clinical and medical directorate structures and the developing audit and clinical audit initiatives, the groundwork was laid for a more effective and accountable organisation.

5.11   The 14 Regional Health Authorities in England were abolished by Secretary of State on 31 March 1996. In their place, the NHS Executive established eight Regional Offices in England whose role it was to performance-manage the NHS in the region through Health Authorities and directly with NHS Trusts. That performance management role exists to this day.

6.   The University

6.1   The University of Liverpool and the Royal Liverpool Children's Hospital NHS Trust
have a responsibility to deliver training and education for medical students and to
facilitate research in medicine. This demands a productive relationship between the
University and the Trust, with shared managerial responsibilities and established lines
of communication.

6.2   Medical students, as part of their education and training, require access to clinical
situations and to patients. Students need to be taught by clinically expert academic staff
who are actively involved in research. This is essential and forms the basis of complex
relationships between the University's Medical Faculty and the Trust. The Medical
Faculty or Medical School at the University has relationships with a number of local
Trusts known as teaching hospitals, and one such is with the Royal Liverpool
Children's Hospital NHS Trust. Students are supervised and taught by both University
and NHS staff. Clearly these arrangements need to be regulated.

6.3   Academic staff of the University and Medical School are responsible directly to the
University through the head of the University department and then the Dean of the
Faculty of Medicine. In turn the Dean is accountable to the Vice Chancellor. However,
academic staff are also accountable to the Trust for their clinical teaching duties and
clinical activities in the NHS. This dual accountability is achieved through a contractual
arrangement with both the University and the Trust. For example, a University clinical
professor would have an honorary NHS consultant contract. Such a member of staff
would have fractions of time, e.g. 5/11ths with the University for teaching and research
purposes and 6/11ths dedicated to the relevant Trust patient clinical care activities. Thus
the individual would be responsible to the head of the department of the University for
one part of the contract and to the clinical director at the Trust for the other. Generally
this individual would be paid through the University with the NHS clinical part of the
salary paid by the NHS. Both the University and the Trust would perform recruitment
but the University is the main employer. This dual responsibility was explored in oral
evidence given by Professor Orme. He said,

> 'all University clinical academics in the Faculty of Medicine have a contract
> in which they provide six sessions to the NHS, … and their responsibility in
> that lies not to the Dean of Medicine but to the Chief Executive and Medical
> Director of the Trust, and they are answerable in disciplinary terms to the
> NHS in exactly the same way as an NHS consultant.'

6.4   Frequently, full-time NHS Trust clinical staff are asked to contribute to the teaching
of medical students. Those individuals may be given an honorary contract with the
University to perform this task and 1 or 2/11ths of their time would be dedicated

accordingly. Funding for the training of medical students from the NHS viewpoint is through a mechanism called SIfT (Service Increment for Teaching). The NHS Regional Office controls allocation.

6.5 In addition to the University's formal responsibility for educating medical students, it should provide facilities for research in medicine. For this purpose it receives a grant for medical and educational research from the Higher Education Funding Council for England (HEFCE).

6.6 All University clinical staff are expected to undertake teaching and research. Additional funding for research is received in a variety of ways: NHS Research and Development funding, commercial support for clinical trials, support from UK Research Councils, or from charitable or commercial sponsors. Responsibility for monitoring expenditure depends on the source but HEFCE funding is managed by the University and NHS Research and Development levy funding by the NHS.

6.7 These complex sets of arrangements involve both the Trust management and University, the latter via the Faculty of Medicine. The two organisations should maintain constant and close dialogue. Relationships are normally directed between the Dean of the Faculty of Medicine and the Medical Director of the Trust, or at the immediate level below being the head of the University Clinical Department and the relevant clinical director at the Trust.

6.8 The potential for confusion in lines of accountability for jointly appointed academic staff is summed up by Professor MacSween from Glasgow. Writing on 29 October 1992 to Professor Orme about academic appointments he said,

> 'where appointments of this type have been made the routine has not always been satisfactory, leading to separation of the academic and service (NHS) components with eventual and undesirable fragmentation. I think this must be avoided.'

6.9 A further complexity relates to accommodation. Medical Schools are usually located within the NHS Trust or Trusts. The Liverpool University Medical School is located within the Royal Liverpool and Broadgreen University Hospital NHS Trust but has a range of teaching facilities located in other local NHS Trusts including the Royal Liverpool Children's Hospital NHS Trust. In the case of the latter, the accommodation of the Institute of Child Health, part of the Medical School, is located on the Alder Hey site. Universities usually pay for teaching accommodation through leasing arrangements.

The Audit Structure

7.   Internal Audit

7.1   Internal audit was predominantly focused on finance, but not clearly defined before the 1974 reorganisation. New management arrangements in 1974 defined internal audit of hospitals as within the Regional and Area Treasurers' responsibilities. Until the early 1980s the function tended to be performed by small teams of middle ranking grades, although larger authorities could attract more qualified staff. The state of internal audit is captured in a 1981 Public Accounts Committee report by the description 'weak and ineffective'.

7.2   Developments in the 1980s, such as production of the NHS Internal Audit Manual in 1987, led to an agreed definition of internal audit and minimum accepted standards. These covered 'soundness and adequacy of financial and other management controls, compliance with established policies, plans and procedures, suitability and reliability of financial and other management data within the organisation'. Emphasis was given to the management's 'responsibility to establish systems of internal control for operations for which it is responsible to ensure that these are properly run.' However, in general, internal audit plans continued to focus on internal financial control rather than the wider managerial or policy areas.

7.3   The emerging Corporate Governance agenda in the last decade has driven the establishment of Audit Committees in every NHS Trust and Authority. This provided internal audit with an independent reporting line to the Board and outside the direct control of Executives. It also gave internal audit greater freedom to move away from finance-led audit to the wider management and health policy agenda, the latter covered by the developing area of medical audit and clinical governance.

8.   External Audit

8.1   In the 1970s and 1980s, the Secretary of State for Health appointed auditors for external audit of NHS bodies. The Finance Division of the Department of Health was responsible for undertaking this statutory duty. The key objectives of external audit were primarily financial but some Value for Money audits were undertaken. Hospital pathology departments would have been scrutinised from the point of view of the use of resources, staffing, accommodation, cost, output and accounting.

8.2   Responsibility for external audit passed to the Audit Commission in 1990. The Commission is an independent body with statutory responsibilities to ensure efficiency and effectiveness of public services, including the NHS. It appoints external auditors to Health Authorities and Trusts, from the District Audit Service or from private firms. They review and report on all financial aspects, performance, efficiency and effectiveness of use of all resources. They also sign off annual accounts and produce reports of national and local efficiency studies.

9. Clinical Audit

9.1   The NHS reforms of 1991 established the principle that all clinicians should participate in medical audit and in 1993 a strategy was established to move towards multi-professional clinical audit. Progressive implementation has been given greater emphasis and impetus through the introduction of the clinical governance agenda in 1997/98. This provides a framework through which NHS organisations are accountable for continuous improvement in the quality of services, involving full participation by all doctors including specialty and sub specialty in external audit programmes.

9.2   The most recent development is the establishment of the National Institute for Clinical Excellence (NICE) and the Commission for Health Improvement. NICE is developing national clinical standards, oversees a range of functions at the Department of Health and is the national centre for clinical audit. The Commission, currently being established, will have a performance management role to ensure minimum clinical standards are met, maintained and improved.

10. Ethics Committees

10.1   Medical research is widely considered to be essential. Ethical approval for medical research is of equal importance. Whilst management responsibility ensures the availability and use of resources and finance, independent advice needs to be sought regarding ethical considerations. During 1991, District Health Authorities in England were required to take responsibility both to establish Local Research Ethics Committees (LRECs) and to provide administrative support. Each committee must have procedures in place for appointing members and have Terms of Reference agreed with the NHS organisations it advises.

10.2   The LREC exists to provide independent advice to any NHS body about proposed research projects within the geographical area of the health district. It is neither representative of nor beholden to any NHS organisation. The NHS organisation involved makes a final decision on whether to proceed with the research project, taking account of advice received from the LREC. Liverpool Health Authority has two Ethics Committees, one for adults (aged 16 and over) and one for children (aged under 16).

10.3   Members do not sit on the committee in any representative capacity. The meetings are held in private and the minutes taken are confidential to the committee to promote free discussion.

10.4   The LREC must be consulted about research proposals involving NHS patients, the recently deceased in NHS premises, the use of fetal material and IVF involving NHS patients, where access to patient records is required or where access or use of NHS facilities or premises is required. Once approval for a research project has been given, it is the NHS organisation, research sponsor and researcher who are responsible for ensuring the research follows the agreed protocol and for monitoring progress. No NHS body should agree to such a research proposal without the approval of the LREC. No such proposal should proceed without the permission of the responsible NHS body.

10.5   Universities have no remit to provide a clinical service and therefore rely upon their staff to work through the respective NHS Trust to obtain ethical approval for research from the LREC. University staff are also bound by their own discipline's ethical standards. Any significant deviation from the original proposal should be reported to the LREC.

10.6   From July 1997, in addition to a Local Research Ethical Committee, a Multi-Centre Research Ethics Committee (MREC) was established in each of the eight Regions across England. The Research and Development Directorate of the NHS Executive was given the responsibility for the MREC system. The purpose of the MREC is to advise the LREC on research proposals that will be carried out within five or more LREC geographical boundaries. Once MREC approval has been obtained, the LRECs in each locality will have the opportunity to then accept or reject the proposal for local reasons.

10.7   Now, after simplified charts of the organisations, the detailed account can begin.

Simplified NHS (England) Organisation Chart 1974

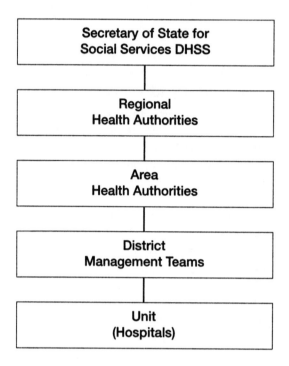

Simplified NHS (England) Organisation Chart 1982

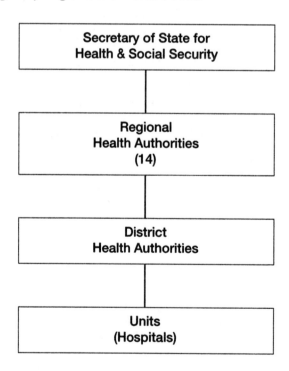

Simplified NHS (England) Organisation Chart 1991

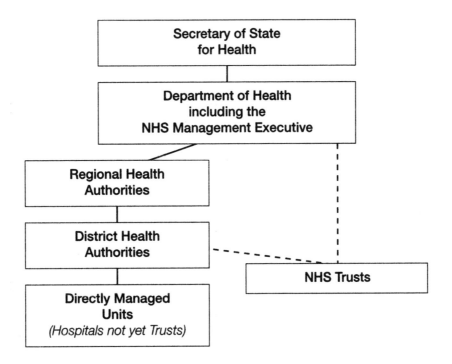

Simplified NHS (England) Organisation Chart 1996

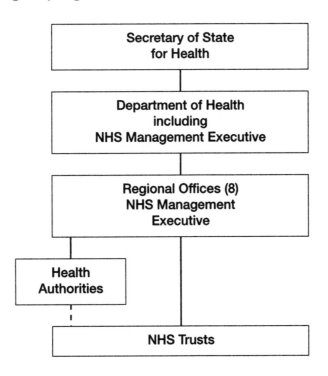

Chapter 7. Collections

The Other Collections, the Institute of Child Health and the Pre-van Velzen period

Contents

1.   Introduction

1.1   In Chapter 3 we explained that the wholesale retention of organs between 1988 and 1995 marked Alder Hey out from other hospitals where there was organ retention. We explain in Chapter 8 'The van Velzen Years' how it was that those organs were allowed to accumulate at Myrtle Street. We were able to identify a number of other collections and they are the focus of this chapter.

The Heart Collection at the Institute Of Child Health

2.   History; Personnel; the Institute of Child Health; Contents of the Collection

2.1   The heart collection at the Institute of Child Health (ICH) at Alder Hey is well known within the medical community in the UK and abroad. It has been difficult for the Inquiry to establish the exact number of hearts within the collection. In October 1999 Hilary Rowland, Chief Executive at Alder Hey, reported that there were 2087. The heart record books released to the Inquiry contain 2128 sequential entries. The collection is widely considered to be one of the leading two collections in the country, the other one being The National Heart and Lung Institute, Royal Brompton Hospital, London, and one of the most extensive in the world. It includes many rare and unusual congenital abnormalities of children's hearts and has been the basis for teaching trainee paediatric cardiologists, paediatric cardiac surgeons, nurses, echo-cardiographers and medical students.

2.2   In 1939 Dr John Hay (subsequently Professor of Child Health) was appointed as Physician to the Royal Liverpool Children's Hospital. From early in his appointment he took an interest in cardiology. In 1948 Mr Ronald Edwards was appointed as Surgeon and the surgical service in Liverpool began. Although the official date of starting the collection was said by the University of Liverpool to have been 1954 there is at least one heart in the collection from 1948, which was joined by numerous others in 1949. During the period 1948–1954 the collection was clearly established and continued to grow.

2.3   Dr Rewell, Pathologist at Myrtle Street Hospital and Dr Bouton, Pathologist at Alder Hey, co-operated from an early stage. From 1954 onwards there is a record of monthly meetings attended by anatomists, physiologists, pathologists, anaesthetists, cardiac surgeons and cardiologists. These were both NHS and University personnel including consultants, trainees and researchers. The results of surgery were reviewed and the findings from examination of hearts following unsuccessful operations were discussed to determine the causes of failure and to improve future operative procedures. This would hopefully benefit children with congenital heart abnormalities in the future.

The categorisation of congenital defects was also discussed. Dr Hay was joined in his work by Dr R S Jones, Dr E Goldblatt and Dr G Farquhar, who were all at the time substantive NHS appointees, save that Dr Goldblatt was also a part-time lecturer in the University of Liverpool.

2.4   At the time the collection was established, treatment for heart abnormalities was ineffective and mortality was high. There was a limited understanding of the anatomy and the pathology of congenital heart disease. The nomenclature of various defects was confused. Very little had been written about the pathology of the malformed heart. Early attempts at diagnosis and surgery often foundered because of inadequate knowledge of morphology, especially of complex defects. The heart store stimulated study of structural and functional anatomy of the normal and abnormal heart and was first used for surgical training in the Children's Hospital in 1958.

2.5   Until the mid-1950s the diagnosis of congenital heart abnormalities during life was made by a combination of clinical and X-ray examination. This was somewhat inaccurate and meant that many abnormalities were not diagnosed until the heart was opened at operation or at post mortem examination. Precise diagnosis became possible with the introduction of cardiac catheterisation in the 1950s. This allowed the injection of contrast media into the heart and the vessels around it so that any anatomical or functional abnormalities could be defined on X-ray screening. It also enabled measurements of the blood pressure and oxygen saturation to be made at various critical sites in the heart itself and in the great blood vessels close to it.

2.6   The combination of radiology and applied physiology produced accurate diagnoses of abnormalities of the heart because, for the first time, the tip of the catheter could be located in precisely the correct place for injection and sampling. Failure to ensure the correct position of the tip could lead to false and misleading information. Correct data meant that the best operation for that child could be planned in advance, which eliminated having to make the diagnosis at the time of operation.

2.7   Previously faulty or incomplete information led to poor planning and poor results. Stitches interfered with contraction of the heart or damaged the coronary circulation. Incisions, flaps or repairs were misplaced and harmful. Placing the catheter tip in the correct position ensured accurate information on the interpretation of X-rays, blood pressure and oxygen measurements, and on electrical measurement of the activity of the heart. This skill was learned from study of the structure of the hearts in the collection, and feedback from surgery and post mortem examination. Many of these diagnostic techniques were explored and developed using hearts in the collection before they were employed for the benefit of live children.

2.8   In 1966 the first funding was obtained by way of a grant for study on the histopathology of the outlet of the heart in various congenital malformations by a paediatric cardiologist. The grant from the Greenwood Trust (Children's Research Fund) allowed for the employment of Dr Audrey Smith as a Research Technologist.

She was employed essentially to perform histopathology work for Professor Bwczynski, Professor of Cardiology in Warsaw, Poland, who had access to material in the heart collection which was stored at Myrtle Street Hospital. Her role was to work with the hearts and process some of the microscopy. The laboratory facilities were in the old Dental Hospital, although in due course Dr Smith, who worked initially on a half-time basis, was given laboratory space in the Developmental Anatomy Laboratory of the newly opened ICH at Alder Hey. The collection of hearts, however, remained housed at Myrtle Street Hospital. The appointment of Dr Smith coincided with formal documentation and categorisation of the entire collection, and a series of research grants permitted her continued employment.

2.9 From 1968 Dr Robert Anderson, a pathologist then working in Manchester, started to take an interest in cardiac morphology and travelled to Liverpool to use the collection. It was, of course, Dr Anderson (by then Professor Anderson) who subsequently gave evidence to the Bristol Inquiry in 1999, which led to the existence of the Alder Hey heart collection coming into the public domain.

2.10 In the early 1970s the mortality rate for open heart surgery for neonates and infants dropped dramatically. This surgery, developed in Liverpool, transformed an 85 per cent mortality rate in the first year of life in some severe conditions into an 85 per cent survival rate.

2.11 In 1978 the National Heart Research Fund started to provide funding to back a long series of research projects.

2.12 Dr Smith was encouraged to perform her own research and obtained an MPhil in October 1979. She was appointed to the academically related staff as research fellow thus relieving the medical and surgical staff of the running of the laboratory, the straightforward laboratory work and the care and maintenance of the collection.

2.13 On 1 January 1986 another Research Technologist was appointed, Mrs Gwen Connell. Her role was to assist Dr Smith with her research, and to undertake the technical work involved. Essentially she did some histology work and helped Dr Smith with her studies on the heart collection.

2.14 In 1986 the new ICH building was opened at Alder Hey. The building included two rooms specifically designed for the heart store and fetal store (see below). There was a large developmental anatomy laboratory with a number of storage spaces designed to store preserved human material. These storage spaces were cooled and had security locks. There was also a dry room for the storage of blocks and sections. The expanding heart collection was not re-housed in the new ICH until 1989 prior to closure of the hospital site at Myrtle Street and the transfer of services to Alder Hey. By this time the number of hearts was in the region of 2,000, and transfer of the collection made work at the laboratory more efficient.

2.15   Until 1990, funding for any research, which also supported Dr Smith's salary, came solely from charities whose primary concern was pure research. The Greenwood Trust, the National Heart Research Fund, the British Heart Foundation and the Endowment Fund of Royal Liverpool Children's Hospital, all eminent bodies, offered support. The care and maintenance of the collection was subsumed as an integral part of the research.

2.16   In 1994 Dr Smith retired as a Research Fellow. She still holds an Honorary Research Fellowship and has continued to work in the ICH on a part-time basis working predominantly with the heart collection.

2.17   Since 1990 the Head of the Department of Child Health has been Professor Cooke, Professor in Neonatal Medicine at the University of Liverpool since 1988. His immediate predecessor was Professor Lloyd, Professor of Paediatric Surgery, who was acting Head for a short time following the departure of the previous Head, Professor Frank Harris, who held the post from October 1974 until leaving the University in December 1989.

3.   Source of the Hearts

3.1   The initial source of the hearts was from children who had died after unsuccessful heart surgery at Liverpool Children's Hospital. The Inquiry's formal investigations begin in 1962, the Human Tissue Act having come into force in 1961. Professor van Velzen took up post in 1988. Retention today of organs removed during the period 1962 to 1988 has been confined to heart and lung specimens. However, it should be understood that a standard way of removing the heart and lungs at post mortem was to take the tongue and neck tissues in addition. Many of the heart and lung specimens contained within the ICH include other organs/tissue such as, for example, the tongue, thyroid, larynx and trachea. This retention does not arise as a result of any particular need for such material but as a consequence of the method used to obtain the heart and lung specimens.

3.2   For much of this period the pathologist at Alder Hey was Dr Bouton, who retired in 1986. We were unable to take evidence from Dr Bouton on grounds of his ill health. A detailed medical certificate was provided by his treating doctor and we were entirely satisfied that to interview Dr Bouton would have been inappropriate and unhelpful. Evidence as to his practices, however, has been obtained.

3.3   It is clear that Dr Bouton did not retain organs beyond hearts and lungs, except those included due to the method of removal explained in paragraph 3.1. The need to fix the brain for a period of several weeks following post mortem examination meant that there would have been initial retention of some brains (probably followed by disposal), in accordance with usual procedures prevailing nationally. The recollection of those clinicians who gave evidence to the Inquiry was that Dr Bouton did undertake histology. He was considered to be a good pathologist, although someone from whom it was often difficult to get prompt reports and who would often have to be chased. It was felt that as he grew older he lost some of his enthusiasm, that he was somewhat irascible and that there was no real desire on his part to advance the Department of Pathology. It would be fair to say that the service was considered satisfactory, but nothing more.

3.4   The Inquiry's clinical expert, Dr Keeling, did examine a number of hearts from this period and found them to be fully dissected with detailed requests available. The post mortem reports during this period were rarely more than two pages in length. A brief clinical history was given. Weight and body measurements were included together with an external description. Organ weights were recorded. Variable microscopic examination was done, which on occasion was confined to two or three organs. The reports written by senior trainees or the forensic pathologist were more detailed than those done by Dr Bouton. His reports were sometimes unacceptably brief which made it difficult to confirm or refute the syndrome diagnoses. A final diagnosis or summary was rarely included so that the significance of findings was, in some cases, in doubt.

3.5   There was a general expectation that hearts/hearts and lungs would be made available to the ICH and retained. In her witness statement of 6 June 2000, Dr Smith stated,

> 'Generally accepted practice within Alder Hey was that the cardiologists or surgeons would hope to be able to see the heart in cases of congenital heart disease for the purpose of clinical audit. The pathologists would understand that and would allow the heart following post mortem to be transferred to our Department. It was generally expected that where a post mortem had been performed with relevant findings (ie malformed heart) the heart would be preserved. I am not, however, aware of any standing instructions in writing. … It was never the practice that we would obtain every single heart from each post mortem. We would sometimes be sent normal hearts which we would use, together with fetal hearts, as control material and we have also done studies on the hearts of babies who have died from Sudden Infant Death Syndrome where generally the heart would be of grossly normal anatomy.'

Dr Smith's statement was confirmed by Professor Cooke,

> 'I cannot say whether in every case where there was a PM following death due to congenital heart disease, the heart would make its way into the ICH, but I would say that it certainly did in most cases.'

3.6   The practice of sending the heart and lungs to the Institute was clearly well established. The locum Consultant Pathologist, Dr Ibrahim, who worked at Alder Hey from November 1986 to August 1988, following Dr Bouton's retirement, confirmed that his practice was not to retain any organs at post mortem, other than the heart:

'I would generally meet with the surgeon, cardiologist and Audrey Smith at Myrtle Street to look at the heart in detail, and the heart would be kept in the collection in the ICH. Audrey Smith would look carefully at the conducting system, and even by the time I left Alder Hey I would not say that I was an expert cardiac pathologist. The custom was very much to retain the heart.'

3.7   Indeed, the pathologists as a whole were clearly well aware of what was 'expected' of them. The culture of expectation, on the part of both clinicians and pathologists, may well have been such that the issue of requisite consent from parents became, if not a secondary consideration, something viewed as a mere formality. There was little change in the era of Professor van Velzen. Dr Khine stated,

'In Alder Hey if a child had died of congenital heart disease then it was expected that one would retain the heart and lungs so that the specimens could go to the ICH. It would have taken a very brave person not to have sent those specimens through. If a congenital problem were suspected I would therefore have retained the heart and if there was a need to look at the conducting system I would probably retain a large part of the heart if not the whole. There was pressure to retain the heart and lungs in appropriate cases as every so often there would be telephone calls either from Dr Audrey Smith at the ICH or from the Cardiologists such as Miss McKay or Mr Franks who would provide a list of names where heart retention might be appropriate.'

3.8   However, Professor van Velzen himself was to prove somewhat less accommodating. This was not because of any qualms on his part as to retention but rather his own desire to have personal access to the hearts, which he removed at post mortem examination. In 1990 Dr Smith noticed that the transfer of hearts to the ICH from Alder Hey began to decrease and eventually it ceased altogether. This caused her obvious concern as she appreciated the importance of updating the collection on a regular basis,

'Within the laboratory at the ICH it was clear to see the slowing down of new material. I did discuss this with the cardiologists and the surgeons to tell them that material was not coming through, and I also rang Professor van Velzen's department on a number of occasions to try to ask him if I could view a particular case. I did not generally however, have any positive response from him.'

3.9   In her oral evidence Dr Smith felt that it was probably during 1993 when the flow of hearts to the ICH from Alder Hey dried up altogether. On 11 August 1994 she wrote to Professor Cooke bemoaning the 'dearth of new material arriving in the laboratory, although I understand that deaths are occurring at the rate of approximately 40 per year. The scarcity of new material naturally contributes to lack of stimulus for anatomical research by our clinicians and surgeons.'

3.10   She asked Professor Cooke to encourage Professor van Velzen to establish a better throughput. There is no evidence to suggest the situation changed even after Professor van Velzen's effective removal from Alder Hey in December 1994. Dr Kokai, who took up his post of Senior Lecturer in Paediatric Pathology in January 1996, did not send hearts through as a matter of routine. This was despite the fact that Dr Smith had written to Henry Meade, the Pathology Service Manager, on 16 May 1995, explaining the benefit of the heart collection as a 'very valuable teaching resource' and setting out a protocol in an attempt to ensure continuity of her work investigating the morphology of congenital cardiac malformations.

3.11   In December 1995, following the decommissioning of the Myrtle Street building and the break up of Professor van Velzen's department, a batch of 50 hearts was transferred from Myrtle Street to the ICH. Some of these hearts dated back to 1989 but Dr Smith was not able to deal with them as she would have liked, due to her other commitments. Counsel to the Inquiry asked Dr Smith whether she could remember the condition of these particular hearts when they arrived and queried whether Professor van Velzen had attempted to examine them himself. Dr Smith responded,

> 'I cannot answer that because ... I did not get a chance to look at them. Of the 50, there were seven that we actually took out and gave a catalogue number. Four of those we selected for special study which, in view of what happened afterwards, did not take place and all those hearts went back eventually to the Pathology Department. So I did not get a chance to look at all of them.'

3.12   However, the flow of hearts to the ICH had not dried up completely. Dr Smith confirmed that hearts from children who had attended the heart clinic but who had died outside the area would still be sent by the hospitals where Alder Hey cardiologists had regular peripheral clinics, in places such as Manchester, Blackpool, Preston or Wrexham. Dr Arnold confirmed in his witness statement dated 19 June 2000 that hearts would be sent to Dr Smith for examination 'from all over the country: many of the hearts in the ICH collection are not local.'

3.13   This was confirmed by Liam Nolan, who commenced employment at Alder Hey in November 1999 as a locum Medical Laboratory Scientific Officer (MLSO), with a Master's Degree in Pathology. He had access to the containers in the ICH as part of the recataloguing process undertaken by Alder Hey in July 2000. He confirmed that the ICH books showed that various hearts dating back to the 1970s were in fact sent to the ICH in the early 1990s. By inference those hearts must have been stored at hospitals elsewhere and sent to Alder Hey as a result of the reputation acquired by the heart collection. Hearts from Addenbrookes Hospital, Cambridge, were sent to the ICH in this way, but the more usual source of hearts external to Alder Hey was North Western hospitals where clinicians based at Alder Hey had out-patient clinics.

3.14   It appeared to be recognised locally that there was the facility at Alder Hey for the specialist examination of hearts taken at post mortem. In particular the Inquiry has seen documentation focusing on the transfer of hearts from Royal Preston Hospital to Alder Hey. The Preston documentation was of particular note because an investigation by the Medical Director of Preston Acute Hospitals NHS Trust had been undertaken in May 2000 to establish why in some cases the tongue, thyroid, larynx and trachea had been removed in addition to the heart and lung. The investigation confirmed that this was a consequence of the way in which the heart and lungs had been removed at post mortem. We believe that many of the heart and lungs specimens contained within the ICH include similar organs and tissue. The Alder Hey recataloguing process confirmed this in July 2000. This calls into question the integrity of the information about retention initially given to parents by Alder Hey, when the presence of such other organs was not specifically mentioned.

4.   Cataloguing; Storage; Maintenance and Procedures

4.1   Dr Smith confirmed that the system of registration/cataloguing evolved over the years. The procedure initially adopted was not quite the same as the later more definitive version. Essentially the heart was collected from the histopathology department, and then recorded in the daybook as it was brought into the laboratory. The daybook recorded the child's identification information and the heart was allocated a chronological number. The heart was then examined to identify any major malformation and placed broadly into an alphanumeric classification in a different catalogue book, for example C18 or J23, the C or J being a code for the individual anomaly and the number reflecting the number of hearts with that particular anomaly. It was then placed on the shelf, in its container, until required for further detailed examination. The alphanumeric classifications were then listed at the back of the catalogue (for example C1–C18, J1–J23). By reference to the catalogue and daybook one could, in theory, trace any individual heart and ascertain the identity, or alternatively trace any heart within a particular anomaly. The container itself bore the alphanumeric classification. Sometimes the organ carried this classification itself, by way of a dymo tape tag. Dr Smith felt that there was always sufficient information to identify the heart. It would certainly have been possible for researchers to trace hearts with a defect in which they were particularly interested but identification of the source of the heart was not consistently clear.

4.2   Throughout the Inquiry we received a significant volume of evidence outlining the benefits of the heart collection. This is explored in greater detail later. We were urged by both Alder Hey and the University to consider the heart collection in a completely different way from the collection of organs assembled at Myrtle Street under Professor van Velzen. It was stressed that the heart collection had been accessed frequently, had been a valuable tool in terms of research, education and training, and that the collection had been well respected and cared for and properly maintained. We accept this evidence.

4.3   However, the re-cataloguing exercise undertaken by Alder Hey in 2000, which included the hearts and lungs in the ICH, did reveal cause for concern in relation to the proper identification of the individual child from whom the heart had been removed. Liam Nolan suggested that there were in the region of 150 hearts where identification was uncertain and explained some of the problems which had arisen. In some cases hearts had been entered in the daybook with no identification of the child. For example 'Bangor' was not an infrequent entry. We understand that Bangor is the hospital from where the heart was received. Some jars had no numbers and in the absence of tags these hearts were unidentifiable. In other cases up to ten hearts (usually 'normal' and listed as controls) had been stored together in one container and whilst the books allowed identification of the group of ten, the individual tags attached to each had fallen off. This meant that for identification purposes no distinction between the hearts could be made. The collection therefore achieved its aim of summarising the particular defect associated with an individual heart, but its priority had not been the identification by patient name of each heart. That information was therefore not as accurate as it should have been. In August 2000 Alder Hey confirmed publicly that hearts in the ICH could not be accurately identified.

4.4   We had already noted these difficulties in identification following witness evidence relating to the initial cataloguing of the containers in October 1999. We heard of ten hearts that had been labelled and re-coded only as 'baby' with a case sheet number from an unknown hospital. Mrs Elizabeth Clapham, one of the MLSOs involved in the initial cataloguing confirmed that 'in some instances there would have been organs the identification of which was unclear. Anything which could not be identified positively was not put on to the database.'

4.5   Whilst she felt this only represented a handful of cases she accepted,

    'It is however, therefore the case that a parent may have rung up subsequently and been told that there had been no organ retention whereas in fact that parent's child's organs could have been amongst the unidentifiable specimens.'

4.6   Because of the concerns raised in relation to identification we have had to study the validity and consistency of the various heart books. There are four in total. Heart Book I begins in January 1955 and ends in April 1971. In fact it includes information on hearts retained from at least 1948, as explained earlier. Heart Book II begins in May 1971 and ends in May 1982, Heart Book III begins in June 1982 and ends in September 1988. Heart Book IV begins in October 1988 and continues until the present.

4.7 Heart Book I contains a number of discrepancies. In two cases there is no evidence whatsoever of the date or origin of the heart being recorded, whilst the 'Bangor' references mentioned above are common within this Heart Book. From a period of approximately October 1966 to May 1967 (Heart Log No.520–564) no dates are recorded as to when hearts were received. It is difficult to say with complete certainty if any of the dates are correct because occasionally the dates when the heart has been received are inconsistent, a trend which continues throughout the Heart Books. There is similar failure to record dates during the period May 1967 to July 1969.

4.8 Heart Book II contains a smaller number of discrepancies and this seems to be a much fuller and complete Heart Book.

4.9 Heart Book III contains numerous discrepancies, including 265 hearts recorded without any note of when they were received. 155 of these are near to the end of the book, which suggests that it became common practice at the time. There are also two log number entries that do not contain any details as to origin or the dates when the hearts were received.

4.10 Heart Book IV also contains discrepancies, there being 174 instances when no date was recorded for when hearts were received, including some with no details of the origin of the hearts. There are also entries where the source is recorded but no date given. Towards the end of the book 42 hearts are added to the collection but no medical classification under the alphanumeric system has been recorded. This raises concern, as unless and until those hearts have been correctly catalogued they will be of little teaching or research benefit.

5. Consent

5.1 The value and benefits generally of the cardiac collection are obvious. This does not in itself justify the collection. There has to be appropriate consent.

5.2 The hearts were taken at both Coroner's and hospital post mortem examinations. In the case of hospital post mortem examinations specific consent – or more properly 'lack of objection' – from parents was required under the Human Tissue Act 1961. The question of whether consent was obtained properly by clinicians from parents under the Human Tissue Act is addressed in Chapter 10. We note that Mrs England, in her capacity as Acting Director of Operational Services, wrote to the solicitor to the Bristol Inquiry on 13 September 1999 and said,

> 'The specific issue about retained tissue was probably not discussed in detail, if at all … It was agreed that no-one was asking specifically if the heart could be kept… Specific training in obtaining consent was not undertaken.'

Mrs England made it clear that she understood this to be in accordance with national standard practice at the time.

5.3   A Coroner's post mortem examination does not require consent. It is a matter of law. However, the consent of the parents should be obtained to authorise the retention of hearts removed legitimately for clinical purposes at Coroner's post mortem examinations. We consider this further in Chapter 9. The recent approach adopted by the Paediatric Research Ethics Committee at Alder Hey is perhaps significant. In April 2000 the Committee made it clear to Dr Smith that consent should be obtained from parents for 'the re-use of retained tissue' despite concerns that this requirement might carry the risk of causing distress to parents whose children had long since died.

6.   What was the Purpose of the Collection; Who Used It; What Were the Benefits?

6.1   There can be no doubt that use of the heart collection has been invaluable in terms of research, education and training. In 1985 Dr Smith started a programme of regular lectures and demonstrations to nurses. In 1993, following a request by Dr Pozzi, Consultant Cardiac Surgeon, she established a course of 20 lectures and demonstrations, using the material from the collection, especially for the surgical team, but open to any other interested parties. Dr Smith was invited to demonstrate hearts on many occasions at prestigious meetings, both at home and abroad, including the European Association of Cardiothoracic Surgery. The collection provided specimens for the opening sessions on specific malformations at various Study Days that attracted international delegates. In May 1995 there was an International Congress when 170 people registered, from 12 different countries.

6.2   Dr Smith confirmed that staff often found it invaluable to review examples of a particular anomaly, on an individual basis or in small groups. This was useful for diagnosis, correlation with echo-cardiographic and angio-cardiographic results, or as a preliminary to operating on a specific anomaly. Newly acquired specimens were used for many years at meetings now classified as audit. Here the echo- and angio-cardiographic findings, diagnostic surgery and post mortem findings and the pathology of the heart were discussed together. She indicated that surgeons found it invaluable to review their operations on the autopsied heart and confirmed that this was an essential part of surgical audit, was fundamental in the process of the constant striving for surgical improvement. The constant aim was to minimise the mortality rate of cardiac surgery.

6.3   Heart specimens have also been used to study the detailed anatomy of cardiac abnormalities, to develop methods of diagnosis in life, to develop operations and techniques, to review the results of surgery and for training. Some of the most unusual have been used by visitors from both the UK and abroad to plan operations on these rare conditions. The collection has been a significant factor in the development of neonatal and paediatric cardiac surgery not only in Liverpool but throughout the world. In 1999 a surgeon came from Japan to examine two examples of a very rare congenital abnormality of the heart which are in the collection so that he could understand the abnormal anatomy and plan the operation which his patient required.

6.4   There is also evidence of developments through research as a result of use of the collection. More than 200 scientific papers including information derived from the collection have been produced. In the early years much work was done to establish an international system to describe abnormal hearts so as to ensure conformity in discussion. The congenitally abnormal heart may have many significant differences from the normal. One of the most important is the position and structure of the tissues which control the contraction of the heart. These are normally in the middle of the heart but in the malformed organ are often at the back or front so that they may be damaged at operation if the malposition is not known and understood. These tissues and other aspects of the disturbed anatomy of abnormal cardiac development were extensively studied in the hearts of the collection, producing significant advances and improvement in the techniques and results of cardiac surgery on children. A number of pioneering techniques for unusual and complex abnormalities were developed from intensive and detailed study of the hearts in the collection.

6.5   Interestingly, many of the most valuable hearts are those which originated in the very first years of the collection, as they demonstrate anomalies which have not been operated upon. However, it is important to keep adding new hearts to the collection as certain investigations require destruction of specimens through dissection and the creation of sections.

6.6   Perhaps the most compelling evidence of the value of the collection was the dramatic reduction in the mortality rate following complex cardiac surgery. Two-thirds of babies born with severe abnormalities of the heart die in the first week of life if they are not operated on and more will not survive the next three weeks. To prevent such early deaths and to improve the health of children with severe abnormalities approximately 6,500 open-heart operations have been carried out since 1970 on children of all ages at Myrtle Street and Alder Hey. Some were done in the first month of life, some in the first year and some in the next few years. The younger the baby or child and the more complex the abnormality, the greater the risk of surgery. The mortality rate following all such surgery has fallen from 20 per cent in 1970 to 3.6 per cent in 1999. The improvement is particularly striking in the 2,000 or so children operated on in the first year of life. Their mortality following surgery fell from 75 per cent in 1970 to 32 per cent in 1984 and has continued to fall since then, to 6 per cent in 1999. There are now more than 1,600 living children who would have died in infancy or childhood without the improvements in surgical techniques and care which were pioneered in Liverpool.

6.7   Whilst it would be disingenuous to suggest that the lowering of the mortality rate is solely due to use of the heart collection alone, there can be no doubt that pioneering positive developments have resulted directly from work undertaken surrounding the heart collection. One cardiac surgeon who illustrated this graphically was Dr Pozzi,

> 'I used that collection extensively and it has been an invaluable experience for me. It has improved my surgical results, reducing the number of deaths and serious complications. It is regrettable from a training and education point of view that our acquisition of heart specimens has been in decline, but I accept that public perceptions and feelings have changed. We have to accept that.'

7.   Who Knew of the Heart Collection?

7.1   The existence of the heart collection at Alder Hey was no secret; in fact quite the contrary. The reputation of the collection was such that its existence was known widely both within Alder Hey and the University and externally in the medical world. In her witness statement of 2 June 2000 Ms Rowland stated,

> 'No-one would deny that they were aware of the heart collection.'

8.   Whose Responsibility was the Collection?

8.1   It is clear from the evidence that the practical day-to-day responsibility for maintenance of the heart collection lay with Dr Smith. However, as Head of the Department of Child Health, Professor Cooke was ultimately responsible for all collections within the ICH. Dr Smith did not see Professor Cooke as a line manager as such. She explained that if she had problems regarding the heart collection she would go to the cardiologists or the surgeons. Essentially, she regarded herself as, and was, autonomous within the Department. Similarly, Professor Cooke did not really see himself as exercising a co-ordinating function. We found the absence of a proper management structure concerning. Fortunately Dr Smith was clearly a woman of integrity who did not abuse her position and who was well aware of her responsibilities. However, proper management controls did not exist.

8.2   Professor Cooke's predecessor, Professor Lloyd, agreed that the Institute constituted a disparate collection of individuals doing research and that there was no co-ordinated function as such,

'The fetal collection and the cardiac collection was a bit out on a limb, because it did not belong to paediatric surgery or paediatric medicine, it was really in the ambit of the Cardiology Department, and they are not a University Department. So there was no clear line of responsibility, but ultimately from the University side, given that Audrey Smith was a University employee, then in that direction, it went up to the Head of Department.'

He accepted, however, in oral evidence, that ultimately as Acting Head of the Department he was responsible for the collections, and, of course, that responsibility would have passed to Professor Cooke when he became Head of the Department.

8.3 We were surprised at the clear disagreement between Alder Hey and the University about the ultimate responsibility for the heart collection. In its closing submissions Alder Hey emphasised the fact that the ICH was a University Department run by a University researcher, and that whilst many of the hearts came from patients of Alder Hey, hearts from all over the country would have been sent to Dr Smith. It was accepted that Alder Hey had undoubtedly received clear benefits for its patients by having access to the ICH collection. It also had particular benefit from access to Dr Smith, from whom clinicians had received a great deal of help and information of undoubted clinical benefit. It was further accepted that there had been research projects involving Dr Smith and the clinicians at Alder Hey using the collection and Alder Hey therefore accepted some 'moral' responsibility for the heart collection having contributed to and used it. However, Alder Hey submitted that the administrative responsibility for heart collection continued to lie with the University of Liverpool.

8.4 However, Mr Robert Francis QC, on behalf of the University, stressed that overall responsibility was that of Alder Hey. In his opening submissions he accepted that University staff, in an academic sense, had had access to the heart collection, had written papers, that the collection had been maintained by a University employee, and that the collection was housed in a building leased from Alder Hey by the University. He also pointed to the fact that it was Alder Hey staff, under the direction of Alder Hey management, who identified the organs in response to the parental requests, that it was Alder Hey management who arranged for the transfer of material from Myrtle Street in 1995, and that it was Alder Hey which accepted responsibility for the reporting of the collection to the Chief Medical Officer's (CMO) Survey.

8.5 The Dean of the Faculty of Medicine of the University of Liverpool, Professor Peter Johnson, observed in his witness statement of 5 June 2000,

'I had been aware of the existence of the heart collection because of the specific references in Stephen Gould's report and also because of comments made by Hilary Rowland to the effect that the hospital was very proud of its heart collection which it perceived as its own, and which was considered immensely valuable for training in cardiac surgery.'

8.6   We found the concept of 'ownership' unhelpful. The issues were essentially possession and control. In his oral evidence Professor Johnson accepted that the cardiac collection was within the University site, and that there was University and clinical use. On this basis we must conclude that the ultimate responsibility for the cardiac collection was joint.

The Fetal Collection at the Institute of Child Health

9.   History; Personnel; Contents of the Collection

9.1   Within the ICH there is a collection of fetal material. In February 2000 the University of Liverpool returned information to the CMO relating to the collection, to comply with the CMO's census to determine the scale of retention of organs, body parts and tissues. The completed census form confirmed that the ICH held 1,564 stillbirths or pre-viable fetus. That figure includes 52 late premature or term fetus although none since 1973.

9.2   The store of primarily intact fetal tissue started in 1955, with identification details from 1975, and the collection ceased in 1992. As in the heart collection, the instigator of the collection was Dr Hay. The collection was initially stored on the old Dental Hospital site and the fetus were obtained from Broadgreen, Mill Road, Walton (later Fazakerley), Whiston and St Catherine's Hospitals. In 1986 the new ICH building was opened and included a room specifically designed for the fetal store. At one stage the collection contained a total of 3,575 fetus but in the three years before transferring to ICH a substantial number were incinerated. Decisions about disposal were made according to the state of the tissue and the organs which had been removed. However, problems were then experienced with the Alder Hey incinerator and this practice ceased.

9.3   Collection continued until 1992, although there was no conscious departmental decision to cease collection at that time. When Ms Connell, who looked after the collection on a day-to-day basis, took up her position in 1986, the number of hospitals providing fetal material to the ICH had diminished. Only Fazakerley and Mill Road were still involved in supplying fetus. Fazakerley stopped providing material shortly afterwards, leaving Mill Road as the sole source of material. In 1992 Mill Road closed and fetal material was no longer offered to the ICH. In addition there were no new postgraduate students coming through with an interest in this type of work.

9.4   In August 1992 a working party was set up by Liverpool Obstetrics and Gynaecology Services NHS Trust to consider the question of disposal of fetal tissue. Recommendations were that whilst fetus of less than 14 weeks gestation should be 'cremated on hospital premises' the parents' views in relation to the burial or cremation of fetus from 14 weeks gestation up to the legal age for viability should be respected. The ICH took the view that it did not have funding to introduce any such practice of dignified disposal and so the disposal of the fetal tissue simply did not take place.

9.5   The fetus within the ICH collection include miscarriages, therapeutic and social terminations. After Professor van Velzen took up his post in September 1988 procedures were changed so that the ICH would forward to him any fetus from therapeutic terminations or miscarriages which it might receive but would retain the fetus from social terminations. If, however, a fetus were observed which was thought to be slightly abnormal then that too would be transferred to Professor van Velzen. Similarly, a fetus from a termination where the mother had, for example, a history of drug-taking would be sent to Professor van Velzen because of his specific interest in fetal pathology.

10. Cataloguing; Storage; Maintenance and Procedures; Consent

10.1   The system for collection was that the Institute would receive a telephone call from someone on a hospital ward, confirming that a fetus was available for collection. A special Howie box was used for the collection and for carrying pathological material. The usual source was Mill Road Hospital, and the technician collected the fetus from a fridge at the end of the ward and put it in the Howie box. A form was completed by the referring hospital containing certain information as to the identity of the mother, her partner, and their smoking and alcohol history. The form was later amended by Professor van Velzen, to make it clear that social terminations only should go to the ICH and all other fetal studies to his department, and also it removed the need for information about the father to be recorded. There was no other documentation, so Ms Connell would not know the extent of any discussion between clinicians and the mother regarding consent. She assumed however, that consent had been given because in some instances mothers ultimately asked for the return of the fetus for burial. Ms Connell says that such requests were probably only made five or six times a year. There would be one or two new fetus coming into the ICH each week.

10.2   There were two cross-referenced books cataloguing the fetal specimens. The 'mother book' contained the patient's name and hospital patient number and recorded whether the termination was induced, spontaneous or therapeutic. The 'baby book' confirmed the date upon which the specimen arrived at the ICH, the sex, the foot length and weight in order that an estimated age could be attributed to the fetus. The 'baby book' entry was anonymous, but had the same number as that allocated in the 'mother book' so that the two books were cross-referenced. The 'baby book' confirmed the condition of the fetus and recorded the container number in which the fetus was to be stored. Any specimens removed for serial sectioning were recorded in the laboratory histology books and cross-referenced to case numbers. The University is presently cataloguing the entire store in substantial depth. The forms referred to above were kept within the ICH, but no specific consent documentation was held.

11.   Polkinghorne Report

11.1   The absence of specific consent documentation is particularly significant, given the findings of the Review of the Guidance on the Research Use of Fetus and Fetal Material (CM 762 HMSO), known as the Polkinghorne Report. The report was published in July 1989 and gave guidance on the research use of fetus and fetal material. The report makes it clear that the written consent of the mother was required for fetal research after July 1989, even though strictly the pre-viable fetus and the mother had no rights in law. In section 6.3 of the report the committee stated,

> 'We recommend that positive explicit consent should be obtained from mothers to the use of the fetus or fetal tissue. We see the process of consent as requiring the mother to be counselled and given all the information, in a form that is comprehensible to enable her to make a proper judgement of whether or not to allow the fetus to be used for research and therapy, including transplantation.'

11.2   Despite the clear recommendations of the Polkinghorne Report it seems that they were essentially ignored. The ICH continued to receive fetus with no written consent and in circumstances where the University ignored its own duty under section 3.8 of the Code of Practice,

> 'On the same principle the user should be able to satisfy itself that any material it receives has been procured in accordance with the requirements of this Code. It must keep records indicating the appropriate source of any fetal tissue and of the use to which it is put, but should not reveal details of the use to the source.'

11.3   The forms which accompanied the fetus (see paragraph 10.1) were not consent forms and in reality were nothing more than information sheets completed by the referring hospital, and did not provide evidence that any relevant discussion had taken place resulting in consent to research being given by the mother. The problem was highlighted by Dr Smith prior to the Polkinghorne Report and following the introduction of the new Anatomy Regulations in 1988. She wrote to Professor Harris on 15 February 1988,

> 'We understand that the mothers are always consulted about the material coming to Alder Hey but I do not think that permission is given in writing. Perhaps we should have written permission. This would mean setting out a standard form. Who would be responsible for that?'

11.4 It seems that this specific query was never followed through properly. Professor Harris could not recall taking matters further. The present Head of Department, Professor Cooke, admitted in oral evidence that he 'naturally assumed' that appropriate consent documentation had been obtained. He submitted that the obstetricians were people known to the ICH and it could be assumed that proper consent had been given. That did not satisfy the Department's duty under section 3.8 to assure itself that the fetal material had been obtained with appropriate consent.

11.5 The problems in this area were also highlighted in the oral evidence of Professor Lloyd who confirmed that there was no individual designated with overall responsibility to ensure compliance with the Polkinghorne Report. He admitted that there was no perception of the importance of the recommendations, and also that there was no formal mechanism within the ICH to ensure compliance with such issues. The present Dean, Professor Johnson, expressed his surprise at the failure of Professors Lloyd and Cooke to be aware of and act upon the Polkinghorne Report. The failure to comply with the Code of Practice established by the Polkinghorne Report emphasises the lack of proper management systems and accountability within the ICH on the part of the University.

12. What was the Purpose of the Collection; Who Used It; What Were the Benefits?

12.1 At a meeting of a special working group (established by Professor Johnson in December 1999 to consider the fetal collection) there was discussion of the fetal collection. It was confirmed that 47 publications had been produced from work on the collection, beginning in 1959 and ending in 1993. Six papers were published in the period 1989 to 1993, and research on the fetal collection had actually stopped in 1992. The collection was used to facilitate work on the development of the gut in relation to Hirschprung's disease, work in relation to adrenal glands to assist with the treatment of neuroblastoma and work on the development of ureters. Work had also been undertaken on other sections of the gut and pancreas, and on the development of the fetal heart and conduction tissue. In earlier years there had also been important projects on cranio-facial abnormalities. Approved students would have access to the collection through the usual channels. Anyone beginning a research project would have required ethical approval from one of the appropriate ethics committees.

12.2 The methods used for the research often demanded fresh tissue and work was sometimes undertaken on specimens from fetus obtained within two hours of the termination procedure. The papers indicate the number of fetus used and most of the material was published in high quality peer reviewed journals.

12.3　　It is a matter of concern that the fetal collection has essentially lain dormant since 1992. Professor Cooke speculated that it might be possible for limited research to be undertaken but he had previously doubted the collection's value for research purposes because of the age of much of the material. It appears unlikely that the collection can still be considered a useful research tool. In her witness statement dated 6 June Ms Connell stated,

> 'I cannot explain why the fetus collection has been maintained in view of the fact that collection has ceased and there has been no recent research. I know that the incineration facilities at the hospital closed in or around 1992/1993, and I also believe that the regulations regarding disposal may have changed due to the input of SANDS (Society for Stillbirth And Neonatal Deaths) and so it could be that a reason for the collection remaining is difficulty as to the appropriate method of disposal. I know that those fetus that were previously regarded as of no further use or those which were badly macerated were incinerated. It is not necessarily essential to have fresh material to undertake research. Whilst immunocytochemistry work would require fresh material, developmental work would not necessarily.'

13.　Who Knew of the Fetal Collection?

13.1　　It is clear that the fetal collection was treated much more sensitively than the heart collection in terms of the dissemination of information as to its existence. Ms Connell said in her witness statement dated 6 June,

> 'Whilst the heart collection was very widely known within the Trust I do not know how many people knew or know about the fetal collection. I did treat the fetal collection with more sensitivity although I cannot remember whether this was on anyone's specific instructions. I felt however, that as many of the fetus were social terminations that some people would not agree with the collection in the sense that they objected to terminations per se.'

13.2　　In her witness statement also dated 6 June Dr Smith said,

> 'Some people at Alder Hey would have known about the existence of the fetal collection and some people who undertook research on it came to be employed on the hospital staff. The collection was obviously sensitive and was never publicised widely although its existence was never denied. The heart collection was obviously well known and used for teaching purposes by the Trust. The fetal collection was not used for teaching but only ever for research purposes by people specifically appointed to do so. There would therefore be no reason for individuals from the Trust to be accessing the fetal collection. Professor Lloyd

(Paediatric Surgery) and Professor Cooke (Paediatric Medicine) would have known about the existence of the fetal collection. They would have been required to approve the appointment of any research fellows, as were their predecessors, Professor Lister and Professor Harris.'

13.3   Professor Cooke also confirmed the potential sensitivity of the collection,

> 'There was also published work on the fetal material, although that collection was dealt with discreetly and people knew as much as they needed to know.'

13.4   Knowledge of the existence of the fetal collection does not appear to have been widespread. Indeed, Professor Orme, who was Dean of the Faculty of Medicine at the University of Liverpool from August 1991 to July 1996, was unaware of the fetal collection. He felt that this was something to which his attention should have been drawn, presumably by Professor Cooke as Head of Department of Child Health,

> 'Even at that time I would have expected to have been informed of a collection as sensitive as that.'

13.5   His successor as Dean, Professor Johnson, did not discover the existence of the fetal collection until visiting the ICH on 7 December 1999. He was concerned enough to ask Ms Connell to take immediate steps to change the lock and code of the room holding the collection and to ask her to collate appropriate research papers in relation to the material.

14.   Whose Responsibility was the Collection?

14.1   Despite the present and previous Deans' ignorance of the existence of the fetal collection, it is clearly the University which bears responsibility for the collection, as confirmed in the CMO census. Professor Johnson said,

> 'In terms of "ownership" of the various collections, it was clear that the fetal store in the ICH belonged to the University. Whilst the Myrtle Street store had been put together as part of the NHS diagnostic service work, that did not apply to the ICH store and indeed all of the fetal material had been derived from hospitals other than Alder Hey.'

14.2   As Head of the Department Professor Cooke accepted overall responsibility for the collection, although the day-to-day maintenance was carried out by Ms Connell. However, it was not to Professor Cooke, but to Professor Foster, Head of the Department of Pathology, that Professor van Velzen expressed some of his concerns regarding the collection in March 1995,

'I take this opportunity to inform you that at the Institute of Child Health an archive exists of fetal specimens, dating mainly before and the first year after my arrival, which were sent there when the Liverpool Eurocat Registry resided at the Institute of Child Health and amateurish, non-specialist reports were sometimes made and issued to clinicians and patients by researchers (mainly paediatric surgeons and non-medical cardiac researchers) on congenital abnormalities and syndromes. This archive still resides there, even after the data of the registry, which closed down approximately 2 years ago, and has been placed in the custody of Professor P Pharaoh. This archive of specimens is not based on parental consent, has no pathologist supervision, no Ethical Committee approval and is not part of an officially licensed Anatomical Institute as far as I know.'

14.3   This letter should be placed in its proper context. Professor van Velzen was going on the attack in defence to questions from Professor Foster regarding his use of fetal tissue at Myrtle Street. Professor Foster did not act given that the collection had been 'closed down'. It is however, regrettable that this letter was not dealt with substantively because some of Professor van Velzen's observations had validity.

The Fetal Collection at Myrtle Street

15.   History; Contents of the Collection

15.1   Following Professor van Velzen's arrival, fetus began to be referred to his Unit of Infant and Fetal Pathology by the Unit III Management Group. Prior to Professor van Velzen's arrival in Liverpool non-viable fetus had been incinerated, although fetus from various hospitals had been referred to the ICH (see paragraph 9.2).

15.2   Unit III included Mill Road Hospital, which subsequently closed in 1992, Liverpool Maternity Hospital, which closed in 1995, and the Women's Hospital in Catherine Street, which also closed in 1995. The three hospitals were incorporated into the new Liverpool Women's Hospital, The Liverpool Obstetric and Gynaecology Services Trust (later renamed Liverpool Women's Hospital NHS Trust) established in April 1992 to manage the hospitals.

15.3   Neither Unit III nor the subsequent Trust possessed pathology laboratories dealing with fetal or infant pathology and after Professor van Velzen took up post a significant amount of fetal material, largely deriving from miscarriage and therapeutic termination, was sent to his unit for histology and subsequent sensitive disposal. This was essentially a diagnostic regional service for fetal abnormalities and approximately 100 fetus per year would be received.

15.4   The fetal pathology service had not existed prior to Professor van Velzen's appointment
        and it was not until the late summer of 1991 that a service agreement was entered into
        providing the funding for this service. By October 1991 a backlog of approximately
        240 fetus was awaiting disposal because of the failure to provide funding for the service
        immediately after Professor van Velzen's arrival and because of factors explored in
        Chapter 8 parts 1 and 2. Under the service agreement Alder Hey was to dispose of
        fetus following examination by means of burial in consecrated ground at the rate
        of 20 per month.

15.5   The backlog was specifically brought to the attention of Mr Pearse Butler, Chief
        Executive at Alder Hey, by Professor van Velzen who wrote to him on 5 November
        1992. Mr Butler responded that some fetal material was being sent which did not
        require formal reporting and anticipated that the tendering process, which was then
        being addressed with a view to a contract being finalised, would achieve a more
        explicit agreement as to what should be sent. He also expected that there would be
        disposal of the backlog,

                'The arrangements for disposal should apply both to the backlog and to new
                material that came in the future.'

15.6   It would appear, however, that funding for the sensitive disposal of the backlog was
        never resolved, and in December 1999 it was identified that 445 fetus were retained at
        Myrtle Street, many dating back to 1989–1991. Of those 445 fetus 198 were intact.
        A table was prepared breaking down the numbers as follows:

	Total	Intact	Other
Name and case sheet number present	197	74	123
No name or case sheet number	20	6	14
Name but no case sheet number	76	37	39
Case sheet number but no name	105	52	53
ICH number present (many no names/case)	47	29	18
TOTAL	**445**	**198**	**247**

        Subsequently in February 2000 Professor Johnson identified a further 30 fetus,
        23 of which could be identified by name, and 22 of which were intact.

15.7   The vast majority of fetus emanated from Unit III work, although fetus were also sent
        by other hospitals including the Countess of Chester and (rarely) Whiston. Whilst a
        decision was apparently made following Professor van Velzen's arrival for fetus from
        social terminations to go to the ICH collection there are nevertheless a number of such

fetus within the Myrtle Street store. Louise Costi, who began work as a Medical Laboratory Assistant (MLA) at Myrtle Street in November 1991, gave evidence that perhaps two fetus per week would come into the laboratory. Most were therapeutic terminations of pregnancy, although there was the occasional social termination. All miscarriages were dealt with in the same way as terminations.

15.8   There is confusion as to the source of some of the fetus. Dr Vyvyan Howard (Senior Lecturer in Anatomy) was asked by Professor Johnson to log the fetal collection in October 1999. He identified that an ICH collection, started under Professor Harris for the study of Hirschprung's disease and collected prior to 1989, had been sent to Professor van Velzen. It is certainly true that a number of ICH fetus made their way to Myrtle Street. Dr Howard also identified the presence of a clinical genetics collection stored by Professor Christine Gosden, Professor of Medical Genetics, between 1990 and 1992, extending to 30 or so cases. However, it would appear that Dr Howard was mistaken about the Gosden collection. We understand that Professor Gosden did bring with her to Liverpool a number of genetically abnormal fetus collected in Edinburgh. These were subsequently stored and catalogued within her laboratory at the Women's Hospital, and despite Dr Howard's comments, there is no evidence of the collection being relocated to Myrtle Street or indeed to the ICH. It would seem therefore that the majority of fetus at Myrtle Street came through the NHS diagnostic route, the remainder being transferred by the ICH.

16. Cataloguing; Storage; Maintenance and Procedures

16.1   Louise Costi and Jason Sweeney both began work as MLAs at Myrtle Street on 18 November 1991. They were employed specifically to assist with the fetal work undertaken for Unit III, although they assisted with other work within the laboratory, and were responsible for booking in the fetus. A driver brought the fetus (and placentae) to Myrtle Street, and they entered the names and details into the logging in book. The fetus normally came with a form from the Liverpool Women's Hospital setting out the details of the mother. The information was entered into a separate fetal book, and the forms stored in an A4 folder. The containers were opened to check that the fetus had been stored properly in formalin.

16.2   Mr Sweeney and Ms Costi gave evidence that the work on the fetus was undertaken much more regularly than the clinical work on the post mortems, evidence which was confirmed by the Chief MLSO, Ms England. She agreed that the fetal work did not involve specialised techniques and could therefore be processed relatively quickly.

Mr Sweeney and Ms Costi confirmed the change in procedure whereby fetus would be sent for burial. The Co-operative Funeral Service collected the fetus which were placed into small coffins for burial at Calderstones Park.

16.3   Both Mr Sweeney and Ms Costi were surprised to learn of the extent of the fetal retention at Myrtle Street. Mr Sweeney stated,

> 'It is only through the Inquiry process that I discovered that there was a large number of fetus retained at Myrtle Street, and that information surprised me because I thought we had got through most of the fetus and arranged for the burial.'

16.4   His views were echoed by Miss Costi,

> 'I am led to believe that in the region of 450 fetus were found to have been retained and stored in Myrtle Street, and that figure very much surprises me. Given the progress that we had made in dealing with the backlog I thought that we were up to date, and so am a little confused as to where the fetus have come from… I dealt with a lot of the fetus from therapeutic terminations before I left, and the only fetus that I can think were still stored were those that were being retained for a study on club feet.'

16.5   Professor van Velzen also expressed surprise when interviewed by the Solicitor to the Inquiry as to the extent of the retention, but we have seen a helpful document prepared by Dr Howard logging the retained fetus. The majority of the retained fetus relate to the period 1989 to 1991, although there was substantial retention in 1995, possibly because by then Professor van Velzen's commitment to the workload reduced in light of his impending departure from Liverpool. There are in the region of 100 fetus where even the dates cannot be ascertained, let alone the identity.

17.   What was the Purpose of the Collection; Who Used It; What Were the Benefits?

17.1   It is clear that some research has been undertaken on the fetal material. In a significant number of cases the left leg is recorded as having been removed, possibly in connection with a study into club foot deformity, and in a number of cases the brain has been removed. Eyes have also been taken from some of the fetus. We have considered elsewhere (see paragraph 28) the validity of any such research on the fetal eye tissue.

18. Who Knew of the Fetal Collection?

18.1 We accept the evidence of Mr Sweeney and Ms Costi that they were unaware of the full extent of the retention at Myrtle Street. However, all those working within the laboratory would have known that there was a backlog in respect of the fetal work and that not all the fetus had been disposed of sensitively. Issues as to whether higher management knew, not just of the fetal collection at Myrtle Street, but of the organ collection generally, are addressed in Chapter 8 dealing with the 'van Velzen years'.

19. Whose Responsibility was the Collection?

19.1 It is clear that the Myrtle Street store arose predominantly as a result of the NHS diagnostic service work. Initially there may have been some suggestion on the part of management at Alder Hey that Unit III might assume some responsibility, but this was quickly rejected by Peter Herring, Chief Executive of Liverpool Women's Hospital NHS Trust. Mr Herring wrote to the Inquiry on 15 February 2000,

> 'When the situation regarding the existence of the store of organs and fetus was revealed to the hospital and its staff in October last year we were very surprised and concerned. There was an initial assumption by the Alder Hey management that this Trust should assume responsibility for the retention of those organs and fetal material that originated from our hospitals' patients. I subsequently made clear that we did not believe this to be appropriate on the basis that this Trust had no operational management responsibility for the department and obviously no knowledge or control over the actions of its staff. There are, nevertheless, implications arising from this situation in relation to consent and the monitoring of service provided, even where these comprise other NHS organisations.'

19.2 Mr Herring also pointed out to Ms Rowland that the fetal material retained at Myrtle Street came from a variety of different sources, and not just the hospitals falling within his remit. He wrote to her on 4 January 2000,

> 'As far as the fetus were concerned it was the department's clear responsibility to sensibly dispose of this material, and, as with organs, that responsibility cannot be passed back to the organisations from which the child or baby originally emanated as they clearly had no control or responsibility over the actions of the department or its staff.'

19.3 We note that Alder Hey accept broad responsibility for the Myrtle Street fetal collection. However, its uses included research activity by the University who must accept some responsibility for its existence.

The Collection of Children's Body Parts at the Institute of Child Health

20. History; Personnel; Contents of the Collection

20.1   In December 1999 Professor Johnson became aware that in addition to the heart and fetal collections within the ICH there was a third store consisting of a relatively small number of children's body parts. He caused investigations to be made.

20.2   The history of the store dates back to the 1950s, when the Department of Child Health began to collaborate with the old Dental Hospital, which was demolished in 1967/1968, to pursue its research interest in developmental anatomy. Dental and facio maxillary research transferred to the ICH from the Dental School in 1966, and one of the principal researchers was Dr Ralph Latham, Lecturer in Oral Anatomy. In the 1960s and early 1970s research on the development of the ear and nose was undertaken, and this research involved the use of human anatomical specimens of the head and neck. Some of these specimens remain in the ICH, and some, but not all, have identifying labelling.

20.3   The store contains a number of children's heads and intact bodies dating back to dental cleft palate research work in the 1960s undertaken by Dr Latham who left the University in December 1970. Some material was disposed of by proper funeral arrangements during Dr Latham's time and much of the material was disposed of at the time of the move from the Dental Hospital. The material transferred to the ICH did form the basis for research by others until 1973/1974. A number of hospitals supplied Dr Latham with the bodies once consent had been provided, including Alder Hey, Wrexham Maelor, Broadgreen, Whiston and St Catherine's Hospital, Birkenhead. Correspondence shows that Dr Latham endeavoured to build good working relationships with the pathologists working at the hospitals.

20.4   Professor Johnson, as part of his investigation into the store, spoke at length to a former colleague of Dr Latham. He confirmed that Dr Latham had acquired fetal and paediatric material from a number of sources and that the collection had consisted of peculiar developmental abnormalities as well as cleft palates, and was not confined to human tissue. He was able to confirm that Dr Latham had acquired a wide variety of material, some of which had been stored in bathtubs in formalin with a lid over the top. It was considered unlikely that the Alder Hey pathologist, Dr Bouton, would have provided material to Dr Latham, as his relationship with the University was apparently not good. However, Dr Latham's own thesis published in September 1967 acknowledges the assistance of a number of pathologists, of whom Dr Bouton was just one, in making post mortem material available. Further documentation makes it clear that Dr Bouton was involved in the removal of heads in cases where appropriate consent (see paragraph 21.2) had been obtained.

20.5   The children's body parts remaining within the store were catalogued by Gwen Connell in as much detail as could be gleaned from the limited amount of documentation still available. The census returned to the CMO by the University confirmed that there were retained 22 body parts from 15 children. Ms Connell went through the various containers and books, and the summary of the collection makes sobering reading. She identified 13 post natal heads/parts of head from children from a few days old to 11 years of age dating back to the 1960s and 22 heads from late premature/term fetus. There are containers with a whole body of a child in one jar with a separated head in another jar. Perhaps the most disturbing specimen is that of the head of a boy aged 11 years old. The most recent specimen was obtained in 1973.

21.   Cataloguing; Storage; Maintenance and Procedures; Consent

21.1   The University has been able to trace some consent documentation, but the process of checking procedures has been hampered by the fact that the specimens date back almost 40 years. The University's position is that parents were told very frankly of the intended research which was primarily into the development of cleft palate. The University said the parents were willing to donate their children's bodies for the purposes of research, but the disclosed documentation on its own does not justify the University's conclusion that all relevant information was given to parents. Professor Cooke did give hearsay evidence that Dr Latham had apparently had very detailed discussions with families to obtain consent to retention of tissue and had given an undertaking to bury the child once his work was complete.

21.2   A number of relevant consent forms are still in existence. These specifically confirm consent to 'donate the body' of the deceased child to the Cleft Palate Unit or Oral Morphology Research Unit 'for the purpose of research'. It is further recorded that the Unit will undertake 'all responsibility for the proper burial'. There is also correspondence from Dr Latham to one parent explaining that 'it would greatly help our research if you would think of giving me permission to retain the body of your child until investigations are undertaken and authorising me to arrange for the burial in due course'. Under cover of that letter was enclosed the consent form referred to above. A similar letter to another parent queried 'would you consider donating the body of your deceased infant to the Cleft Palate Research Centre of the ICH and leaving the funeral arrangements and expenses to us?'

21.3   The consent forms are clearly broad, specifically referring to donation for research. But were parents told exactly what that research work would include? Given that the research was likely to be in relation to cleft palate it might have been expected that there would be work undertaken on the face or skull, but did parents appreciate that there would be decapitation? The letters referred to above were certainly not explicit and there are no records from that period to confirm full and frank discussion. We have not felt it appropriate to contact those parents identified in the documentation. Whilst Dr Latham was traced to Canada he failed to co-operate with the Inquiry (or indeed the University) and did not provide any additional information. What is clear is that there was an expectation on the part of parents and indeed an assurance on the part of the researcher that there would be a proper burial.

21.4   This clearly calls into question the retention of the body parts which should have been disposed of sensitively by way of proper burial/cremation long ago. The problem is worsened by the fact that many of the retained body parts cannot be identified positively.

21.5   There is documentation to show that there were some burials. By linking such documentation to those details which can be confirmed in relation to the retained body parts it is evident that such burials were not always complete and that in other cases burial has simply not taken place. For example, there is a consent form donating the body of a stillborn child for research, with the University, through the Unit, undertaking all responsibility for burial. The body of that stillborn child remains in a jar in the ICH, with the head in a second jar, some 30 years after the stillbirth. In another case, relating to a neonate who died shortly after birth, a similar consent form was signed. There is evidence of burial and yet 'pieces of head' remain in a container, more than 30 years later. Was this really what parents envisaged when giving the consent?

21.6   Documentation which would confirm the circumstances in which other material has been disposed of is also missing. In one case there is correspondence from the appropriate Registry Office querying the position in relation to a burial. The Registrar had been told, following the death more than two years previously, that burial would be arranged and the disposal certificate returned to him afterwards, but had heard nothing further. The Registrar indicated that burial must take place within two years according to the Regulations and was therefore anxious to conclude matters. The disclosed documentation simply indicates that burial will take place 'in the next few days' but there is no further relevant documentation. Indeed, in one particular case of which we are aware the University has been unable to confirm the circumstances of any proper burial in response to a family request.

21.7   Professor Johnson was asked whether his investigations had revealed why it should be that there had been no burial when research had ceased 27 years previously. He was unable to throw any light on this issue,

> 'It is clear that it also came to a point whereby the body parts had been left and those involved were not motivated to dispose of them, either because of the difficulty of disposal or because of neglect.'

21.8 Given the circumstances in which it was discovered by the Dean, the maintenance of the collection must also be dubious. Certainly the impression is that the 'store' had simply been left within the fetal room where, if it had been known about in the first place, it had certainly become forgotten. Consent to research should not constitute an open-ended ticket whereby material can be kept for years on end without any research work being undertaken.

21.9 Some of the remaining documentation reveals a lack of respect and a failure to appreciate the circumstances which led to the donation or taking of human material. Two entries relating to material which has not been retained refer to fetal material of 9 weeks' and 45 days' gestation respectively. The comments next to each entry read 'Inflated monster. Humpty Dumpty' and 'Neck deeply lacerated. Pull it to pieces some time and reject'. Such entries do the researcher no credit. They are shocking and disrespectful.

22. What was the Purpose of the Collection; Who Used It; What Were the Benefits?

22.1 Dr Latham did publish extensively in relation to the work undertaken in respect of cleft palate malformation. We have reviewed a number of the papers from the oral surgery and dental departments. Some papers related to the development of the facial skeleton, both normally and in the presence of some congenital abnormalities, in particular cleft lip and palate. Some of the work was undertaken on normal fetus acquired following social termination of pregnancy and other work on fetus with cleft lip and palate. Some of the work was carried out on children who had been patients in the Facio Maxillary Unit and confirmed that specific consent had been obtained for the use of infants' heads. On the evidence this does not necessarily follow. The work itself was of high quality. Our concerns relate to the extent of discussions securing consent and the lack of clarity regarding burial. In particular we are concerned by the simple fact that heads and bodies remain within a store in the ICH many years after the research has been published and despite undertakings given as to respectful burial.

22.2 From a positive perspective the research undertaken has increased medical understanding of the proper treatment of cleft palate. Professor Cooke confirmed,

> 'As a result of his (Dr Latham's) work it has now been established that the palate should be repaired as late in childhood as possible, and he obtained very rare material from children who had died after palate repair.'

23. Who Knew of the Collection?

23.1 It is clear that the finding of the paediatric collection came as a great shock to the Dean, Professor Johnson, when he discovered it together with the fetal collection, on 7 December 1999. He had been asked by Alder Hey many months previously to be one of three people judging their research poster day and had attended the hospital that evening for that purpose. He was then approached by Professor Cooke who had mentioned the fetal collection, much to his surprise. Professor Johnson asked to see the collection and it was during that tour of the ICH that he noticed heads stored within the fetal collection. There had been no attempt to hide the children's body parts and Professor Johnson immediately asked Ms Connell to place them on a lower shelf out of view, and to take steps to change the lock and code of the room in which the body parts were stored. He told the Inquiry that he was 'saddened at what I had seen, and also confused'. His initial reaction was to set up an internal inquiry, but a University decision was made by the Vice-Chancellor, Professor Love, to co-opt a special working group to investigate internally.

23.2 Professor Cooke had some knowledge of the paediatric collection, but did not appreciate the true extent. He said in his witness statement dated 2 June 2000,

> 'I knew, through Audrey Smith, of the fetal collection, and I also knew that there was some other paediatric material dating back to the Dental School but I did not know the extent or the nature other than that it related to the cleft palate work.'

23.3 In oral evidence he expanded those comments, confirming that Dr Smith had told him of the collection soon after he became Head of the Department, telling him that there were 'very rare, unusual specimens' which were 'part of the museum collection'.

23.4 We accept the evidence of Professor Johnson that he did not know of the collection. We give him credit for not destroying the collection when he became aware of its existence in December 1999. He was aware of its sensitivity, particularly at a time when there was considerable public concern in relation to the retention of organs, and any temptation to dispose of the material, however great, was resisted.

23.5 Dr Smith confirmed that she was aware of a collection of residual material relating to cleft palate and other facio maxillary research undertaken by Dr Latham and others many years previously. Her understanding was that the bodies had been given over for research and once the pertinent organ (either head or part of the head) had been removed, the body itself would have been stored. What knowledge there was of the paediatric collection was extremely limited. Essentially this had been a collection used in years gone by but then left on shelving without arrangements being made for proper disposal. Because the children's body parts were stored amongst the fetal collection it is probable that persons having access to the fetal store would have noticed the various paediatric parts, particularly as no attempt was made to separate them from the fetal collection as a discrete store.

24. Whose Responsibility was the Collection?

24.1 Clearly the responsibility lay with the University given the nature and purposes of the collection.

The Eye Tissue Collection at The Royal Liverpool University Hospital

25. History; Personnel; Contents of the Collection

25.1 On 7 December 1999 Professor Johnson had become aware of the fetal and paediatric stores within the ICH and a few days later he was told by Professor Malcolm Jackson, Head of the Department of Medicine, that there was a 'fetal eye collection' held within the Department. Professor Johnson instituted investigations through the special working group which he had already established.

25.2 He arranged for a complete inventory of the collection to be prepared and asked for a list of publications resulting from the collection. He established that the collection had begun with a pilot study by Professor Ian Grierson, Professor of Ophthalmology, Professor van Velzen and Dr Howard in 1993 which had resulted in a successful application for a Wellcome Trust grant. He queried what consent had been given and was reassured that proper consent had been obtained. The University notified the Inquiry of the 'fetal eye collection' on 24 March 2000.

25.3 The question of consent was put to Professor Johnson and in his witness statement he said:

'I was told that Professor Grierson's understanding in relation to the issue of the consent was that this related back to the consent obtained on the original post mortem consent form which specified that tissues could be used for teaching and research. I was also reassured that the eyeballs were taken from fetus, and not neonates or older children, and the collection remains secured in the Department of Medicine.

I was somewhat taken aback by the news of the fetal eye collection, but my initial reaction was tempered by the fact that the research work performed in ophthalmology was generally of an excellent standard, and the clinical work of the Royal Liverpool University Hospital was excellent. I therefore felt that the likelihood was that the work had probably been done properly. I nevertheless instructed Professor Jackson and Professor Grierson to catalogue and secure the tissues in a locked place not generally known to other staff and to await the outcome of the due process which was occurring.'

25.4   Apparently the eye collection was limited to fetal tissue. We were concerned, however, to eliminate the possibility that eyes had in fact been taken from children at post mortem examination at Alder Hey. Initial documents which we obtained suggested that we could not rule out this possibility.

25.6   A document prepared by Professor Grierson in 1994 in support of a proposed research paper entitled 'The Development of the Extra-cellular Connective Tissue Matrix and Macroglia at the Lamina Cribrosa Region of the Human Optic Nerve' stated,

> 'Several studies have looked at the fine structure, three dimensional topography and immunochemical composition of the lamina in the adult eye but much less work has been done on the fetal and infant tissue. We have available to us approximately 200 fetal, neonate and infant specimens from the Department of Infant and Fetal Pathology, University of Liverpool. …No major immunohistochemical studies of human fetal material have been undertaken to our knowledge. It is fair to say that there are a large number of questions about the developing human lamina cribrosa that we do not know. … A total of 80 fetal and infant eyes are available to us at present. These range from the fourth fetal month to four years of age. All specimens have been either fixed in 10 per cent formol saline or 2 per cent buffered glutaraldehyde and then processed for wax histology. A total of two to three suitable specimens come to the Department of Fetal and Infant Pathology each week so that it is our expectation to have between 100 and 150 specimens for the optic nerve investigations. Enucleated eyes with malignant melanoma of the choroid and eye bank eyes from the Manchester eye bank will serve as adult control material. 20 such eyes are embedded but as yet not sectioned and a further five specimens have been stained and sectioned to test out the reconstuctive software.'

25.7   A formal application for a research grant from the Wellcome Trust was submitted by Professor Grierson, Professor van Velzen and Dr Howard on 8 March 1994. The summary of proposed research referred to the intention that the work be conducted 'on an archival series of over 150 fetal specimens and the predicted prospective series which is expected to accumulate at a rate of approximately 1–2 specimens per week'. The application confirmed,

'A total of 150 fetal and infant eyes are available to us at present and have been introduced into the database as part of our pilot feasibility investigation. The specimens range from the second fetal month to term and then there are eyes from neonates and infants up to four years of age. …Between one and two suitable specimens come to the Department of Fetal and Infant Pathology each week so that it is our expectation to have an additional 50–100 specimens per year for the optic nerve investigations.'

It was therefore quite clear that the proposal envisaged the use of neonatal and infant eyes, notwithstanding the fact that we had been told the collection related exclusively to fetal material.

25.8   The conclusion that neonatal/infant eyes were made available was supported by study of the thesis submitted by the research fellow Mr Alan Kosmin in July 1998. His thesis refers to the use of 17 fetal eyes between 12 and 35 weeks post conception, and one eye from a 3.5 month neonate.

25.9   We were able to clarify matters by obtaining evidence from Professor Grierson. A list purporting to identify the sources of the eye tissue, either by post mortem number or by reference to histology day book numbers, was also disclosed. We have established that the store contains 188 eyes and 2 optic nerves from 109 specimens. The majority consists of both left and right eyes but there are some specimens where only one eye is present. Whilst referred to as the 'fetal eye collection' by both the University through its solicitors and Professor Johnson personally in his witness statement, we have determined that a number of the eyes were removed from children at post mortem examinations at Alder Hey. We (and indeed Alder Hey to whom the list was similarly disclosed in August 2000) have had problems in making the necessary identification but were able to highlight at least 12 cases where eyes had been taken from identified neonates and children. The youngest child lived for only an hour, the oldest for 21 months.

25.10   The list of specimens also makes it clear that eyes were taken from fetus as long ago as 1988. Professor Grierson gave evidence that prospective collecting for the purpose of the Wellcome Trust study only began at the very end of 1993/start of 1994 and stopped in 1995. Eyes in the collection which pre-date that could only have been collected retrospectively from material already held by Professor van Velzen.

26.   Cataloguing; Storage; Maintenance and Procedures

26.1   The specimens were provided by Professor van Velzen's Unit of Fetal and Infant Pathology. The issue of the removal of fetal eyes was discussed with Professor van Velzen in his interview with the Solicitor to the Inquiry. He explained that in about

10–15 per cent of cases eyes would be removed from fetus 'as part of a routine service, normal diagnostic purposes'. The justification advanced by Professor van Velzen was that a proper examination of the eye was demanded in certain cases to determine the genetic consequences of any disease process. It is clear from the list of the retained fetus at Myrtle Street as logged by Dr Howard in October 1999 that eyes were removed from fetus. An examination of Dr Howard's log reveals that a total of 44 eyes had been removed from those retained fetus. The vast majority of removals could not in fact be dated as in some instances the fetus were not properly identified other than by a case number. This was unhelpful in terms of further identification.

26.2   The actual collection of the specimens was carried out by Mr Michael Birch and Mr Kosmin, who were both research fellows. Eyes were brought to the Ophthalmology Unit in the Department of Medicine at Royal Liverpool University Hospital. When they were dissected segments of tissue were given a unique reference code. The coding was done by Mr Birch and Mr Kosmin and the Wellcome Trust funded technician working on the project. Remnants of eye material after dissection and eyes not dissected would retain their original Myrtle Street numbers.

26.3   The material required for Professor Grierson's project was eye tissue in the developmental stage. Professor Grierson's interest was in glaucoma of the eye. This is a problem where high pressure in the eye causes collapse of the optic nerve head. Where the optic nerve enters the eye it is vulnerable to collapse and is supported by a connective tissue skeleton. The skeleton is vulnerable in some individuals but not others and Professor Grierson wanted to find out how the skeleton was constructed. As glaucoma is a disease believed to start during development but which expresses itself in old age it was important to look at eyes still in the development phase rather than adult eyes. This was why fetal eyes were so important. Fixed tissue was perfectly satisfactory for these purposes, there was no requirement for fresh tissue.

26.4   A total of 79 of the 109 specimens have been used in the research. The other specimens in the collection remain intact, stored in fixative. There are 100 'analysed' eyes to 88 'unanalysed' eyes. All the eyes have been retained and are stored in a double-locked room within the Unit of Ophthalmology on the third floor of the Royal Liverpool University Hospital. None of the eyes have been disposed of save for any material used up during research.

27.   Consent

27.1   Professor Grierson's evidence was that Professor van Velzen assured him that the material which he had collected could be used for the purposes of research. Professor Grierson had no reason to doubt that this was correct and assumed that the relevant consents had been obtained. He had never done any research on fetal material before and has conducted none since and was totally reliant upon Professor van Velzen's guidance. He told us that had he had any concerns about Professor van Velzen in the first place he would not have proceeded with the project at all.

27.2   We accept Professor Grierson's evidence. However, the use of fetal material meant that the recommendations of the Polkinghorne Report, discussed above (see paragraph 11), should have been followed, although under the Code of Practice there was no sanction for non-compliance. There is no evidence that appropriate consents for the research use of fetal tissue were ever obtained. Professor Grierson told the Inquiry that he was unaware of the Polkinghorne requirements. In Liverpool at that time he would not have been alone in this. The failure of researchers to understand or comply with Polkinghorne – or the lack of proper dissemination of the report – was a constant theme throughout the Inquiry.

27.3   In relation to the eyes from neonates and older children there is no evidence that any consent, other than the usual consent obtained at the time of a hospital post mortem, was in fact requested. It would have been good practice to obtain specific consent for removal of eyes at post mortem examination. The procedure could result in an external change to the body which could be noted on viewing the body following the post mortem examination. There may well have been instances, although probably relatively infrequent, where parents have buried children without knowing that eyes have been removed.

27.4   Professor van Velzen made it clear in evidence to the Inquiry that for the purposes of research he did not distinguish between Coroner's and hospital post mortems. He took the view that research was permissible on any material legitimately removed at post mortem for clinical purposes. The validity of this approach is addressed more fully in Chapter 9. Given that a Coroner's post mortem would not have required any formal parental consent there might have been instances where eyes were removed at post mortem examination and where the consent of parents has never been a relevant issue. However, it is reasonable to assume that the Coroner would not give consent for eyes to be removed unless there was, for example, an allegation of a traumatic injury in which case a Home Office pathologist would have been involved in the examination, with or without the involvement of an Alder Hey pathologist. We have not seen any Coroner's post mortem report which confirms the removal of eyes.

28.   What was the Purpose of the Collection: Who Used It; What Were the Benefits?

28.1   Before considering the research papers generated as a result of the consideration of the fetal, neonatal and infant eye tissue it is helpful to consider the events of early 1995, when concern as to the position regarding ethical approval was first raised by Professor

Neilson. In January 1995 Professor Neilson was Clinical Director of Obstetrics and Gynaecology at Liverpool Women's Hospital. He received a telephone call from Mr Kosmin. Professor Neilson said,

> 'He told me that he was undertaking some research work with Professor van Velzen which involved the study of eyeballs and that he was concerned about the cosmetic appearances of babies after they had had their eyes removed to facilitate this research. He suggested some sort of cosmetic procedure to improve the appearance and queried whether this was acceptable to me. I said to Mr Kosmin that this was the first I had heard of this project and I queried whether he had valid Ethical Committee permission to do the research. He was unclear about that and I think he had felt that issue had probably been dealt with by Professor van Velzen but I said that there was no question of the research continuing until those matters had been clarified, and so I wrote to him asking him to clarify the position, and copied Professor van Velzen, amongst others, in on that correspondence.'

28.2   Professor Neilson's letter to Mr Kosmin was dated 20 January 1995,

> 'Following your telephone call two days ago, I have failed to establish that the research project you describe has received approval from the Ethics Committee at the Royal. I speak here not only with my University hat but also as Clinical Director for Obstetrics in Liverpool Women's Hospital NHS Trust and I know that I speak for all my colleagues in saying that continuation of this project in an area of such sensitivity is quite unacceptable without approval from a properly constituted Research Ethics Committee. It may be that such approval has in fact been given either by the Committee at the Royal or by the Committee at Alder Hey and if you can furnish me proof of this, I would be delighted to discuss the cosmetic details that you discussed on the telephone. If you can also find no evidence of such approval, then it is essential to seek this before the project is re-started.'

28.3   The letter was copied to Professor Foster as Head of the Department of Pathology. Professor Foster immediately raised the issue with Professor van Velzen in a letter dated 27 February 1995. This was a long letter dealing with a number of concerns in relation to the service being offered by Professor van Velzen, and the use of the eye tissue was but one issue raised,

> 'Finally, I address the question of the authorised use of human tissues used for "research" purposes. It has been brought to my attention (see enclosed copy of letter from Professor Neilson) that you have been supervising a project in which eyeballs from fetus and from children dying in the neonatal period have been removed by yourself and/or by Mr Kosmin. As far as I am aware, no approval for this or any allied project has been obtained from any Ethical Committee – at the Royal, Alder Hey or at the Women's Hospital.

You must know that such use of human tissues is a highly sensitive issue that would have disastrous consequences for the University and for the involved NHS Trusts if leaked to inappropriate third parties. As the Director of Pathology, I am now asking for your guarantee that all of your research projects that involve the use of human tissues are not only approved by the relevant Ethical Committee but that the approval is available in a written and dated format. Any such project that is not suitably approved must be stopped forthwith until the requisite approval is obtained.'

28.4 Professor van Velzen's response was to go on the attack, and he wrote to Professor Foster on 7 March 1995. This is the letter referred to above in the section regarding the fetal collection at the ICH in which Professor van Velzen queried the legitimacy of that collection (see paragraph 14.2). The letter copied Professor Foster in on Professor van Velzen's response to Professor Neilson, also dated 7 March 1995, dealing with the latter's correspondence to Mr Kosmin. He stated,

'Mr Kosmin and BSc students up to today have only studied in detail eye specimens obtained by ourselves as part of legitimate routine analysis. As you will appreciate there are quite a few indications for eye examinations in fetal and perinatal pathology, especially in a University which prides itself on the depth of its post-natal care for infants with retinopathy of prematurity. Rest it to say that the exclusion of retinal dysplasia, toxoplasmosis and rubella associated ophthalmo-pathology regularly require detailed studies of this part of the human fetus. We more than others are aware of the sensitivities in these issues (I am one of the regular informants to enquiries by the Department of Health with respect to the practical details of fetal tissue) and as such we only report on those eyes in which clinically relevant pathology was found. The subsequent research on the stored specimens, was in line with current practice in all pathology laboratories and as long as patient privacy issues are not at stake no further Committee approval is required although we often submit protocols on such projects for confirmation of our opinion in such issues by the Committee itself.'

28.5 Professor van Velzen went on to indicate that in any future project in which a number of normal eyes of varying gestational age would need to be studied, full Ethics Committee approval would be requested. He indicated that in fact that had been done for a project related to fetal development of intestinal disaccharide transferase and that approval had been forthcoming through the Ethics Committee at the Royal Liverpool University Hospital, the Chairman of which was Dr Bell. He continued,

'It was for the purpose of discussing the various aspects of practical organisation of the future study and its feasibility, that Mr Kosmin was to contact you, so that a proposal (if the whole study proved feasible in the first place) could be properly written and not, once the procedure was completed be met with justified criticism of colleague obstetricians having not been involved with the project in an early stage. Perhaps he was not very clear, and we perhaps should have addressed you ourselves, but your anxiety, I can assure you, is not justified.'

28.6   Professor Neilson's reaction to the letter was not to accept what Professor van Velzen had said. In his evidence to us Professor Neilson made it clear that it was untrue that Mr Kosmin's contact with him had been for the purpose of discussing the various aspects of practical organisation of a future study and its feasibility,

> 'Mr Kosmin had made it very clear to me that the research project was ongoing and involved the removal of eyes from stillborn babies, and his query to me had been in relation to the cosmetic arrangements to be made thereafter.'

28.7   Professor Neilson made these points to Professor van Velzen by way of letter dated 16 March 1995,

> 'With respect to my telephone conversation with Mr Kosmin, he was clarity itself. He was describing to me an ongoing research project which involved the removal of eyes from stillborn babies. He telephoned me not to discuss the project nor whether ethical permission had been given, but details of the cosmetic arrangements to be made after removal of the eyes. I accept entirely that there may be circumstances in which there may be sound clinical indications why the eyes should be removed at autopsy for specific investigative reasons. I would, however, have to say that I cannot recollect ever having seen mention of eye histology in any autopsy which I have read over the years. I also have no difficulty whatsoever with the concept of using fetal tissue for legitimate research purposes – indeed, a major part of our research work is based on the use of fetal tissues. What I do feel very strongly about is that for any research, and especially research involving such a sensitive subject, the proposal should be accepted by the properly constituted Ethical Committee. I am still unclear at the end of your long letter whether Dr Bell's Committee has actually given permission for this specific project or not. Perhaps you could clarify this for me.'

28.8   In subsequent evidence to the Solicitor to the Inquiry, Professor van Velzen explained that he had taught Mr Kosmin how to remove fetal eyes 'in such a way that the fetus was not damaged to the extent that it could not be repaired, so that the parents could see the baby and viewing the baby wasn't impaired.'

28.9   In his witness statement to the Inquiry, Professor Neilson resumed the story,

> 'The issue over ethical consent was resolved to a certain extent. It became clear from correspondence from one of the three Ethics Committees that were in existence at the time that approval had not been sanctioned, although that, of course, did not mean that the research had not been approved by one of the

other two Committees. However, the ball was effectively in the court of
Professor van Velzen and Mr Kosmin as I had made it clear that the research
could not continue until evidence of approval had been produced and that was
never done. My interpretation of my discussions and correspondence on this
issue was that research was being done on the eyes of babies which were going
to Professor van Velzen's Unit for service post mortem examinations. My
understanding was that the eyeballs were not being taken from fetus following
terminations of pregnancies, but in situations were there was parental consent to
a hospital post mortem in respect of either a stillbirth or a perinatal death. The
sensitivity of the project clearly had a major impact. The consent form for a
hospital post mortem would have specified consent to the use of tissue for
teaching and/or research, and obviously there are well recognised problems as
to the interpretation of the term 'tissue' and what access consent affords
pathologists in such circumstances. In this particular case I do not know if the
specific research was discussed although I believe that Professor van Velzen said
that the eyes were being removed for clinical reasons in any event. However, I
was particularly concerned that eyes are clearly a part of the body which everyone
would regard as particularly sensitive structures and I recognise that there
would be very serious concern amongst parents if they felt that their children's
eyes were being removed for research purposes without specific consent.'

28.10 Professor Foster's view was also that no 'ethical permission' had been obtained and he
too recognised the sensitivity of the project,

'It duly transpired that there was no ethical permission for the project being
undertaken by Professor van Velzen and Mr Kosmin. At that point we were in
a transitional period in that it was normal for pathologists to work on human
tissues although there was not carte blanche. An issue such as the removal of
eyes which would disfigure the body and would be very obvious to relatives
post death was particularly sensitive and would be extremely disturbing. There
is an obvious distinction between taking something from the body out with the
practice necessary to complete a post mortem and in doing additional work on
material which would have been taken in any event.'

28.11 Professor Johnson's subsequent investigations in 1999 led him to conclude that ethical
permission had, in fact, been granted,

'I was told that Ethical Committee approval had been sought, and had been
formally approved by Dr Bell, the Chairman of the Royal Liverpool University
Hospital Ethics Committee by way of letter dated 10 December 1993. I was told
that the research had included work which had attracted a Wellcome Trust
Research Grant and that there had been publications, although not as many as
had been hoped for.'

28.12   We have obtained a copy of the letter written by Dr Bell as Chairman of the Ethics Committee and Royal Liverpool University Hospital dated 10 December 1993. The letter is interesting in that it refers to one specific project 'The Development of the Extra-cellular Connective Tissue Matrix and Macroglia at the Lamina Cribrosa Region of the Human Optic Nerve'. This was the project undertaken by Mr Birch, Professor van Velzen and Professor Grierson which subsequently attracted the Wellcome Trust Grant (in excess of £110,000) in August 1994. There is no reference to the involvement of Mr Kosmin, who of course undertook a separate thesis. Professor Grierson gave evidence that Mr Kosmin's thesis merely took the information which was being accumulated for the Wellcome Trust study and put another angle on the work emphasising other possible clinical relationships. He said in his witness statement,

> 'Mr Kosmin's thesis merely reviewed data already accumulated for the optic nerve study in a different light and did not involve the use of additional eye material, tissue blocks or sections. I believe this is why he did not consider that it was a separate study requiring separate ethical approval. Mr Kosmin was using exactly the same tissue slides and sections as had been used in the main project.'

28.13   We do not question Professor Grierson's integrity. As soon as he became aware of Professor Neilson's concerns regarding Professor van Velzen's activities in 1995 he immediately sent a memo to Mr Birch and Mr Kosmin instructing them not to collect any more eyes. Professor Grierson is highly respected and the Wellcome Trust project clearly had proper ethical approval.

28.14   We have to query however, whether Dr Bell's letter did in fact cover the specific work being undertaken by Mr Kosmin in conjunction with Professor van Velzen, which was not necessarily the same work as that covered in his thesis. We also note that the letter of approval specifically asks Mr Birch to check with his 'obstetric colleagues involved in the trial, that this sensitive issue as addressed in terms of fetal material disposal, as addressed in your protocol, is within current legislation'.

28.15   The outcome of the research itself remains unclear. Mr Kosmin's thesis was never published, although Professor Grierson explained that was not particularly unusual in the field of ophthalmology and the work undertaken was of a good standard. The final writing up and publication of relevant data under the Wellcome Trust project is expected to take place in 2001. We are told that the research has helped identify which cells are responsible for the production of the optic nerve skeleton, when and how it develops and the strengths and weaknesses. A very important incidental development from the work is that a new generation of machines are being developed in the UK and elsewhere which image the skeleton from outside the eye. These machines are of vital importance to the diagnosis of glaucoma.

29. Who Knew of the Collection?

29.1   Ms Costi, the MLA employed specifically to deal with the fetal work, confirmed that she had some knowledge that research work on fetal eyes was being undertaken. In her witness statement dated 30 May 2000 she said,

> 'I am not aware of any work being done on the fetus save the club foot study, and also I knew that Mr Kosmin, one of the research fellows, was doing some work on fetal eyes, although I do not know exactly what that research involved. I am unaware of eyes being taken from neonates or older children and believe that this was limited to fetus.'

29.2   In his subsequent investigations in 1999 Professor Johnson clarified through Professor Jackson and Professor Grierson that the collection was known to three ophthalmic research fellows and the technician, Mr Daniel Brotchie. Professor Neilson and Professor Foster, as is evident from the correspondence referred to above, were aware that work had been undertaken but had made it clear that such work should be stopped in the absence of specific ethical approval. The then Dean, Professor Orme, was unaware of the collection:

> 'I am aware of the correspondence in early 1995 regarding the research work undertaken by Professor van Velzen and Mr Kosmin on fetal eyeballs. I was not aware of eyeballs being stored, and if I was still Dean now I would expect to be told of something like this.'

29.3   His successor, Professor Johnson, was unaware of the collection until it was brought specifically to his attention in December 1999. It is clear that knowledge of the collection was extremely restricted and this was apparent when we inspected the collection at Royal Liverpool University Hospital. The collection was secured in a locked room with a notice prohibiting entry. The room itself was a disused darkroom. The collection was kept in three cardboard boxes, the first containing the eyes yet to be 'worked up', the second containing the remaining tissue following initial work, and the third blocks and slides.

30. Whose Responsibility was the Collection?

30.1   The collection in the Department of Medicine at the University of Liverpool is clearly a store for which the University has ultimate overall responsibility. We are disappointed that the late disclosure of the collection referred specifically to 'fetal tissue' and did not make it clear that the collection included some eyes taken from children at post mortem examination.

31. Footnote

31.1   We recognise that the possibility of eye removal will cause parents great distress, particularly if our Report is the first indication of such a possibility. Alder Hey were given a list by the University in August 2000 which led to their identifying a number of children affected by eye retention and where parents had made general inquiries of Alder Hey as to the position in relation to organ retention. Those parents should have been told of the eye retention immediately identification was complete. It was suggested that repatriating eye tissue to parents would have set a dangerous precedent, given that the research work was ongoing. We believe that this should not be a consideration if the material has been obtained improperly.

32. Animal Material at the ICH/Myrtle Street

32.1   The question of the animal material can be dealt with quite succinctly. We include reference to the animal material because we know that is a specific concern of parents. Within the heart collection as a whole there are a small number of animal hearts retained essentially for comparative work. Dr Smith confirmed that there was access to a small number of pig hearts which were used for the examination of specialised conduction systems, some lamb hearts, and the hearts of some rats and a few chicks. There are also hearts from some very rare species of animal including a red kangaroo, a gibbon and a giant tortoise given to the ICH for comparative studies. Apart from the gibbon there are no other monkey hearts in the collection. Rat and mouse material obtained from elsewhere is also held within the University but not stored within the ICH. The small number of animal hearts held are kept on a completely separate shelf from the human hearts and all are clearly identified. There can be no suggestion that the animal hearts have been stored in the same pots as human hearts.

32.2   It is also the case that some animal material was stored at Myrtle Street in the basement. Indeed an animal researcher, Dr Paul Sibbons, was working at Myrtle Street. He joined the Unit in order to test further in animal studies some of the hypotheses being explored by Professor van Velzen and Dr Howard in relation to 'cot deaths'. Studies on lamb and piglet in particular were undertaken. The containers in which such animal material was stored were held separately from the containers of human material and, again, there can be no question of animal material having been held in the same containers as human tissue or organs.

32.3   It was regrettable that during the course of the Inquiry a story appeared in the Liverpool Echo in or around March 2000 which focused on an allegation that monkey parts had been stored next to human material. This story was considered front page news and prompted numerous worried parents to contact the Inquiry to ask whether there was any truth in the story. Due to the confidential nature of the Inquiry it was not possible to advise those concerned parents of the truth, because otherwise it would have been necessary to comment on any story which subsequently appeared in the media, thus jeopardising our policy of confidentiality. We were aware that the incident to which it referred had no connection with the retention of organs at Myrtle Street, but in fact related to the University Department of Human Anatomy. The history was that fetal material had at one point been stored in a freezer next to some monkey parts. The Department was aware of that situation, but could not explain precisely how that fetal material had ended up in that particular freezer. The situation had been dealt with, in that the fetal material had been incinerated. The extent of the fetal material was understood to be in the region of 10 fetus at very early stages from social terminations of pregnancy. It was never satisfactorily established from where that fetal material emanated.

32.4 We found it surprising that anyone purporting to have parents' interests at heart should consider that release of such information to the local media could in any way be helpful to parents affected by organ retention.

33. Final Observation

33.1 We have described all the existing collections of organs from 1947 onwards but more particularly within the period 1962–2000 specified in our terms of reference. Clearly organ retention before 1988 was not restricted solely to hearts and lungs. However, we have seen no evidence of individual organ retention beyond that contained within the collections we have described. The general view we have is of organ removal, examination and return to the body for funeral purposes. However, if brains and hearts were retained they would have to be fixed, which itself took at least eight weeks, and it is likely they were not returned to the body. Whether other organs were retained and then disposed of is a matter about which we can only speculate.

33.2 We have also chosen not to highlight in this chapter the cerebellum collection which came to light in August 2000. The cerebella had been taken from brains already held at Myrtle Street and in 'the van Velzen years' we explore how the organs stored there were allowed to accumulate. We also deal specifically with the cerebella in Chapter 3 when we comment on Alder Hey's handling in 1999/2000 of the organ retention.

Chapter 8. The van Velzen Years

The van Velzen Years: Part 1
November 1986 – August 1988

The Appointment of Dr van Velzen to the new Liverpool Health Authority Chair of Fetal and Infant Pathology

1. Introduction

1.1 Having considered in Chapter 7 the various other collections we now move on to explain the background to the extraordinary retention of organs between 1988 and 1995 which we have called 'the van Velzen years.' To understand how this situation developed it is necessary to consider the events leading up to Professor van Velzen's ultimate appointment.

2. Initial Contact of the Foundation for the Study of Infant Deaths (FSID)

2.1 In 1986 Dr Bouton retired after many years of service as Consultant Pathologist at Alder Hey. A locum Consultant, Dr Ibrahim, was appointed in his place.

2.2 There was a proposal that the Health Authority should convert what was the vacant consultant post in Paediatric Pathology at Alder Hey into a Chair. This was in the hope and expectation that lectureships and other supporting staff might be provided by charities interested in promoting research and training in paediatric pathology.

2.3 On 26 November 1986 Professor John Davis, Professor of Paediatrics at the University of Cambridge Clinical School based at Addenbrooke's Hospital, wrote to Alder Hey in his capacity as Chairman of the Scientific Advisory Committee of FSID. He addressed Professor Frank Harris, Professor of Child Health at the University of Liverpool (the University) based at the Alder Hey site, who was also the Dean of the University Medical School and Head of the Institute of Child Health (ICH). Professor Davis requested details of the University's confidential proposals for converting the consultant post, and what resources might be available in Liverpool for such a Chair. The resources to be clarified included the likely access to cases of fetal, neonatal and infant death, particularly cot death, and the kind of support the University would need from FSID to make a Chair academically viable. Professor Davis asked about the nature of the support to be expected from the Departments of Pathology, Paediatrics and Obstetrics at Alder Hey and from Community Health in Liverpool.

3. The University Response

3.1 Professor Harris replied to Professor Davis on 9 December 1986, in his capacity as Dean of the Medical School and Professor of Child Health. He assured FSID that the venture had the unreserved support of the Departments of Pathology, Paediatrics, Obstetrics and Community Health. He said that both the Chairman of the Royal Liverpool Children's Hospital Board (Alder Hey) and the Chairman of the Paediatric

Medical Executive Committee of the District Health Authority were wholly supportive. The District Medical Officer and the Vice Chancellor of the University awaited a formal proposal with interest. Professor Harris gave an outline description of the resources available. He described the premises as,

> ' … from the NHS, a well-found NHS diagnostic laboratory (including an electron microscope) and a mortuary with supporting medical, laboratory, scientific staff and records staff … housed in purpose built units with a separate, recently re-built mortuary.'

While this was true, it hid the reality of the cramped conditions and split sites that were later described by an applicant for the Chair (see paragraph 17.1). In addition, the University would make a laboratory suite available at the ICH. There was said to be 'total access' to neonatal and infant deaths in the Children's Hospital and Maternity Units within the Liverpool District Health Authority. Professor Harris saw no reason why the Coroner would not use the Professor as his Consultant Paediatric Pathologist for 'cot deaths'.

3.2   Professor Harris then set out what he considered to be the minimum academically viable package. He suggested in a formal proposal from the Health Authority and FSID to the University that:

(a)   a Chair in Paediatric Pathology be established in the University Department of Pathology, to be based at Alder Hey and funded through the National Health Service; and that

(b)   a Lecturer (Clinical), together with a research technician and secretary, be established in Paediatric Pathology and based with the Professor at Alder Hey.

These posts were to be established on funds provided by FSID. It is necessary to understand that clinical lecturer posts as envisaged by the University and FSID are training posts in University terms and beneath consultant status in the NHS.

3.3   Professor Harris would make the academic case for this proposal, and he closed his letter highlighting the support and co-operation of the Unit General Manager of the Children's Hospitals.

4.   The FSID Offer and University Acceptance

4.1   FSID considered its position and wrote to Professor Harris on 20 March 1987 making an offer of £250,000, over a five-year period, to fund supporting staff for the Chair. The letter came from Dr Pamela Davies, Secretary to the Scientific Advisory Committee of FSID.

4.2   FSID envisaged that the sum could provide salaries for two clinical lecturers, as opposed to the minimum of one proposed by the University, a research technician and a secretary. The grant would not meet future wage awards. Support from FSID was to be on the understanding that a substantial part of the research effort would be devoted to the problem of cot death. This support could not be guaranteed beyond the first five years, but, provided there were satisfactory yearly reports and the standard of excellence remained high, at the end of a three-year period, it might be continued.

4.3   Professor Harris responded accepting the offer, subject to the approval of the other interested parties. He wrote to the Vice Chancellor of the University, Professor Graeme Davies, on 31 March 1987 describing the venture as 'a considerable investment' on the part of FSID. He proposed that the Chair be awarded the title of Liverpool Health Authority Chair in Fetal and Infant Pathology in order to 'ease the negotiations'.

4.4   There appears to have been little difficulty in gaining approval for the translation of the NHS Consultant's post into funding for the Professor. The only written evidence of any attempt to cast the net wider in terms of resource is in a letter from Professor Harris to the District Medical Officer in May 1988. He suggested that Mersey Regional Health Authority fund one of the new Professor's six clinical sessions in return for the Regional Referral Service in Perinatal Pathology. This was an attempt to spread the cost rather than an effort to provide a further clinical resource. In any event the request was politely refused on the ground of lack of funds.

External Advisers and Soundings

5.   The External Advisers

5.1   The University swung into action. Two external advisers for the creation of the new Chair were appointed: Professor John Emery, Emeritus Professor of Paediatric Pathology at the University of Sheffield and Professor Jonathan Wigglesworth, Professor of Perinatal Pathology at the Hammersmith Hospital in London. As early as 14 July 1987 Professor Emery wrote to the Registrar of the University, Mr Nind, suggesting that it would be best to explore one or two particular names before advertising the post. He mentioned two people in particular, one of whom was Dr Dick van Velzen at Delft, in the Netherlands. So even before the advertisement of the Chair, Professor Emery had suggested Dr van Velzen as a candidate well worth considering.

6. Professor Donald Heath

6.1 Various people were asked for their views on the Chair and how it should be supported.

6.2 Professor Donald Heath, the Head of the Department of Pathology at the University wrote with his suggestions for the new Chair. He expressed his full support for what he described as 'this welcome initiative'.

6.3 There were two features that he considered important. The person appointed to the Chair had to be able to initiate and execute a programme of basic research into infant and neonatal pathology. They should also be capable of providing a service in paediatric pathology for Alder Hey Hospital. He evidently overlooked the service provision in neo-natal and fetal work that would be required.

6.4 Professor Heath believed that the appointee must be a member of the Royal College of Pathologists and preferably by examination rather than by exemption. The competence of the appointee would have to be clear to the Liverpool Heath Authority, to the clinicians at Alder Hey and the pathologists in the Eastern Sector Division of Laboratory Medicine. He concluded his letter with the following observation,

> 'To find this combination of capacity for high quality research and competence to provide a service to the NHS is not going to be easy. However, the Chair is unique and the opportunities offered by it are great. The challenges and the possibilities of gaining a national or even international reputation in this field may provide the magnet for attracting the outstanding candidate we are seeking.'

7. Professor Jonathan Wigglesworth

7.1 However, all was not well. Professor Wigglesworth, the second external assessor, had substantial reservations about Professor Harris' proposals. He developed them in a letter in October 1987 to Mr Cudmore, Consultant Surgeon and Chairman of the Medical Advisory Committee at Alder Hey (see paragraph 12.1). In essence he did not believe that the planned resources were sufficient to underpin the successful provision of a clinical service and felt that the Chair would fail on that ground. He had already voiced his concerns and on 31 July 1987 Professor Harris wrote to the Vice Chancellor,

> 'I am afraid one of our external assessors has the bit between his teeth!'

Professor Harris questioned Professor Wigglesworth's motive and his ability to serve as an external assessor. As will be seen, this questioning was mistaken. Professor Harris went so far as to say,

'This does not mean that all criticisms are likely to be unfounded but I do sense that there is a personal element behind his approach. In addition, I am not sure whether he understands that he is there to help the University and not primarily to serve the College of Pathologists.'

Precisely why Professor Harris considered it unhelpful for Professor Wigglesworth to make constructive criticism of the resources to cover the clinical requirements remains a matter of speculation at this point. Dr Barson, a potential applicant for the post, ascribed a potential motive in later correspondence. He suggested that the use of charitable funding for the Chair was more important to the University than the long-term development of the clinical service (see paragraph 17.1).

7.2   Professor Heath and the Vice Chancellor both wrote to Professor Wigglesworth in August 1987 in an effort to calm his fears. They explained they knew the workload at Alder Hey. Professor Heath made particular reference to the average current service load, comprising some 150 post mortems (55% of which were performed for the Coroner) and reporting on 1,500 surgical specimens annually. He believed that a Professor, two clinical lecturers and a rotating NHS Registrar should find that workload well within their capacity and would allow adequate time to initiate and carry through a vigorous research programme.

7.3   Neither Professor Heath's nor the Vice Chancellor's letter showed any understanding of the main thrust of Professor Wigglesworth's concern. Neither made any allowance for the entirely new workload in fetal and neonatal pathology that the Chair would attract, both on Merseyside and on a regional basis. Nor did they make any allowance for an increase in workload at Alder Hey, whether through the introduction of more modern techniques or simply through greater enthusiasm under a new regime.

8.   Further Soundings

8.1   Meanwhile, further soundings were received. Dr Helliwell, Senior Lecturer in Pathology at the University wrote to the University Registrar, Mr Nind, on 11 August 1987. He stressed the substantial clinical commitment associated with the Chair. He said the Professor would need to spend most of his time, and be based, at Alder Hey. Consultant level cover would be necessary for clinical work.

8.2   Dr Nash, another Senior Lecturer in Pathology at the University wrote to Mr Nind on 26 August 1987,

'There are certain aspects of the post that require consideration and no doubt the Committee already has these mind. The diagnostic commitment for the NHS is vital and the new incumbent will have to be prepared to undertake this, or at least its organization, including the provision of cover during staff absence at meetings, conferences, etc. A further point is the fitting of the two proposed clinical lecturers into the existing training programmes and their access to research facilities in the University Department of Pathology. It will also be necessary to come to an agreement with the NHS on the effect of these two new posts on Senior Registrar numbers in the Region.'

The NHS diagnostic commitment was certainly in the mind of Professor Wigglesworth and had been communicated to the Committee by both Dr Helliwell and Dr Nash. However this was not reflected in drafting the job description to advertise the Chair later that year (see paragraph 13).

9. The Eastern Division

9.1 The Eastern Division of Pathology, which included Broadgreen, Mill Road and the paediatric hospitals met to consider the Chair. Dr Kenyon, Consultant Histopathologist, wrote to the District Medical Officer, Dr June Phillips, in September 1987 to tell her what the Eastern Division recommended,

> ' …. That the two Clinical Lecturers should be replaced by a single Senior Lecturer with Honorary Consultant status in order to provide satisfactory cover for the service needs of the paediatric hospitals. This was the view discussed at a meeting chaired by Dr Wilkinson and we still await Professor Harris' reply to this proposal. It is the view of the Royal College of Pathologists as recorded at the Annual General Meeting of the College in 1986, that there should be two Paediatric Pathologists (Histopathologists) in each Region.'

The Inquiry has no documentary evidence of any reply from Professor Harris, but he wrote to Professor Heath in October 1987,

> 'I cannot see that the recommendation of the Eastern Division of Pathology that the two Clinical Lecturers should be replaced by a single Senior Lecturer is a matter for the Job Description. The staffing and the use of the grant are a matter for the new Professor and yourself.'

10. The University and FSID Response to the Concerns

10.1 Professor Wigglesworth's concerns reached the ears of FSID and, according to Professor Harris, in a most unusual way. Professor Wigglesworth, external advisor to the University, communicated them himself.

10.2   The Vice Chancellor wrote on 21 September 1987 to FSID in an effort to steady their nerves. He stated that the University was committed to ensuring that the Chair was properly resourced both through the University's own processes and through dialogue with the Health Authorities. In fact in Professor Harris' first proposal the University's sole contribution was the laboratory facilities at the ICH. The only resource suggested through dialogue with the Health Authorities was the funding of the Professor's salary. The Vice Chancellor attempted to avoid Professor Wigglesworth's criticisms saying that the resources and support for the Chair had yet to be finalised and presented to the Committee, including Professor Wigglesworth.

10.3   Evidently, Dr Pamela Davies from FSID had a meeting with Professor Harris and Professor Heath on 23 September 1987, without Professor Emery. The Vice Chancellor's letter concluded,

> 'As there has been considerable local and national publicity, interest and commitment to this joint venture, I firmly believe we should endeavour to avoid a mutually embarrassing and damaging situation arising from the prejudicial action of Professor Wigglesworth.'

10.4   Mr Charles de Selincourt, the Chairman of FSID, wrote to the Vice Chancellor on 6 October 1987. Far from criticising the view of Professor Wigglesworth, he understood that Professor Emery shared his belief that three Consultant Paediatric Pathologists would be needed to cope with the workload. The clinical responsibility for seeing that workload done would almost certainly fall on the holder of the Chair.

10.5   It was not clear to FSID whether the necessary resources would be available when the new Professor was appointed.

10.6   FSID believed that adequate backup for routine work was vital *from the outset* (emphasis added) if the venture was to succeed. Until an assurance was given that these resources would be in place FSID was to hold the promised monies. FSID hoped that the venture would continue,

> 'secure in the knowledge that the new Professor will have adequate support at NHS Consultant level of the sort felt necessary by the Paediatric Pathologists who advise us – and yourselves.'

11.   University Reaction

11.1   Meanwhile, Professors Heath and Harris were in communication. Professor Heath wrote to Professor Harris on 12 October 1987 agreeing absolutely with Professor Harris that it was not necessary for the Regional Adviser of the Royal College of Pathologists to see the job description for the Chair before the post was advertised. He agreed that staffing and use of the grant was a matter for the new Professor. It was inappropriate for the Health Authority's representatives to suggest that the University take such decisions away from the new Professor.

11.2   The University was worried about creating a dangerous precedent, not only for any future laboratory-based Chairs but also for Clinical Chairs. Professor Heath said that,

> 'All along the representatives of the Health Authority have been trying to exert an undue influence on this appointment in accentuating the details of the light service commitment and forgetting that they are sitting on a Selection Committee for a Professor of this University, rather than an NHS Consultant.'

A picture was emerging in which the University was not just irritated by, but hostile to, outside advice from any quarter that did not blandly support the venture.

11.3   A little later the Vice Chancellor wrote to Professor Harris and said of the FSID correspondence concerned with the clinical resources,

> 'I suspect that this one will continue to run for some time yet – *sic transit gloria mundi!*'

12.   Professors Wigglesworth and Risdon, and their Letter to Alder Hey

12.1   On 27 October 1987 Professor Wigglesworth wrote with Professor Risdon, Professor of Paediatric Pathology at Great Ormond Street, to Alder Hey. They wrote on behalf of the British Paediatric Pathology Association and expressed their major reservation over the implication that the routine service was to be provided on what amounted to a part-time basis. Professor Wigglesworth had already resigned as an external adviser, another step which Professor Harris stated in evidence to us was highly unusual. They wrote and gave advice in straightforward, practical terms. The letter is now set out in full.

> 'We write on behalf of the British Paediatric Pathology Association to express our concern about proposals for the histopathology service at Alder Hey. We do so with some diffidence since this is obviously an internal matter for Alder Hey, and hope that you will understand that we are motivated purely by our interest in the future of the sub-specialty, particularly as it is practised in specialist children's hospitals.
>
> Our major reservation is over the current proposals for setting up a Chair based at Alder Hey and the implications of this on the routine service. As we understand it, it is envisaged that the salary for the Professor would be derived from NHS funding but with a commitment of only 6 sessions for running the

routine service. Although the present workload at Alder Hey does not appear great, we feel that the figures seriously underestimate the potential. Alder Hey is the largest children's hospital in Europe, yet has roughly half the workload in histopathology at Great Ormond Street, which has many fewer beds. This would seem to suggest that both the surgical pathology and post-mortem demand is being held in check. A modern histopathology service would provide rapid diagnosis over the full range of paediatric material, including neuropathology, using techniques in histochemistry, immuno-chemistry and electron microscopy as well as more traditional methods. Rapid diagnosis, particularly in diseases such as Hirschsprung's requires an out-of-hours emergency service such as that at Great Ormond Street. In addition, a histopathology service at a large centre like Alder Hey should be concerned with the rapidly expanding field of fetal pathology. We really cannot see how a satisfactory service to the clinicians at Alder Hey can be provided on a part-time basis. With an able and enthusiastic person in post the present service could be rapidly enlarged to the advantage of all the clinical services. Indeed, if the full potential could be exploited, there would probably be justification for at least two consultants. For purposes of comparison, Great Ormond Street has two full-time Honorary Consultants, a part-time Neuropathologist and a full-time, non-medical Professor of Histochemistry.

If it would be of any use to the medical staff at Alder Hey, we would both be happy to visit Liverpool and discuss the matter.'

The letter speaks for itself. Two full-time equivalent consultant posts within the NHS are roughly comparable to three academic posts, providing six clinical sessions each per week, with honorary consultant status. References elsewhere to three posts are to such academic positions. The advice was to provide two full-time equivalent consultant posts.

12.2　Mr Cudmore did not circulate the letter widely at Alder Hey and he did not discuss the detail with the Unit General Manager, Miss Sheila Malone. He should have done, since he received it in an official capacity as Chairman of the Medical Board. Instead, having worked with Professor Harris for many years and holding him in high regard, he went to him. He was reassured that the venture proposed by the University was the best way forward given the historical under-funding of children's services particularly in Merseyside. Mr Cudmore decided to support Professor Harris. Sadly this proved costly for Alder Hey, as did Professor Harris' failure to reconsider and reopen inquiries for the University.

13. Job Description

13.1 This is how the final job description came to be published in November 1987. Probably in response to the concerns with regard to the clinical workload, the University promised that a currently vacant, established senior lecturer (clinical) post in Pathology would be filled with a two or three session commitment to Alder Hey. This modest contribution of 1–1½ days' clinical work a week was the University's total contribution. The FSID research award was stated to provide for a research technician, a secretary and two clinical lecturers. The University had not acknowledged Eastern Division's suggestion that, in order to service the clinical need, these two clinical lecturers' posts should be converted into senior lecturer posts of Consultant status.

13.2 No checks appear to have been made that the two training posts would fit in with the allowed numbers of senior registrar posts in the Region, as Dr Nash had warned they should. Registrars were to work in the unit on a rotation basis, each spending four months on the Paediatric Unit. However, an inexperienced and junior doctor, of registrar status, was more likely to 'cost' the Professor clinical time in terms of training required than relieve the clinical burden. Even two clinical lecturers would require substantial training followed by supervision from the Professor if they were to contribute clinically. The workload from Alder Hey was set out as described earlier in Professor Heath's letter (see paragraph 7.2). How the Professor was to cope with the responsibility for both the Obstetric and Gynaecology service in fetal and neo-natal work was not clear.

13.3 The NHS was to provide and fund four service technicians. There was a vacant post for a Chief Medical Laboratory Scientific Officer (Chief MLSO), two further MLSOs and a Mortuary Technician. As it worked out later, the Chief MLSO post was filled from one of the existing two MLSOs, and a trainee MLSO was recruited.

13.4 All the University promised to provide was two to three clinical sessions from a senior lecturer.

14. FSID Reaction to the Advertisement

14.1 An advertisement for the Chair was placed in *The Lancet* in early November 1987 and was seen by the Officers of FSID. On 11 November 1987 Dr Pamela Davies wrote to Professor Harris reiterating FSID's concerns about the clinical workload. Professor Emery, both a member of the Scientific Advisory Committee of FSID and an external assessor for the University, had said at the Committee meeting in October that three consultant paediatric pathologists were needed. Dr Davies referred to Professor Emery's concerns and wondered if approval for these posts had been forthcoming. She mistakenly believed that there were to be three Consultant posts in addition to the Professorship. In confidence she also passed on concerns that no paediatric pathologist practising in the UK was to be an assessor for the Chair.

15. Interest in and Reaction to the Chair

15.1 The advertisement for the Chair attracted the interest of a number of pathologists. Some came to view the facilities and consider whether they should apply. All except two applicants were from overseas.

16. Dr D G Fagin

16.1 Dr D G Fagin was a Senior Lecturer and Honorary Consultant in Perinatal Pathology at Nottingham University. He wrote to Mr Nind on 24 December 1987,

'I find the whole concept of this post and the potential absolutely enthralling and I appreciate fully the boldness and generosity of the Sudden Infant Death Foundation's offer to fund supporting staff. The overall depth of vision in attempting to create such a post in the present day climate is breathtaking and deserves to succeed.

That being said, I'm sorry to have to introduce a note of caution. Although the proposed staffing may be adequate to update the Routine Histopathological Services and start a School of Research, the hospital accommodation is NOT ADEQUATE to even supply a satisfactory service at the present level, let alone produce any improvement. The same is true of the equipment.'

17. Dr A J Barson

17.1 Dr A J Barson was a Senior Lecturer and Honorary Consultant Paediatric Pathologist at St Mary's Hospital, Manchester. He wrote to Mr Nind on 30 December 1987. His letter contains such important criticisms of the premises, equipment and resources that it is now set out in full.

'As a prospective applicant for this Chair who has spent two days examining the facilities provided, it has become very evident that serious difficulties face any successful candidate. The University's formal job description is in itself a deterrent to the few trained paediatric pathologists who exist in the UK and abroad. I fear this situation is unlikely to be reversed by those who inspect the premises.

The creation of the Chair, even with the help of a three session commitment from a senior lecturer will actually reduce the current number of consultant sessions in paediatric pathology, which in any case are half those which existed a decade ago in Liverpool. This has occurred at a time when the discipline has expanded its consultant posts in other University cities. Over the last generation, fetal and infant pathology, rather like neonatology within paediatrics, has become a distinct sub-discipline. Like neonatology it has to be located in proximity to an intensive care unit, a cytogenetics service and obstetric staff who usually far out-number the paediatricians benefiting from the pathologist's expertise.

Despite this the proposal is to locate the Professor in Fetal and Infant Pathology four miles distant from the maternity beds and the new-born intensive care unit. There is no accommodation for the two clinical lecturers with their Professor. There is no room for them in the Alder Hey pathology laboratory and the new Institute of Child Health provides neither the equipment nor research milieu suitable for someone pursuing research in histopathology. The lecturers would be more properly accommodated in the University Department of Pathology. However, this would necessitate the Professor supervising his research staff from a distance of four miles. They in turn would be dependent for their research on mortuary facilities four miles from them. The Maternity Hospital being the source of material for both the Professor and his research staff would be separate from both. To attempt to provide research and a comprehensive clinical service at three such locations with inadequate staff is clearly not possible.

The following changes are the minimum necessary to bring paediatric pathology in Liverpool to a standard which already exists in most other provincial universities in the UK:

In addition to a Professor (or Reader/Senior Lecturer) there should be two Senior Lecturers in Paediatric Pathology, each with six NHS sessions in Alder Hey Children's Hospital.

The laboratory space at Alder Hey should be doubled to include three more offices, two more laboratories and a storeroom.

The Alder Hey mortuary requires structural alterations and equipment to facilitate postgraduate teaching.

Mortuary facilities removed from the Liverpool Maternity Hospital should be re-opened.

Space for a Professor, secretary and two lecturers or research staff should be provided in proximity to the Regional New-Born Intensive Care Unit. Routine laboratory facilities may profitably be combined with those required for gynaecological pathology.

Appointment of a Senior Registrar in Paediatric Pathology to be rotated between Alder Hey and the Liverpool Maternity Hospital.

I must emphasise that these are modest improvements necessary through long-standing neglect of paediatric pathology in Liverpool. It would not be unreasonable for what I am told is the largest children's hospital in Europe to aspire to an academic standing comparable to Great Ormond Street or other international paediatric centres of excellence. In that event staffing levels and facilities would have at least to be doubled.

Not unnaturally I found most enthusiasm for a clinical service in paediatric pathology amongst those clinicians with experience of it at other centres. A Chair in Fetal and Infant Pathology would fit in well with planned developments in obstetrics in Liverpool, although I feel it is unlikely that proper accommodation can be found for such a Chair before obstetrics is unified in a refurbished Liverpool Royal Infirmary. Senior University staff appeared to be more anxious about using charitable monies which are temporarily available than with the long term development of the clinical service. Whilst I understand the financial pressures on University authorities, clinical and academic excellence are mutually dependent. The wisdom of spending charitable money intended for clinical research where there is a virtually non-existent clinical service is very questionable. The appointment of a Chair will not by itself rectify this situation and the Area Health Authority, perhaps more than the University, has an obligation to show faith in Liverpool comparable to that shown by the Foundation for the Study of Infant Deaths.

I trust you will find these observations helpful for what is clearly a very difficult situation.'

Dr Barson did not apply. The significance of his letter is clear in the light of the history of the Chair.

18. Concerns brought to the Attention of the Vice Chancellor and Dean

18.1 On 5 January 1988 Mr Nind passed on the letters from Dr Barson and Dr Fagin to the Vice Chancellor and Professor Davies with the following note,

'You will wish to see these two letters. The closing date for applications was the 31 December but at the moment we have only three firm ones. We have notes of up to six more in the pipeline, so I am not closing off yet. I have sent copies of these to Frank Harris [the Dean] – should you discuss?'

The Vice Chancellor wrote a letter to Professor Harris to set up a meeting, or at least a discussion on the telephone. No note of any such meeting or discussion appears within the papers of the Inquiry. No action appears to have been taken to meet the constructive criticism within the letters.

18.2   In oral evidence Professor Harris agreed that the clinical workload could not have been borne within the proposed arrangements without a substantial service element from the clinical lecturers. It is not clear how it was all to work, nor why the University failed to appoint even one of the two clinical lecturers before the end of 1991.

19.   References from the External Advisers

19.1   The University Selection Committee obtained references and met. Professor Emery wrote to Mr Nind on 1 February 1988. Out of the eight potential candidates he dismissed two and listed the remaining six in order of preference, stating that the list was 'very adequate'. At the top of his list was,

> '1.   <u>Dick van Velzen</u> – being by far the most able and dynamic of the younger generation of paediatric pathologists in Europe – a vast potential. Could Liverpool control and contain him?'

While Professor Emery had identified Dr van Velzen as a prime candidate in the summer of 1987, he did not apply for the Chair until 1988. In fact Dr van Velzen gave evidence to the Inquiry that he was invited initially to appraise the post and advise the University. This seems unlikely, which reinforces the rumour prevalent at the time that the post had been earmarked for him. This rumour, together with the standard of facilities, may explain what was, objectively, a poor field of applicants.

19.2   Professor Huber, who was appointed as external advisor to replace Professor Wigglesworth, wrote on 11 February 1988. He maintained that the field was strong but, apart from Dr Fagin, there was a striking absence of UK applicants. He believed that this was the 'result of some sort of campaign amongst the paediatric pathologists in the UK to discredit the whole idea of establishing a strong academic paediatric pathology unit in Liverpool, on the grounds of lack of facilities, poor support, a too heavy routine workload etc. etc.' He continued,

> 'Even though we may have more positive thoughts and expectations, nevertheless we should take these negative vibes seriously. David Fagin is the only one of the candidates who sounds a note of caution in this respect, also because he knows the ins and outs of the UK system better than any of the foreign candidates. He is in a better position to appraise the job description realistically, to weigh the possibilities in the NHS and University setting.

Having said this I should state that in my opinion, at least initially, people are more important than rooms or instruments. Drive, ambition, ideas are the essence in starting this new venture.'

Professor Huber, who seems not to have seen Dr Barson's letter because he did not apply for the post, went on to review the field in greater detail than Professor Emery. Of Dr van Velzen he wrote,

'Young, brash, ambitious, very energetic, highly intelligent. Does not always deliver the goods. Conceptually very strong, willing to take intellectual risks. Thoroughly committed to developmental and paediatric pathology. He does inspire young people (he is himself only 38) but has no track record yet of leading. One would wish that for a few more years he would have a benevolent but strong boss on whom he could lean and who would ride hard on him. He has matured over the last years. Little experience in cot death. Able and energetic organiser, tends to have one too many irons in the fire. On the whole a bit risky but could, given a bit of luck and favourable circumstances, certainly become the leading paediatric pathologist in the UK.'

20. Professor Heath's View

20.1 Following Dr van Velzen's visit Professor Heath was impressed by his vigour, optimism and sense of humour. He turned his lack of experience and peer-reviewed publications into a virtue, and wrote,

'He has the right level of seniority for the Chair but has not yet developed academic specialisation that would make him unsuitable for his appointment.'

Bearing in mind the criticisms of Dr Barson of the premises and resources, Professor Heath noted that,

'It was very pleasing to find that having seen the facilities offered at Alder Hey he was still very keen to apply for the Chair which he felt presented both challenge and opportunity.'

21 The Selection Committee and Interviews

21.1 The Selection Committee for the Chair was made up of:

the Vice Chancellor,
Professor Harris (the Dean),
Professor Beazley (who was to become the next Dean),
Professor Heath (Head of the Department of Pathology),
Mr Bibby,
Mr Bruce,
Professor Hart,
Professor Ritchie,
Mr Cudmore (the Chairman of the Medical Advisory Committee at Alder Hey) and
Dr Kenyon.

21.2 Whilst Dr Kenyon was a practising histopathologist in the UK he was neither a paediatric nor perinatal specialist. Professor Emery, the external assessor, was retired. Professor Huber, the other external assessor, was from the University of Utrecht in the Netherlands. Professor Emery had already identified Dr van Velzen from the Netherlands as one of the two prime candidates before Professor Wigglesworth resigned as external assessor in August 1987 requiring the appointment of a replacement. There is no evidence as to how Professor Huber, also from the Netherlands, was chosen.

21.3 Overall, there had been eight applications for the Chair, from which four people were invited to meet the Selection Committee on 25 April 1988. Of those, one withdrew his application shortly before the interview date and another was unable to attend. Two candidates, Dr van Velzen and Dr Fagin, remained to be interviewed.

21.4 Professor Hart and Mr Cudmore, the Alder Hey representative, had significant reservations about the appointment of Dr van Velzen. He had only published about 27 papers, 20 of which were in Dutch although English is the language of choice in international publications. However, the Vice Chancellor spoke to them outside the Committee Room and the final decision was unanimous in favour of Dr van Velzen. Mr Cudmore said in evidence that it was obvious that Dr van Velzen was to be appointed and had he protested, the appointment would still have followed. Essentially Mr Cudmore trusted Professor Harris. In late 1999 Professor Hart remembered that a deciding factor in the appointment of Professor van Velzen was the strong support from the two external advisers, Professor Emery and Professor Huber.

22. The Result – August 1988

22.1 So Professor van Velzen was appointed to the Liverpool Health Authority Chair of Fetal and Infant Pathology. He was not a Member of the Royal College of Pathologists and even his supporters identified him as a risky appointment. He was only 38, with little published work and was to attempt to set up a unit in a foreign country. Miss Malone, Unit General Manager of Alder Hey, was subsequently to realise that he had lied to the Selection Committee. He had told them that prior to interview he had been to see Miss Malone to discuss the clinical service. This was untrue.

22.2 The appointment was against a background of almost unanimous concern for the resources available. The premises and equipment were inadequate. The clinical resource in terms of consultant support for the Chair amounted to 1–1½ days per week. The appointment and integration of the two clinical lecturers remained to be resolved. It was still not clear how the work from the Obstetric and Gynaecological Units was to be financed and serviced. Expansion and modernisation of the service at Alder Hey did not appear feasible on the proposed resources.

22.3 In effect, the historical NHS resource of one whole-time equivalent consultant histopathologist (11 sessions) was to be exchanged for the Chair (six sessions), the senior lecturer post (two to three sessions) and whatever useful clinical work could be gained from the two clinical lecturer training posts, after off-set for lost time in training and supervision. The University authorities had simply ignored all convincing advice and informed warnings. Through Mr Cudmore's faith in the University in the person of Professor Harris, Alder Hey had been swept along.

22.4 While the Senior Lecturer (Clinical) position was advertised on 28 May 1988 it remained unfilled and there is no advertisement available in evidence until 1991 for either of the clinical lectureships. FSID's concern that the supporting resources be in place from the outset had been ignored.

22.5 Professor Harris retired as Dean on 31 August 1988, the day before Professor van Velzen took up his Chair.

23. The Service Provision 1986–1988

23.1 Throughout the period between November 1986 and the end of August 1988, Dr Ibrahim, as locum Consultant Histopathologist at Alder Hey, had been gaining friends and providing a timely and professional clinical service. However, before Professor van Velzen formally took up his post he made it clear that he was unshakably opposed to Dr Ibrahim obtaining the position of senior lecturer. The hospital community wanted him appointed as senior lecturer and he was keen himself, but Professor van Velzen considered him unqualified for the position. In evidence before the Inquiry Professor van Velzen maintained that he would rather have done all the work himself than appoint someone with Dr Ibrahim's qualifications at that stage. The locum position covering the clinical need terminated upon the arrival of Professor van Velzen. He was left, or chose to be left, to work alone.

24. Dr Ibrahim, the ICH, the Coroner and Consent

24.1 Whether there was more to Professor van Velzen's opposition to Dr Ibrahim must remain a matter of speculation. Dr Ibrahim played a role in February 1988 that was of importance to this Inquiry. He had read the new Anatomy Regulations 1988 when they were published and was concerned about the retention of the Heart Collection in the ICH at Alder Hey. He discussed this with Dr Audrey Smith, a Senior Research Scientist at the ICH, who was effectively in charge of the research using the Heart Collection. She wrote to Professor Harris, then both Dean and Head of the ICH, on 15 February 1988,

> 'I should like to draw your attention to the new Anatomy Regulations, 1988 which are in force from now.
>
> The matter was raised with me by Dr Ibrahim last Friday. He was planning to speak to the Coroner in regard to our heart material. There is no mention of fetal material here but I think we may be placed in a delicate position.
>
> We understand that the Mothers are always consulted about the material coming to Alder Hey but I do not think that permission is given in writing. Perhaps we should have written permission. This would mean setting out a standard form. Who should be responsible for that?
>
> In regard to heart material – perhaps the standard post mortem forms could be modified so that the signature covers retention material for more than one month.'

Professor Harris annotated the letter, 'Audrey. Are we licensed in any way?' At the side of the text suggesting the modification of the standard post mortem forms with regard to the heart material, Professor Harris wrote, 'Yes'. Above that he wrote the names 'Arnold [Dr Arnold, Consultant Cardiologist] and Miss McKay [Consultant Cardiac Surgeon].'

24.2 Dr Ibrahim had told Dr Smith that he was also writing to the Coroner. Professor Harris' file at the ICH holds two copies of his letter of 16 February, addressed to Mr Barter,

'Please find, enclosed, a copy of the new Anatomy Regulations 1988 that I received recently. The current practice regarding heart (heart/lung) specimens from coroner's autopsies is to study them histologically and then to discuss them at regular sessions with Cardiac Surgeons and Physicians. In fact, most of these specimens from both coroner's and hospital autopsies over the last 35 years have been properly preserved and filed with relevant data.

In the light of the new Anatomy Regulations, I am not sure if the authority for possession of these specimens has been sought from the relatives of the deceased. I therefore wonder if it is possible to ask the relative for such a consent. If a consent is withheld then we have to dispose of the specimen properly after we have studied it microscopically.

I would much appreciate your advice.'

Immediately before this letter in the file lies a memo from Professor Harris to Dr Smith, which reads, 'Audrey, please see me for a chat about this.'

24.3　In evidence before the Inquiry Professor Harris did not remember Dr Ibrahim, nor did he remember any discussions or action arising out of Dr Smith's letter to him regarding the issue of consent. Mr Barter said he never received the letter and we have found no reply from the Coroner on file. Dr Smith did not remember, other than to say that if she had been asked to discuss the matter with Dr Arnold and Miss McKay, she would have done so. She could not remember any substantive discussion. For some reason unknown to the Inquiry, the initial reaction of Professor Harris to move the issue forward, annotated on the letter of Dr Smith, came to nothing. The opportunity to review the issue of consent and retention of hearts/lungs at the ICH was ignored. The concern at the collection of fetus for research, without written consent, was ignored. And Dr Ibrahim, too, was ignored after August 1988.

The van Velzen Years: Part 2
September 1988 – December 1990

Clinical Practice, Zero-money Research and the Fight for Resources (Fetal Pathology)

1.   The Resources: September 1988

1.1   Professor van Velzen took up his Chair on 1 September 1988. He arrived fired with enthusiasm and ambition. The laboratories and resources were as he had found them earlier in the year and as described by Dr Barson in his letter of December 1987. There was no clinical support at all. One of the first jobs was to appoint a Junior 'B' MLSO to the team of technical staff. It then consisted of Mrs Karen England, the new Chief MLSO, Mr Paul Dearlove, MLSO 2, Miss Fiona McGill, Junior 'B', appointed on 30 January 1989, and Mr John Kenyon, Senior Anatomical Pathology Technician who worked in the mortuary. There was no room in the laboratories at Alder Hey for any expansion of either personnel or equipment.

2.   The Professor's Diary

2.1   Prior to appointment, the University had agreed to allow Professor van Velzen to have leave of absence in order to fulfil commitments made in the Netherlands. His family remained there. He also had a commitment to the SSZD Laboratory in addition to private contract work with CIBA-GEIGY in Switzerland.

2.2   During the early period of his tenure, Professor van Velzen was away from Liverpool roughly once a fortnight. Every other weekend he visited his family, leaving on the Friday morning and returning on the following Monday afternoon. The opportunity for productive clinical work on the Friday before he left was limited. About once a month, Professor van Velzen tended to incorporate some working commitment with SSDZ and/or CIBA-GEIGY. Mostly the work was with SSDZ, where he had ongoing commitments in the running of a diagnostic laboratory. In that case he returned usually on the Wednesday. This arrangement lasted for about 18 months after he took up the Chair. Occasionally, if the work encompassed CIBA-GEIGY as well, he was away effectively for a whole week. With CIBA-GEIGY he worked as a consultant to various research projects begun before he became Professor. His commitment was for eight days a year in all, petering out in 1990/1991. It did not involve the use of any of the human material forming the subject matter of this Inquiry.

3.   The Challenge in Liverpool

3.1   In Liverpool Professor van Velzen had two main tasks.

3.2   Somehow he had to establish what he called the University 'Department' of Fetal and Infant Pathology which was in fact a 'Unit' or at best 'Sub-Department' of the main Department of Pathology (referred to as the 'Unit' in this report). In practice he had autonomy which had both advantages and drawbacks. He had to devise a programme of research attracting funding and personnel.

3.3   He also had to provide a clinical service to the Department of Histopathology based at Alder Hey. Even though the resource was not in place, fetus and stillborn babies were beginning to be delivered to him for specialist examination and report as part of this clinical service.

3.4   In order to achieve his goals Professor van Velzen had to make friends and allies within the close knit community of the Alder Hey Children's Hospital, within the University and across Liverpool. The environment was alien. While many people took to him in the early months, impressed, as had been Professor Heath, by his dynamism and vigour, it is clear that Professor van Velzen always considered himself an outsider and ill at ease.

4.   The SIDS-IUGR Hypothesis, Dr Howard and Stereology

4.1   It did not take Professor van Velzen long to realise that he had to develop what he called 'zero-money' research. There were simply no established resources for his research beyond the FSID support and until he had a track record there was little chance of any additional substantial grant.

4.2   There had been a hypothesis around for some time in which Sudden Infant Death Syndrome (SIDS), or 'cot death', was linked with babies of low birth weight and particularly those who were considered to have suffered from Intrauterine Growth Retardation (IUGR). By coincidence, the University had expertise in three-dimensional measurement in microscopy, known as stereology. Dr Vyvyan Howard, Senior Lecturer in the Department of Human Anatomy and Cell Biology, was one of the leading scientists in the field, and between 1984 and 1991 he was the general editor of the *Journal of Microscopy*.

4.3   The hallmark of stereology is a quantitative against qualitative study of a sample. In a qualitative study, sections are taken across a sample and then viewed under the microscope to reveal the inside of the object and interesting detail of the structure. It can only do so at the point of sectioning. However, in a quantitative stereological examination, sub-samples on an unbiased random basis are taken from the whole sample and the 2-D slides from these random samples are used to make highly relevant and intuitively understandable 3-D measurements. Stereology enables the accurate counting of structures throughout a sample, without having to count every such structure, using mathematical and statistical theory.

4.4   In Professor van Velzen's work his 'samples' were to be organs. He was to explore the hypothesis that SIDS babies were vulnerable as a result of the effect of IUGR which had left a permanent legacy on the structure of an organ in development. Different organs develop at different times in the womb. Depending on the timing of the growth retardation, different organs might be affected and in different ways.

4.5   Dr Howard met Professor van Velzen at a conference before he came to Liverpool. They discussed the hypothesis that SIDS and IUGR were linked. The application of stereological techniques was of obvious relevance, as instead of just measuring the weight of an organ, it would be possible to measure its component structures to see if IUGR had affected the development and number of those structures. It was this technique applied to the SIDS-IUGR hypothesis that was to mark the research of Professor van Velzen into SIDS throughout his time in Liverpool.

5.   Confocal Technologies Limited

5.1   Dr Howard was also director of a company, set up with University permission, based upon a collaboration between various academic scientists in the north of England. The company was called Confocal Technologies Limited. Professor van Velzen spent his professorial starting grant on a Confocal laser scanning fluorescent microscope. He had the hypothesis, the mathematical and statistical support of Dr Howard, the equipment and was already collecting samples. What Professor van Velzen now needed was time from technicians and researchers in order to found what would be, in his words, 'zero-money' research.

6.   Move to the Myrtle Street Laboratories

6.1   Professor van Velzen needed more people within the Unit, but first he had to
      obtain larger premises. By coincidence, the Myrtle Street site of the Royal Liverpool
      Children's Hospital was being closed down and all departments gradually moved up
      to Alder Hey. Laboratory facilities became available on Mulberry Street, part of the
      Myrtle Street site, known as the Myrtle Street laboratories.

6.2   In the summer of 1989 Professor van Velzen's Unit of Fetal and Infant Pathology
      moved from Alder Hey to Myrtle Street. Only the mortuary with the facility for
      carrying out the autopsy itself remained at Alder Hey. The Myrtle Street laboratories
      were on the edge of the University site. The move was always seen by those in charge
      at Alder Hey as a temporary one. Getting the Unit back on site at Alder Hey was to
      become a major task for the hospital management in the first half of the 1990s.

7.   Recruitment and Integration of Research and Clinical Work

7.1   Professor van Velzen now had to recruit more staff. He developed his
      collaboration with Dr Howard who was still in a different department, embarking
      upon the supervision of research students who were invited into the Unit. That cost
      him nothing, other than some of his precious time, already over-stretched. 'Soft' monies
      from relatively small research grants could attract an established research scientist here
      and a technician (MLSO) there. However, additional 'technician time' was vital for
      the processing of research samples and Professor van Velzen decided to 'integrate' the
      NHS and University elements of his Unit making the workforce interchangeable in
      terms of function. As early as 20 March 1989 he wrote to FSID,

> 'I have decided not to have a separation of research staff from the routine. First
> of all the routine staff is more experienced and of higher training level than any
> research staff I can lay my hands on. They thoroughly enjoy being involved with
> the research as a team and sometimes four people are active in different projects
> while only one is doing the last bits of the daily routine surgicals. I think our
> capacity and capability have through this measure increased multiplefold over
> what a single technician on her own could have provided us with....'

7.2   This kicked-off a tactic and correspondence that continued for years, with the research
      and clinical aspects of the Unit being played off, one against the other. FSID and the
      University were told how well they were doing in terms of clinical staff in fact

supporting research. Alder Hey was told the opposite, namely how much additional clinical work was carried out by those funded from research monies. The detail of this letter will be seen to conflict with later complaints of lack of resources for clinical work.

8.   Workload 'Laundering'

8.1   In addition to the propaganda in correspondence, manipulation was required of data regarding the clinical workload. In the 1980s and early 1990s clinical audit was becoming more established in the NHS. Various methods, such as Körner and Welcan, were developed for estimating the true amount of work completed in a department and its cost efficiency.

8.2   Various methods began to be used in the laboratory day book to enhance the appearance of the clinical workload. In 1989, there were 1,813 booked requests. However, 159 requests were for post mortem histology, which Professor van Velzen did not in fact do. It was unusual to give post mortem histology a number in a routine day book at all. The laboratory statistics for 1989, compiled by Mrs England, included 163 post mortems with 24 blocks per case. 145 fetus were included that were not examined, as well as 133 placentae. All had extensive photography included in the statistics which was not carried out to the extent claimed, if at all.

8.3   Another document compiled by Mrs England entitled 'Morbid Anatomy 1989' converted the workload into Welcan Units. This document included footnotes indicating that work had not been done even though the figures had been calculated and included in the body of the report. Later documents included no such disclaimer. All of this made a substantial increase in the apparent clinical workload of the Department of Histopathology for Alder Hey. Some 25 research requests were included in the day book in 1989, with substantial numbers of sections, 24 were double entries.

8.4   All this exaggeration and occasional falsification fuelled the assertion that the NHS was doing well out of the research-funded technicians and provided the basis of repeated applications for further staff at NHS expense on the grounds of increased workload. The figures were effectively being falsified or 'laundered' throughout Professor van Velzen's tenure, which required the complicity of the Chief MLSO. After initial denials this falsification was admitted before the Inquiry by Professor van Velzen, Mrs England and later Mrs Jacqueline Waring. The documentary evidence in respect of the period when Mrs England worked as Chief MLSO with Professor van Velzen was overwhelming, showing falsification of important documents regarding clinical workload.

9.   Overview of *Modus Operandi*

9.1   It is important to appreciate the *modus operandi* [method of operation] to understand later events.

9.2   It is also important to understand this *modus operandi* operating against the backdrop of poor resource forced upon Professor van Velzen. No-one working at the interface of clinical service and academic research has ever had unlimited funds: part of the job is to make do and campaign for more funding. This does not excuse his working practices which went beyond harmless exaggeration in order to make his case. What happened after his appointment can only be understood in the context of his need for 'zero-money research'. The fact that he was critically short of clinical resources provided at the creation of the Chair was also highly relevant. It was made worse when the University reneged on the provision of the Senior Lecturer (Clinical) and the clinical lecturers.

10.   The Clinical Practices of Professor van Velzen

10.1   Within a week of taking up the Chair Professor van Velzen issued an instruction in the Unit that there was to be no disposal of human material. The store of material began to grow and, due to his practice and need for samples, this meant whole organs. Until then human material had been disposed of once the histological or microscopic analysis had been completed, apart from the sections on slides and hearts, including lungs and often upper respiratory tract, which were destined for the ICH. Occasionally an interesting specimen had been retained for use in teaching.

10.2   The decision not to dispose of any material was taken before any backlog developed and indicates that lack of resource was not the overriding motive for the retention of organs.

10.3   The technical staff soon realised that Professor van Velzen's clinical practice in the removal and retention of organs was unlike anything they had seen before. Until now pathologists had retained sections only of the relevant organs and returned everything else to the body except heart/lungs and possibly brains in relevant cases. Professor van Velzen removed every organ in every case and retained every organ in every case.

10.4   This was the protocol that he laid down as Professor of Fetal and Infant Pathology at the University and Head of the Clinical Department of Histopathology at Alder Hey. Professor van Velzen insisted that histopathologists who joined the Unit later also follow the same protocol. By and large they followed the protocol. Additionally, there was no taking of blocks from the relevant organs at the time of the evisceration. Organs, in the case of small infants these had often having been dissected out in one block, were placed in a receptacle and transported to Myrtle Street. Not only were all the organs to be taken, they were to be kept whole and all were to be fixed before histological examination, something usually reserved for the brain and heart before processing. The technical staff noted the change of protocol, and whilst surprised, they accepted it from their new Professor without question.

10.5   So began the Myrtle Street collection. Containers, usually two per child, were stored on shelves. Later, as the numbers increased and they ran out of space, containers were stacked on top of each other in the reception area of the laboratory.

11.   Clinical Post Mortem Reports

11.1   How Professor van Velzen managed to balance his commitments abroad and to the University with his clinical work in the early months is unclear. He worked extremely long hours, often late into the night and over the weekends when he was in Liverpool.

11.2   Soon after taking up the Chair in September 1988 he stopped histological analysis of the organs as part of his routine clinical analysis. Instead he prepared a lengthy and apparently detailed report based upon the macroscopical, (naked eye), findings at the time of evisceration. In his first few months the typing of these lengthy reports posed problems in the main typing pool for the Department of Pathology at Alder Hey, as the typists were quite unused to Professor van Velzen's detailed dictation.

11.3   In 1989 a computer system was installed at Myrtle Street, a template was stored on the computer and Professor van Velzen, an able typist, amended the template himself in each case. While it was true to say that he typed his own reports, as he was later to stress when attempting to obtain further resources, this ignored the fact that he was able to type as quickly as he could dictate and he worked from a standard template. Later he was to insist that other pathologists type their own reports as well.

12.   'Preliminary' Reports only in Majority of Cases

12.1   Clinicians now received Professor van Velzen's reports without histological analysis. They were headed 'preliminary' and clinicians had to wait increasing periods of time even for a preliminary report. If they complained and chased, or if they were important individuals, they sometimes obtained a final post mortem report following histological analysis. The more junior the doctor and the greater distance from the hub of power in Liverpool, the less likely they were to succeed in obtaining a final post mortem report.

12.2 A backlog of these preliminary post mortem reports built up, in addition to a backlog of post mortem histology and final reports. In fact, whether the latter should really be called a *backlog*, implying there was a genuine expectation that clinical post mortem histology would be done, is an issue that will develop. It is convenient here to refer to a backlog generally.

13. Fetal Pathology

13.1 While not all hospitals in the Obstetric and Gynaecological Unit known as Unit III began to send fetus and stillborn infants immediately, some did so believing that the new Professor of Fetal and Infant Pathology would indeed provide a fetal pathology service. These cases Professor van Velzen simply could not do. Fetus remained stored, awaiting any examination, let alone a histological examination. As the backlog of final post mortem reports grew quickly after Professor van Velzen started work, so did the backlog of even preliminary reports in respect of fetus.

14. Motivation

14.1 In certain circumstances the lack of both time and resource could have been the reason for Professor van Velzen's failure to carry out post mortem histology, and provide final post mortem reports. However, the potential for a motive in relation to research cannot be understated. The research tool of stereology required whole organs. In the case of small organs the entire organ was used in the sampling. In the case of larger organs, while substantial parts of the organ remained after sampling, the sampling techniques required samples to be taken from the *whole* organ. In addition, it was Dr Howard's preferred course to fix certain organs before attempting to take samples, so blocks for clinical analysis could not be taken at the time of evisceration as a matter of routine. Professor van Velzen set out on his SIDS-IUGR research with no clear idea where it would lead in terms of which organs he would ultimately wish to analyse in relation to the hypothesis. He did not know which organs would be required and which would not. The procedures and protocols did not change in later years when Professor van Velzen had clinical assistance. If routine post mortem histology remained undone when there was ample resource, the relevance of lack of resource is substantially undermined.

14.2 The scope of organ retention, including every organ in every case, together with the continued widespread retention when no clinical examination was carried out over many years, support the conclusion that research purposes were the main, if not only motivation.

15. The Senior Lecturer Post – the Selection Committee and the Application of Dr Y F Chan

15.1   The University has provided the Inquiry with the files of the relevant Deans of the Faculty of Medicine and the Heads of the Department of Pathology. There are no documents to show that the post of senior lecturer was advertised between 23 May 1988 and 13 April 1991. The report of the Selection Committee meeting in 1989 states that there was no response to the original advertisement. Word had got round that the set up in Liverpool was unattractive.

15.2   One application was received subsequently from Dr Yuen-Fu Chan and he was called for interview towards the end of 1989. He lived and worked in Hong Kong but was a member of the Royal College of Pathologists in the United Kingdom. He had been a Lecturer in the Department of Pathology at the University of Hong Kong between 1979 and 1986, when he was appointed as a consultant pathologist in the Clinical Pathology Unit at the Princess Margaret Hospital in Hong Kong. He had relatively few publications to his name on the academic side but, as became clear when he came to Liverpool, he was a more than competent histopathologist in clinical terms and worthy of his consultant status. Professor Beazley, who became Dean after Professor Harris, chaired the Selection Committee. Of the other members, Professor Heath, Professor Harris and Dr Kenyon had been involved in the appointment of Professor van Velzen, who was himself on the Committee. The Committee was completed with Dr Gosney, Professor Petersen, Dr Chubb and Dr Smith.

16. The Terms of Engagement

16.1   The Committee made no mistake in appointing Dr Chan but there may have been a mistake in the terms upon which he was appointed. Having called Dr Chan half way round the world for an interview, in circumstances in which he had effectively been told the job was his, Dr Chan was only offered a clinical lectureship for a period of three years as a special appointment with honorary consultant status. Contrast this with the expectation of a senior lecturer's post of at least five years' tenure to coincide with the FSID grant. Status and security of tenure are of vital importance to someone attempting to make his way, like Dr Chan. Professor van Velzen was deeply disappointed at the terms, which provided for a review at the end of the three-year period, following which the appointment might have been confirmed at lecturer level, improved to senior lecturer status, or allowed to lapse altogether. The review criteria were to be solely academic, centred around the number of papers in refereed journals of national or international repute and on studies preferably supported by grants obtained from external bodies. Dr Chan took the position at lecturer status on the terms that were available. According to Professor van Velzen, and with his knowledge from the outset, Dr Chan was looking for an alternative appointment and he did not move his family to Liverpool.

16.2 Professor Heath died. While there is no documentary evidence, all oral evidence points to him as the driving force behind the three-year limit to the appointment. Dr Chan did not have a track record in research and it may have been strictly correct, in academic terms, to appoint him at lecturer rather than senior lecturer level. However, this decision can now be seen as both devaluing and destabilising. The new Chair had run-down and dislocated premises, inadequate resources on a clinical basis and was required to effect 'zero-money' research. Whether or not Dr Chan really had the academic background in terms of published research to justify senior lecturer status, there was an overwhelming need to secure someone to provide the long term bedrock of the clinical service. In offering Dr Chan a three-year lectureship the University did nothing to enhance the prospects of the Unit.

16.3 Dr Chan began work in Liverpool on 1 November 1989. As a newcomer he felt unable to object to Professor van Velzen's protocol on organ retention but otherwise gave good service. His memory regarding his disenchantment at the appointment with lecturer status only does not tally with that of Professor van Velzen. He maintains that he was simply happy to come and work at the world famous Alder Hey Children's Hospital. He only started to look for another post when he realised that his working relationship with Professor van Velzen had become unsustainable and he had to get out to save his career. He left for the Children's Hospital in Auckland, New Zealand on 31 March 1991. He is now a Consultant Senior Paediatric Pathologist in Australia at the Children's Hospital in Melbourne, a well known major teaching hospital.

17. The Two Clinical Lectureships

17.1 No-one was appointed to either clinical lectureship in the early years. There may have been thought of using the available resource from FSID intended for two clinical lecturers to provide a different package, as seemed a possibility in the correspondence between Professors Harris and Heath when the Chair was created (see Part 1, paragraph 9.1). Perhaps there were plans for a senior lecturer fully-funded and dedicated to fetal and infant pathology rather than the two to three sessions at Alder Hey. As there is no documentation or oral evidence to prove this it remains a speculative debate. The known facts are that not only had Dr Chan been appointed on a three-year basis at lecturer level, in circumstances in which he was always likely to leave, but no concerted attempt was made to appoint the clinical lecturers. One advertisement seems likely to have been placed in 1989, according to a reference in one of Professor van Velzen's documents, but it cannot be traced. Again, this decision or lack of decision, has to be viewed against the backdrop of all the other deficiencies and difficulties.

18. The Battle for Resources – Fetal Pathology

18.1   The narrative in the foregoing paragraphs during this period (1988–1990) is taken largely from uncontested oral evidence, admission and matters of obvious inference. There is little documentary evidence. However, such evidence will now come to the fore in the account of the battle for resources – fetal pathology.

19. Alder Hey and the University

19.1   Professor van Velzen attempted to obtain further resources at Alder Hey itself. Soon after coming to Alder Hey he realised that the Unit General Manager, Miss Sheila Malone, simply had no further resource to make available to him. The University failed to deliver the resource of senior lecturer and clinical lecturers other than through the short-term provision of Dr Chan.

19.2   It appears that Professor van Velzen, young and utterly inexperienced in University politics, accepted his position in terms of the University without serious challenge. Contrast this to the attitude of Professor David Lloyd, Professor of Paediatric Surgery, appointed by the University and Alder Hey at the same time as Professor van Velzen. He wrote to Mr Sell, the Assistant Personnel Officer at the University in September 1988 in the following terms,

'I have received your response to my letter about secretarial support. However, your note does not tell me anything about what is being done nor how long it is likely to be before I obtain secretarial support. I really find it unacceptable that the Head of a Department should have to waste time doing his own filing, photocopying and, for typing, have to depend upon the good nature of the Institute Secretary who is already over-burdened with her own responsibilities. These were not the conditions advertised to me when I was appointed to this post. If there were hurdles to be overcome all this should have been done prior to my taking up my appointment. I would appreciate your urgent attention to this matter.'

19.3   This letter was copied to Professor Harris. Two appointments cannot form the basis of any serious conclusion, but echoes of Professor van Velzen's appointment ring out. Later on, in another context, others noted that if Professor Lloyd were to be left working single-handed for much longer he would not put up with it and be off! Somehow Professor van Velzen did not have the confidence to tackle the University directly. He did not understand the lines of communication and the channels through which he should operate. He lost the support of his Head of Department, Professor Heath, but why remains unclear from the evidence until a reference in a note of a meeting in 1993 (see Part 5, paragraph 16.1).

20. Mersey Regional Health Authority

20.1   Having drawn a blank at Alder Hey and with the University, Professor van Velzen turned to the Regional Health Authority, particularly with a view to resourcing the fetal and stillborn pathology service.

21. August 1989 – Letter to RHA Identifying the Mischief

21.1   On 30 August 1989 Professor van Velzen wrote to Dr Peter Simpson, the Regional Medical Officer at the Regional Health Authority,

> 'The major change anticipated will be that in addition to an approximate 40% volume increase in the workload as a paediatric hospital, the workload comparable to the final volume for the paediatric hospital needs to be developed for fetal and perinatal pathology services to the Obstetrics and Gynaecology Units, which is at present non-existent and not provided for....
>
> It will be necessary to enlarge the present professional staff and more importantly they will have to be trained in the use of new techniques, specifically molecular biology and image analysis, and applications of flow cytometry....
>
> The most important feature of our service requiring priority recognition is the development of adequate fetal and perinatal pathology services as at present **nothing** is provided but for which I am, however, expected to provide a service, especially in fetal pathology, but am totally unable to do so without unacceptable levels of extra hours which my present staff can no longer provide....

Quality of care and value of service can be evaluated only indirectly in the sense of reduced recurrences of the congenital abnormalities which result in human suffering and require great costs for hospital care, the reduction of cot death mortality rates, and the reduction of complications of clinical therapy by adequate diagnosis of paediatric disease.'

22. December 1989 – Widely Copied Request for Technical Resource

22.1 On 1 December 1989 Professor van Velzen wrote to Mr Robert Atlay, Chairman of the Division of Obstetrics and Gynaecology, Professor Beazley, Head of the University Department of Obstetrics and Gynaecology and also Dean, Dr John Martin, Chairman of the Medical Division at Alder Hey and Professor Lloyd, Chairman of the Surgical Division at Alder Hey. The letter was copied to Dr David Isherwood, Head of Pathology at Alder Hey, Miss Sheila Malone, Unit General Manager and Mr Preece, Hospital General Manager, both at Alder Hey, Mr Collier, District General Manager, Dr June Phillips, District Medical Officer, Dr Peter Simpson, Regional Medical Officer and finally Mr Geoffrey Scaife, the Regional General Manager.

22.2 Professor van Velzen referred to the unacceptable backlog in the typing of post mortem reports earlier in the year *but made no reference to any continuing backlog or inability to carry out post mortem histology*. He referred to the advertisement for a clinical lecturer/honorary senior registrar as having gone out. With that post filled, and with Dr Chan now in Liverpool, Professor van Velzen felt that he would be able to cope with the fetal and perinatal pathology workload from the point of view of clinical staff. In fact, no clinical lecturer/honorary senior registrar was appointed until as late as October 1991, after Dr Chan had left. Professor van Velzen continued in his letter seeking technical staff and secretarial staff for the fetal and infant pathology work. He maintained that the three NHS MLSOs were wholly dedicated to surgical biopsy production, which was inaccurate. While post mortem histology was carried out on neither infants nor fetus, a large proportion of the time of the Chief MLSO at this stage was being spent in developing new techniques both for clinical and research reasons. However, the point that he did not have sufficient technical staff to handle the fetal service was well made.

22.3 Professor van Velzen was looking to the Regional Health Authority to provide funding to complete the service capacity of the Unit. He hoped that the details he had given would go some way to answering the 'justified complaints that the Department has received'.

23.   The Financial Vacuum

23.1   It was Professor van Velzen's misfortune to be making his case to the Regional Health
Authority at a time of change within the National Health Service. In late 1989
Mr Pearse Butler arrived as Alder Hey's Project Manager and to begin its transition
towards Trust status. He was under pressure to run a tight ship financially and
applications for special monies from the Regional Health Authority were not
encouraged. Together with this change in management was a move towards charging
for services on a contractual basis between what would be Trusts and Health
Authorities and a lessening of the monies provided directly by the Regional and District
Health Authorities. Trust status would not arrive at Alder Hey until April 1991, so there
could be no contract with the new Women's Hospitals Trust until the late summer of
1991 and so no formal arrangement which would provide the necessary funding.
Mersey Regional Health Authority was not keen to make a financial commitment in
the run up to Trust status. The effect would be to stultify the position until late 1991.

24.   'The Five-Year Vision' Paper

24.1   On 13 December 1989 Professor van Velzen provided a 'Five-Year Vision' paper for
Regional Paediatric, Fetal, Placental and Perinatal Pathology. He sent it to the Regional
Health Authority. Mr Butler had a copy at Alder Hey. A number of important points
arise out of the document.

- No complaint was made about the lack of resources for post mortem histology in the
paediatric field, i.e. the historical workload from Alder Hey. The existing resources
were said to be enough.

- Capital investment in more modern technology was sought to expand the diagnostic
service at Alder Hey.

- No increased resource was sought for administrative staff or typists on the traditional
Alder Hey work; and only a half-time audio typist was requested in relation to fetal
pathology. There was slight exaggeration here, since the fetal pathology reports were
also to be produced from a computer template by the pathologist, rather than a typist.

- Cases for important staff increases revolved around four further MLSOs and a trainee.

- Professor van Velzen sought an MLSO Grade 2 and MLSO Grade 1 for an expanded
paediatric pathology service which he envisaged using modern techniques. This had
nothing to do with the post mortem histology service and related to new diagnostic
services yet to be provided.

- Professor van Velzen sought two similar MLSOs and a trainee to service fetal pathology. He undoubtedly required technical staff for the fetal pathology service.

24.2 The requirements sought in this Paper should be seen as an opening gambit. In the end Alder Hey agreed with the Women's Hospitals Trust funding for the equivalent of 1.2 MLSOs, out of which monies a decision was then made to obtain the services of two lower grade Medical Laboratory Assistants (MLAs).

24.3 These requests should be read in the light of Professor van Velzen's *modus operandi*. He lacked no reasonable technical support in terms of NHS provision, leaving aside the inadequate provision for fetal pathology up to the end of 1991. Since neither Alder Hey nor the University saw through his workload laundering there was no disciplinary action taken, but an ultimatum was issued that services should be provided.

25. The Simpson–Butler–van Velzen Negotiation – Early 1990

25.1 Dr Simpson, the Regional Medical Officer, was the interface between Professor Velzen and the Regional Health Authority (RHA).

25.2 During the period of preparation there may have been some uncertainty regarding who was in charge at Alder Hey, but strictly the old regime remained accountable until 1 April 1991. There was no such ambiguity with regard to Professor van Velzen, as Mr Butler was in charge. Mr Butler had been handpicked as a high-flying Health Service Manager to be Project Manager in the preparation of Alder Hey for Trust status. Miss Malone, the Unit General Manager, left early in the summer of 1990 after a short power struggle with Mr Butler that neither now remembers.

25.3 In January 1990 Mr Butler and Professor van Velzen met. The meeting was referred to in letters in similar terms dated 17 January 1990 from Professor van Velzen to Mr Butler and Dr Simpson. Reference was also made to discussions between Dr Simpson, Mr Scaife, the Regional General Manager and Professor van Velzen. The discussions centred on funding for the Regional Fetal Pathology Service, for which everyone agreed no budget existed. Professor van Velzen felt that the issue needed to be addressed urgently.

25.4 With these letters Professor van Velzen included an example letter of complaint dated 10 January 1990 from Miss Thom, Consultant Obstetrician and Gynaecologist at the Mill Road Maternity Hospital. It was said to be one of at least 40 such letters held on file. It was written to Professor van Velzen himself and copied to Mr Atlay, the Chairman of the Division of Obstetrics and Gynaecology. It was a short letter but gives a clear idea of the mounting complaint.

'I wonder if you are yet in a position to let me have a report on this lady's fetus delivered at 21 weeks gestation on 30 July 1989.

Both [the mother] and her general practitioner are very distressed that, as yet, we still have no information from the examination of the baby.

I have to say that as time goes on I find it more and more embarrassing having to deal with these bereaved parents, who have to wait so long for any information to come from the investigations.

I would be most grateful if you could look into this for me.'

There can be no other conclusion than that it was imperative for Mr Butler to investigate and resolve the problem which was so upsetting both parents and a respected consultant.

25.5   In his letters of 17 January 1990 to Mr Butler and Dr Simpson, Professor van Velzen went on to discuss other matters of funding and concluded,

'These are all interesting consequences of funding the Unit to full size, (which we have by no means reached yet) which I assume were foreseen when the appointments were made. Therefore I assume that the consequences of providing a service were foreseen, and any proposals arising from this could be dealt with.

I feel I am obliged to run such a service as economically as possible, even to the extent of doubling output with my existing group, but feel however that any capacity to increase throughput has reached its end, as we are seeing more patients and doing more investigations per patient than the small unit in Birmingham, which has more than nine technicians in the Paediatric Hospital Pathology Department alone.

We very much appreciate all that you are doing on behalf of this department and hope for a rapid resolution of this matter, and would appreciate your guidance as to what to say to the clinicians and present laboratory staff, and when.'

There is some exaggeration in the second paragraph in the comparison with Birmingham, but the overall complaint was clear and realistic.

25.6   On 31 January 1990 Dr Simpson replied,

'The fact that we are having this correspondence demonstrates that the consequences of funding the unit to full size were not foreseen at the time of appointment but that should not daunt our determination to tackle the matter now. As you know Pearse Butler is looking at all the services in Alder Hey as a matter of emergency and there is considerable support for this review amongst the medical staff. I am following up the initiative you suggested with regard to reviewing Pathology Services across the City and hope that we can make progress there in the next few weeks. I hope that we shall have answers by the summer and am grateful to you for all you have done in developing your department.'

Dr Simpson had not been in Liverpool when the negotiations for the establishment of the Chair were taking place. In the light of all the advice in 1987–1988, which was unknown to him, it would have been more accurate to say that the likely funding consequences had been consciously ignored.

25.7 There is no letter of reply from Mr Butler on file. However, Dr Simpson and Mr Butler were copied into correspondence from Professor van Velzen in February 1990. In two letters he wrote to acknowledge complaints, one from the Mill Road Maternity Hospital and one from the Liverpool Maternity Hospital. In those letters Professor van Velzen made it clear that there was no budget for the service.

> 'The best we can offer at present is that in limited occasional cases of extreme urgency or anxiety we will perform a provisional macroscopical examination and give an oral report. In view of the extremely stressed budget within which we have to operate, we regret to say that the number of cases that can be dealt with in such a way must be limited to less than five per annum.'

26. Professor van Velzen –'Agent Provocateur'

26.1 Behind the scenes the RHA was indeed looking at the reorganization of Pathology Services in the form of the Pan-Liverpool Review. The aim was to make Pathology Services self-financing, but the meetings promised in late January 1990 as a matter of urgency did not materialize until later in the year. However, Professor van Velzen was being used by the RHA to provoke a response in what was perceived as a cautious pathology community. On 26 February 1990 Dr Simpson wrote to Mr Atlay,

' … to put your mind at rest that we are not asking Dick van Velzen to chair a group on Pathology Services, but rather to act as *agent provocateur*, raising the question whether reorganization of Pathology Services would make the whole of their part of the service self-financing.'

26.2 Elsewhere, Dr Simpson referred to Professor van Velzen, in a memo dated 11 May 1990 to Mr Scaife, not as *agent provocateur* but as 'the Exocet'.

26.3 At Alder Hey Professor van Velzen was known as 'the Flying Dutchman' and he was to have an even more descriptive title at the University Review in 1993 (see Part 5, paragraph 12).

27. Negotiations Fruitless – a Real 'Cry for Help'

27.1   On 27 March 1990 Professor van Velzen took the extreme step of writing to the
Vice Chancellor, Professor Davies, and sending copies to the following people:

Mr Butler, Project Manager and 'Chief Executive Elect' at Alder Hey,
Miss Malone, Unit General Manager at Alder Hey,
Dr Simpson, Regional Medical Officer,
Professor Beazley, Dean of the Faculty of Medicine and Head of Department of
    Obstetrics and Gynaecology,
Mr Atlay, Chairman of the Division of Obstetrics and Gynaecology,
Dr Helen Carty, Head of the Department of Radiology at Alder Hey,
Dr Martin, Chairman of the Medical Division at Alder Hey and
Professor Lloyd, Chairman of the Surgicial Division at Alder Hey.

In this important letter, desperate for funds, Professor van Velzen suggested a novel but
unrealistic financial solution under which the University would fund the clinical work
and then attempt to reclaim the cost from the NHS. Professor van Velzen also set out
the history of his difficulties at the beginning of the letter and made a powerful 'cry
for help' at the end.

'Over the past 18 months in a series of communications too long to summarise
even in the most brief of forms I have had consecutive dealings with the
Hospital General Manager, the Unit General Manager and finally in December
the Regional General Manager and Regional Medical Officer related to
providing fetal and perinatal and placental services to the Unit, District and
Region. Separate from the fact that on a very rare occasion no mail has ever
been answered formally, I have now been informed on a meeting with my
intended future Chief Executive for the self-governing Trust, Mr Pearse Butler,
that there will be no staff forthcoming and no budget forthcoming from Region
to be used in providing this service to patient care.

The expected expansion of demand to the pathology services at the Royal
Liverpool Children's Hospital, Alder Hey, from the paediatric and paediatric
surgeons' side similarly requiring expansion of staff has similarly been dealt
with in a long series of communications with a similar, that is totally negative
outcome. Again here I have been informed last week by same Mr Pearse Butler
that no budget in staff or consumables is to be forthcoming for the expansion
of this service.

… The reason why I am approaching you with some, if not considerable urgency is that I am continuously under pressure from gynaecologists, obstetricians, social workers, legal advisers, hospital managers, Coroner's officers for supplying acute diagnosis on cases long since submitted to us and for which we have at present until recently been able to keep the clients at bay expecting any moment to be supplied with the means to provide this service.

In view of maintaining my own credibility and no longer willing to accept legal responsibility for what may happen in these families who are depending for future counselling on appropriate pathology services, I find that having been informed last week that there is no budget forthcoming I cannot delay a reaction on my part and feel I have to deposit, being primarily a University employee, the situation into higher authority's hands, i.e. that of my Vice Chancellor.'

The main thrust of the letter was clear and accurate in relation to the fetal and perinatal service, spoilt only by reference to lack of resource on the paediatric side. Nevertheless, that Professor van Velzen wrote such a letter at all on the issue of service provision, copied widely, to the Vice Chancellor who was effectively the Chief Executive of the entire University, not the Faculty of Medicine, shows how desperate he had become.

28. Rationale of Mersey Regional Health Authority

28.1 There is no record of any reply from the Vice Chancellor to the above letter but, of those copied into it, Dr Simpson replied by return of post. The letter reveals the thinking at the RHA.

'Firstly with regard to the future financing of medical services, they are all to move on to a contractual basis whereby the provider, in your case the laboratory, will be paid for the work carried out either on an individual case basis or as a batch contract.

With regard to the individual Regional Units within Alder Hey, their interrelationships and interdependence are such that we intend to think of them as a single Regional Unit rather than separate entities. Regional Units will look to the Regional Health Authority for pump-priming monies but will ultimately recharge their services as described previously.

When you described to Geoffrey Scaife and myself the intermediate stage in development of your own unit, we asked whether your colleagues in pathology might similarly be short of important staff and equipment and whether this might be financed by reorganisation within the Pathology Services. As you know following a series of individual discussions I have now asked pathologists as a group to meet and discuss this possibility with me.

The important step to be taken now is to identify those districts and departments for whom you are providing a service and to let them know what the future charges are likely to be and the extent and timeliness of the service you have to offer. I know Pearse Butler has such work in hand and trust we can move forward from the current budgeting on to the new basis for funding.'

This letter, copied to all those received the letter to the Vice Chancellor on the previous day, shows the financial vacuum in which Professor van Velzen had to operate. Alder Hey either had no money or had more pressing need for their limited funds. The University was certainly not interested in providing funding for 'pump priming' (initial funding to kick start a new project or new appointment) on the technical support side for the clinical service. It all boiled down to the RHA not being prepared to provide such funds for technical and support staff to establish the fetal and perinatal pathology service.

28.2   The Trust status was still a year away. Fetus continued to be sent to Professor van Velzen only to be stored. Parents continued in their distress and clinicians in their embarrassment. There was no prospect of money becoming available until contracts could be signed, after both Alder Hey and the Women's Hospitals had achieved Trust status.

28.3   Mr Butler regretted in his oral evidence continuing to allow fetus to be sent to the Myrtle Street laboratories only to be stored, with all the expectations and distress caused to parents. He was correct to do so.

28.4   As Professor van Velzen had pointed out in his letters (echoed by Professor Lloyd in relation to his secretarial provision) the responsibilities accepted at the creation of the Chair should have been honoured and the pump-priming monies provided by Mersey RHA or otherwise found at Alder Hey. The political climate change did not absolve anyone. The dogma of 'market contracting' and political expediency, in not being seen to favour Professor van Velzen with funding, came before service provision. All for a pathetically small sum in real terms – 1.2 MLSO WTE (whole time equivalent), or £15,492 as negotiated with the Women's Hospitals Trust in 1991.

29.   Mounting Complaint

29.1   June 1990 saw the first direct letter of complaint to the management at Alder Hey in relation to the fetal service. It was a moving and powerful letter on behalf of a mother who had suffered a stillbirth in mid-1989. Permission for post mortem examination had been obtained on the basis that the baby would be returned for burial. The baby was sent to Professor van Velzen but there was no examination. The mother and the treating obstetricians continued to expect a report. After two months the mother became pregnant again and her general anxiety about having another stillbirth became a specific worry for the second baby she was carrying. Still no report was forthcoming and she gave birth to a healthy baby in May 1990, never having been told the result of the post mortem for the simple reason that it had never been done. She had yet to bury her first baby.

29.2 Miss Malone replied to the complaint, it being one of the last jobs she did before leaving Alder Hey. Her response was inadequate and would not have reassured the mother. She simply explained that Professor van Velzen did not have enough resources and he had been asked to determine his priorities in order to avoid repetition. There is no other evidence of any reorganization of priorities in 1990 in order to establish or suspend the fetal and perinatal service. Babies continued to be sent to Professor van Velzen. Everyone simply marked time waiting for Trust status and competitive tendering to provide the funding.

29.3 A number of letters of complaint have been set out in this narrative. One of them was specifically an example of about 40 similar letters. Since those in senior management at Alder Hey, the RHA and the University knew both of the non-existent fetal service and of its consequences in human terms, the precise number of complaints is irrelevant. However, the Inquiry has heard oral evidence of mounting complaint on a day-to-day basis.

29.4 The staff at the Unit of Fetal and Infant Pathology remained loyal to Professor van Velzen and did their best to hold off the numerous complaints both written and over the telephone. Negotiations for resources revolved around the fetal and perinatal service, and so did the written complaints up to this point. The complaints at the level of service provision also included cases of paediatric post mortem examination. Some clinicians pressed for a final report after histology had been completed. In a small number of cases the pressure caused staff within the Unit to prevail upon Professor van Velzen and Dr Chan to provide a final report. In addition, all clinicians were waiting a very long time for even the preliminary macroscopic report. Parents underwent bereavement counselling without the clinician having received a definitive post mortem report including histology. Often even these unsatisfactory consultations were cancelled and rearranged to await preliminary reports, embarrassing doctors and causing parents further anxiety and distress.

30. Overview of the Service Provision and Lack of Resource

30.1 Professor van Velzen had been short of clinical support until late 1989 when Dr Chan arrived. Dr Chan carried out some research but was principally to service the clinical work. If they had both done six sessions of clinical work, it would have amounted to about 1.2 whole time equivalent (WTE) consultants. Professors Wigglesworth and Risdon had advised that two WTE consultant pathologists were required to carry the clinical workload in an expanded regional service, but the actual workload in 1990 does not excuse failing to carry out post mortem histology and provide a fetal service. There were now four technicians. Research projects had yet to get underway in any great volume and again there was no real excuse why paediatric and neonatal post mortem examination should not have included histology.

30.2   No one appears to have seen the issues clearly in 1990. Professor van Velzen appeared plausible and he had the sympathy of the clinicians at the Unit III/Women's Hospitals on the issue of resources. This is shown in the evidence to the Inquiry of Mr Stephen Walkinshaw, Consultant in Feto-Maternal Medicine and Mr Atlay, Chairman of the Division of Obstetrics and Gynaecology (see also Part 4, paragraph 20). It was his very *modus operandi* to make all those around him feel that he was under-resourced in order to attract more resources. The Chief MLSO, Mrs England, provided figures to support the supposed lack of resource and managers examining the position did not address the true situation. Either Professor van Velzen was not in fact lacking in resource, or he lacked such a small amount that once given it he could be required to implement the service and disciplined if he did not do so. It is doubtful whether the provision of additional technical support alone in 1990 would have established the fetal service, nipped the problem in the bud and avoided major disaster. By failing to provide the additional resource and continuity of clinical support in the form of the senior lecturer, the authorities did not see the lack of service provision clearly for what it was. The seeds were sown, so that neither the Hospital nor the University felt confident enough at any stage to institute disciplinary proceedings for fear of a defence of lack of resource. This was particularly so on the side of the University which had failed to provide a senior lecturer.

31.   The Polkinghorne Report

31.1   The period of 1988–90 cannot be concluded without mention of the *Review of the Guidance on the Research Use of Fetuses and Fetal Material* which was published in July 1989, commonly referred to as the Polkinghorne Report. In the Department of Health Circular HC(89)23 the Code of Practice recommended in the report was adopted as proper practice.

31.2   Not only were abnormal fetus being sent to Professor van Velzen for the non-existent clinical examination but fetus from social terminations in Liverpool Hospitals were being collected and taken to the ICH for research. Many women were more than willing for the hospital staff to take responsibility for the disposal of the fetus following a social termination. Rather than being buried as women were led to believe, many fetus ended up being stored at the ICH.

31.3   The Polkinghorne Report made it clear that the written consent of the mother was required for fetal research after July 1989, even though strictly the pre-viable fetus (now 24 weeks and previously 28 weeks gestation) and the mother had no rights in law. Section 6 of the Report dealt with the issue of consent and the Committee considered the form of words to be used,

> '6.2   Discussion of consent has been affected by the consideration that a woman undergoing an abortion may be distressed if she has to consider too closely the possibility of her fetus being used for research or transplantation. The Peel Committee had this in mind when reaching the form of words, in their code, at Paragraph 3(ii) that there should be 'no known objection on the part of the parents.' We regard this as insufficient. We are conscious of the need to avoid distress but are even more strongly opposed to formulations which disguise the reality of what is to take place. Distress will be caused to the mother if she later feels that she did not know what was going to happen to her fetus.

> 6.3   We recommend that positive explicit consent should be obtained from mothers to the use of the fetus or fetal tissue. We see the process of consent as requiring the mother to be counselled and given all the information, in a form that is comprehensible, to enable her to make a proper judgement of whether or not to allow the fetus to be used for research and therapy, including transplantation. This may take the form of an information sheet which might be supplemented with discussion. The information will have to be general because it must embrace all uses to which the fetus may be put.'

The final sentence of 6.3 has caused some difficulty in practice. It is difficult to get the mother's consent to research without giving some details, as the mother will often ask what research is envisaged. Apart from that, this Inquiry has heard evidence from numerous doctors and there is no other disagreement or practical difficulty in the Polkinghorne Committee recommendations. The same formulation as paragraphs 6.2 and 6.3 with *child* substituted for *fetus* has been acceptable to those giving evidence in relation to obtaining consent for an infant post mortem examination. It is a matter of regret that the Polkinghorne Report and the Code of Practice went unheeded.

31.4   The ICH continued to receive fetus where there had been no written consent and in circumstances where the University ignored its duty under 3.8 of the Code of Practice,

> 'On the same principle the user should be able to satisfy itself that any material it receives has been procured in accordance with the requirements of this Code. It must keep records indicating the proximate source of any fetal tissue and of the use to which it is put, but should not reveal details of the use to the source.'

Dr Smith and Professor van Velzen amended the standard paperwork for the collection of fetus in 1990 but they ignored the need for anonymity set out at 3.8. They drafted a dual-purpose form, covering both clinical and research referral, which included details of the mother and the clinical history in each case.

31.5 Professor Harris made a brief contribution for the consideration of the Polkinghorne Committee, as appears from Appendix 4 to their Report. This contribution is relevant as it shows that he was aware of the Review at about the same time as Dr Ibrahim was attempting to set up a system of written consent for hearts in the Heart Collection at the ICH. Professor Harris was still Head of the ICH when the Polkinghorne Report was published. He cannot remember even having made a contribution let alone having acted upon the Report.

31.6 Successive Heads of the ICH after Professor Harris must also take responsibility for failing to implement the Code of Practice. Professor Richard Cooke has been Head of the ICH since 1991 and Professor Lloyd was Acting Head for a short period in 1990 between Professor Harris and Professor Cooke.

31.7 The irony of the Polkinghorne recommendations in the context of this Inquiry is inescapable. From 1989 onwards 'informed consent' was the standard required in respect of fetal research, the fetus and mother having no rights in law, and yet 'ill-informed lack of objection' remained the actual standard applied for retention of organs at post mortem examination in respect of children and their parents.

The van Velzen Years: Part 3
1991 – June 1992

Fetal Resources Provided, but Post Mortem Histology 'Still not Possible'.

1. The Fetal and Perinatal Contract

1.1 In February 1991 Mr Butler sent funding proposals for the provision of Fetal Pathology Services to Mr Keith Haynes, the Unit General Manager at Mill Road Maternity Hospital. The letter was copied to Mr Atlay, Chairman of the Division of Obstetricians and Gynaecologists. The proposal was for the Unit III hospitals to provide a capital sum of £7,000 to cover tissue processing equipment and then to provide the gross salaries and on-call costs for two technicians: an MLSO 2 and an MLSO 1, costing £28,423 per annum. In return the Unit III hospitals were to receive a combined full placental and fetal service, with an expected annual volume of some of 120–200 fetus and 700–1,200 placentae. Reports on placentae were to be provided three days after the receipt of specimens. Macroscopical reports on fetus were to be provided within two days and a final report, following histology, five working days after receipt of the specimen. All special tests, documentation and X-ray investigations were to be included in the study. These terms had been suggested by Professor van Velzen to Mr Butler at the end of November 1990 and on the basis that he was prepared to catch up the backlog within six months at the latest, probably counting on Dr Chan to help achieve this. Dr Chan gave three months' notice to leave at the end of December 1990.

1.2 The proposals were not acceptable to Mr Haynes and the Unit III hospitals that were to become the Liverpool Women's Hospitals NHS Trust. Both doctors and administrators were aware of Professor van Velzen's staffing difficulties, as he had made a point of letting them know about them to avoid alienation. Indeed, as late as 10 April 1995 Mr Atlay wrote to the Dean at the University,

> 'Since his arrival in Liverpool some years ago, Professor van Velzen has frequently visited us to outline his difficulties regarding his working environment, his support staff, etc but whatever the reasons, the fact remains that the fetal pathology services to our unit have never been satisfactory.
>
> There have been isolated periods of time when excellent reports came through, very detailed, and this was under the guidance of a senior lecturer who was there at the time.'

1.3 The spring of 1991 was not a time of such excellence. In July and August 1991 terms were agreed. No capital provision was made and an allowance of 1.2 full-time equivalent MLSO manpower was given. There was to be no placental service from the outset unless in conjunction with fetus, although the laboratory day book reveals that separate placentae were delivered and reported. The backlog of 240 fetus was to be cleared without additional payment. Crucially, the Women's Hospitals Trust would only agree to pay in arrears after the completion of the report in respect of each fetus because of the poor service that it had received in the past, and despite the way in which the annual cost was calculated by reference to MLSO wages. Mr Haynes wrote to the key players in the Women's Hospitals on 6 August 1991,

'The terms of this agreement are set out in the enclosure. You will see that we incur no capital costs, the staffing implication is reduced from the previous proposal and I have agreed payment on a fee basis for work done. This latter point should ensure the necessary stimulus to us getting a service and if it does not we will all know where we stand.

The backlog of fetus is being disposed of by Alder Hey by means of burial in consecrated ground. I have reminded Pearse Butler that we will need a schedule together with details of whether Professor van Velzen proposes any more with the fetus or not.'

The Inquiry has not seen any such schedule.

2.   The Backlog of Fetus

2.1   The Inquiry has discovered that, contrary to the contract, the backlog of fetus was never buried. Professor van Velzen maintains that funding was never provided for the burial of the backlog by Alder Hey. Mr Butler cannot remember the provision. Substantial numbers of fetus from the period 1988–91 remain unburied. Although Professor van Velzen wrote to Mr Butler and to the clinicians at the Women's Hospitals implying that he was catching up and that the backlog was being buried, in fact the backlog remains. Many fetus are intact and post mortem reports have not been issued. Professor van Velzen did not catch up.

3.   Resources and the Arrival of Dr Khine

3.1   It was decided to spend the 1.2 whole time equivalent MLSO salaries on two Medical Laboratory Assistants (MLAs) and they were appointed with effect from 18 November 1991, shortly after the contract commenced on 1 October 1991. Mr Paul Eccles, an experienced MLSO, was taken on in early September 1991, funded through soft research monies linked to Confocal Technologies Limited.

3.2   Professor van Velzen now had five MLSOs and two MLAs and certainly did not lack technical support at this stage. However, he had lost Dr Chan. An advertisement for a Senior Lecturer (Clinical) appeared in the *British Medical Journal* on 13 April 1991 and again at about the same time in *The Lancet*. Apparently there was no response and the post does not appear to have been re-advertised. Instead an advertisement appeared in the *British Medical Journal* on 6 July 1991 for a clinical lecturer as against senior lecturer. Dr Myat Mon Khine was appointed to the post, funded by the FSID grant, for three years from 14 October 1991 but she had virtually no experience in fetal and perinatal pathology. While she would become the mainstay of the clinical provision in later years, when she first took up her post with an Honorary Senior Registrar's contract at Alder Hey, she was not in a position to provide the service because of her lack of experience. After all she had taken up a training grade position.

4. The Start of the Fetal Contract

4.1 We have seen how while the lack of technical support was being remedied there was a lack of clinical support.

4.2 The fetal service got off to a bad start. At a Pathology Directorate Budget Meeting in December 1991 it was noted that only five post mortems had been carried out in the first two months of the contract to the end of November 1991 rather than the expected coverage of 16 or 17. Importantly, no reports or test results had been sent out and consequently no bills either. Mr James Birrell, the Financial Director at Alder Hey, was notified. The Women's Hospitals were complaining to the Service Manager, Mr Henry Meade. Professor van Velzen was complaining that he had not got adequate secretarial backup, a smokescreen tactic since secretarial backup was not needed for fetal post mortem examinations which were completed from the template by the pathologist. The reports were always to have been done. Interestingly, Professor van Velzen did not complain of his lack of clinical support which was where he had a real case. The note ends,

> 'I had to tease this information out of Henry Meade who is obviously embarrassed .... Reading between the lines he blames Professor van Velzen .... Please get Pearse Butler to get this problem looked into.'

4.3 Mr Walkinshaw, wrote to Mr Haynes on 2 December 1991 complaining that there were still considerable problems with delayed reports and delays in burial. Autopsies were not being carried out within the contractual arrangements. However, by April 1992 Mr Walkinshaw wrote to Professor van Velzen complimenting him on the service that was now being provided. He was then under the impression that a little bit of a backlog remained but the autopsy and pathology reports were timely and clinically helpful. He was mistaken about the backlog and the quality of service overall. Professor van Velzen almost certainly set out to make an ally of Mr Walkinshaw and did his best to impress him while the service remained generally slow and the backlog was essentially untouched.

5. 'Post Mortem Histology is Still not Possible' – Contribution to Business Plan

5.1 Going back in time slightly, during 1990 in preparation for Trust status various drafts of an Overall Business Plan were completed with contributions from each department. Towards the end of 1990 Professor van Velzen had compiled an inappropriate contribution running to over two hundred pages. Most is now missing, but part, taken from the files of Mrs England, was available to the Inquiry. In early 1991 a contribution to the Second Alder Hey Overall Business Plan was produced. It was delivered to the Executive Board in Waiting, which was:

Mr Pearse Butler – Chief Executive,
Mr James Birrell – Director of Finance,
Dr John Martin – Consultant Oncologist and Medical Director,
Mr Peter Tallentire – Director of Personnel and
Ms Patricia Hooton – Director of Nursing.

5.2 The relevant section is set out below.

'The dislocation to Myrtle Street continues to interfere severely with service. The additional staff time required to serve clinicians especially in urgent requests in theatre is very considerable. The facilities at Myrtle Street, however adequate from an area point of view, will require continued investments to correct back-maintenance and make working conditions acceptable. The doubling of productivity, in addition to developing a service in an additional series of techniques has eliminated the need for sending material elsewhere. Still there is a capacity deficiency. **Post mortem histology is still not possible, final post mortem reports are not delivered.** The Fetal Pathology Service has in part been funded by ourself. As still no new budget has been identified for staffing, the service has not begun. It is hoped that through external contracting a joint budget between Unit III and RLCH Alder Hey may be developed to fund the required staffing.

The senior consultant staff will be severely affected by the departure of Dr Y F Chan, Senior Lecturer/Consultant Paediatric Pathologist. Replacement is urgently sought but may be affected by University staffing reductions. This is all the more pressing as the Head of Department functions as Clinical Director.'

Emphasis has been added for the general reader only. No such emphasis should have been needed for the Medical Director of a new Trust, particularly (like Dr Martin) an oncologist of many years' experience of post mortem procedures.

6.   Response of the Executive Directors

6.1   As Medical Director Dr Martin was responsible for providing advice to the executive directors on matters requiring clinical expertise. He was an oncologist of great experience. In oral evidence he conceded that he must have seen a copy of Professor van Velzen's contribution and he must have read it, but he does not remember it. Consequently he does not remember giving any medical advice to the executive directors as to the importance of the problems described in the above extract. This is both astonishing and the subject of deep regret.

6.2   Mr Butler was the only other Executive Director to remember this contribution, but he is clearly mistaken in his memory. He remembers reading the above passage and believing that post mortem histology was to be a new development as part of a service not previously provided. In effect, he considered the provision of post mortem histology and final post mortem reports generally at Alder Hey on a par with the fetal pathology service. This was something new to have been provided upon the arrival of Professor van Velzen but for which there was no existing funding. With respect to Mr Butler this cannot be right. The plain wording of the contribution shows that post mortem histology generally and the fetal pathology service in particular were separate and had separate considerations. If Mr Butler sought advice from any clinician and in particular Dr Martin as Medical Director, he would have discovered his mistake. Dr Bouton and Dr Ibrahim provided post mortem histology relevant to the diagnosis and cause of death. Correspondence between Mr Butler and Dr Heather McDowell, Consultant Oncologist, in the autumn of 1991, will reveal Mr Butler's understanding as it was then, rather than as it is now, some nine years later (see paragraph 12).

6.3   Any thorough investigation of the backlog in 1991 would have revealed Professor van Velzen's unacceptable practice of retention of all organs in every case. It should have led to the re-establishment of post mortem histology as a matter of routine.

7.   Uncertainty of not Knowing – Waiting Times

7.1   On 15 March 1991 Mr Butler produced a paper entitled 'Waiting Times' to set the benchmark for the new Trust. In a general context, as against one where parents were left waiting for information about the cause of their child's death or genetic counselling, Mr Butler wrote,

> 'General practitioners are anxious to ensure that children are seen quickly so that parents are reassured as it is the uncertainty of not knowing anything that creates the most considerable concern.'

So how could parents at Europe's largest children's hospital have been left waiting without post mortem histology between 1988 and 1996, other than in exceptional cases? This will take considerable explanation.

8. The Proposed New Department for Pathology

8.1 On 15 March 1991 Mr Butler produced a capital programme for the early years of the Trust. It allowed £2 million for 1992/93 and £2.5 million for 1993/94 for a new pathology department. Mr Butler was thinking of and acting on the needs of the Department of Pathology at Alder Hey. From the earliest days of the Trust the plan was to move the laboratory back from Myrtle Street to Alder Hey.

9. Scott-Grant Report

9.1 In May 1991 Scott-Grant Management Services Limited produced a preliminary report for Mr Butler with the following terms of reference,

> 'To carry out a preliminary survey of Pathology looking at the organization and staffing levels. The aim of the survey is to provide an estimate of potential efficiency and cost improvement measures, organizational changes and quality enhancements, together with a time-scale for the implementation of any recommendations.'

The report described the laboratory at Myrtle Street as 'out on a limb' and recommended that it be moved back to Alder Hey. Over-staffing was identified in certain areas but a detailed 'skill-mix analysis' was not carried out. Attempts were made to evaluate the real workload using Welcan statistics applied to raw data provided by the Unit. The exercise did not include an analysis of the primary source materials such as the laboratory day books. Calculations of the workload in histology included the following tasks even though they had clearly not been done:

- post mortem histology processing at 24 blocks per post mortem;
- 101 fetal specimens; and
- 229 placental specimens.

2,268 routine histology specimens were allowed, a total that was an overstatement in itself, if based on the numbers in the laboratory day book for 1990. Double-entries and research projects, together with corresponding numbers for post mortem histology, fetal and placental specimens should have been subtracted. Despite not being completed, fetal and placental specimens were calculated separately and they were given a number in the routine laboratory day book.

10. Mrs England's Response

10.1 Mrs England prepared a response to the report dated 7 June 1991. She took a number of straightforward points but, far from correcting the mistaken impression of workload, she criticised the use of the Welcan data as underestimating it. Specifically, she added in a further 6,000 Welcan units on account of specimen handling of post mortem tissue. She increased the number of Welcan units to be attached to placental and fetal specimens without admitting that the work was not being done. As a result when Mr Butler wrote to Professor van Velzen on 20 June 1991 he accepted that the Scott-Grant report was poor, but apparently believed that it underestimated the work rather than grossly over-estimated it.

10.2 The acceptance of the figures provided, in this case by Mrs England and later by Mrs Waring, without an effective audit of the primary source documents, is a theme that runs throughout.

11. Professor van Velzen as Clinical Director – Another 'Cry for Help'

11.1 On 5 July 1991 Professor van Velzen wrote to Mr Butler in the most surprising terms. He was having difficulty in fulfilling his duties as Clinical Director. He called for a meeting with Mr Butler, Mr Birrell and Mr Tallentire and threatened to go to the Trust Board.

> 'The reason is I feel there are different messages coming to me in relation to the achievables, targets and goals in our financial plan for the remainder of this year and the next.

> ...I would like an urgent meeting in which we establish 'goal posts' again as I find it difficult to clarify to staff at meetings a changing set of achievables. It increases my workload considerably.

> In addition the mess this hospital's finance, personnel and organization is in is much bigger than ever appreciated and I very much feel pathology is getting the wrong end of the stick by combined efforts of all clinical directors with some of the more interesting new power alliances that arise.

Frankly the workload and hassle that arises from all this is getting to levels where I cannot continue to cope on all fronts and deliver. I will have to make some decisions pretty soon as to my priorities and to do this properly I need to know a few firm facts before I continue to commit myself....

I for one will not commit a second of further effort, or allow any of my Heads of Department to spend time on any of these issues, without some guarantees that promises will materialize, or conversely facts admitted so that I and my staff can then react to these appropriately without further hassle, time, cost or anxiety on my part....'

In his evidence Mr Butler described this as a 'wild letter'. It was three months since Trust status was achieved. Professor van Velzen had only been in the official post of Clinical Director for these three months, although Mr Butler had given him similar unofficial status from June 1990.

12. Specific Complaints at Absence of Final Post Mortem Reports – Lengthy Discussions Revealed

12.1   Mr Butler did not act upon the letter of July 1991 and remove Professor van Velzen as a Clinical Director. He did so in January 1992 after Professor van Velzen had made himself thoroughly unpopular.

12.2   Between July 1991 and January 1992 there were two specific complaints in writing over the failure of Professor van Velzen to provide *final* post mortem reports.

12.3   Dr Heather McDowell, Consultant Oncologist, wrote to complain to Professor van Velzen on 15 November 1991 and copied the letter to Dr Martin and Mr Butler.

'As you are only too aware, I have attempted to obtain the final post mortem report on ... for several months now. You will recall he died at the end of July and I informed the parents that I would see them six weeks after this event. You have already received a copy of a letter to them offering an apology for the delay.

These parents are now finding the situation intolerable and I cannot make an appointment until I have this report in writing. I would expect this to be remedied within the next week.'

12.4   Mr Butler wrote to Professor van Velzen on 20 November 1991.

> '<u>POST MORTEM REPORTS</u>
>
> Further to our conversations on this subject I am afraid I am in receipt of two further letters, one with regards to … who died in April 1991 and a further one with regard to ... who died in July 1991. In both cases individuals are very unhappy that the post mortem reports have yet to be submitted.
>
> ***I am desperately disappointed that we have discussed this matter at length, that I was reassured that the problems of backlog were now resolved***, and yet I still have correspondence on this subject which suggests the contrary. I will be grateful if you could let me have a detailed breakdown of the post mortem backlog, i.e. on post mortems that have been undertaken but yet to be reported back to the referring clinician. I look forward to hearing from you.'

Emphasis is added in the above passage to stress the ongoing difficulties and lengthy discussion. This shows that the problem of the backlog in final post mortem reports was well known to Mr Butler and that he had at least taken the trouble to try to resolve it. All clinicians including Dr Martin himself agreed in evidence before the Inquiry that the failure to provide post mortem histology was a serious matter, particularly for a hospital of Alder Hey's status, and it should not have been ignored. It is clear to the Inquiry that the problem was never resolved and that no effective step was taken towards its resolution.

12.5   Mr Butler does not remember the context but this short letter tells us more than any other document about the true state of affairs in the early years of Professor van Velzen's tenure. Dr McDowell was an impressive and straightforward witness when giving evidence. We have no difficulty in preferring contemporaneous documents from her and Mr Butler's written response to Mr Butler's memory nine years later.

13.   The Removal of Professor van Velzen as Clinical Director for Pathology

13.1   Professor van Velzen continued with the initiative instigated by the RHA in 1990 concerning the centralization of pathology services in the Mersey Region and entered into negotiations with a private laboratory, Unilab. He went beyond his authority and upset pathologists at Alder Hey and other hospitals. Centralization ran contrary to the commitment of the Trust Management to a pathology service on site at Alder Hey run by the Trust's own staff. On 18 December 1991 Mr Butler wrote to Professor van Velzen in no uncertain terms,

'I am sorry to be so directive in this letter but the confusion that exists at the moment I think is damaging, upsetting and unnecessary. Please cease any discussions with the firm.'

13.2   At the same time as alienating clinical colleagues Professor van Velzen upset the veterinary scientists at the University. He had begun to offer a service in veterinary pathology based at the Myrtle Street laboratories. He had spent some considerable time and money setting up the service with a glossy brochure. He did not have the necessary qualifications to offer the service in law, as management should have known, quite apart from poaching work from the Professor of Veterinary Pathology at the University. A row followed which was finally settled in the spring of 1992 with a directive, again from Mr Butler but via Dr Isherwood, that the service cease. Quite apart from the ill-will, Mr Butler simply did not think that the value of the work obtained was worth the effort and time.

13.3   Dr Isherwood, a Consultant Biochemist with a scientific background, was involved because he had become Clinical Director in January, following the removal of Professor van Velzen. It had been necessary for Mr Butler to make it plain to Professor van Velzen that he should resign his Clinical Directorship.

13.4   While there is no hard evidence, Mrs England conceded in oral evidence that the veterinary venture might have had to do with the transfer of Dr Howard into the Unit from the Department of Human and Cell Anatomy and there had been a broadening of the SIDS research to include animal models. In fact, Dr Howard had been in the Unit throughout 1991 with the FSID grant for one of the clinical lecturers being used to fill his place in the Department of Human Anatomy and Cell Biology with a fixed-term lecturer. Dr Paul Sibbons, an animal researcher, joined the Unit to test the SIDS-IUGR hypothesis further in animal studies. Whether this *was* the motive for taking on veterinary work, it must have been a motive that animal tissues would be available for research.

13.5   By now Professor van Velzen had shown himself to be unreliable in a number of ways. His lack of judgement as Clinical Director and his inability to handle the political situation were obvious. Apart from the re-organization of the Clinical Directorate in April 1993, when the number of Clinical Directors was streamlined, no witness from whom we took evidence could ever remember a Clinical Director effectively being sacked from that position.

14. Service Management of the Alder Hey Department of Pathology

14.1   Shortly after Trust status was achieved in April 1991, a job description was drafted for the NHS Service Manager of the Department of Pathology, Mr Meade. Mrs England had two versions of a job description, one drafted by herself and one by Professor van Velzen, in the context of virtual autonomy down in Myrtle Street. She remained effectively 'part of the problem' whatever her duties and lines of responsibility under her job descriptions. She was loyal to Professor van Velzen and did not alert the Executive Directors or the Trust Board to what was happening. It was therefore all the more important that the role of service manager provided a safeguard. While Mr Meade was formally accountable to the Clinical Director (Professor van Velzen himself until January 1992 and then Dr Isherwood) he also had a line of liaison with the executive directors. He had the following relevant general management functions to:

- manage the functions and services of the Directorate, including designated staff, liaising with other Directorates and colleagues as necessary;

- establish service agreements between the Directorates and support/diagnostic departments;

- foster a sense of Directorate identity, common purpose and shared values in pursuit of organisational and individual objectives and targets;

- develop the positive and responsive employee/customer relations climate that had been established; and

- monitor performance of activity, financial and quality against targets.

14.2   Under 'financial functions' he was to:

- support the Clinical Director with sufficient and accurate information about the activity and staffing of the Directorate to facilitate negotiation of the annual budget;

- take delegated responsibility for managing the budget, further delegating responsibility to the appropriate levels;

- manage the Directorate cost improvement, service development and income generation programmes in conjunction with the Clinical Director;

- ensure that changes in workload and patterns of service were brought to the attention of the Clinical Director and that the necessary corrective action was taken.

14.3   Mr Meade has been described in evidence as 'of the old school' and as 'a decent man'. He was excused on medical grounds from giving oral evidence before us but he gave a statement to the Solicitor to the Inquiry and provided a further statement in answer to detailed written questions. In those documents he admits that he was unable to cope with Professor van Velzen. Once the Unit was moved to Myrtle Street he was made more and more unwelcome so that in the end he hardly visited. Professor van Velzen and Mrs England effectively excluded him from their meetings and Mrs England was elevated to 'Chief Executive' of the Unit, as described in a document by Professor van Velzen. He described how he could out-manoeuvre Mr Meade. Regrettably, Mr Meade allowed himself to be made redundant from the running of the Alder Hey clinical department.

14.4   In the context of this Inquiry Mr Meade is unlucky as he is one of very few people to have held a formal written job description, against which he can be seen to have failed. However, while he must have been aware of the lack of post mortem histology and did not warn management at the outset, his position was a difficult one. He was initially deceived and excluded by Professor van Velzen and Mrs England.

14.5   The problems in the fetal/neonatal service were well-known to the highest levels of management from the very beginning. That post mortem histology was 'still not possible' was known to Mr Butler, the Chief Executive in 1991 and to most senior doctors in practice before that time. It would be unfair to make too much of Mr Meade's formal job description in those circumstances.

15.   Professor van Velzen's Personal Secretary

15.1   Mrs Margery Clark was Professor van Velzen's personal secretary, appointed shortly after he arrived. She was loyal to him and fielded numerous upsetting complaints. By 1991 the working relationship was under strain and Mrs Clark had begun to see through him and his schemes.

15.2   Matters came to a head between Mrs Clark and Professor van Velzen in late 1991 when Mrs Clark refused to fabricate the minutes of a meeting. She was transferred out of his department and served in numerous short-term positions, including as secretary to Mr Butler, Ms Hilary Rowland the next Chief Executive and Dr Martin, before ending up in the Legal Department. Mr Tallentire, the Director of Personnel, organised her move but nobody appears to have properly 'debriefed' her of her experiences in the Myrtle Street laboratories.

15.3   She was sent back from Myrtle Street to a remote office at Alder Hey where she had little contact with anyone other than Mr Meade who worked nearby. She spoke with Mr Meade about her problems with Professor van Velzen. There is no doubt that from 1991 Mr Meade knew of Professor van Velzen's idiosyncrasies and tendency to fabrication.

15.4   Nevertheless, although the executive directors did not appreciate the detail of Professor van Velzen's fabrication they had come to distrust him. They claim to have lacked hard evidence upon which to discipline Professor van Velzen. Their difficulties have been detailed above and will become evident in the future. However, there was no lack of hard evidence with regard to the failure of the post mortem histology service.

16.   Dr Isherwood as Clinical Director

16.1   Dr Isherwood, who had a scientific background, took over as Clinical Director in early 1992 and remained until April 1993 when the Clinical Directorate structure was re-organized. He was either taken in by or followed Professor van Velzen's line. He supported Professor van Velzen in March 1993 when he circulated his paper 'Re-establishment of Histopathology and Neuropathology Reporting at Alder Hey' (see Part 4, paragraph 22). Since Mr Butler himself and the other executive directors to a lesser degree took actual responsibility for managing Professor van Velzen, it is not necessary for the Inquiry to consider Dr Isherwood's role in greater detail. Mr Butler was more aware of the issues than Dr Isherwood and he took charge.

16.2   Apart from the removal of Professor van Velzen as Clinical Director little of note happened in the first half of 1992 until, with the removal of the laboratories back to Alder Hey in mind, Mr Butler and Mr Birrell visited Professor van Velzen in Myrtle Street.

The van Velzen Years: Part 4
July 1992 – end April 1993

The Pressure Mounts on Professor van Velzen

Professor van Velzen's Handling Strategy with Regard to Service at the University Review

1.   Mr Butler and Mr Birrell Visit the Myrtle Street Laboratories

1.1   On 3 July 1992 Mr Butler and Mr Birrell visited Professor van Velzen in his Myrtle Street laboratories. The discussions were summarized in a letter from Mr Butler to Professor van Velzen on the same day. The important paragraph in the letter reads,

> 'We discussed the most appropriate geographical location for your department. I was surprised that you appeared to have changed your mind and that you appear to prefer to be based within Myrtle Street for the future. That is not our view. We would hope to move you to the Alder Hey site as soon as possible, particularly given the fact that the lease for the building is due for renewal in the very near future. To that end, you agreed to provide me with a list of all staff working within the department, for whom they work and how they are funded, in order to enable us to plan the move of the department to Alder Hey. As I said to you, our thoughts at this stage are to see if we could take over space in the Nurses Home which would initially house Histopathology, but eventually a centralized pathology service on the Alder Hey site. I am anxious to proceed with this as soon as possible so would be grateful for the information on staff numbers, and the nature of their work and how they are funded, as soon as possible.'

A little later on Mr Butler recounted his impressions of that visit to Professor Michael Orme, appointed Dean of the Faculty of Medicine at the University in September 1991.

He said,

> 'You are no doubt aware that we are considering how and when we can move the Fetal and Infant Pathology Department from the Myrtle Street site up to Alder Hey. This is part of a long-term aim to centralise pathology services within the Trust, not only to Alder Hey but indeed within Alder Hey to the one site.
>
> Clearly our first aim would be to move the services from Myrtle Street and I have had discussions with Professor van Velzen on the possibility of doing this, although I sense that he is not now keen.
>
> As I walked around the offices recently I was surprised, perhaps staggered is a better word, at the number of individuals working from these offices, many of whom I was totally unaware.'

The letters speak for themselves expressing surprise both to the 'staggering' number of people working in the Myrtle Street laboratories, and the change of heart of Professor van Velzen in terms of the move back to Alder Hey. The reader will remember from Part 2 of 'The van Velzen Years' Professor van Velzen's need for space and personnel in order to carry out his 'zero-money' research. He now realised that a move back to Alder Hey could not accommodate his large number of research staff.

Neither Mr Butler nor Mr Birrell remembers seeing huge numbers of 'containers' of organs at their visit, although by now they were probably mounting in the reception area.

2. The List of Personnel at Myrtle Street

2.1 On 11 August 1992 Professor van Velzen responded enclosing part of a working document dated 2 July 1992 entitled 'Fetal and Infant Pathology located at the Alder Hey site.' The background section of the document and the introduction to the list of staff stressed the fully integrated nature of the research and clinical aspects of the department. The tactics of the document, bearing in mind Professor van Velzen's *modus operandi* (see 'The van Velzen Years' Part 2, paragraphs 7–9) are clear. The point was to show that the research side of the work was so interlinked with NHS patient care that it would be impossible to split the clinical side away and return it to Alder Hey. The description went well beyond exaggeration.

- Dr Michael R Ashworth was included as Senior Lecturer responsible for day-to-day management of patient care but he had never been appointed and indeed had decided not to take up the position in Liverpool but in fact took up a position in Bristol.

- The registrars on rotation from Broadgreen and Arrowe Park Hospitals were included as if members of the department, when they were not.

- Numerous research fellows and students had the description of their function extended to include references to NHS clinical support work, when in fact they had no such function and were demonstrably unqualified to carry out such a function.

- Research students who had not joined the Department but who had simply expressed the wish to come at some stage were included as if present and working in order to bolster the numbers.

- One MLSO 2, who was really part of the Department of Microbiology was included in the list.

- Even though there were by now seven technicians (five MLSOs and two MLAs) excluding the two mortuary attendants, Professor van Velzen envisaged a total establishment of 13–14 technicians (12 full-time equivalent), again inflating the numbers and the requirement for space.

- Five administrative staff were listed, including an agency audio typist (3.2 whole time equivalent). A further 1.5 was envisaged on the same basis.

3.   NHS and University Audit

3.1   Mr Butler sent the list of personnel to Professor Orme in September 1992, asking for his views. A joint NHS and University audit was commissioned and Mr Highcock and Mr Harris, representatives of the University and the Trust respectively, met at the Senate House on 21 October 1992. Mr Harris confirmed the names of Trust employees on Professor van Velzen's list. Both sides agreed to investigate. Mr Highcock believed a joint approach was required and a visit to the Unit was to be arranged which would be treated as an audit visit.

3.2   There are repeated references to audit in the University documents in late 1992 and 1993 but for some reason the audit was delayed. In the end it was carried out by a trainee at Mersey Internal Audit Agency (MIAA), under the overall supervision of Mr Crowley, Chief Internal Auditor. It may be a coincidence but Professor van Velzen and Dr Howard were interviewed on 2 June 1993, the day after the meeting of the University Review Committee for the Unit of Fetal and Infant Pathology which will be covered in Part 5 of 'The van Velzen Years'. The preliminary report was circulated in June 1993 at the same time as the conclusions of the University Review were being circulated for final approval. It is impossible to say what the point was for carrying out an audit immediately after the University Review.

3.3   Mr Birrell at the Trust was far from happy with the audit report. He complained to Mr Crowley that it posed more questions than it answered and a good deal of clarification was required before they could 'sign off' the audit. Mr Crowley agreed.

An outstanding balance of £16,469 required funding, a significant figure in relation to the overall turnover of the Department. Effectively Dr Sibbons, who had been taken on with six months funding from FSID utilising another project grant as an interim 'loan' measure, was kept on in the Department without funding and the deficit built up rapidly.

3.4   In early 1996, after Professor van Velzen had left, that there was a deficit of about £70,000.

4.   The Net Beginning to Close

4.1   Mr Butler's visit in early July 1992 signalled an increase in the pressure on Professor van Velzen. The purpose of the visit, the move back to Alder Hey, was a potential disaster for him. His tactical response, the list of personnel exaggerating the size and clinical integration of his Department, led to a real threat of an effective joint audit. He did not then know that it would be delayed and ineffectual. He was having little success in obtaining even modest further grants from FSID. His five years of major FSID funding would end in September 1993 and there had been no extension. Although the original £250,000 could be strung out for another year or so, given the savings that had been made on the lecturers, the money was running out. Over the winter of 1992/1993 the clinicians' complaints became more serious.

4.2   At the same time, with the imminent retirement of Professor Heath as Head of the University Department of Pathology, a University Working Party met to discuss the whole future of academic pathology. Professor van Velzen rose to the challenge and produced a lengthy paper for the University in which he outlined two options for the future. In his favoured option he took over from Professor Heath. If he seriously entertained hopes of doing so, he was quickly disabused of them. He would have to fight his way out and resorted, initially, to tried and trusted methods.

5.   The Smokescreen of Research Support for Clinical Work

5.1   Professor van Velzen wrote both to Mr Birrell and Mr Butler in the autumn of 1992 maintaining that although 29% of his technical staff budget came from 'soft' research monies, only 5% of technical time was actually spent on research. Perhaps realising that with seven technicians in his Department the 'technical' card was a weak one to play, for the first time recorded in any document before the Inquiry he went to the University to complain that he was lacking his senior lecturer. He said he could not, on that score, continue to carry the workload.

6. Professor Orme's Choice of Letters

6.1   In late October 1992 Professor van Velzen drafted two letters to Professor Orme. They amounted to a complaint as to the lack of his senior lecturer and yet another 'cry for help'. The chosen letter was to be copied to Mr Butler at the Trust. Crucially, the longer version made specific complaint about the inability to carry out routine histological analysis of post mortem tissues. Professor van Velzen complained,

> 'I however, have been left to carry a double clinical workload in addition to the academic workload for a developing department for the largest part of four years. The NHS presently in the form of the RLCH NHS Trust, Alder Hey, have been fully funding my Chair as part of their continued commitment. They have been given six honorary sessions of my time in return, expecting these to be completed by six similarly honorary sessions of a fully qualified senior lecturer/honorary consultant. This has however not materialised and as such clinical care towards Alder Hey is presently not optimal. For example, histological analysis of post mortem tissues is not routinely reported on with a resultant reduction of perceived value and a subsequent fall in post mortem rates.
>
> I am sorry to say that under the present circumstances I cannot continue to take responsibility for both clinical service to Alder Hey, Unit III as well as full academic responsibility.'

He concluded by making a strong case for the University funding of an NHS locum consultant and for funding in respect of Dr Sibbons whose continued presence in the Unit was building up a deficit. He concluded,

> 'Without intending to create undue unrest I hope I have conveyed to you the urgency of this matter and the seriousness of the predicament I find myself in. If only for reasons of my personal health and wellbeing I must ask you to urgently take action and inform me of the outcome so that I can allay any undue anxiety in my staff, both those of NHS and academic origin.'

6.2   Both drafts were sent to Professor Orme for him to choose which one he would prefer to receive, that is to say which one he would wish Mr Butler to see when copied. He chose the longer and more explicit of the two letters, quoted above making a minor amendment. However, for some reason the politics of which no one has been able to explain, both versions of the letter appear in Mr Butler's file at the Trust.

6.3   The University and Trust were therefore in possession of another explicit complaint including reference to the lack of routine histology following post mortem examinations.

7. Trust and University Response to the Suggestion of NHS Locum Cover

7.1   Mr Butler accepted gratefully the suggestion of University-funded locum cover. In his oral evidence to the Panel he accepted that Professor van Velzen had lacked a senior lecturer and had been working as a sole consultant. He criticised himself for not having pursued the University more vigorously after the departure of Dr Chan in March 1991. Operating without clinical consultant support was a real lack of resource for Professor van Velzen.

7.2   In mitigation of Mr Butler, Professor van Velzen had not complained of it until this point. His position before the Inquiry was that he was not afraid of working long hours. On its own the lack of clinical support does not begin to explain the practice of organ retention and the lack of histological examination of post mortem tissues. Indeed, Professor van Velzen found time for his Unit to do research on some of the very organs on which he had not found time to report clinically. Mr Butler felt vulnerable in any future wish to discipline Professor van Velzen given the likely defence of lack of resource.

8. Working Party Meeting

8.1   Professor Orme gave the University-funded NHS locum concept his backing but stated that there was no precedent for such a scheme.

8.2   Trenchant views were expressed when the University Working Party met on 7 December 1992 to consider the Chair to be vacated by Professor Heath and to consider the dynamics of the Unit of Fetal and Infant Pathology within the overall Department of Pathology. Ms Gillian Bridgett, the Administrative Sub Dean, made notes of the meeting, and what follows is her transcript. It is set out verbatim right down to the structure, given the important matters discussed.

> 'Working party on pathology: 7 December 1992
>
> Present: Dean (Chair), Shields, Kenyon, Kelly, Hart, Cawley, Scott, Shenkin, G B.
>
> Apologies: PM [Johnson]
>
> Paper tabled at meeting: George Holt Chair in Pathology from Myskow

Questions posed at last meeting:

1. Clinical Histopathologist but with track record in research.

Indicate that have rejected idea of a pure scientist.

2. Relationship with Fetal and Infant Pathology.

   Current situation:

   Van Velzen is a member of Department. Chair of Pathology is Head of Department. Senior Lecturer in Department seconded to Fetal and Infant Pathology.

   Tension re Senior Lecturer post.

   Shields: important that freed up and made available to new Professor. (Not part of original deal. Van Velzen salary provided from ex-Consultant post).

AGREED

LOOK AT FUNDING OF LECTURER POSTS

– should new Professor be allowed to ignore Fetal and Infant Pathology altogether?

   Chair within Department

   Department should be seen as focus for all areas of Pathology

   Personality is not good reason for policy.

   Dean's concerns – Alder Hey will feel we have reneged.

   Van Velzen is being paid for six clinical sessions – not being provided.

   If Van Velzen left – would expect post to revert to Health Authority.

   Therefore try to give it University support

   Need to talk to Pearse Butler.

   Converting Senior Lecturer post temporarily to NHS Consultant post – now clouding issue. To put one in and try to change it afterwards – flagging up message.

   Alternative – Van Velzen becomes University Funding Council funded. Dean has resisted this.

   Hart: University would get nothing. Ossify things.

   Shields: salary is paid by Health Authority. Must really do six sessions.

Hart: University's responsibility to make sure he does.

Putting in locum will muddy issue.

No precedent for University resource being used for NHS post.

Prime Academic Committee to say no.

AGREED

Senior Lecturer should revert to Department of Pathology and to stay vacant or fill as temporary Senior Lecturer. Van Velzen should stay in Department of Pathology.

What commitments were made?

Pressure on Van Velzen to provide service.

Collaboration re research?

?Who owns Van Velzen's equipment?

most – University or NHS (Dean)'

8.3   A number of points emerge from this note. The first is that the Working Party, without recorded dissent from Professor Orme, primed the Academic Committee to say 'no' to the concept of a University-funded NHS locum. The Dean was concerned that Alder Hey would feel that the University had reneged on the initial agreement to provide the senior lecturer and did not want to 'flag up the message'. After this reference someone is noted to have said that Professor van Velzen was being paid for six clinical sessions but not providing them. In oral evidence Professor Orme denied having said this, notwithstanding its position in the note, and claimed that he believed Professor van Velzen was in fact providing his six clinical sessions. No dissent is recorded in the note on that score either and no corrections to the minute were suggested by Professor Orme. Indeed, Professor Shields went on to make the point that Professor van Velzen must really do six sessions and Professor Hart said it was the University's responsibility to make sure that he did. There is no evidence that the agreed plan to put pressure on Professor van Velzen to provide the service was ever put into effect by Professor Orme.

9.   A Full Six Sessions? The Alder Hey Standpoint

9.1   Professor van Velzen worked at odd hours. The routine surgical reporting was being done. Autopsies were being carried out and preliminary post mortem reports issued albeit late. Professor van Velzen was working as a sole consultant, with Dr Khine in a training position. In reality Dr Khine was Professor van Velzen's clinical 'dogsbody'.

Although only of Senior Registrar status, she bore the brunt of the work so much that the view expressed at the Working Party concerning the Professor's failure to fulfil his clinical sessions is likely to be accurate. However, the management at Alder Hey assumed that Professor van Velzen was carrying out his six sessions because work was being done. This was the view expressed by the Trust representative at the University Review in 1993. Nevertheless, the notes of the Working Party at the University are unequivocal in expressing that Professor van Velzen was not doing his six clinical sessions.

9.2   Another way of looking at the issue of clinical sessions is to note the evidence of Professor Christopher Foster, who took over as Head of the Department of Pathology in 1994. He said that when Professor van Velzen's clinical sessions were stopped at Alder Hey in December 1994 he noticed little difficulty in continuing to service the work overall, so little had Professor van Velzen been doing.

9.3   While it was agreed at the University Working Party meeting that there should be pressure placed on Professor van Velzen to provide the service, nothing was done by the University. Only they were aware that Professor van Velzen was not carrying out his sessions.

9.4   In evidence before the Inquiry Mr Butler was upset to be shown the notes of the Working Party and to realise that Professor Orme had not passed on this information. Professor Orme had recently carried out a confidential appraisal of Professor van Velzen in his capacity as Dean and Line Manager. In normal circumstances this would have been carried out by Professor Heath, but he did not do so because of a communication breakdown. How useful a totally confidential appraisal might be when unrecorded, and there is no job description against which to judge performance is hard to understand. In evidence Professor Orme was unable to identify who else in the Working Party said that Professor van Velzen was not carrying out his six clinical sessions.

9.5   It is extremely difficult to interpret the note of the Working Party as Professor Orme would wish, with all the attendant circumstances. We prefer the more obvious reading of the contemporaneous note, and conclude that Professor Orme knew Professor van Velzen was not fulfilling his clinical commitment.

10.   Professor van Velzen – 'Millstone'

10.1   The Working Party met on four occasions. Professor van Velzen gave evidence to it on 23 November 1992 and immediately after he had left Ms Bridgett recorded the following,

> 'Reality and what is said are on parallel tracks.'

At the end of the overall discussion, in the context of deciding whether a scientist or a clinician should be appointed as the new Professor, Ms Bridgett recorded the following,

'BUT – van Velzen problem is structural, is a millstone.

Has to be marginalised at Alder Hey.'

When the conclusions of the Working Party were distributed for approval Professor Orme received the following advice,

'My final concern is that there is unfinished business around van Velzen. Quite simply I believe Liverpool will be far better off without him.'

10.2   There is no expression of dissent within the notes of the Working Party with regard to the assessment of Professor van Velzen at the end of 1992. There was no communication of these views to the Trust.

11.   The Move to Alder Hey and the Fetal Backlog

11.1   Meanwhile Professor van Velzen wrote further tactical letters.

11.2   On 5 November 1992 he wrote one of considerable audacity to Mr Butler amounting to complete fabrication. Professor van Velzen attempted to ease the mounting pressure by claiming that he had cleared the full backlog of fetus and placentae from 1991 and had progressed by about 50 reports into 1990. The laboratory day book and the remains of these fetus demonstrate that this is not true. Mr Butler took the letter at face value and until he gave evidence to the Inquiry he believed that the backlog had been cleared.

12.   Mayoral Visit to the 'Department'

12.1   Professor van Velzen now decided to play to the press and to public opinion. His first move was to arrange for a tour of the Unit by the Lord Mayor of Liverpool followed by lunch attended by Professor Orme. The propaganda campaign had begun in earnest, as shown in an article in the 18 December 1992 issue of *Precinct*, the newspaper for the staff and students of the University. It describes the visit of the Lord Mayor and tells how Professor van Velzen had built up the department over four years from an original staff of three to a present staff of 34. The Myrtle Street laboratories were described as ideal. Worries were outlined about the expiry of the lease and that

'any relocation will inevitably cause severe disruption to the Department's busy and important research efforts, as well as patient care.'

13. Laboratory Move – 'Threat to Children'

13.1   On 8 January 1993 the *Liverpool Echo* ran a story under the above headline. It was leaked by Professor van Velzen and linked specifically to the proposed move from Myrtle Street up to smaller premises at Alder Hey. Professor van Velzen said,

'There is no way the Department could survive intact if it is moved to Alder Hey. We have nine laboratory spaces. At Alder Hey we would only have two because of pressure on room.'

13.2   Mr Butler was quoted as denying the story but the *Echo* gave Professor van Velzen the last word,

'Some researchers, who would not be employed at Alder Hey, spend 95 per cent of their time on patient care. It would be impossible to maintain the service.'

13.3   Mr Butler wrote a letter dated 20 January 1993 reprimanding Professor van Velzen for leaking the scandalous story but he did nothing further to discipline him.

14. Pressure on the University – Publication of SIDS Research

14.1   Professor van Velzen also used the national press to raise the research profile of the Unit to make it that much more difficult for any hostile action to be taken. Somehow he managed to get University approval for a press release which previewed his findings on cot death. The story was run in the *Observer*, the *Telegraph*, the *Guardian*, the *Independent* and *The Times*. It was run in Liverpool by the *Daily Post*. It described the combination of the painstaking collection and cataloguing of post mortem material by Professor van Velzen with the new 3-D measurement and microscopic techniques developed by Dr Howard.

14.2   There is no document indicating any reprimand on the part of the University but the situation was such that Professor Orme visited the Vice Chancellor on 10 February 1993 to discuss Professor van Velzen.

15. The Vice Chancellor's Note of 10 February 1993

15.1 The Vice Chancellor, Professor Philip Love, made a detailed note of the meeting with Professor Orme immediately after it had finished. It should be realised that Professor Love was not a medic and outside the Faculty of Medicine. The importance of this note merits it being set out in full here.

> 'This morning the Dean of Medicine called to see me to discuss a number of matters including the position of Professor Dick van Velzen. He explained that there was a feeling of unease amongst his colleagues about Professor van Velzen, both on the University and Health Board fronts.
>
> Professor Orme has no criticism of the efforts being put in by Professor van Velzen but he takes the view that they are being misdirected. Professor van Velzen is a great entrepreneur but so far he has not delivered the goods.
>
> The paediatric pathology service which he provides at Alder Hey is not good. He was for some time Clinical Director of Pathology Services at Alder Hey but was removed from that post.
>
> The obstetricians used to be unhappy about the service provided by him but they appear to be reasonably happy just now.
>
> Professor van Velzen would claim that all his troubles stem from the fact that he has not been able to fill a senior lecturer vacancy.
>
> With regard to the funding which he receives from the Sudden Infant Death Society (SIDS) [FSID], the Dean explained that SIDS are not happy about the work which he has done. All his recent applications for project grants have been turned down and his programme grant from SIDS will end in September/October 1994.
>
> Basically SIDS is unhappy about his science. They are now more interested in putting money into the sociological aspects of cot death following the efforts of Ann Diamond.
>
> The Chairman of the Alder Hey Trust (Pearse Butler) is not happy with the paediatric service being offered by Professor van Velzen. The Trust is insisting that the Paediatric Pathology Department moves back from the precinct to Alder Hey, but Professor van Velzen does not want this and has campaigned in the press against such a move saying that infant deaths would result. In addition Professor van Velzen called in the Lord Mayor and tried to persuade her to lease the building, currently occupied by his Department, to the University or to himself.

In connection with the planned move to Alder Hey, Professor van Velzen was asked to produce a list of posts in his area of activity. He prepared a list of 25 posts, 6 of which were erroneous. As a result a financial audit is now being carried out at the instigation of both the Health Service and the University.

I had a discussion with the Dean about the recent publicity on the apparent 'breakthrough' by Professor van Velzen's team in relation to one of the causes of cot deaths. The Dean said that an article written by Professor van Velzen is due for publication in an American journal in May, but Professor van Velzen, with the approval of that journal, has gone to the media prior to publication. The Dean thinks that this is a tactic to put pressure on the University and the NHS.

Pearse Butler would like Professor van Velzen to go (he is paid for by the NHS, although he is a University employee).

The Faculty Board of Medicine will almost certainly approve the recommendation that the vacant senior lecturer post in Professor van Velzen's area be returned to the Department of Pathology. This will annoy Professor van Velzen who may raise the matter in the press. I told the Dean that he must tell Professor van Velzen that, if there are complaints about decisions, they must be raised internally and not externally. When the Dean told Professor van Velzen what was to happen to the senior lecturer post, Professor van Velzen threatened to sue the Dean and claimed that the Faculty was at fault for his divorce, for the inadequate service he provides and for his poor research track record!

The Dean believes that Professor van Velzen will complain about Donald Heath, Head of Department, who has really done very little for the Department as such and who has not encouraged younger staff.

The Dean confirmed that he appraised Professor van Velzen last year – because Donald Heath had done nothing about it – and told him that his research needed to be improved. He has, in fact, improved his output of research publications in peer reviewed journals.

Professor van Velzen has raised a very small amount of research money if the SIDS support is disregarded.

The Dean said that Professor van Velzen is 'articulate, plausible and streetwise'. He will not go without making a fuss.

I thanked the Dean for alerting me to the potential problems in his area. He will keep me informed of developments.'

16.   Analysis of the Vice Chancellor's Note

16.1   The following points arise out of the note.

- Professor Orme did not pass on the trenchant views of the Working Party to the Vice Chancellor nor the criticism that Professor van Velzen was not actually providing his clinical sessions.

- Nothing good was said about the clinical service at Alder Hey. Indeed it appears that Mr Butler wanted Professor van Velzen to leave.

- The obstetricians were said to be reasonably happy 'just now' in terms of the service, but no more than that.

- The research was discussed in negative terms. Professor Richard Cooke, the Head of the ICH, was then a member of the Grant Review Committee of FSID and he kept Professor Orme informed. There was to be a shift in emphasis towards the sociological aspects of cot death, Professor Orme said more about this in oral evidence. By February 1993 he had been told that FSID was to look towards epidemiological and multi-disciplinary research in the future.

- There was specific discussion of the date when Professor van Velzen's project grants would run out in the autumn of 1994.

- Professor Orme had seen through Professor van Velzen's tactics in recent months. However, he does not appear to have mentioned his own attendance at the Mayoral luncheon or the 'spinning' of the two letters to be copied to Mr Butler in the previous autumn.

- There was detailed discussion of how Professor van Velzen might react to the news that he would lose the senior lecturer post and how he might react if disciplined.

- The University's vulnerabilities were discussed.

- The note concludes without any plan of action other than with various considerations relevant to a handling strategy in order to avoid a fuss.

17.   Reaction to the Loss of Senior Lecturer – University Review

17.1   The decision ratifying the recommendation of the Working Party to remove the senior lecturer post from Professor van Velzen was taken at a Faculty Board Meeting on 3 March 1993. He reacted angrily, as expected, and demanded a review of his Unit in order to make his case for the return of the resource. At this point Professor Orme was happy to agree to a review and the senior lecturer issue was put on 'hold'. The scope of the review was defined as follows,

> 'It should look at the service aspects of the Unit as well as the teaching and research performance, and should take into account the historical position since the formation of the Unit. It should also give advice on the future of the Unit.'

An internal University or Faculty review of this type is extremely rare.

18. Composition of the Review Committee

18.1   By 16 March 1993 the Review Committee had been drawn up by Professor Orme:

- Professor James Neilson – Chairman – Professor of Obstetrics and Gynaecology and a newcomer to Liverpool.

- Professor Cooke – Head of the ICH.

- Dr James Burns – Acting Head of the Department of Pathology.

- Professor Jem Berry – Professor of Paediatric Pathology at the University of Bristol – as external assessor.

The following were later nominated by the relevant Trusts or co-opted by Professor Neilson:

- A representative of the Alder Hey Hospital Trust – Dr Helen Carty, now Professor Carty, Clinical Director of Support Services.

- A representative of the Obstetrics and Gynaecology Hospitals Trust – Mr Walkinshaw, Consultant in Feto-Maternal Medicine.

- A senior non-clinical scientist from the Faculty – Professor Graham Dockray, Professor of Physiology.

18.2   Professor Carty, a Consultant Radiologist, became the Clinical Director of Support Services at Alder Hey from 1 April 1993. Under the new structure devised by Mr Butler the Departments of Radiology, Pathology and Pharmacology were merged into one Directorate of Support Services on that date.

19. The Net Tightening Further

19.1   Professor van Velzen now had to deal with the University Review on top of the pressures of the proposed move, the audit and mounting complaint over delay. It was obvious from the start that no review could exclude service considerations. However, as he said in evidence to us, he was not really concerned to retain his senior lecturer for the purposes of service delivery, but rather to maintain status and scientific output. His *modus operandi* had been to keep the University and Trusts apart, playing one off against the other. Now he had the prospect of a review where those very parties would meet and discuss the position. Once the service issue had been raised it required active management. Further pressure would be required to prevent all the issues running out of control. Professor van Velzen said himself in interview with the Inquiry when considering the overall balance on service and scientific issues in 1993 that his position was untenable.

> 'So it comes to follow if you bring all of them in, then the only response to the system is, well, if its that complicated that's 'non-viable', 'no go' anyway. Let's eliminate it totally! What a mess!'

The elimination of the Unit was not Professor van Velzen's preferred course.

Professor van Velzen's Handling Strategy with Regard to Service at the University Review

20. The Women's Hospitals

20.1   We have abundant evidence that the service offered to the Women's Hospitals was always poor and never remotely lived up to the tender documents. However, there was also considerable sympathy for Professor van Velzen from that quarter over what was considered to be an impossible situation, as indicated by the evidence of Mr Atlay and Mr Walkinshaw. He had cultivated this sympathy over the years. From the perspective of the Women's Hospitals it was apparent that the Chair had been inadequately set up and resourced from the beginning, little wonder that without a senior lecturer Professor van Velzen could not provide the service. Mr Walkinshaw told the Inquiry,

> 'Effectively the situation was tolerated because we knew that whatever complaints were made the response would be that Professor van Velzen needed medical support and that as a single-handed academic consultant he could not possibly fulfil the workload.'

20.2   Against this background of sympathy, Professor van Velzen believed that he would have support from the Women's Hospitals on the basis that if he were to leave there would be no service at all in Liverpool.

20.3   The above analysis ignored the fact that by 1993, the Women's Hospitals had Trust status and could buy the services from wherever they pleased. However, Mr Walkinshaw gave evidence that no other Centres had bid for the contract leaving Alder Hey to succeed without competition. There was no certainty that a reasonable alternative contract could be negotiated quickly without substantial disruption. Given the scarcity of trained fetal and perinatal pathologists, Mr Walkinshaw thought it highly unlikely that a replacement could be found for Professor van Velzen if he were to be forced to leave.

20.4   The various representatives of the Women's Hospitals Trust deny that they were consciously motivated at the time of the University Review by the fear of Professor van Velzen leaving. It is difficult to find any other reason why, whether consciously or not, they should have held back from comparing the actual service (poor) at the time of the review with that expected under the tender document (perfect). We have seen from the Vice Chancellor's note in February 1993 that they were prepared to say they were reasonably happy and not make further difficulty. Mr Keith Haynes, Chief Executive of the Women's Hospitals Trust, wrote a bland letter for the review with no critical analysis of the service. Mr Walkinshaw accepted in evidence to us that the letter did not amount to a fair summary of the problems afflicting the service. At the time, despite being a member of the Review Panel he wrote,

> 'The services required were clearly laid out in the tender documents for the Pathology Services contract which has recently been agreed. This especially dwelt on the speed of the service in terms of making reports available to clinicians. Although there have been difficulties in the past with this, the turnaround time in the main is now acceptable.

> There is little doubt that the quality of the service is excellent from a clinical point of view with detailed autopsy reports and further guidance where necessary ....

> ... During the review of the Pathological Services, considerable surprise was expressed by the expert panel that there was only a single perinatal pathologist in the Mersey Region. The recommendations of the various Colleges including the Pathology College suggest much more generous staffing than this. Some disquiet was expressed by the expert panel that stated turn around times could be met by a sole consultant service and these criticisms were taken very seriously by the Clinical Directors and by the Trust Board. We would therefore be keen that no further inroads were made into the Clinical Fetal Pathology Service.

Whatever the internal politics, it was with dismay that the Trust learnt of the transfer of the senior lecturer post out of the Department of Fetal and Infant Pathology. This would have gone some way to alleviating the clinical difficulty.

... I think in conclusion that clinicians within the Trust feel that the clinical service is adequate although there may be improvements still to come. The difficult comparison is that the service was so poor prior to the appointment of Professor van Velzen that it is difficult to know how much better it ought to be.'

20.5 Whatever the difficulties and the real standard of the service, Professor van Velzen expected and got, if not support, at least lack of complaint from the Women's Hospitals.

21. Alder Hey

21.1 Professor van Velzen knew that the attitude at Alder Hey was entirely different from that at the Women's Hospitals. There were mumblings as to inaccuracy of reporting but this was not a serious threat at this time. However, detailed complaints were building about both delay and the lack of post mortem histology. He knew that Professor Carty as the new Clinical Director would not be generously disposed towards him. He had to go on the attack and exploited the previous inertia of management at Alder Hey.

22. The Paper 'Re-establishment of Histopathology and Neuropathology Reporting of Post Mortem Service in RLCH Alder Hey NHS Trust'

22.1 A paper with the above title was delivered to Mr Butler and Dr Martin with a covering letter dated 12 March 1993. It was immediately copied to the Executive Board and shortly afterwards to the new Clinical Directors.

22.2 The authors of the paper appeared on the front page as Professor van Velzen and Mrs England. While Mrs England denied that she had any real input to the paper when giving evidence to the Inquiry, Professor van Velzen maintained that she had. Despite the danger in accepting the uncorroborated word of Professor van Velzen on any matter, there is substantial corroboration. There is nearly five years of fabrication and 'workload laundering'. Mrs England remained loyal to the last and received a Psion organizer as a personal present from Professor van Velzen when she left the department in May 1993. Notwithstanding the wide circulation of the paper there is no evidence that she attempted to distance herself from it at the time. Nevertheless, while the figures for the paper were provided by Mrs England the serious 'spin' was 'vintage van Velzen'.

22.3   The paper passed responsibility for the failure of post mortem histology back to the managers of the hospital and the senior doctors. Most of the groundwork had been done in previous correspondence but a new spin was applied. The apparent increase in workload was stressed, particularly with regard to new techniques. The familiar story of lack of technical and administrative support was trotted out. All of this was old hat. However, whereas what had really happened was that management had simply failed to respond to the lack of post mortem histology and the complaints, Professor van Velzen now alleged a management decision to suspend the service. He maintained that he had complained specifically about lack of resources causing delay in post mortem reporting and that management had specifically told him to stop carrying out the histological and neuropathological examinations and reserve the tissue in pots for further study if resources became available. He alleged that this management measure had been conveyed to the doctors but no-one had found it appropriate to express their concern.

22.4   The management was put in a difficult position precisely because of its inactivity, failure to see through the 'workload laundering' and Professor van Velzen's general *modus operandi*. The above narrative sets out all the crucial documents, and shows that Professor van Velzen had neither complained to hospital management about the lack of resources for post mortem histology, nor the inability to carry it out, until early 1991. There is simply no evidence other than this paper of 12 March to suggest that management actually suggested the suspension of post mortem histology and the reserving of tissue in the pots for further study if resources became available. The reader will remember that upon his arrival Professor van Velzen ordered that there was to be no disposal of material at all.

22.5   The allegation that the suspension of post mortem histology was a specific decision of the management, at a time before the Trust team was in place, represents the crowning glory of Professor van Velzen's web of fabrication. That Miss Malone was no longer at Alder Hey to deal with the allegation, together with the inactivity of the management of the time and in the face of numerous references in other documents, made an effective response difficult. Only by confessing previous management inactivity and clinical neglect, from the Medical Director down to the wider body of clinicians, could the Trust make powerful criticism of the Professor.

23.   The Reality Underlying the Fabrication

23.1   The detailed reasons within the paper were false despite being spun around real resource difficulties. The reality remained that there had been no routine reporting of post mortem histology since Professor van Velzen arrived in September 1988. The paper presented the position as follows,

'I feel that all throughout these years, I, and lately we, have done the utmost to maintain service and clinician satisfaction. However, I must say that not carrying out histology and neuropathological assessments leaves us very vulnerable (there for example are only 'preliminary post mortem reports' on file!!), does not comply with postgraduate training requirements, and in fact constitutes an incomplete and professionally and clinically speaking unsatisfactory if not unacceptable service. None of the clinicians originally involved however found it useful to complain to past and present management.'

The analysis was correct and should have alerted management to immediate action. It did not.

24. The Climax of the Paper – an Attempt to Head Off Service Criticism

24.1   Professor van Velzen concluded the main section of his paper by attempting to head off the very complaints that were putting him under pressure and could condemn him at the University Review. He wrote,

'The problems arise from the fact that newly appointed clinicians (Jane Ratcliffe, Imti Choonara, Brian Judd) who are used to a proper service make (in my opinion justified) demands with respect to the service. If we have made any mistakes it was in trying to comply and 'promising to do our utmost' 'hopefully having something available next week', which has repeatedly been taken as a normal service commitment and when not met, has resulted in dissatisfaction. More importantly when results have been promised to parents, this has led to embarrassment. It is this group of consultants who is writing to the both of you. [Mr Butler and Dr Martin].

In addition a number of cases from the past years have gone on to have medico-legal consequences and in some cases there are now consequences for further family counselling and issues related to additional children. Senior consultants such as L. Rosenbloom are now asking for results on some of these as they are by now (urgently) required. The Coroner's Office similarly is beginning to press for results on some long outstanding cases.

I have indicated this problem in many meetings and on many occasions and am appreciative of the limited financial margins within which the Trust has had to function over the past years and generally have supported the priority of larger issues.

However, I am coming under increasing pressure to now provide a service.'

24.2   This was as careful a piece of fabrication as Professor van Velzen ever compiled. The key to it was, of course, a substantial element of truth with heavy spin applied, playing upon the weakness of previous management inactivity.

25.   The End Game?

25.1   The major work to head off criticism of the service and prepare for the University Review had now been accomplished. Professor van Velzen had just the final touches to put in place.

25.2   The first touch involved the composition of the Review Committee and letters of 1 April 1993 to Professor Orme. The second was to try to influence Professor Carty, the new Clinical Director, who was to attend the review on behalf of the Trust.

26.   Letters of 1 April 1993

26.1   Professor van Velzen wrote two letters to Professor Orme on 1 April 1993.

26.2   In the first letter he objected to Dr Burns being a member of the Committee. Dr Burns was to be the Acting Head of the Department of Pathology from 1 May 1993 upon the retirement of Professor Heath. He did not want anyone from the Adult Main Department on the committee, due to the history of tension between it and his Unit. He wanted the composition of the Committee reviewed at a higher level in the University. He continued,

> 'However, you will no doubt ask me not to hang out the dirty linen, not rock the boat and again ask me to trust you, which again I will.

> In this same vein I am interested why, if you chaired the previous Committee, the Faculty of Medicine is not represented either by yourself or in any other way? Is there an answer to that question that you can release to me?'

The letter then entered the realms of wild conspiracy theory before coming back to conclude,

> 'I will be guided by your judgement and advice, but I hope and know that you will understand how this in itself is still very, if not increasingly difficult.'

26.3   Professor van Velzen appeared to have a trust in Professor Orme that things would work out to his advantage in the end. The question why Professor Orme did not chair the review is a good one.

27. The Second Letter of 1 April 1993

27.1   The second letter was headed 'Strictly Personal and Confidential'. It shows Professor van Velzen at his lowest ebb, believing that his fight to save the Unit would be unsuccessful. He feared that there was a hidden agenda to move paediatric pathology to the Royal Liverpool University Hospital (RLUH), because it would attract academic papers and funding. He feared that the move would be without him, and the blame for all the ills in the pathology community in Liverpool would fall on him. He was beginning to doubt his faith in Professor Orme and to consider reacting publicly. He subscribed to a conspiracy theory against him at Alder Hey and thought, wrongly as it turned out, that Alder Hey was looking to save money by sub-contracting to the RLUH and doing away with paediatric pathology at Alder Hey. He believed that the Women's Hospitals would have to find their own budget for a consultant perinatal/fetal pathologist. He concluded the letter,

> 'This is what will be cooked out by a Committee on whom the proponents of this strategy have now been carefully manoeuvred to be in a majority ….
>
> I would like your personal views on this matter and, rather than asking you to commit yourself in writing will come to visit you to talk this through as soon as possible, not just as a desperate Professor would like to be allowed to talk with his Dean but more precisely as a desperate academic, who feels that not rocking boats leaves him no better off, in fact, much worse off, than doing the opposite.'

What Professor van Velzen termed the 'hidden agenda' is essentially what happened two years later, following the appointment of the new Professor.

27.2   Readers will probably be aware that Professor van Velzen survived the University Review. Documents show that in the spring of 1993 he had nothing going for him at all in real terms, except the pressure he could generate through his fabrication and the expectation that he would make a fuss. Even he agreed in evidence that his Unit was not viable. How it survived the University Review will take considerable telling.

28. Reaction to Continuing Complaint – Letter to Professor Carty

28.1   In April 1993 Dr Choonara continued his complaint regarding delay and lack of post mortem histology through Professor Carty. Professor van Velzen had to react and wrote to Professor Carty on 27 April 1993, reiterating his position in the March 1993 paper. He gave the impression that Mr Butler and Dr Martin had requested him to prepare that paper with costings to reinstate the post mortem examination histology service. This was not true, as the covering letter to them with the paper in March 1993 shows. Professor van Velzen reiterated the fabrication to Professor Carty,

> 'Let me therefore repeat again to avoid any misunderstandings. There is no long delay in receiving post mortem histology. This hospital does not receive any post mortem histology, as by managerial combined with clinician decision, dating from at least three to four years ago. I feel that the reinstatement of this service will be in the interest of the hospital and is essential to a teaching hospital and we need to do this as has been indicated at least once or twice a year, by me to management in the past years.'

All Professor van Velzen could do now was to hold his nerve and await the review.

29.   Paediatric Research Ethical Committee at Alder Hey

29.1   Meanwhile the Paediatric Research Ethical Committee at Alder Hey had held one of its regular confidential meetings on 21 January 1993 under the Chairmanship of Dr Campbell Davidson, Consultant Paediatrician. Professor Lloyd and Dr McDowell gave their apologies to that meeting. Dr Smith and Dr Jackson attended from the ICH in order to present two research projects for approval. The first was,

> 'The Association between Abnormalities of the Coronary Arteries and Reduced Blood Supply to the Muscle of the Heart in Congenital Heart Disease. A Study of Anomalous Vascular Patterns and the Implications for both a Reduction in the Oxygen Supply to the Heart Muscle and also for Surgical Treatment. Smith A; Jackson M; Connell G; Anderson R H; Arnold R; and van Velzen D.'

29.2   The specimens were to be hearts of children who had died of congenital cardiac disease obtained at autopsy under the supervision of Professor van Velzen. Dr Smith was looking for approval for the continuation of the work that had been running for many years. The minutes reveal,

> 'Discussion centred around the ethical issue relating to tissue obtained at the time of post mortem for research purposes. The Chairman agreed to contact the Chairman, Royal College of Physicians Ethics Committee, London, for his view.'

29.3   Dr Davidson wrote on the minutes,

> 'Report: post mortem consent embraces consent that post mortem material be available for teaching and research. This should be fully explained when consent is obtained.'

29.4   At the following meeting in February 1993 at which Professor Lloyd and Dr McDowell were present, the minutes read in relation to this point,

> 'The Chairman reported that the report from the Royal College of Pathologists entitled 'Autopsy and Audit' dealt with this issue and that when post mortem consent is obtained this allows for material to be used both for teaching and for research. This should be ***fully explained when the consent is obtained.***'

Emphasis has been added, but hardly needs to be.

30.   An Opportunity Lost

30.1   In the early part of 1993 Dr Davidson, despite his own note on the minutes, did nothing to change his own practice. Nor did he alert clinicians and management at Alder Hey to what would have amounted to a practice of 'informed consent'. Dr McDowell took over the Chair of the Committee later in 1993 and she too failed to act. The annual report of the Committee failed to make any mention of the issue so as to inform proper practice. Whereas Dr Davidson in his evidence refused to accept any mistake, Dr McDowell acknowledged with the benefit of hindsight that she should have taken steps to inform management and doctors of best practice. Indeed she conceded that even without the benefit of hindsight she should have done just that. She is to be congratulated on her openness and clarity of thought.

31.   Fetal Research

31.1   At the same meeting in January 1993 Dr Jackson sought approval for a similar study relating to the growth and development of the human fetal myocardium. The note in January reads,

> 'The Committee informed Dr Jackson that they were not fully aware of the legal aspects of using fetal tissue and decided to look further at the issue. The need for a patient information document and consent form was questioned and the Chairman agreed to contact Steve Walkinshaw for an independent view.'

31.2   Dr Davidson endorsed the minutes,

> 'Polkinghorne Report – ***permission to use fetal tissue should be obtained at time of obtaining consent for the abortion.*** Consent to use tissue for 'general purpose of research' – rather than elaborate details. – Patient information sheet not considered necessary.'

Again emphasis has been added. The minutes for February 1993 reflect Dr Davidson's endorsement.

31.3   Nothing was done to change practice in Liverpool in relation to the obtaining of fetal tissue for research purposes. Not only was the issue ignored immediately after the publication of the Polkinghorne Report in 1989 it was again ignored in early 1993 when express reference was made to the Polkinghorne Report and the need for the mother's permission.

The van Velzen Years: Part 5
May – June 1993

The University Review and its Final Preparations

1. Alder Hey Reaction to the March 1993 Paper

1.1 While many of the witnesses were vague about what happened in response to the paper of Professor van Velzen and Mrs England in March 1993, the documentation of the period reveals no ambiguity.

1.2 Mr Butler copied the paper to the executive directors. Mr Birrell as Financial Director took the paper at face value and sent a response on 29 April 1993. He was not concerned with the accuracy or otherwise of the history but where the requested funds should come from to re-establish the service, if that was to be the decision. He wrote,

> 'Having read the above paper, I would comment as follows:
>
> i. the proposal represents a clinical development and as such should come out of the Clinical Development Reserve. It should be assessed by Clinical Directors.
>
> ii. Capital costs should be a charge on Pathology's 1993/94 Capital Allocation.'

1.3 The agenda for the meeting of the clinical directors on 6 May 1993 shows that the paper was to be circulated then for discussion at the next meeting. The minutes of the meeting on 6 May do not show any discussion. The witnesses' oral evidence differs regarding discussions at the meeting on 20 May 1993. Mr Butler remembers detailed discussion leading to a policy in which the Trust would seek the appointment of a senior lecturer by the University and would carry out an audit of the Department. However, there was already the joint NHS-University audit in the course of preparation. The external audit of the overall Department of Pathology at Alder Hey carried out by Mr Lewis in the summer of 1993 does not appear to have been commissioned specifically to consider Professor van Velzen's problems and was coincidental, as Mr Alan Sharples maintained. He was to take over from Mr Birrell as Director of Finance in December 1993 soon after this meeting. Indeed, the Lewis audit was silent on the issue of post mortem histology and it does seem to be a response to the March 1993 paper. Clinicians present at the meeting do not remember much by way of discussion at all. Other executive directors remember little. There are two slightly different versions of the minutes of the meeting, but in the essential detail they are identical, and reveal no discussion and/or policy decision. One set of the minutes reads,

> 'Re-establishment of Post Mortem Histology
> Mr Butler is dealing with the further requirements to progress this paper.'

The other set is slightly differently worded but amounts to the same thing.

2.   Mr Butler Seeks Clarification

2.1   In line with the impression from the minutes, Mr Butler wrote to Professor van Velzen on 11 May 1993 requesting clarification of the problem,

> 'Many thanks for your very full report, which was initially considered by Clinical Directors on 6 May 1993. Whilst there is real desire to develop the service in the way that you have outlined, there was some concern as to the exact nature of the problems within the department.
>
> It appears, partly, to be a clerical matter, although I am not sure that is the case. Equally, it appears to be a problem of capital equipment, as well as being one of technical staffing. It would be very useful if you could clarify the exact role these areas play, then we can judge the developments you have outlined against other priorities across the Trust. We certainly need a picture of all the current staff within the department to try and evaluate what difference these extra posts could make.
>
> Many thanks.'

2.2   Evidently Professor van Velzen's tactics were working. How the re-establishment of histopathology could have been considered a development, as against reintroducing an essential clinical service, is beyond belief. Mr Butler should have by now appreciated the exact nature of the problems within the Unit. Unfortunately, either Professor van Velzen succeeded in deceiving everyone or no-one was willing to intervene to expose the deceit.

2.3   When Professor van Velzen replied to the above letter on 8 June 1993 following the University Review he simply repeated his previous deception and this time described himself spending $1\frac{1}{2}$ hours per case typing preliminary post mortem reports. This was not a true picture.

3.   Alder Hey's Written Submission for the University Review

3.1   Professor Carty, the new Clinical Director, was given the task of preparing a paper. Nevertheless, various endorsements on different drafts show that Mr Butler had editorial input. The text of the submission is set out below with only minimal abbreviation because of its importance,

'At the request of the Executive Board I have discussed with several members of staff the service they receive in Histopathology. I have sought on every occasion to ensure that there is a fair request for information, and have insisted that good points were highlighted, as well as bad points.

I have consulted the Surgeons, Nephrologist, Oncologists and Clinical Geneticist. I have also been independently approached by two Physicians who wanted to express concern about the failure of delivery of post mortem histopathology, the failure of provision of post mortem reports within a reasonable length of time and failure to respond to requests for the issuing of definitive post mortem reports, so that death certificates could be issued. This last point has led to a major concern of the parents that there is a hospital cover up taking place. In this particular instance, the Coroner has been extremely patient and has leaned over backwards to protect the hospital. Professor van Velzen has written a letter to the Medical Director, Chief Executive and myself, explaining why there are no histopathology reports for post mortem.

GENERAL HOSPITAL HISTOPATHOLOGY

1. All clinicians state that the reports are extremely long, and one has to read a lot of detail before coming to a conclusion.

2. When the clinical problem (e.g. an inflamed appendix) is what they expect from a report, then the clinical conclusion is reliable, and they have no concerns about the accuracy of the histopathology. If there is a difficult clinical problem, however, the conclusion is not always clear, in that there is not always a definitive answer.

3. Two colleagues have commented that the opinion they have been told, on initial review of the material, has not been confirmed in the final written report. This has led to the incorrect management of cases.

4. One colleague said he was prepared to go and learn his own histopathology, in which he has not been trained, so that he can interpret his own slides. He has found that having taken the slides from Alder Hey for a second opinion elsewhere, he gets a definitive opinion rather than an inconclusive answer.

5. There are some complaints about the time taken to provide the definitive report, but these complaints are variable and not totally consistent.

6. There are complaints regarding the non-availability of a report during periods of the Professor's absence. These absences appear at times to be prolonged. Adequate cover is not always available at a weekend; this can lead to difficulty in initiating treatment.

7. One clinician when approached said that though the reports were very unreliable, and caused great concern on the Professor's arrival in Alder Hey, of more recent years he has found the reports reliable and he has no longer any concerns about his clinical competence, although this was questionable in the beginning.

8. There is real concern about the Professor's attitude to the development of Clinical Genetics....

9. [Concerning the secondment of monies to develop a service in molecular genetics.]

10. CARDIAC MORPHOLOGY

I made specific enquiries as to the question of problems associated with obtaining good quality cardiac morphology reports on children who die. I have been informed that it has now been established that the heart is taken out intact and is not interfered with and dissected before the specimen is received by the Specialist Cardiac Morphologist.

11. An independent and totally uninvolved source who knows nothing of this enquiry has commented that the quality of research is very dubious. I have not tried to verify this comment, but it might be worth getting this assessed formally.

12. A consistent comment made by many, was that Professor van Velzen often has good ideas and has enthusiasm, but when he embarks on a project he does not see it to conclusion, and has no follow through. His management decisions are perceived as erratic.'

3.2 The reader will notice the slant of this document in the light of Professor van Velzen's tactics. Some clinicians did have concerns about the accuracy of Professor van Velzen's reporting, others did not. Numbered points 1–7 in the main text of the report could not have amounted, on the quality of the evidence available then, to sufficient grounds for the disciplining of Professor van Velzen. The nub of the clinically important complaint, that could and should have led to the disciplining of Professor van Velzen, was lost in the second introductory paragraph.

3.3 Professor van Velzen's tactics did not dispose of the underlying complaints about delay and lack of post mortem histology, but his tactics did undermine Alder Hey's confidence in confronting him with those complaints.

3.4   Alder Hey's submission was upside down. The numbered points should have been the general points by way of introduction, giving flavour to the submission, and the serious complaints in the introduction should have been highlighted as the main numbered complaints. This document did not even challenge Professor van Velzen's version of events leading to the supposed suspension by management of post mortem histology.

3.5   It should be made plain that reference in paragraph 11 to the dubious quality of research is a general statement and not related to the cardiac research in the previous paragraph which was of high quality.

University Preparations for the Review

4.   Contribution of Professor Orme

4.1   Professor Orme set out a good deal of the history of the establishment of the Chair and the difficulties in obtaining a senior lecturer. He recorded but did not describe the disagreement between Professor van Velzen and Professor Heath. He also noted that Dr Chan had only been appointed at lecturer level, after a delay, and left early. He described the move of Dr Howard into the Department and the appointment of Dr Khine. He dealt briefly with service problems as follows,

> 'It is clear that there have been service problems in the Unit over the years and no doubt others will comment on this. There are letters on file dating back to early 1990 concerning this issue and on 27 March 1990 Professor van Velzen wrote to the then Vice Chancellor, Professor Graeme Davies, over the lack of support given to him for service work. The complaint was mainly directed to management at the Royal Liverpool Children's Hospital Alder Hey and to the Regional Health Authority. No further resource was available to the Unit as far as I am aware as a result of this complaint. Professor van Velzen made further attempts to fill the senior lecturer position but without success.'

4.2   Professor Orme described the difficulties that Professor van Velzen had, leading to his removal from the post of Clinical Director. He touched on Confocal Technologies Limited to say that he accepted Professor van Velzen's word that he had never received payment in a personal capacity for any work that he had done with the company.

4.3   Professor Orme dealt with the list of personnel dated 2 July 1992 which, as we have seen, exaggerated the numbers of people in the Department. Of that he said,

'It has to be said that there are other posts on that list where it is stated that an appointment was made through the University of Liverpool, and the staffing office of the University has no record of any such appointment being made. These are posts numbered 009, 018, 021, 022, 023, and 024.'

He concluded giving an account of his appraisal of Professor van Velzen,

'I took over the appraisal of Professor van Velzen following the breakdown in communications with his Head of Department. Clearly the details of that appraisal are confidential. However, I can say that one of the things I asked Professor van Velzen to concentrate on was his research output into peer-reviewed journals. Professor van Velzen will have submitted to you the research publications of the unit. At the time of his first appraisal by me in November 1991 there were very few publications but there has been a very considerable improvement since, with at least 10 research based publications in 1992 and more appear to be forthcoming in 1993. I was disappointed that Professor van Velzen went public to The Observer in February over his research findings prior to scientific publication but it was done with the consent of the journal editor concerned and both the Faculty of Medicine and the University were briefed.'

4.4 The contribution of Professor Orme was straightforward and balanced in the areas that it covered. However, its importance lies in what it left out. It did not reflect the trenchant views expressed without recorded dissent by the Working Party (see Part 4, paragraph 8.2 of 'The van Velzen Years'). It did not reveal the concerns and difficulties communicated to the Vice Chancellor and recorded in his note in February 1993 (see Part 4, paragraph 15.1 of 'The van Velzen Years'). Despite being aware of Professor van Velzen's tactical manoeuvres Professor Orme did not discuss them. Crucially, there was no suggestion that Professor van Velzen was not fulfilling his contract and providing the clinical sessions for Alder Hey.

5. Contribution of Professor Cooke

5.1 Professor Cooke was nominated to be a member of the Working Party in his position as Head of the ICH. He wrote on 20 May 1993,

'1. The initiative for the creation of the post of Professor in Fetal and Infant Pathology came from the Department of Child Health, although it was supported by the Department of Pathology. Until that time services in paediatric pathology were entirely provided by the NHS at Alder Hey and Liverpool Maternity Hospital. Although the Foundation for the Study of Infant Deaths were initially enthusiastic about creating a funded unit of fetal and infant pathology, they were advised strongly that staffing and facilities for paediatric pathology were grossly inadequate in Liverpool. They were nevertheless persuaded to go ahead with their support, partly I believe by the offer of the Department of Pathology to second a Senior Lecturer post to the Unit to improve manpower.

2. Professor van Velzen was appointed before I assumed the headship of the Department of Child Health, and I have always been unclear as to his relationship with this Department. His relationship with the Department of Pathology has similarly been vague, and this has enabled him to appear to head his own department in an independent manner, contributing to some extent to the development of the present problems.

3. Professor van Velzen has always expressed great enthusiasm for undergraduate teaching. Certainly occasional groups of students taken to his laboratory have found the experience stimulating. CPC's for the paediatric undergraduates proved rather tedious, and I allowed them to lapse. His post-graduate contributions tend to be rather longwinded slide shows with not a lot of planning to them and for the most part have not been popular.

4. Professor van Velzen enthusiastically adopted the 'market philosophy' of the recent NHS changes, and was initially welcomed by the management as a doctor with the right attitudes. He was given management training and became Director of Pathology Services, but soon took this too far by taking on veterinary pathology as an income-generating sideline. This was stopped and he was asked to resign. During this period, research output was very little as he was occupied by other things.

5. The research output of the Unit has been largely from Dr Howard and his research associates. I am unclear as to Professor van Velzen's contributions in this area.

6. As Chairman of the Grants and Scientific Advisory Committee of the Foundation for the Study of Infant Deaths, I am under considerable pressure to account for the large sum of money entrusted to Liverpool University to support this post and am keen that these matters are resolved speedily and satisfactorily.'

5.2   Given his position at FSID Professor Cooke's assessment of the research output, dealt with in three lines at paragraph 5 of the letter, could hardly have been more damning. Professor Neilson who chaired the Committee conceded as much when he gave oral evidence to the Inquiry. Professor Cooke did not deal with the clinical service in his letter.

5.3   By way of contrast, when asked by the incoming professor, Professor Foster, to express a view he said in a letter dated 9 March 1994,

'At present anyone doing the job reasonably will look better compared with what has gone before!'

6.   Contribution of Dr Burns

6.1   Dr Burns provided his contribution earlier – it was dated 1 April 1993. He spoke of the very poor research record over five years, but which may have recently blossomed. He referred to Professor van Velzen, not the University, having difficulty in filling the senior lecturer position and interpreted this difficulty as an indication of the Unit's poor academic standing. He described minimal teaching but to a high standard. There was grave concern that the Unit had made no contribution to the SIDS Symposium of the Royal College in 1992. He wondered if there was a conflict of interest with Confocal Technologies Limited. He called for much closer co-operation and mutual support between the main Department of Pathology and Professor van Velzen's Unit. He criticized what he called the 'outrageous situation' in which Professor van Velzen and another colleague, Dr Ian McDicken, were bidding against the main department to provide a histopathology service to the Women's Hospitals Trust. He concluded,

> 'We trust that the Working Party will find these comments of some use in its deliberations and we would state again, by way of emphasis, that it is the earnest wish of the senior staff of the Department of Pathology that the Unit of Fetal and Infant Pathology flourish and be recognized as a centre of true academic excellence.'

7.   Contribution of FSID

7.1   The FSID response was dated 28 May 1993. It was from Dr Shireen Chantler, Secretary to the Scientific Advisory Committee, of which Professor Cooke was the Chairman. Evidence provided on behalf of FSID to the Inquiry reveals that the contribution was sought at the very last moment. Whereas the University files reveal extensive correspondence in March and May asking for views and setting up arrangements, there is no letter seeking a contribution from FSID. There is only a telephone attendance note dated 27 May 1993 recording that Professor Neilson should telephone Dr Chantler that evening. She wrote the next day and set out the now well-known history. On the issues of the review this is all that was said,

> 'Professor van Velzen's commitment to, and support for, the Foundation has been exemplary. He served on the Scientific Advisory Committee, never failed to attend the Grant Holders Research Meetings, participated in the National Conferences for parents of his own volition, and assisted with the Appeals Department on many occasions.
>
> As far as research, his original findings have been published in peer review journals. Evidence of work from other centres is compatible with his findings.'

There was no more analysis than that.

8. Review Committee Meeting

8.1   The Review Committee met on 1 June 1993. Ms Bridgett, the Administrative Sub
        Dean, was the secretary for the meeting and took detailed notes. The Committee visited
        the Department but no comment appears within the notes, nor does anyone remember
        consideration of the huge number of specimen containers on racks and stacked in the
        reception area. After the tour, in which there was no examination of the laboratory day
        books, the meeting reconvened and heard evidence.

9. Evidence of Professor Orme and the Comments of Professor Cooke

9.1   Professor Orme gave evidence in line with his written submission. In the course of that
        evidence is the following note when discussing the senior lecturer post,

> 'There is a Hungarian with track record interested but – post now withdrawn –
> to make Chair of Pathology as attractive as possible.
> It is for this group to consider the importance of the Senior Lecturer post.'
> '…Cooke – FSID.
> At least superficial impression that things are going well, but more privately –
> there is some unhappiness. Letter from FSID – understanding of Foundation
> includes the secondment of Consultant.
> Cooke – it is also in the Job Description.
> FSID will NOT give more money.
> Delays in appointments – will last until October 1994.'

9.2   The evidence given by Professor Cooke ties in with the impression given by Professor
        Orme to the Vice-Chancellor in February 1993. The 'Hungarian with track record' was
        in fact Dr George Kokai, who was keen to come to Liverpool and would have come in
        1993 had the post been available. He was appointed in mid-1995, started in January
        1996 and is now an NHS consultant in Paediatric Pathology at Alder Hey.

10. Description of the Original Resources for the Chair

10.1   Professor Cooke is noted to have said the following,

> 'FSID sent a team to look at Alder Hey. It was horrified. Requirement for three
> full time equivalents for Alder Hey and Unit III.
> Withdrew a £¼m.
> Persuaded only on condition University put in some help. Alder Hey actually
> <u>lost</u> sessions.'

10.2 At numerous points in the discussions there were references to the inadequate resource both in terms of the overall number of clinical sessions available and the lack of consultant cover. Someone expressed a view that it was an injustice that Dr Chan had not been made a senior lecturer. While there was a perception that Professor van Velzen was an extremely strong personality and people might not wish to work with him, there was general agreement that the resources issue should have been considered far more carefully at the time of the creation of the Unit. Their view was that it was impossible for one man to do everything expected. Against this overall background of the failure to resource the Chair, it is easy to see how the Review Committee overlooked the shortcomings that might otherwise have forced a different result.

10.3 Professor Orme did not mention the discussion at the differently constituted Working Party which implied that Professor van Velzen was not fulfilling his clinical sessions. The strategic view that Professor van Velzen was a *millstone* and was *to be marginalized* at Alder Hey was not expressed.

11. Evidence of Professor Johnson

11.1 The present Dean of the Faculty, Professor Johnson, who was then in charge of the Faculty Research Strategy gave evidence after the Dean. Ms Bridgett noted that he found considerable difficulty in gaining information from Professor van Velzen that could withstand audit. It was clear that a substantial number of grants were not administered through the University. While a number of publications had just come out, the publication record was previously very poor. Professor Johnson observed that the Unit had not fallen into the University structure and that the finance office, staffing office, etc were not aware of what was going on. Even on the issue of research the discussion returned to the issue of lack of resources and personnel.

12. Professor 'Munchausen'

12.1 Towards the end of the note while Professor Johnson attended Ms Bridgett recorded,

> 'Johnson:- concerned re: funding – not being properly administered through the University.
> 'Professor Munchausen'.
> Burns: – recent Symposium – not invited? – van Velzen – not member of College........'

12.2 Professor Carty was able to assist the Inquiry with evidence as to the meaning of the nickname, although she as with all other witnesses who gave evidence did not remember the use of it at the meeting. Munchausen's Syndrome and Munchausen's Syndrome by Proxy are well known conditions. In Munchausen's Syndrome the sufferer inflicts injury on himself in order to seek attention, usually of the medical profession. In Munchausen's Syndrome by Proxy the sufferer inflicts damage on another, usually a child, again as a form of attention-seeking behaviour. Quite how the term was meant to apply to Professor van Velzen is unclear, but there is abundant evidence of attention-seeking behaviour in his correspondence and general *modus operandi*. Whatever was meant and how far the term was to be pressed, it was clearly not intended as a compliment.

13. Evidence of Dr Howard

13.1 Dr Howard gave relatively brief evidence and was supportive of Professor van Velzen as one would expect. That is not to say that it was inaccurate evidence. While there is evidence of friendship between Dr Howard and Professor van Velzen with scientific camaraderie, Dr Howard's evidence to the Committee was straightforward. One of Ms Bridgett's notes gives an important insight into Professor van Velzen's motivation in removing and retaining body parts. Speaking of what happened when Professor van Velzen arrived in Liverpool Dr Howard is noted to have said,

> 'van Velzen started collecting material which is priceless.'

14. Evidence of Professor van Velzen to the Committee

14.1 Professor van Velzen prepared a paper for the Committee that ran to about 100 pages. It was a reworking of earlier material, all of which has been covered in the earlier part of this account or will be covered elsewhere in the wider Report. His oral evidence compounded the deception. He presented a picture in which he himself was attending to substantial clinical duties. He repeated all his deceptions in terms of research staff supporting clinical work and regarding the suspension of post mortem histology.

15. Professor Carty's Contribution

15.1 Professor van Velzen's evidence went essentially unchallenged by Professor Carty according to the notes. Of course it had been Mr Butler and not Professor Carty who had dealt with Professor van Velzen over the previous years. It is less of a criticism of Professor Carty, a consultant radiologist and newly appointed clinical director, that she did not intervene than it is of the long-term inability of the management at Alder Hey to manage Professor van Velzen. The notes of Ms Bridgett reveal the following,

> 'Carty; post mortem histology.
> The hospital does not want to see the situation arise *again*. There *is no* routine post mortem histology service. Two particular problems recently; the Coroner would not issue death certificate until he had histology report. There was a long gap – several months.
> Shortage of staff.'

The above note reflects an uncertainty and a conflicting impression which has been emphasized. On the one hand there is the impression that the problem has been solved and there is a wish that it will not arise *again*. On the other, the next sentence uses the *present tense* and is explicit in the continuing absence of the routine post mortem histology service. What Professor Carty does not appear to have done is to state that the service had been lacking for the best part of five years. Apart from the lack of post mortem histology speaking for itself as a criticism of Professor van Velzen, no specific criticism of him on that score appears anywhere in the notes of the University Review.

16. Deterioration in Relations between Professors Heath and van Velzen

16.1 Ms Bridgett's notes record that Professor Cooke asked Professor van Velzen about his relationship with Professor Heath and why it had deteriorated. Professor Heath was stated to have been very enthusiastic for the new Chair initially. The notes then reveal the following explanation from Professor van Velzen,

> 'Heath began to feel more and more threatened. Distance from staff increased. Dominant style.
>
> VV – sent anonymous letter re Ph.D student.
> VV – approached Heath. Never heard from him again.
> Heath = v. ambivalent re that.
>
> Heath = felt v. threatened.'

Professor van Velzen told the Inquiry that the anonymous letter concerned a student and allegations that a thesis was being written for him by Professor Heath. He himself did not think the allegation particularly important but there is secondhand evidence before the Inquiry that lends it support. It is not a matter for us but for the appropriate University authorities. Nevertheless this is the only evidence available as to why Professor Heath failed in his 'line management' of Professor van Velzen, leaving him alone and, later, to the management of Professor Orme.

17. Review Committee Recommendations

17.1   The recommendations of the Review Committee were bland and lacking in teeth. Granted that there was no immediate prospect of any increased resources, this blandness was no doubt because of the view that it was impossible for Professor van Velzen to satisfy his commitments.

17.2   The Committee recommended that the senior lecturer post be returned. It recommended that an agreed job plan be drawn up between the Trust and University and that the University, preferably through the Head of Department of Pathology, should support and supervise more closely. In short, apart from agreeing with Professor van Velzen that he should have a senior lecturer, the Review came up with nothing and discovered nothing. This was despite the apparently wide terms of reference for the Review covering service, teaching and research and with a view to giving 'advice on the future of the unit'.

17.3   The reader will have noted the lengthy history suggesting why that result came about. However, final resolution of the issues raised by the University Review will have to await the development of another strand in the story to do with FSID (see Part 7, paragraphs 29–33 of 'The van Velzen Years').

The van Velzen Years: Part 6
July – December 1993

Political Concerns at the University, the Senior Lecturer's Post and Farewell
to Mr Butler

1. Mr Butler's Stand over the Senior Lecturer Post

1.1 On 5 July 1993 Mr Butler met with Professor Orme. They discussed a number of different matters but here is Mr Butler's note in relation to Professor van Velzen,

> 'Fetal and Infant Pathology
> Professor Orme reiterated the view of the University that they would not wish to put the promised money for the Senior Lecturer into Professor van Velzen's Department. He accepted that this was a breach of the agreement that had been reached in setting up the post and was not surprised at my line, which had been reinforced by Dr Carty, that we would take away the funding from Professor van Velzen's post and create an NHS post in Paediatric Pathology. I indicated I would write to him by the end of the week. The view of the University is that the greater priority is to put the Senior Lecturer money into the new Chair in Histopathology which was advertised this weekend. I indicated that if we went down the line of appointing an NHS Consultant Paediatric Pathologist, we were likely to separate out the Paediatric Pathology service from the Fetal and Infant Pathology service and move only the Paediatric one up to Alder Hey. That clearly would change the nature of Professor van Velzen's clinical sessions which would no longer be with the Royal Liverpool Children's Trust. I indicated that I would try and see Professor van Velzen before the end of the week, when I understood that he was to go on leave, to put him in the picture with regard to these moves.'

1.2 Mr Butler wrote to Professor Orme on the following day setting out in writing what they had discussed. In the letter Mr Butler identified the consequences of the University's continued failure to provide the senior lecturer,

> 'This is clearly a breach of the three-way agreement between the University, the NHS and the Foundation and leaves the NHS Service Provision, particularly the Children's Pathology Services at Alder Hey, severely undermined. I cannot accept that.'

1.3 Mr Butler said that he would take the matter to the Trust Board at the end of July. The letter was copied to the executive directors, the Chairman of the Board, Professor van Velzen and Professor Carty. Mr Butler presented his letter of 6 July 1993 before the Trust Board on 26 July 1993 and received its support.

2. Professor Orme Reports to the University Registrar

2.1   On the same day as he met Mr Butler, 5 July 1993, Professor Orme wrote to the University Registrar at the Senate House, Mr Michael Carr. He enclosed the report of the Review Committee and summarized it briefly. He explained that the recommendation of the Committee to restore the senior lecturer post to Professor van Velzen had been rejected by the Faculty Agenda Committee sitting as the Board of Faculty,

> 'The Committee felt that it was more important that the vacant senior lecturer position was kept available for the new holder of the George Holt Chair in Pathology. I accept that view and I am in discussion with the various parties to see what can be done to prevent too much damage.'

2.2   Professor Orme then went on to speculate about the potential damage and to consider damage limitation exercises. This echoed his briefing to the Vice-Chancellor as recorded in the note in February 1993,

> 'I can foresee two scenarios here. One is that Alder Hey Trust, where Professor van Velzen is unable to provide the full clinical service required, will not accept the recharge for his salary and will utilize the resource to make their own NHS appointment in Pathology. This would leave us having to pay van Velzen's salary. They would also move part of Professor van Velzen's unit up to Alder Hey (but not him) thereby breaking up the unit. I shall move to try to head off this eventuality by talking to Alder Hey Trust and the Region. The second scenario envisages the FSID suing the University for the return of part of the £250,000 since we have not kept our part of the bargain. I do not think this is a very likely position, but clearly do not want relationships to deteriorate with a major charity. Professor Cooke is closely involved with FSID and will keep me briefed.'

2.3   As with many other documents, this colourful passage speaks for itself. Professor Orme was dealing with an ever apparent conflict of interest, which was a legacy of the under-resourcing and lack of supervision of the Chair from the outset.

3. Meeting of 12 August 1993

3.1   On 12 August 1993 Mr Butler and Professor Orme met again. The note began,

> 'There is great dissatisfaction at Alder Hey over the service provided by Professor van Velzen and this is not just due to a shortage of consultant staff to provide the service. Professor van Velzen has apparently offended a number of managers at Alder Hey over some actions taken and letters written.'

Professor Orme then set out what he understood to be Alder Hey's position. There had evidently been discussion as to the type of appointment that was acceptable,

> 'In this case both scenarios mean that we will have to find the senior lecturer (clinical) salary and thus our move should be to offer Alder Hey a senior lecturer post. They would not accept a one-year (locum type) post but would accept a five year post.'

3.2   Professor Orme noted considerable concern at the lack of suitable candidates,

> 'Initial searches suggest one candidate only, a 'Yugoslavian' working in Hungary, who would not be acceptable to Alder Hey since he is a perinatal rather than a paediatric pathologist. To advertise and fail to appoint – a likely scenario – would waste time from the Alder Hey perspective.'

3.3   This was another reference to Dr Kokai. A year later Dr Kokai was a satisfactory candidate to Alder Hey. Perhaps there was a change of heart or Professor Orme was mistaken as to the acceptability of Dr Kokai. In early 1994, in correspondence with Professor Foster, Professor Carty questioned his experience in paediatric as against perinatal pathology, but certainly she did not rule him out. In the meantime Alder Hey was to search for a candidate itself on the footing that the department would be moved back to Alder Hey, leaving the fetal and neonatal work behind for Professor van Velzen. Professor Orme concluded,

> 'I think we should now make the offer of a five-year senior lecturer post.'

This is an odd way to close if a genuine intention to fill the five-year senior lecturer post already existed.

4.   Conversation of 16 August 1993

4.1   Mr Butler and Professor Orme spoke on 16 August 1993. Mr Butler recorded how matters were left. In the light of the University's attitude it was now Alder Hey's policy to appoint an NHS Consultant in Paediatric Pathology and move the Department up to Alder Hey. Mr Butler

> 'restated the position of the Royal Liverpool Children's NHS Trust in having as a major concern the provision of a high quality Paediatric Pathology Service.'

5.   The University Concedes

5.1   Professor Orme sent a copy of his note of 12 August 1993 to Mr Carr and set up a meeting with him and Professor Ritchie, Chairman of the Academic Committee. They met on 23 August 1993 and Mr Carr's note begins,

> 'Agreed that the University had little alternative but to make available to Alder Hey a five-year senior lecturer in Paediatric Pathology. This level of resource was assumed when Professor van Velzen's post was being considered and is now necessary if Alder Hey's requirements are to be met and indeed if disciplinary action is ever to be taken against van Velzen who would otherwise claim lack of resources as the explanation for the problems being experienced.'

5.2   So Professor Orme wrote to Mr Butler on 24 August 1993 offering a senior lecturer (clinical) in Fetal and Infant Pathology to be appointed for a five-year period. This was a special appointment and not the original senior lecturer's post, occupied for a short time by Dr Chan at lecturer status and taken back for the new George Holt Professor of Pathology. The offer was accepted by Mr Butler, despite his previous stated intentions to 'take the NHS route'. He continued to express the worry that the post might not be filled and he would be left paying for a professor without an adequate clinical service. He wanted to see an appointment before Christmas.

6.   Filling the Senior Lecturer Post with a Locum

6.1   The documentary evidence available gives an impression of the University's reluctance, even in 1993, to honour its original commitment, the breach of which it acknowledged but never really explained. In response to our requests the University provided details of the advertisements placed between 1988 and 1995. None of the documents before us shows any actual advertisement of the post in 1993, nor does the more recent evidence from the advertising agencies which reveals advertisements in other years. This is of interest, given the University's general reluctance to fill the post, to make the post again available for a five-year period and then, it seems, to advertise it. What happened next is unclear, but someone mentioned that Professor Kaschula, a well-known paediatric pathologist in South Africa, was looking to have a sabbatical for one year in the United Kingdom. Professor Orme had no difficulty in persuading the University authorities to authorize the filling of the new five-year senior lecturer post with a locum for 12 months. How the Trust was persuaded to accept this against both its interests and stated position is a mystery. It may be connected with the departure of Mr Butler towards the end of November 1993, following which the Medical Director, Dr Martin, was Acting

Chief Executive. Ms Rowland took up her post on or about 21 December 1993. By the time Ms Rowland arrived Professor Kaschula had already been appointed, although he had not yet taken up his post.

7. Audit

7.1 The combined NHS and University Audit was considered briefly earlier (see Part 4, paragraph 3 of 'The van Velzen Years'). Mr Crowley, the Chief Internal Auditor, and Mr Birrell agreed that matters were unsatisfactory. Mr Crowley suggested that it be signed off on the basis of various investigations to be carried out by the University. The situation was still far from satisfactory. Mr Birrell left in the autumn of 1993 and Mr Sharples began work soon after in December 1993 as Director of Finance at Alder Hey.

7.2 Various documents show that Mr Harris made some investigations himself in the autumn of 1993. He had originally been given the task of pursuing the audit for the Trust together with Mr Highcock on the part of the University. There are about 30 pages of papers including printouts of figures and handworked reckonings.

7.3 Mr Harris identified an interesting question. The figures themselves are not important for the purposes of this analysis but the trend is. There was a slight drop in the number of requests recorded in histopathology between the years 1991/92 and 1992/93. Yet total expenditure rose substantially, so the unit cost rose from £157.46 in the year 1991/92 to £196.54 in the year 1992/93. The first six months of the year 1993/94 revealed a unit cost of £173.13, still a substantial increase over 1991/92 and this at a time when unit costs in pathology were supposed to be dropping nationally, and savings were to be made. Differences in wages and recharging in the different years may have contributed to the result and perhaps the 1991/92 figures in the early days of the Trust were unreliable. However, Mr Harris asked 'why had there been the increase in unit cost?' but the papers do not reveal an answer. In evidence before us neither Mr Birrell nor Mr Sharples was able to give the answer.

8. The Lewis Audit

8.1 Mr Lewis delivered his audit in draft dated 29 September 1993. It formed no conclusion of any great weight on the financial side of the situation. There was no analysis of the primary source data, nor discussion of the increased unit cost question posed shortly afterwards by Mr Harris. The audit is only really of interest in relation to the following section,

'A number of Clinicians were interviewed to assess their degree of satisfaction with the pathology service they received. On the whole their comments were positive but some did identify concerns that had not been addressed, specifically:

- <u>All</u> considered the quality of service from Histology and Microbiology had deteriorated over the last two years through:

- Histology being based at Myrtle Street Hospital; and

- The introduction of 'academic' appointments whereby the departments' consultants are frequently away from the laboratory. Users considered the service involving technicians to be adequate. The Consultant service was severely criticized both in terms of timeliness and quality. The lack of consultants' access was considered a major issue by the users;'

How many times did this criticism have to be made?

9. The Pathology Directorate Response

9.1   The response was co-ordinated by Dr Isherwood as Head of the Department of Pathology. He collaborated with Professor van Velzen with regard to histopathology. Again, the response, a document of some 50 pages, is largely irrelevant for present purposes. It is of importance only in that it was yet another reminder of the lack of post mortem histology and the problems with Unit III,

> 'It is also important to note that two issues which could have improved perceived quality of the service, the provision of PM histology and the development of staff from the Unit III bid funds have similarly been delayed by the issues with respect to the University and lately the waiting for the outcome of this Review. Documents provided for Management on these issues have been resting at Management for almost one year. We are however sure that these will be addressed with great urgency now that these matters are coming to a conclusion.'

10. Re-establishment of Post Mortem Histology?

10.1   So how was post mortem histology re-established in the second half of 1993? In fact it was not re-established until after Professor van Velzen left and Dr Kokai took up his post in January 1996. On 6 July 1993 Professor Carty came away from the University

Review with some vague recommendations for a job plan and greater supervision. She wrote to Mr Butler with 'the way forward in pathology', which does not mention post mortem histology let alone its re-establishment.

11. Professor van Velzen Suggests the Answer

11.1   The re-establishment of post mortem histology was broached at a meeting of the Department of Fetal and Infant Pathology on 12 November 1993. Mr Peter Tallentire, the Director of Personnel, had some dealings with Professor van Velzen in the early years, and with the departure of Mr Birrell and Mr Butler it was his turn to deal with Professor van Velzen again. They met with Mr Meade and Mrs Jacqueline Waring, the successor to Mrs England as Chief MLSO, who began in the autumn of 1993. Mrs England became Service Manager in the Cardiac and Intensive Care Directorate at Alder Hey in May 1993. Mrs Waring was persuaded by Mrs England to move from Broadgreen Hospital to head the technical staff in the Myrtle Street laboratories.

11.2   At this meeting in November 1993 Professor van Velzen himself suggested the reinstatement of the service through the purchase of a Microtome machine for the mortuary and then training of the mortuary technicians in their idle time to block, stain and mount the specimens. This suggestion was minuted and a copy sent to Mr Butler and Dr Martin. Professor van Velzen followed up his suggestion with a letter to Mr Tallentire on 26 November 1993 which was also copied to Mr Butler and Dr Martin.

12. An Unrealistic Suggestion

12.1   The suggestion for re-establishment came to nothing, probably because it was an unrealistic suggestion and a ruse. In oral evidence Professor van Velzen maintained that it was a realistic proposition and that he had instituted such a system elsewhere. However, in the UK problems existed relating to the demarcation and skills of mortuary technicians.

12.2   Professor van Velzen maintained that the Alder Hey management were unwilling to overcome elementary health and safety difficulties in the mortuary. A short consideration of Professor van Velzen's clinical practices reveals that it was unlikely that he intended to change his practices to have the mortuary technicians mount specimens. It was his practice to take all organs in every case, keeping them intact and fixing them all before any analysis. He wanted whole organs for research. Even when he had manpower he had not carried out routine histology on post mortem specimens.

He seldom even opened organs at autopsy, let alone take sections for others to mount. At one stage Mr Dearlove and even Mrs England had begged him that if only he would take the blocks they would mount them and they could all catch up.

12.3   References to the proposal simply died away in 1994 and no other proposal was ever forthcoming.

13.   Irregular Applications for Research Grants

13.1   The autumn of 1993 saw a disagreement between Professor Lloyd and Professor van Velzen. Professor Lloyd was the Chairman of the Research Advisory Committee at Alder Hey. On 8 October 1993 he wrote to Professor van Velzen after his submission of a number of grant applications. In one Professor Lloyd described the signature as a forgery, the person had not seen the application before its submission and had not signed it themselves. In another application a doctor's name appeared amongst the list of applicants on the original application but she had not seen the document and the signature was not hers. In the final case an application had been sent without signature and was forwarded on to the doctor concerned. He also complained that he had never seen it before. Professor Lloyd concluded,

> 'I regard this behaviour as highly irregular and unprofessional. I am therefore not allowing applications from you … to be considered by the Research Advisory Committee until the matter has been discussed by the Trust Endowment Committee. I am also informing Mr P Butler by copy of this letter.
>
> Under the circumstances I think it would be inappropriate for you to continue to serve on the Research Advisory Committee, at least until this matter has been resolved.'

13.2   Professor van Velzen's initial response was to accept responsibility but minimise it. In characteristic fashion he then went on the attack in correspondence, maintaining that Professor Lloyd had a personal vendetta against him. He sought the intercession of the Dean, Professor Orme, but there is no documentary evidence of any reconciliation or intercession. All witnesses trivialised this episode in oral evidence at the Inquiry. Nevertheless, Professor Lloyd who appeared to us as a man of integrity and good judgement evidently thought the matter serious at the time. Indeed, he did take matters before the Committee and there is the following note,

'There was some discussion on the final minute *'Applications not Reviewed'*, which related to seven applications submitted by Professor D van Velzen. Professor Lloyd was extremely concerned about irregularities in these applications and Mr Davies had a brief chat to the Chief Executive and the Chairman about the issue, following which it was agreed that a two-year ban would be placed on Professor van Velzen making applications to the Research Advisory Committee for funding support. The possibility of routing future pathology funding bids via [Professor] Carty was discussed.'

This was a serious penalty indicating a serious irregularity.

14.   Conclusion: July–December 1993

14.1   Not only will readers be dismayed to have heard that there was no re-establishment of post mortem histology but no job plan as recommended by the University Review was ever agreed between the Trust and the University. Sadly, neither was there any more forceful supervision of Professor van Velzen and his activities.

The van Velzen Years: Part 7
1994

New Regimes at Alder Hey and University Lead to Realignment of Professor van Velzen's Clinical Duties and Effective Suspension from Alder Hey

1.   The Arrival of Ms Hilary Rowland – the Handover

1.1   Ms Hilary Rowland took up her post as the new Chief Executive on 21 December 1993. It would be some months into 1994 before the transition was complete and Ms Rowland had worked herself into her new post. Mr Butler had not left her with any formal briefing on pathology services, Professor van Velzen or the absence of post mortem histology. However, while neither she nor Mr Butler can remember any specific references to Professor van Velzen, they had discussions amounting to handover briefings. Ms Rowland had the benefit of Dr Martin, who had been Medical Director since the inception of the Trust, and Professor Carty, who had attended the University Review.

1.2   Ms Rowland did not complain to us that her briefing was inaccurate or inadequate in the sense that the evidence available to her predecessor was not available to her. For instance, she knew pretty quickly of Professor van Velzen's unreliable behaviour. His reputation as a 'maverick' was well established. It was obvious to all concerned that he was a University-appointed clinical professor, working in a unit remote from the hospital and as a sole consultant, with all the difficulties that entailed. Ms Rowland did not read all the correspondence files to see for herself the mounting complaints, the findings of the University Review and the important 'Re-establishment of

Histopathology …' Paper from March 1993. Nevertheless, she was shortly to receive the Business Plan for the Department of Pathology dated 3 February 1994 indicating that post mortem histology was 'to be introduced'.

1.3   None of the witnesses gave any detailed evidence either orally or in writing on the nature of the handover. However, the reader may feel it inconceivable that Professor Carty and Dr Martin did not share their concerns in the context of what follows.

2.   Professor van Velzen's Fabrication – 'a New Lease of Life'

2.1   Professor van Velzen was candid in oral evidence, explaining that he saw the arrival of Ms Rowland as an ideal opportunity for him to renew his propaganda battle. There were two issues in particular which interested him at this time. The first and main issue was the proposed move from Myrtle Street back to Alder Hey. Could he influence the new Chief Executive to change the plan? The second issue was the funding for Mr Eccles – the main point was to get Alder Hey to fund his salary so that soft monies could be released for other purposes.

3.   The Opening Gambit

3.1   One of the first items awaiting Ms Rowland in 1994 was a letter from Professor van Velzen dated 23 December 1993. In that letter he told the most blatant of his lies and redeveloped old themes. The lie was obvious from the outset to all concerned,

> 'Today I was informed in a meeting with 'an architect' external to the hospital organization, that, unknown to me and not previously discussed with me, a decision had been taken by 'management' that only 'the service component' of my Department (a fully integrated University/NHS Department) was to be considered for relocation to the Alder Hey site when the Myrtle Street facilities will be vacated.
>
> Clearly this decision pre-dates your appointment and I am therefore writing to you to explain the financial aspects of my Department.'

3.2   None of the existing management team could have been taken in by this fabrication and Ms Rowland asked for and received advice from them. Indirectly Professor Carty responded to the letter on 25 January 1994 rejecting the idea that Professor van Velzen had only just found out about the move,

'I am surprised at your statement that you have only just discovered the proposed move. I know that Pearse Butler has spoken to you on several occasions about the fact that, when histopathology moves from Myrtle Street back to Alder Hey, the accommodation that will be provided within Alder Hey is that suitable to providing proper histopathology services for the hospital. However, I equally know that, in any such move, the future of development of histopathology has to be considered to ensure that it does not cramp developments for you, any future Consultant colleagues, and the hospital in general. I have to say that I do not understand the diagram that you have provided to Hilary Rowland.'

3.3   Mr Butler had not only spoken to Professor van Velzen about the move but also written to him, not least in the letter of 3 July 1992 which led to the exaggerated list of personnel and the joint NHS/University audit (see Part 4, paragraph 1.1 of 'The van Velzen Years'). The reference to a diagram provided to Ms Rowland was to one included in the 23 December 1993 letter, which must have been copied by Ms Rowland to Professor Carty along with the executive directors, as endorsed by Ms Rowland on the letter. In the diagram Professor van Velzen perpetuated the myth that research-funded staff in fact subsidised the clinical care.

3.4   The diagram was somewhat obscure in its presentation but can be translated as follows,

	Proportion of funding provided	Proportion of activity enjoyed
Alder Hey	35%	85%
University Research	45%	10%
Unit III	20%	5%

3.4   The funding aspects of this table were further sub-divided. It was alleged that 90% of the equipment and 30% of the consumables were provided by the research side of the funding, with the balance of those items provided by Alder Hey funding. Professor van Velzen said that the Unit III work led to a £10,000 profit, which was an outrageous statement given the appalling service over the years. The main section of the letter concluded,

'As you will see it is not immediately clear how Alder Hey's interests will be served by such a division [of service and research components with a move back to Alder Hey] especially if one takes into account that the highly profitable contract with Unit III, which depends very much on this integration, will be due for renewal by April 1995.'

4.   Briefing from Mr Tallentire

4.1   Mr Tallentire prepared a briefing paper dated 10 January 1994 to inform the Executive Board on the transfer of histology from Myrtle Street to Alder Hey. It refers to the need for discussion when Ms Rowland returned on 17 January 1994. The paper was kept in neutral terms even though written by a personnel director responsible for transferring the services from one site to another. He envisaged asking Professor van Velzen to set out in writing how many staff he wanted to transfer and identify how much space he required. In this he echoed the ambitions of Mr Butler as early as July 1992. Mr Tallentire began his paper in his characteristic, low-key but plain-speaking fashion,

'For some time there was tension between Professor van Velzen and our former Chief Executive concerning the transfer of services. Pearse Butler had made it plain to all and sundry (but it seems that Professor van Velzen has only just learned about it) that the cost of moving the entire histology department to Alder Hey will be prohibitive and he therefore intended that only people engaged on NHS work would transfer. Professor van Velzen understandably takes the view that this would seriously damage the work of his department. (He at present has about 25 staff and Pearse reckoned only 5 of them were doing NHS work.)'

4.2   Mr Butler was about right as to the numbers and Professor van Velzen was lying as to his date of knowledge of the move.

5.   Demarcation of Service and Research – Mr Tallentire's Briefing Note Taken Up by Professor Carty

5.1   There was no record kept of any executive directors' meetings at Alder Hey under either Mr Butler or Ms Rowland. So there is no note to the effect that Professor van Velzen was discussed in January 1994, but he clearly was and the issue surrounding him aired. It seems unlikely that the specific problems regarding the absence of post mortem histology were presented to Ms Rowland with any force, if at all. It would be surprising if they had been, given the lack of interest shown by the management team up to then. This time the management team was not taken in by the broad thrust of Professor van Velzen's propaganda. Professor Carty, in her letter of 25 January 1994, rejected the idea of his late knowledge of the proposed move, expressed surprise at the assertion that the University owned 90% of the equipment and pointed out confusion in the funding arrangements for various staff members, in particular secretaries and Mr Eccles. She said,

'It is therefore, I believe, essential that the precise distribution of resource in your laboratory is now sorted out. The hospital cannot be expected to provide, on NHS premises, the facilities that you have acquired in Myrtle Street over the last few years. I have no idea what cross charging is made to the University for the use of these premises. I have already had correspondence with you over the Photography Unit and I am awaiting the information from the Finance Department as to precisely what has and hasn't been paid for....

...You have my total support in introducing developments that are pertinent and relevant to our patients. Beyond that, however, if there is to be a move of what is clearly purely University-based activity in laboratory research, then I believe that the hospital requires an appropriate cross charge from the University for whatever use of facilities is made on this account.... I will, therefore, ask Henry Meade to provide the inventory of equipment, which I believe he has, and we can then establish the ownership as appropriate. I would also ask him to give an estimate of space requirements for laboratory work, technical staff, and the accommodation of two consultants, a registrar and two research fellows.'

The last sentence shows that some thought was being given to the size of a potential department at Alder Hey, which would include some element of paediatric research but leave the fetal and perinatal research behind at Myrtle Street. As to the idea of cross-charging or a contribution from the University, Professor Orme conceded in oral questioning that there was never any real chance of that from the University's perspective.

6.   Continued 'Workload Laundering'

6.1   While it is clear that the management at Alder Hey had some appreciation of Professor van Velzen's fabrication, its extent and detail was still beyond them. The workload laundering jointly undertaken by Professor van Velzen and Mrs England carried on into 1994 when the new Chief MLSO, Mrs Waring, took over. On 12 January 1994 she wrote to Mr Tallentire to support the case for the NHS funding of Mr Eccles. She presented the following figures,

CASES	1992	1993	INCREASE
Routine	2,595 (Blocks 3842)	3,339 (Blocks 6241)	29% (62%)
Special Stains	199	323	62%
Immuno-cytochemistry	1,005	1,821	81%
Electron Microscopy	82	110	34%

6.2   Even now it is not clear from where Mrs Waring obtained these figures. The laboratory day book reveals 2,396 booked requests in 1992 which include all the categories set out in the table. Once post mortem histology, research specimens, double-booking of fetus and placentae, examination of old Alder Hey biopsies, research samples and general double entries have been excluded, the actual number of booked requests for surgical biopsy is only 1,676. A similar exercise in 1993 reduces the laboratory day book total of 3,411 to 2,427.

6.3   The letter itself is supposedly written by Mrs Waring and goes so far as to say in the opening paragraph,

> 'Whilst I am aware of your communications with Professor van Velzen regarding the post presently held by Paul Eccles, I felt I must express independently my concern for the potential consequences of the loss of this post.'

In fact the wording of the letter is almost certainly that of Professor van Velzen, as Mrs Waring reluctantly conceded. She did not allege that her signature at the foot of the letter had been forged or that she provided the statistics unwillingly. The letter also included a laboratory work rota for the months January to March 1994 which made false claims for the staffing of the various aspects of clinical work.

6.4   Mr Dearlove was the mainstay of the clinical work but did not carry out flow cytometry. The January and February 1994 rota supposedly had him carrying out such a technique on Tuesdays and Thursdays. The rota included technicians' time on Monday and Thursday afternoons for resin work on bone marrow trephines, yet Professor van Velzen wrote to Mr Tallentire on 10 May 1994 saying that only one research student was then able to prepare the sections and her presence was required to train the technicians.

7. 'This Does Not Add Up in the Normal Commerce of Things'

7.1 More than anyone else up to now Professor Carty was beginning to see the problem with Professor van Velzen, if not seeing through the detail. On 15 February 1994 she wrote to him expressing succinctly what appears to have eluded others,

> 'I find it difficult to accept that people who are funded by research money should spend 90% of their time on patient care. This does not add up in the normal commerce of things.'

7.2 At this point the evidence of Mr Sharples, the successor to Mr Birrell as Financial Director, completes the likely picture. He spoke of taking over and reviewing the work done by his predecessors. He described the previous exercise as 'messy and inconclusive'. He said,

> 'As it was the plans to move the service element from Myrtle Street ultimately went ahead and were achieved successfully. My task was therefore to support that original plan rather than to go in and undertake another similar exercise to try to establish the service/University split. It was in that context that Helen Carty had written to me on 23 March 1994 querying the specific funding of Paul Eccles' salary and the division between service and University work. I think that ideally she wanted another audit, but based on the prevailing plan of action at the time I felt it justifiable to do as I did and simply support the plan to move the service component.'

7.3 There are numerous references to matters of audit in the letters of Professor Carty in early 1994. Time after time previous half-hearted attempts at audit came to nothing. Why was no effective audit now carried out? The role of the clinical director was ill-defined. The training and support available in the early 1990s for newly appointed clinical directors were rudimentary.

7.4 Professor Carty had her own department to run and patients to investigate as well as real responsibilities as Clinical Director for Support Services. She had at last confirmed the suspicions so that vigorous and methodical audit by others should have revealed the detailed falsification. It appears, however, that she did not have the support to carry it through. Indeed, while the Alder Hey witnesses did not agree, there is a strong impression that the Trust management had seen the Professor van Velzen problem as insuperable given the 'University dimension', and the handling strategy was by now well established. The strategy was to move the department come what may and as a by-product of that move the ills in the department would be cured. This was a good medium-to-long-term policy but it ignored the deficiencies of the service in the interim. This strategy also ignored the potential for a maverick professor continuing undiscovered and unprofessional practices.

7.5   There is no evidence up to this point that anyone in management outside the
       Department of Pathology knew of the practice of organ retention, other than
       Mrs England, who had moved up to Alder Hey as a Service Manager. Nevertheless the
       medium-to-long-term plan to manage by simply moving the Department, without short-
       term scrutiny, permitted the unprofessional practice of organ retention to continue.

7.6   Only incompetence, whether through lack of training in management or otherwise,
       can explain the failure to re-establish post mortem histology or even to appear to take
       the matter seriously, unless such a handling strategy played a part. In reality, both
       incompetence and such a policy appear to have contributed.

8.   Ms Rowland Visits the Myrtle Street Laboratories

8.1   When Ms Rowland received the letter from Professor van Velzen dated 23 December
       1993 she endorsed the top of the letter asking her secretary to arrange for her to visit
       Professor van Velzen and his staff at Myrtle Street. The visit took place on 22 March
       1994 but only Ms Rowland and Professor van Velzen remember it. Mrs Waring,
       Mr Dearlove and Mr Eccles cannot be right in thinking that they must all individually
       have been absent on that day. Mrs England had refused to relocate the mounting store
       of containers into the basement at Myrtle Street, but when Mrs Waring arrived in the
       autumn of 1993 she had agreed to Professor van Velzen's suggestion to do so. The vast
       majority of containers were in the basement when Ms Rowland visited. There is no
       evidence that her tour included access to the basement, neither is there evidence that
       her visit made any real difference to the train of events.

9.   Alder Hey Takes the Coroner's Opinion on the Legal Status of Tissue Retained After Coroner's Post Mortem Examinations

9.1   In the spring and early summer of 1994 Alder Hey corresponded with the Coroner.
       Mrs Clark, previously Professor van Velzen's personal secretary but now working in
       the Legal Department, wrote to Mr Barter, HM Coroner, on 9 May 1994,

       'Re: Human Tissue removed during Coroner's post mortem examinations

       We understand that under the terms of the Act relating to the use of human
       tissue, it is stated that the patient retains legal ownership of any tissue removed
       at operation and signed consent of the patient (or the parent(s)/legal guardian in
       the case of children) has to be obtained before any such tissue can be used for
       research purposes.

We are now trying to clarify the position with regard to post mortem tissue. We fully understand that where you feel it necessary to order a post mortem examination, there is no requirement for the consent of the next of kin to be obtained, and that you have authority to order whatever histological/analytical examinations necessary to establish the cause of death. However, we should be grateful if you could give a definitive ruling on the legal ownership of such tissue once the post mortem examination and all subsequent tests have been completed. Do you retain authority for its disposal (or otherwise) at your discretion or, in law, does this revert back to the next of kin of the deceased?

Usually this tissue is ultimately disposed of by the hospital where the patient was treated or by the pathologist who performed the post mortem examination. We have not experienced any problems in the past over this issue, but the potential is always there, and for this reason we are anxious to establish the correct position in this respect.

The position is more straightforward in the case of hospital post mortem examinations, as signed consent from the next of kin for the removal and examination of tissue is a pre-requisite in these cases.

Your assistance in clarifying this matter would be very much appreciated.'

The letter speaks for itself and its relevance to this Inquiry is obvious. There is, however, no reference to whole or multiple retention of organs within it.

9.2   On 13 June 1994 Mr Barter replied to Mrs Clark,

> 'Re: Human Tissue removed during Coroner's post mortem examinations
>
> ...As you correctly say, when I order a post mortem examination my Pathologist has permission to remove for histological examination any organs or tissue necessary to establish the cause of death.
>
> I do not know a definitive answer to the question raised in your letter. The right to possession of a dead body is vested in either the deceased's Executor, if he has left a Will, or in the person entitled to apply for Letters of Administration. It is often necessary for a Pathologist to retain possession of tissue samples etc for some time after the autopsy, either because they may be needed for further examination or because some person properly interested in the death wishes to have his own examination carried out. Having said that, I think that any tissue which remains after all necessary examinations have been carried out belongs to the person entitled to possession of the body. In over 25 years' experience, I have never had a legal representative ask for the return of such material, and I cannot visualise any circumstances in which it would be likely.'

9.3   Mrs Clark at first maintained that she had simply written to the Coroner without prompting. It is true to say that the correspondence occurred at a time when Alder Hey was also considering the legal status of tissue excised in the course of surgery. However, while the minutes of the Board of Clinical Directors reveal open discussion of the other issue, no record of discussion or link with correspondence concerning the status of tissue following a Coroner's post mortem examination exists. Under detailed questioning Mrs Clark conceded that she is likely to have had an instruction to write the letter from someone in senior management whom she cannot now remember. She did not allege any instructions from the Board of Clinical Directors. She does not remember to whom she passed the response or upon which file it was placed.

10.   Concerns About 'Utilisation of Stored Tissue' and 'Potential Pitfalls for the Hospital'

10.1   On 31 May 1994 Professor Carty dictated a letter to Professor van Velzen which was later dated 13 June 1994, the same day as the reply of the Coroner to Mrs Clark. It was a lengthy letter following a recent meeting when they had discussed a number of issues – the letter was intended as a summary of the meeting. At point 7 of the letter Professor Carty wrote,

> '**Storage of tissue**. You indicated to me some concerns about the utilisation of stored tissue and the potential pitfalls for the hospital. You indicated that you would write a short paper outlining the problem for me so that again, this could be brought to the Board of Clinical Directors. I thanked you for bringing this to my attention and said I would further it at the Clinical Director Board.'

10.2   Professor Carty appears never to have received the promised paper despite at least two reminders in the second half of 1994. Again, on the face of it, this paragraph reveals matters of vital importance to this Inquiry. Professor Carty denied that the paragraph referred to the organs stored at Myrtle Street. She explained that the reference was to loss of tumour material stored in a low temperature refrigerator, an issue dealt with by her at point 2 of her letter, two pages earlier,

> '**–70° centigrade Fridge.** I discussed with you the letters of complaint that I had received following the incident with the Fridge. You indicated to me that the loss of tissue was not as great as I had been led to believe. You indicated that there is now a new fridge present which has appropriate alarm systems on it and that a repetitive incident will not occur. I said to you that I would respond to Dr McDowell and ask her if she was satisfied with the new arrangements.'

The *storage* of tissue and its *loss* in Professor Carty's explanation are not easily to be equated with the *utilisation* of tissue and its *pitfalls*.

11. The New George Holt Professor of Pathology

11.1   Dr Christopher Foster, Senior Lecturer and Consultant in Histopathology at the Royal Postgraduate Medical School, London, was appointed Professor of Pathology at the University of Liverpool and Clinical Director of Pathology at the Royal Liverpool and Broadgreen Hospitals NHS Trust in October 1993. He had carried out a preliminary investigation of the task in Liverpool before putting himself forward for interview.

11.2   Following his interview and appointment, although not taking up his post until the summer of 1994, he began to make more thorough investigations into what was required to modernise pathology services in Liverpool and to improve the academic output of the University Department. In late 1993 and early 1994 he had meetings with all interested parties including Professor van Velzen. He determined to form his own view of him and not to be ruled by others' opinions, but he had been told enough to realise that he would have to make a critical decision. He either had to harness him effectively or else somehow let him go.

12. The Carty-Foster Discussions – Alder Hey's Hopes

12.1   Professor Foster had discussions with Professor Carty following which she spoke to her colleagues at Alder Hey. On 23 February 1994 she wrote to Professor Foster about future requirements. She wrote,

> 'The ideal for Alder Hey is currently, and has to remain, the retention of full pathology services on site, excepting that there has to be co-operation between the Units locally for any more unusual investigations across all branches of pathology. This would include unusual techniques which, we believe, should be done where the best service can be offered. It may be that for some of these techniques it is appropriate for machinery and equipment available in the Children's Trust to be used throughout for services elsewhere. This is simply a broad general statement and does not, in any way, relate to specifics.
>
> My concern about your proposal to do the processing of specimens in a general laboratory in the Royal is that it would leave the pathologist(s) in Alder Hey in a difficult situation….. I would find it difficult to see how this could take part at remote distance as a routine, although I accept that, for specialist techniques, this has to be the way forward….

We also feel that this is important to the future as none of us knows how long the present Professor will be around and, should we wish to revert to an NHS laboratory in the future, then it is obviously important that such facilities are available to an appointee. I am sure that you understand the position given the background to our problems.'

Professor Carty went on to discuss a potential candidate known to Professor Foster, who was in fact Dr Kokai. Professor Carty had concerns that his CV was loaded towards perinatal rather than the paediatric work Alder Hey needed. She did not rule out Dr Kokai and who had impressed her when they met, but she was going to see how things worked out with the locum consultant Professor Kaschula and if he might stay beyond 12 months. She concluded her letter,

'I would like to meet with you sometime in the near future on one of your visits to Liverpool to discuss ways forward and, indeed, to discuss the hospital's concerns about Professor van Velzen.'

13. Professor Foster's Overview of Paediatric and Perinatal Pathology

13.1   The sentiments expressed by Professor Carty in her letter to Professor Foster were straightforward and difficult to criticise. She and Professor Foster did meet in the following weeks and, over the dinner table, she explained her concerns to Professor Foster. He thought it was an inappropriate time and method to convey the strength of critical feeling towards Professor van Velzen at Alder Hey. He could not dismiss it or consider it 'hard evidence' on which he could act. On 2 April 1994 Professor Foster wrote to Professor Orme with a summary of his views on paediatric and perinatal pathology,

'Following my recent meetings with Dick van Velzen and with Rock Kaschula, I am now able to give you a full assessment of the status of Paediatric/Perinatal Pathology.

First, I believe that Dick van Velzen (for all his shortcomings) is as much sinned against as he is a sinner. I do not think that he should be 'written off' and I am prepared to support him as a member of my department. However, there are problems – and I believe that these must be addressed and resolved. Not least of these problems is the prejudice and bias against Dick – so that he will always be perceived as a sinner – no matter what he does, particularly by Helen Carty and her like.

Two senior pathologists, together with one Senior Registrar in training are required to fulfil all the diagnostic requirements of Paediatric/Perinatal pathology in Liverpool and provide a good service to the clinicians. This is the view of myself and Rock Kaschula. As I intimated earlier, one pathologist working full time would be able to manage the current Perinatal workload (fetal and infant autopsies) and a small amount of the Paediatric surgical biopsies, although the majority of the latter would be performed in the main Pathology department. If only one senior pathologist remained at Alder Hey, very few of the placentas could be examined and there would be no time for research.

There are two problems at Alder Hey. Only one is Dick van Velzen in that he is not and never will be a main-line diagnostic morphological pathologist. Nevertheless, he is an important member of the group at Alder Hey and I consider him to be an asset rather than a detriment to the Department of Pathology. There is no doubt that his flair and enthusiasm will be beneficial in generating research grant funding and in providing additional 'drive' for research within this Department.

You will note from the letters sent separately to you, concerning the availability of specimens at Alder Hey, that it has been necessary for me to discipline Dick. There is no doubt that he responds to being addressed directly and in a manner by which he is not perceived to lose face. I propose to support and to involve Dick, and his entourage, in the organisation of the reorganised Department of Pathology and to give him both responsibility and a framework within which to operate.

The second problem is the provision of suitable manpower for the Paediatric/Perinatal pathology service. I suggested to Rock Kaschula, as we discussed, that he might let us know by August 1 whether he wanted to remain in the UK permanently. He agreed, but thought it unlikely. I suggest, therefore, that we go ahead in appointing George Kokai to replace Rock Kaschula from October/November. We should also consider funding and appointing another consultant-grade staff member from around the same time – possibly with a remit to participate in some of the adult Pathology. To assume that Dick van Velzen will simply change his working habits and take-on a major piece of the Paediatric/Perinatal pathology as the second pathologist would be erroneous and simply perpetuate the problems that have evolved thus far.

I talked for a long time with Helen Carty the other evening. She is a very intransigent lady who appears to be running a personal vendetta against Dick van Velzen. I cannot and will not allow any member of my department to be singled-out and pilloried. As the Head of Dick's department I will discipline him if and when I consider it necessary – not the member of another department in a different institution. I trust that you will support me as I take this approach.

On our next meeting, I suggest that we agree a clear strategy for finally resolving the problem of the poisoned chalice left to the University by Professors Harris and Emery. Reading the history of the Chair of Fetal Medicine/Pathology, it was the fault of the University that Dick was appointed. His suitability was questioned at the time – and ignored. Now we must accept the consequences and appoint the appropriate person to perform the required service – before Helen Carty and a small band of paediatricians take the initiative.'

14. The 'Poisoned Chalice' and 'Vendetta'

14.1 There are a number of crucial ingredients to Professor Foster's analysis. There was clearly a shortage of suitable permanent clinical manpower, only temporarily overcome in 1994 because Professor van Velzen and Professor Kaschula were available as the two senior pathologists, and Dr Khine was the Senior Registrar. Professor Foster wanted to appoint Dr Kokai right away, but the post was not advertised until 20 October 1994.

14.2 The overall problem amounted to a *poisoned chalice* left to the University by Professors Harris and Emery, relating to both the lack of resource, and that 'it was the fault of the University that Dick was appointed.' Professor Foster accepted that an appropriate person needed to be appointed to perform the required service at Alder Hey. He disliked the high feelings expressed by Professor Carty and a small band of paediatricians. She had long experience of Professor van Velzen although she did not appreciate how serious the situation was. Professor Foster considered Professor van Velzen an asset to the Department of Pathology and an important member of the group at Alder Hey despite not being a mainstream diagnostic morphological pathologist. For all Professor van Velzen's shortcomings he had been sinned against.

15. No 'Vendetta' but a Fairly Broadly Felt View Against Professor van Velzen

15.1 On 14 April 1994 Professor Orme replied,

'I agree with most of your thoughts about Dick van Velzen; he has certainly been sinned against, but nevertheless is *persona non grata* at Alder Hey. I agree with you that his role in paediatric/perinatal pathology should be supported and that he should not be the 'front man' for pathology at Alder Hey. We shall need to support him when Alder Hey move to take the unit back from Myrtle Street to the main site. It will always be unacceptable to us to move back only the NHS paid staff.

I would disagree with you about Helen Carty; any vendetta at Alder Hey is a fairly broadly felt view and the previous Chief Executive was pretty vitriolic about Dick! Helen is undoubtedly a lady with clear views on the world but I would not call her intransigent! She can be very flexible on occasion but here she is speaking from personal experience. I would say that she is one of the very few NHS Consultants who have a credible academic track record. Also I think we need to be a little careful over who disciplines staff over clinical service issues. If a University academic transgresses over a service issue they are responsible to the Clinical Director and thence to the Chief Executive over that issue. You and I are however more than interested bystanders!'

15.2   There are a number of crucial factors to bear in mind in the above paragraphs.

Firstly, the attitude at Alder Hey was not simply a vendetta on the part of Professor Carty as perceived by Professor Foster – it was a broadly felt view. Mr Butler's memory, of trusting Professor van Velzen and taking him at face value, does not match his vitriolic attitude of the time or our assessment of the personalities involved and the evidence of Mr Tallentire. He described Mr Butler's trust in Professor van Velzen as beginning at about 6/10 and dropping quickly to 0–1/10 on a sliding scale.

Secondly, the University's attitude to the proposed move from Myrtle Street back to Alder Hey remained, as late as April 1994, that it will always be unacceptable to us to move back only the NHS paid staff. Mr Butler was disappointed to realise, in giving evidence to the Inquiry, the serious University opposition to the move.

Thirdly, while Professor Orme corrected Professor Foster's view on the issue of discipline, he recognised the practical reality of joint responsibility for clinical academic staff. The theoretical line of responsibility from Clinical Director up to Chief Executive was correctly stated. However, the University was more than an interested bystander.

15.3   In his written statement to us Professor Orme accepted the University's equal moral responsibility for the service provision of Professor van Velzen and some moral responsibility for clinical academics generally, despite the Trust's primary responsibility under the honorary consultant contract. When questioned about all of the matters set out relating to him here he had difficulty in reconciling that statement with his actions. The conclusion is that the University did not behave at all times with the Trust and patients in mind. Professor Foster, Head of the University Department of Pathology, was to state as much in strong terms in a letter to the Vice Chancellor in November 1995 (see Part 8, paragraph 35.2 of 'The van Velzen Years'). In practice Professor Orme placed much greater emphasis on the political and practical considerations at the University than on patient care at Alder Hey. The terrible legacy he had inherited, not of his own making, placed him in a position of thorny conflict. We heard evidence from just one other Dean of Medicine, but Professor Orme's behaviour is probably not unusual. We will make a recommendation covering the close relationship that should exist between Universities and Trusts to help avoid a repetition.

16. Subtle Opposition to the Move Back to Alder Hey

16.1   An example of the way the University attempted to influence Alder Hey's decision to move back the clinical element from Myrtle Street is evident in Professor Orme's letter to Ms Rowland dated 9 May 1994,

> 'When we last met we were discussing, among other things, the potential move of the pathology laboratory back from Myrtle Street onto the Alder Hey complex. I thought it would be useful if I talked to you about this. I am of course aware of the sensibilities around Professor van Velzen but I think the pathology service has improved following the arrival of Dr Kaschula.
>
> The point I should wish to make is that there is a lot in the pathology world that is at the interface between pure service and pure research. It is very difficult in a university pathology laboratory, whether it is haematology or histopathology to separate the two aspects and both contribute to each other. This was one of the main things looked at in Southampton in the attempt to disaggregate 'Knock for Knock'. Some tests are pure service, and some work is pure research; but much of the work done in a pathology laboratory is a mixture of the two and this is greatly to the advantage of patient care as well of course to research.
>
> Thus, when the time comes to move the histopathology laboratory from its present site in Myrtle Street, the quality of service offered will be much enhanced if the research aspects can move as well.
>
> Nearer the time we will need to discuss the details and there may be advantages in placing some of the facilities in the Department of Pathology in the Duncan Building here. I only want at this stage to establish the principle that in a university department clinical service and research go very much hand in hand.'

These sentiments were a more subtle version of those of Professor van Velzen himself.

16.2   Ms Rowland replied on 24 May 1994 thanking Professor Orme, accepting the complex interface between pure service and pure research but maintaining the move back to Alder Hey. She accepted the need to provide some research facilities to accommodate research relevant to a children's hospital, that is to say the paediatric research component as against the fetal and perinatal component. She believed what was at issue was a matter of scale not principle.

17. A Cast-Iron Opportunity to Discipline Missed

17.1   1994 saw the complaint of one particular family following the death of their son in late 1993. The complaint is dealt with fully in Chapter 4 (case of Christopher) and passing reference only will be made here. Professor van Velzen not only went well beyond the limited form of consent obtained from the parents, for a biopsy of lung tissue through a small chest incision, but he also then lied about what had happened. Ms Rowland set up an investigation but failed to expose Professor van Velzen's nonsensical explanation. There was clear evidence to justify serious disciplinary proceedings on the score of fabrication, and in addition the original offence of exceeding the consent at post mortem examination went unpunished. Dr Martin was to have been included as Medical Director in the investigation of the complaint but nothing from him exists in writing. He cannot now even remember the boy who was his patient. This was a cast-iron opportunity to discipline Professor van Velzen, who had damned himself in his own letters. He could not conceivably explain matters away. If the reason for the failure to discipline was not through incompetence or cover-up on the part of management, then this episode must be seen in the context of a medium-to-long-term handling strategy dealing with Professor van Velzen simply through the relocation of his department, ignoring existing difficulties and irregularities.

18. Clinical Practice in 1994

18.1   Clinical practice continued in the same way as before. Professor van Velzen himself was doing little or no clinical work. However, there were fewer clinicians' complaints because of the presence of Professor Kaschula. Virtually all organs continued to be taken in every case. Professor Kaschula followed the van Velzen protocol, as had his predecessor Dr Chan and as did his colleague Dr Khine. However, he did carry out routine post mortem histology, providing 33 final post mortem reports in 1994. Professor Kaschula confirmed he would leave at the end of his one-year locum and it was clear that his appointment had simply delayed the inevitable need for reorganisation by 12 months and there was no-one to replace him.

19. Alder Hey Evidence to Professor Dyson

19.1   It was a coincidence that in 1994 an audit of pathology services across Merseyside was carried out. Professor Dyson and a team from Keele University carried out the task. Each hospital in the Merseyside area completed questionnaires providing workload statistics. Various visits and interviews were arranged. A final report covering the whole of Merseyside reported its findings but with anonymity for the relevant hospitals and departments preserved. However, each hospital had a confidential report of its own. Mr Meade answered the questionnaire on 24 August 1994 based on 2,456 Körner Units. The Department of Fetal and Infant Pathology issued a commentary to be read in conjunction with the questionnaire. It will not take any imagination now, knowing how Professor van Velzen operated, to realise what was said. For instance, as to the overall number of Körner Units,

> 'The Körner units relate strictly to Körner units provided to Alder Hey. The service is largely funded by service to non-Alder Hey clients. The present data suggests that the total expenditure on the Department is related to 2456 Körner Units suggesting a very high cost per unit. In fact the Unit services 4000 Körner Units per annum, approximately 10% of which are related to research. It is important to appreciate however that those units produce a considerable amount of funding that pays for a Senior Registrar, an MLSO 2 Full time and an MLSO 2 part time (0.4 WTE). Thus this is a legitimate denominator in analysing [and] interpreting the subsequent information.'

The commentary is a long tedious document, the minute detail of which is unimportant. It was yet another example of the 'van Velzen *modus operandi*'.

20. Dyson Reports – 'Startling' Findings at Alder Hey

20.1 The Dyson Reports were delivered in draft in October 1994 and not well received in Merseyside. Their merits and demerits as a whole do not concern us but even based upon the limited information provided with all the spin that Professor van Velzen could muster, Professor Dyson concluded of histopathology at Alder Hey,

> 'The organization, funding and cross-charging arrangements within the histopathology department are so labyrinthine as to make it impossible within the scope of this exercise to reach firm conclusions about productivity and efficiency. Nevertheless, the figures as supplied in the statistics in Table 1 raise serious questions that the Trust should address.

6.1 Workload and Productivity

Medical productivity in terms of reports per WTE at 2,020 is the lowest in the Region (3,540 is the second lowest) and is the lowest of any teaching or other hospital in the consultant's database. The calculations are based upon the Royal College of Pathologists' approved assumption that one WTE senior registrar would report 50% of the work of a consultant. The Alder Hey workload implies that each consultant would average eight reports per working day, or nine reports per working day allowing for holidays and normal study leave. Whilst it is recognized that this includes autopsies the total workload across the year is somewhat less than what the Trust Board could be entitled to expect.

The position for MLSO staff within the department is even more startling. If the workload is divided between the MLSOs alone it produces a figure of only three prepared requests per MLSO per day for each working day. This again is so far away from the experience of teaching hospitals in the database as to constitute a legitimate question for the Trust Board to consider. As with haematology this workload should be checked confidentially with another children's hospital to examine the most relevant possible comparisons. Even given the extreme difficulty of working with the tiniest of anatomical specimens this would appear to be a generous allocation of staffing. Another way of presenting this information is to say that after allowing for the small amount of emergency work done at Alder Hey in histopathology there will be only 15 specimens a day arriving in the department.

6.2 Non-pay costs

At £25.89 non-pay costs are higher than the second highest department in the Region by a factor of 10! No teaching hospital in this consultant's database has a higher average cost than £4.63. The variations are so gross as to be unbelievable and this leads to the one firm conclusion for the Trust Board in histopathology.

- **The Trust Board should establish an internal review of the histopathological department with a view to identifying the total workload of the department and the proportion which is service workload as opposed to University or private workload; the total funding of the department in order to isolate the service, University and private funding so as to align the different sections of work and its funding, and should also attempt to establish the grounds for the pay and non-pay costs currently experienced in the department. The private comparison with another teaching hospital recommended elsewhere in this Report will be a part of this exercise.**

In fairness and in mitigation to the head of department it has been argued that if research and consultancy funding coming into the department justifies the staffing employed and the salaries paid, the question of their specific productivity should not be at issue i.e. that without the additional funding the position may be worse because by implication there is a cross-subsidy to NHS work. The reason for the uncertainty in the figures in histopathology is because the author of this Report is still not clear whether they represent a mixture. If they represent purely NHS staff and costs, a closer examination of this expense seems highly justified. If they represent a mixture, it seems appropriate that the Trust Board should attempt some clarification in order to undertake a true assessment of the costs of their NHS workload.'

The emphasis appeared in the original text.

20.2   The 'labyrinthine' organisation has been demonstrated throughout this narrative. Leaving aside medical productivity based upon the consultant's database in the first paragraph of 6.1, as the Alder Hey management did not have access to that database by way of comparison, the startling finding of Professor Dyson is clear. Also leaving aside the lack of comparative evidence available to Alder Hey management in relation to non-pay costs at 6.2, the workload revealed the reality of Professor van Velzen's spin over the year. Dividing this workload between the MLSOs alone produced a figure of only three prepared requests per MLSO per working day. Professor Dyson achieved this taking the higher 'laundered' workload figure of 4,040 requests and leaving out the MLA contribution on the fetal and perinatal work. If true clinical figures are used, the work rate drops to about two prepared requests per working day for each MLSO.

20.3   The Dyson Report concluded that the Trust Board should establish an internal review of the Department to identify the total workload and the proportion relating to service provision as against University or private provision.

20.4   How often had that been attempted half-heartedly in the past without success? The quality of the previous audit methods did not warrant the use of the word audit. In the context of this Inquiry audit simply means a common sense approach to checking if irregularities or problems exist and following the trail of suspicion until they are clearly identified. Yet during audits no-one appears to have examined the source documents, all was taken on trust despite ample grounds for mistrust, much was never followed up at all, let alone the trail of suspicion followed to a resolution. If Professor Dyson could do it on the basis of misleading information in a questionnaire, Alder Hey and the University could and should have done it much earlier.

21.   Disciplinary Procedures Explored

21.1   In the autumn and early winter of 1994 the management at Alder Hey took the decision to relocate the relevant or paediatric elements of the Myrtle Street laboratory back to the Alder Hey site when the lease expired in the autumn of 1995.

21.2   At about the same time, on 3 November 1994, Mr Tallentire produced a confidential memorandum for Ms Rowland in which he set out the result of his investigations into the options for disciplining Professor van Velzen. Even at this late stage the memo shows that Alder Hey did not believe Professor van Velzen's shortcomings amounted to gross misconduct or clinical incompetence. Full disciplinary proceedings might have taken 12 to 18 months. Mr Neil Lewis, Senior Assistant Registrar at the University, suggested an alternative method would be to terminate Professor van Velzen's honorary contract at Alder Hey. Mr Tallentire explained that the honorary contract was valid for so long as Professor van Velzen held the Chair. This final point is important when we see what happened in December 1994. Mr Tallentire's memorandum is now set out,

'Following our meeting this morning, I have spoken to Mr Neil Lewis, senior assistant registrar at the University of Liverpool. I have asked him for a copy of Professor van Velzen's contract and he said he would be reluctant to let me have sight of his particular contract, but he would be happy to send me a blank Professor's contract.

He asked why, and I set out some of the difficulties that we had. He said that Professor van Velzen and his ways of doing things are known to himself, and indeed to Chris Foster and Michael Orme.

It seems that Dick has a permanent contract with the University – they do not have tenure any more since the Education Act of 1988 – and termination of permanent contracts is now possible following a Section 37 procedure. This procedure has never been exercised at the University of Liverpool.

I explained that Dick's shortcomings were not of a tangible sort, i.e. gross misconduct or clinical incompetence, and he had some understanding and sympathy with that because they have experienced similar problems from him at the University. He pointed out that terminating his contract was the same as terminating anybody else's who has a permanent contract i.e. it is a tortuous, long and difficult procedure. It normally has to start, as you know, with informal counselling, moving on to a more formal arrangement in which possible outcomes need to be spelt out and terminating with a recommendation from Chris Foster and Michael Orme to the Vice Chancellor that termination is necessary. The Vice Chancellor would then appoint a committee to consider this recommendation and in fullness of time might act.

He suggested that an alternative back door method would be to terminate his honorary contract with us. I explained I had already looked at that and the opening sentence of his honorary contract says '*it is valid while he holds the chair in fetal and infant pathology*', so I think it would create a lot of noise if we were to try and do it that way. It is true to say though that if we did terminate his honorary contract, then he would be unable to carry out his duties here and the University might then be able to terminate his contract by hiding behind us as it were. Before we would terminate his honorary contract we would have to follow the usual procedure – albeit without Section 37 – that the University would need to follow to terminate his permanent contract. In short it can be done but it will take time, a lot of management effort and a great attention to detail. It needs to start off with a letter recalling past '*misdemeanours*' and set out future expectations and standards and to refer to appraisal/monitoring frequencies.

We are probably looking at a 12 – 18 month procedure.'

22. Alder Hey States its Position to the University

22.1   Ms Rowland wrote to Professor Foster on 29 November 1994 following a meeting between them and Dr Martin and Professor Carty. Clearly matters were beginning to come to a head. Ms Rowland wrote,

> 'i) It will be important to clarify Prof. Van Velzen's role. I think we are all agreed that he is currently spread too thinly and that this clearly needs addressing.
>
> ii) There was considerable support for your proposals of a Senior Lecturer who would be responsible for the provision of on-site advice here in addition to the routine reporting which it was strongly felt should be done at Alder Hey. We look forward to seeing the job description when you have cleared the lines from your end.
>
> iii) The notion of centralizing histopathology processing is supported given our current circumstances. However, this would need to be complemented by a small on-site laboratory facility at Alder Hey and for on-site reporting. The sensitive management of the Trust staff will be crucial in this. It will be important that we co-ordinate our information and timing etc.
>
> iv) It was agreed you would be speaking with representatives of the Women's Hospital Trust regarding their future histopathology needs.

v) The future of the laboratory at Myrtle Street needs to be agreed; our intention is to vacate the premises and hand back the lease.

vi) Clearly all of the moves are dependent on a competitive price and a quality service being delivered. The costs should be exclusive of medical 'on-costs' because of previous funding agreements.

vii) We agreed that we would share the idea with the Board of Clinical Directors this week and that they would then have an opportunity to discuss the proposals in more detail with you (and Michael Orme) at 5.00 p.m. on Monday, 5 December at the Medical Institute.'

23. Checkmate at Alder Hey

23.1 Minutes of the various meetings of clinical directors, executive directors and Trust Board in December 1994 do not reveal what happened next. Shortly before Christmas Ms Rowland and Professor Carty met again with Professor Foster and Professor Orme, hoping for a resolution but far from certain of one. They were surprised as well as pleased when Professor Foster outlined his proposals to solve the problem. The plan fell short of terminating Professor van Velzen's honorary contract at Alder Hey but that was its effect. Professor Foster exploited skilfully what had been the University's weakness, devising a detailed job plan for Professor van Velzen and using the lack of clinical resources argument to advantage. Acknowledging that Professor van Velzen could not do all the work alone, he effectively removed from him responsibility for carrying out the work at Alder Hey, letting him concentrate on the fetal and perinatal work together with his research. Professor Foster would then take responsibility for supervising Dr Khine. She would carry the main clinical diagnostic workload for Alder Hey, with support from the Royal Liverpool University Hospital, until a new senior lecturer could be recruited who would concentrate in the first instance not on research but on providing a service for Alder Hey. The proposal met with easy agreement.

24. Reaction of Professor van Velzen

24.1 Professor van Velzen met with Professor Foster and Professor Orme on 21 December 1994. The documents show the date clearly enough although Professor van Velzen has heightened the drama of this meeting by stressing that it occurred on Christmas Eve. He was taken by surprise and in the aftermath of that meeting he made a political mistake.

24.2   Instead of reacting as the Vice Chancellor's note of February 1993 had suggested
(see Part 4, paragraph 15 of 'The van Velzen Years'), working the press and claiming
constructive dismissal, he went on unauthorised leave from Alder Hey and the
University, losing the initiative for the first time. Although Professor Foster had decided
to reorganise his duties so as to exclude him effectively from Alder Hey, Professor van
Velzen had not alienated Professor Foster up to now. His behaviour breached his
contract at the University and gave Professor Foster 'live' ammunition to fire in 1995.
Professor van Velzen's account that he simply took holidays owing to him, as he had
threatened previously if there was no-one to take over when Professor Kaschula left,
is unsupported by contemporaneous documentary evidence.

24.3   In early 1995 Professor van Velzen busied himself finding an alternative position across
the Atlantic.

25.   Contrasting Expectations of Professor Foster

25.1   Why did the University now accept what it had opposed for so long? It had worked
against the move of the Department back from Myrtle Street to Alder Hey. The
conclusions of one of the Working Party meetings in late 1992 had been to marginalise
Professor van Velzen at Alder Hey, describing him as a 'millstone' for the University.
Professor Foster's solution effectively 'marginalised' him at the University and not
Alder Hey.

25.2   In oral evidence Professor Foster appreciated that this was all a high risk strategy.
He fully anticipated, indeed expected, Professor van Velzen to make 'noise' to use
Mr Tallentire's word, in the local and national press, with FSID and in the national and
international academic community. He expected that the University would be attacked
for failing to provide resources in line with the original agreement with FSID. The
decision to suspend Professor van Velzen from his Alder Hey clinical contract was
likely to cause the fuss Professor Orme had wanted to avoid. Whatever Professor van
Velzen's previous attitude he had no will left to fight without clinical support and
decided to look elsewhere.

26.   Motivation in December 1994

26.1   All major witnesses who gave oral evidence were questioned as to why it was that the
decision effectively to suspend was taken in December 1994 rather than in 1993 at the
time of the University Review. Professor Cooke admitted that there had been no real
change other than Professor Foster's appearance on the scene. The service provision

to Alder Hey and to the Women's Hospitals Trust had not deteriorated – it was generally better while Professor Kaschula was in Liverpool. The research output was no worse at the end of 1994 than in mid-1993. Various strands were now coming together and there had been more work published (although we now know the results of the SIDS research were fundamentally flawed (see Part 9, paragraphs 9 and 10 of 'The van Velzen Years'). 1994 had been a 'quiet year' for Professor van Velzen. In the 18 months that had elapsed, the vacuum caused by the retirement of Professor Heath and his previous indifference had been filled and Professor Kaschula had left without a replacement organised.

27. Professor Foster's Motivation

27.1 Professor Foster came to accept the general grumbles of Professor Carty and Alder Hey but he did not base his decision on Professor van Velzen's failure to provide post mortem histology. He was not aware of the evidence at the University Review. He told the Inquiry that Professor Carty did not make specific mention to him of the absence of post mortem histology prior to 1995. Professor Foster was unequivocal in his criticism when he did find out. He maintained that had he known of the lack of post mortem histology when making his preparations in early 1994, it would have provided him with the 'hard' evidence he needed for a definitive action plan for Professor van Velzen. Professor Foster's evidence was forthright and credible on this point – it is likely that, far from playing any political game in late 1994, he was simply trying to marshal the clinical resources effectively, a task long overdue.

28. University Motivation Generally

28.1 So what motivated the University to accept what had been the 'unthinkable'? It was no less vulnerable to criticism over failure to provide resources. We have no evidence of dissent from Professor Orme, or elsewhere within the University, when Professor Foster devised his plan. The FSID funding for Professor van Velzen had run out completely in the autumn of 1994 and this must have been an important factor.

28.2 We now return to a strand of evidence concerning the University Review and FSID alluded to in Part 5 paragraph 17.3 of 'The van Velzen Years'. It is based entirely upon FSID's own contemporaneous records. Readers will note the facts and identities of those concerned against the composition of the University Review Committee set out in Part 4, paragraph 18 of 'The van Velzen Years'. In particular Professor Orme was briefed by Professor Cooke and was in a position to tell the Vice Chancellor what was FSID's hope for future research in February 1993.

29. FSID Research Funding

29.1 FSID was founded in the early 1970s. It had a number of committees integrating its lay, scientific and clinical membership. Professor Emery served on the Scientific Advisory Committee (SAC) between 1971 and 1988. Professor Peter Pharoah is the Professor of Epidemiology at the University of Liverpool in the Department of Public Health. He served on the SAC between 1980 and 1988. Professor Emery and Professor Pharoah retired from the SAC in 1988 and Professor van Velzen then became a member and remained one until 1995.

29.2 In tandem with the SAC, FSID operated a Grant Review Panel (GRP). Professor Pharoah was a member of the GRP while on the SAC between 1980 and 1988, during the time when the initial grant was made to the University to establish the Chair of Fetal and Infant Pathology.

29.3 In 1992 Professor Cooke, Head of the ICH, became a member of the GRP and in 1993 he joined the SAC as well. He enjoyed rapid advancement and in June 1993 he became Chairman of both bodies and a member of the Council of Management. In 1992 Professor Pharoah also rejoined the GRP.

30. Scientific Advisory Committee and Grant Review Panel to Make Recommendations for Research Expenditure

30.1 On 26 May 1993 the SAC met. As a result of impressive fundraising efforts in the 21st year of FSID's existence, funds were exceptionally high and the Council of Management wanted recommendations for research utilisation. The SAC minutes reveal the following on the above date,

> 'Research Strategy
>
> There was complete agreement on the need for further research and extensive discussion on priority areas for research, the range of funding opportunities and the preferred approach to implementation. The major recommendations are summarised below:
>
> • The strategic plan shall include an appropriate mix of reactive and proactive approaches with defined new initiatives to stimulate interactive research, widen research interest and awareness of issues.
>
> • Submitted research proposals should remain a core activity.
>
> • Good epidemiological research was necessary:

- in relation to infant death, prevalence of and response to infection, regional differences, urban conglomerates, social and cultural issues, nutrition;

- to clarify the contribution of antenatal factors;

- to establish the postnatal effects of smoking, nutrition (breast feeding), and house pollution.

- Early developmental physiology was essential and should be directed towards:

  - comparative pathophysiology of delayed development, instability of systems and their interaction;

  - defective physiology and control mechanisms;

  - mechanisms of interaction between extrinsic and intrinsic factors;

  - early development of mother/child interaction;

  - mechanism of smoking effects.

- Monitor changes in pathological findings with change in incidence.

- Establish/expand database on cot death research.

Funding options

In addition to normal project grants a range of funding options were considered at length. There was some support for establishing a chair in epidemiology of infant deaths but there were some concerns about limiting options at this stage. Priority recommendations were agreed as follows:

Cot death research unit – £500,000 over 5 years to assist in the establishment of an academic unit, (an essential component of which would be epidemiology), for which tenders would be invited. It was considered essential that the proposed unit should have the scope to undertake multidisciplinary research with a clear programme of interactive research focused on the causes and prevention of deaths in infancy. Funding would incorporate a 2-tier system of core and flexible funding, the latter being conditional upon approval of projects. It is anticipated that substantial support will be available from the host institution and the establishment of a chair within the bid would be particularly welcomed. Draft advertisement and further details will be compiled shortly....'

30.2 The SAC and GRP produced a report for the Council of Management Meeting on 30 September 1993. The report identified strategic objectives,

'Despite the recent welcome decline in cot deaths the Scientific Advisory Committee concluded that there was still an essential need for research. This should remain broadly based but with greater emphasis in areas outlined below.

- Further epidemiological research into deaths in infancy was a high priority particularly in relation to infection, social and cultural issues, the contribution of antenatal factors, effects in pregnancy and postnatal smoking, and changes in risk factor profile following the reduce the risk campaign.

- Continuing research into early developmental physiology and pathology was essential and should be directed towards comparative pathophysiology of delayed development before and after birth, instability and the interaction between known risk factors and regulatory mechanisms.'

As to the options for implementation that section ended,

'After considerable discussion it was felt that current research needs would be most effectively achieved by a combination of:

1. The allocation of substantial funds to a major venture which would focus the research effort on essential multidisciplinary research, involving scientists and clinicians.

2. A programme of invited proposals for specific research. This is being actively considered and will be the subject of a further proposal in due course.'

30.3   The proposals were accepted by the Council of Management and the £500,000 put out for competitive tender. The multidisciplinary approach and the importance of epidemiological factors remained part and parcel of the initiative.

31.   The Liverpool Bid

31.1   Professor Pharoah resigned his position on the GRP in January 1994 in order to make a bid but Professor Cooke remained on the Council of Management and Chairman of the SAC and GRP.

31.2   The University made an application for the grant and compiled a Mission Statement which was revised in the light of comments from FSID. While the application was headed by Professor Pharoah as Professor of Epidemiology it was supported by a multidisciplinary team in collaboration. The collaboration was set out within the Mission Statement as follows,

'Collaborating Centres

Department of Public Health, University of Liverpool
Head of Department: Professor POD Pharoah

Department of Fetal and Infant Pathology (DOFIP), University of Liverpool and NHS Departments of Fetal, Perinatal and Paediatric Pathology, RLCH, Alder Hey NHS Trust and Liverpool Gynaecological and Obstetrical Services Trust, Liverpool.
Head of Department: Professor van Velzen

Department of Obstetrics and Gynaecology, University of Liverpool
Head of Department: Professor J Neilson
      Professor C Gosden (Medical Genetics)
      Mr I McFadyen, Senior Lecturer
      Ms A Garden, Senior Lecturer
      Mr S Walkinshaw, Senior Lecturer

Department of Child Health, University of Liverpool
Institute of Child Health, Alder Hey Children's Hospital, Liverpool
Head of Department: Professor RWI Cooke
      Dr M Weindling, Reader
      Dr S Ryan, Senior Lecturer
      Dr J Hawdon, Lecturer

Departments of:

Child and Adolescent Psychiatry:	Professor J Hill
Medical Microbiology, University of Liverpool:	Professor CA Hart
Clinical Immunology, University of Liverpool:	Professor P Johnson
Ophthalmology:	Professor I Grierson
Clinical Radiology, University of Liverpool:	Professor G Whitehouse
Health Services Research Unit:	Professor M Pearson
Mersey Regional CESDI Office	
Mersey Regional Headquarters, Pall Mall Liverpool'	

31.3 In the original application the University sought to obtain and utilise the full potential of an award of £500,000.

32. Liverpool and Bristol Bids Successful

32.1   FSID consideration of the award recognised,

> 'a substantial part of the award at Liverpool would directly or indirectly support pathology which undermines the original intention of the pump priming award.'

32.2   However, the Liverpool bid was judged worthy of sharing an enlarged award of £600,000 with Bristol University. The University of Liverpool, under the directorship of Professor Pharoah, was to receive £250,000,

> 'The proposal from Liverpool had a broader focus with emphasis on infant vulnerability in respect to care and health. The strength in Liverpool was epidemiology with links with paediatric pathology, (already established with FSID funding), microbiology and genetics. The major emphasis was on factors contributing to intrauterine growth retardation and premature birth and their influence on vulnerability.'

32.3   Professor Pharoah was notified of the award in a letter dated 8 August 1994. FSID drafted a press release dated 2 September 1994, to be released on 9 September 1994 and on that date the award was announced to the world.

33. University Review Revisited

32.1   Casting back to the composition of the University Review Committee in 1993 (see Part 4, paragraph 18 of 'The van Velzen Years') the reader will note that key members of that Committee were part of the collaboration in 1994 to obtain the further substantial grant from FSID. The well-being of Professor van Velzen and his Unit of Fetal and Infant Pathology was vital to the bid and to the University's credibility with FSID.

32.2   The timing of the Review, when Professor Cooke and through him Professor Orme knew of FSID's plans, and the decision to let Professor van Velzen go after the bid had succeeded have caused us to investigate at length a potential link with the outcome of the University Review. Professor van Velzen, essential to the interdisciplinary bid, survived only to be cast off when the bid was over and the money secured. Did the prospect of the money influence the result of the Review?

33.3   After persistent and thorough questioning there is no evidence that members of the Committee, other than Professor Cooke, knew of the potential for a bid when the Committee met. The outcome of the Review is much better explained in terms of Professor van Velzen's fabrication, his long-term *modus operandi* and the mistakes already made at Alder Hey and at the University. We have not shirked our responsibility to investigate all matters before us. In retrospect it now appears to us as not entirely surprising that members of a Review Committee, who would need to be close to the discipline concerned, should later be close to a bid in which that very same discipline was an integral part. It has been an unhappy coincidence and an uncomfortable one for those who had to face detailed questioning in retrospect. Nevertheless we see here again the conflict of interest that characterised the University's position throughout the van Velzen years and which will become even more obvious in the correspondence with FSID in 1995 (see Part 8, paragraphs 6–8 of 'The van Velzen Years').

33.4 Incidentally, FSID has nothing but praise for Professor Pharoah and the collaboration in the absence of Professor van Velzen.

The van Velzen Years: Part 8
1995

The Organs at Myrtle Street, Research Materials and the Departure of Professor van Velzen

1.   Loss of the Research Operation and its 'Physical Assets' – No Immediate Threat

1.1   We may only speculate whether Professor van Velzen was away from Liverpool for the whole of January and February 1995, or present for part of the time trying to manoeuvre himself into a better position, but he did not do any clinical work. Having run out of people to mislead at Alder Hey and within the Faculty of Medicine at the University, Professor van Velzen attempted to generate some interest and sympathy. He wrote to Dr Hewitson on the University Committee for Outside Grants and Contracts on 3 January 1995. Again he lied about his surprise at losing his 'asset base (i.e. the independently managed laboratory facility at Myrtle Street)'. He highlighted the 'organisational changes' imposed on the 'Department' on the day before Christmas. Dr Sibbons and Dr Howard were co-signatories to this letter and they attempted to scare the wider University beyond the Faculty of Medicine that they would not be able to comply with obligations on externally funded research projects. Dr Hewitson passed the letter to the Registrar, Mr Carr, who replied on his behalf on 18 January 1995. The Faculty of Medicine had briefed Mr Carr properly and Professor van Velzen failed to drive a wedge between it and Dr Hewitson's Committee. Mr Carr wrote,

> 'I can confirm that there is no immediate threat to your research operation and no immediate loss to the physical assets, which support that research. In the light of this and in accordance with the arrangements outlined in Professor Foster's letter, the University expects that you will be able to meet all relevant commitments.'

This attempt to generate a lever failed from the outset.

2.   The True Position in Perinatal Pathology

2.1   Professor van Velzen was now supposed to be concentrating on the perinatal and fetal service work. Alder Hey had no intention of resubmitting its tender for that work when it expired but in the meantime was still formally responsible for it through Professor van Velzen. It was their contract. Professor Carty set about obtaining information as to the true state of affairs. On 2 February 1995 Professor Neilson wrote summarising his concerns following their conversation. Those concerns related to perinatal pathology services in the recent past. There were three broad areas of concern,

> '1.   Autopsy Reports. These are taking a long time to return. I think I am correct in saying that the original contractual arrangements were that the preliminary autopsy report would be available within a week and we all accept that there may be aspects of the histological examination of various tissues which may take very much longer than this. However, as I understand it, the current situation is that all of my colleagues find that it takes about 6–7 weeks for the reports to be returned. Very frequently, when we see parents back for counselling 6 weeks after the death of the baby, we are obliged to phone up the secretary in the Unit of Fetal and Paediatric Pathology to try and get the report sent across. I am also aware that Dr Olive Frost, who has responsibility for arranging our perinatal mortality meetings likewise spends a lot of time prompting secretaries in the Unit to send out reports. This is the most important service provided by the Pathology Service, and … very clearly [needs] … improving.
>
> 2.   Placenta Pathology Reports. I have already written on this subject. Both in December 1994 and this month (January) I have received reports relating to women who delivered in June and July 1994, enough said!

3. Interaction at Meetings. I refer here to what I see as the vital necessity for a perinatal pathologist to be present at our monthly perinatal mortality meeting. The individual should be able to speak with authority about his/her subject, and have slides to illustrate important points from autopsy examinations on babies who have died and whose deaths are being discussed at that particular meeting. The situation was better last year with the presence of Dr Kaschula, but the visual aids were not present. I see this as a critically important part of the fetal pathology service.

    I hope that there will be substantial improvements in this service in due course.'

2.2   The letter stands as a summary of the service in 1994 and fairly represents the best level of service over the van Velzen years. While Professor Neilson had been a newcomer in 1993 when invited to chair the University Review Committee and unable to bring personal experience to bear, in 1995 he did his best to assist Alder Hey in getting to the bottom of what had happened.

3.   Definitive Job Plan for Professor van Velzen

3.1   Meanwhile Professor Foster was also interested in the Women's Hospitals Trust work as everyone looked to him to ensure the service after the December 1994 reshuffle. Dr Khine could not cope with the whole workload when Professor van Velzen took unofficial leave of absence. When Professor van Velzen returned to Liverpool, Professor Foster wrote to him with a new formal job plan. He dealt specifically with the past misdemeanour of taking extended leave without permission and then continued,

    'Re: Clinical Diagnostic Commitment Liverpool Women's NHS Trust

    …Of greater concern to me is provision of the Fetal and Neonatal Diagnostic pathology service to the Liverpool Women's Hospital NHS Trust as defined in my letter of 22 December 1994 (copy enclosed). The expected service includes a full fetal and perinatal autopsy service, analysis of placentae and performance of sudden infant death autopsies, together with the organization of regular clinico-pathological meetings with the relevant clinicians at the Liverpool Women's Hospital NHS Trust.

    With respect to this service, I understand that there are some 29 fetal and infant autopsies presently outstanding, as of 06.02.95, and some 81 placentae outstanding as of 13.02.95. The individual cases are identified on the accompanying photocopied pages. Since your diagnostic remit has, for the present time, been restricted to the Fetal, Perinatal and SIDS work, I am asking you to concentrate on clearing this backlog by Friday, 19 April – thus giving you just over six weeks (excluding leave-time around Easter).

With respect to the current daily workload continuing to arrive at the laboratory, I anticipate that you will be able to comply with the terms and conditions of the contract already existing for Unit III work. I refer to Section A1b, (page 7) of the contract (written by yourself and by Mrs K. England) which states: "Examinations. Within 3 working days of the arrival of the remains at the laboratory", also (page 7): "Fully comprehensive, developmentally-oriented, histopathological examination of all organs is carried out in all fetus. Full neuropathological examination, macroscopical and microscopical is an integral part of the service." And (page 8) provision of: "A comprehensive, standardized report, inclusive of histopathological and neuropathological findings, listing of all congenital anomalies and structural abnormalities will be delivered within 2 weeks of the receipt of the specimen." (Copies of the contract enclosed).

In terms of fulfilling the contractual obligations of the service contract with the Liverpool Women's Hospital, Alder Hey and other NHS Trusts, such as the Countess of Chester, it is imperative that reports on autopsies and on placentae are issued within the specified times so that parents of developmentally abnormal babies can be counselled appropriately – and know that they are being cared for, as they might expect. Some recent delays have been potentially disastrous for the involved Trusts – for example, the brain on baby … was not reported for 7 months, there was no report on baby … when the mother presented for counselling – and then became pregnant without the relevant autopsy report being available. There have been significant delays on several placentae – for example that on … who delivered on 19 July 1994 and the report was issued only 6 December. I could continue.'

3.2   The importance of the letter, quoted at some length, is not to show what in fact would happen in 1995. The reader can guess that Professor van Velzen would not comply. Nor is it to illustrate past complaints, though it does so admirably. The point of the quotation is to show the contrasting approaches of Professor Foster and previous managers. This is the result that should have been the culmination of the University Review. Here is what Mr Tallentire had advised Ms Rowland should be done in November 1994, recalling past misdemeanours and setting out in clear terms what was required for the future. Much has been made in evidence of the different culture in the NHS and in the early days of Trusts compared with today. However, whether one uses modern jargon such as 'job plan', good management is the same the world over and goes back as long as employment has existed. If someone is failing in their work they are to be corrected and, if not corrected, accommodated in an alternative position or dismissed.

3.3   Before moving on to the main themes of 1995, it is convenient to pick up a couple of smaller points to illustrate previous issues.

4. Financial Audit – £68,000 Deficit

4.1 Professor Orme met with Mr Sandwich, the University Director of Finance, at the Senate House on 9 January 1995.

4.2 Accounts under the control of Professor van Velzen were found to have accumulated deficits of £68,000. There were small accounts yet to be considered and ongoing bills, such as telephone, to add to that figure. It was later suggested that the deficit resulted largely from the provision of the clinical service of Alder Hey, which was far from accurate. Alder Hey had in fact subsidised the research work in terms of technician time and 'consumables'. Professor Foster was later to insist on a full, detailed audit but it was impossible because various accounts had been lost and, perhaps, never existed in the first place. How a deficit of £68,000 could have been allowed in the light of all the warnings and previous attempts at audit is beyond explanation. In addition to the accumulated deficit Professor van Velzen had taken delivery of a reconditioned electron microscope at a cost of £14,000. The sum of £11,000, payable in October 1994, remained unpaid and the balance was due in April 1995. Evidently Professor van Velzen had purchased the microscope on the basis that the University would pay for the capital cost and Alder Hey would contribute to the maintenance costs. There is no record of authorisation at either Alder Hey or the University.

4.3 The above matters were discussed at the meeting on 9 January 1995. With the benefit of hindsight enjoyed by this Inquiry, it seems likely that the above irregularities are the tip of the iceberg. Following the meeting, Professor van Velzen's authorisation for further expenditure was frozen and, as far as possible, even his staff were to be paid through the main department. External funding was to pass to the main department rather than through his Unit. Documents reveal the likelihood of Professor Orme and Professor Foster visiting the Unit at about this time. Against the background above of the documentary evidence of the time there is no reason to doubt Professor Orme's assertion that the discussion centred on financial matters and not on human research material.

5. Future Staffing and Expenditure at Alder Hey Reveal Previous NHS Subsidy of Research

5.1 Alder Hey had to consider the required staffing for the future when the department was transferred. A number of permutations were considered including having two technicians at Alder Hey and funding two technicians at the Royal Liverpool University Hospital in order to provide for more specialist tests. In the end, the Alder Hey work was actually carried out through two technicians, one MLSO at Grade 2 and one at Grade 1, with a small amount of specialist work only sent out. The two MLAs were moved when the Women's Hospitals Trust work ceased. MLSOs Miss McGill and Mr Eccles were switched in 1995. Mrs Waring, the Chief MLSO, moved into a management position. Mr Dearlove and one other MSLO remained under Dr Kokai in the years 1996–2000. While Dr Kokai worked under conditions of intense pressure, himself as a sole Consultant, the department just about coped. This was a far cry from the days when there were five MLSOs and shows how over-resourced the department had been in terms of technicians, bearing in mind the level of clinical work. The same point of over-resourcing with regard to 'consumables' is made graphically in examining expenditure for Medical, Surgical Supplies and Equipment (MSSE) in the accounts. The total MSSE expenditure for the 12-month period to March 1995 was £55,214. In the 12 months to the end of March 1996 when research had ceased it dropped to £10,408, at which level it was stable for the next three years.

6. FSID 'Dismay' at 'Potentially Destabilising Events in Liverpool'

6.1 Professor Orme wrote to FSID on 23 December 1994 to tell them of the re-shuffle of Professor van Velzen's duties. Dr Chantler, Secretary of the Scientific Advisory Committee, replied on 16 January 1995. The main paragraphs of her letter were,

> 'Naturally we are deeply concerned about recent developments at Liverpool and their impact on the outcome of substantial awards made in recent years. I know that the Council wishes to consider possible implications. I would be immensely grateful, therefore, if you could provide us with detailed information relating to current status and future plans regarding the unit of paediatric pathology, current research projects and the collaborative research programme with the Unit of Paediatric Epidemiology.
>
> Personally, I am dismayed that the Foundation has not been informed adequately of events which are potentially de-stabilising. I had assumed, following our correspondence in August 1993 that the Unit of Fetal and Paediatric Pathology was secure.

I note your comment that there is no University Department of Fetal and Infant Pathology. Whilst this may be factually correct, listing the Department of Fetal and Infant Pathology under University of Liverpool on notepaper does pose some ambiguity. Certainly we have had no reason to believe that there was anything other than a thriving department headed by Professor van Velzen. I should say that this was a significant factor in the decision relating to the large, recent grant. Had we known that this was a misrepresentation or that there was likely to be a material change of status prejudicing collaborative studies in the area of intrauterine growth retardation, I believe it would have had a significant bearing on the decision.'

6.2 This is another letter that speaks for itself. The allegation of 'misrepresentation' echoes the concern from the University's perspective in Professor Orme's letter to Mr Carr in July 1993 after the University Review. FSID's belief in a thriving and secure department under Professor van Velzen was stated as a significant factor in the award of £250,000 to Professor Pharoah.

7. 'No Material Change in Potential to Conduct Research'

7.1 Professor Orme replied on 19 January 1995 minimising the problems and focusing solely on the issue of the delivery of the service to the NHS at Alder Hey. He did not believe it was necessary or relevant to have consulted FSID over such an issue. He spoke of there having been some concerns, as FSID were aware, about the delivery of the pathology service to Alder Hey. He dismissed Professor van Velzen's complaints to FSID at his treatment as 'a number of emotional letters which contain some inaccuracies'. He concluded on an upbeat note,

'I hope you will see that I do not believe there has been any material change in the status of the unit or in its potential to conduct research work. Thus the statement in the last sentence on page one of your letter is I believe quite incorrect and based on false information. I am happy to correct that situation now. The unit is active in research and in some ways the new arrangements will allow Professor van Velzen to devote more time to his research. There is no doubt that he was being over-stretched, and in some ways this was no fault of his. I do not think anyone has anything but praise for the hard work and effort that Professor van Velzen has put into his various endeavours. Moves are now in place to support the research endeavours of both Dr Vyvyan Howard and Dr Paul Sibbons in that unit. Both Professor Foster and I believe that there is a considerable future in the research work being undertaken by the unit and I hope you will accept this.'

8.   'Character Assassination' – 'Quite Unprofitable'

8.1   Towards the end of February 1995 Professor Orme met with some of the leading lights in FSID in an attempt to explain the situation in Liverpool. Not surprisingly Professor Orme said, when he wrote to Professor Foster on 27 February 1995,

> 'They [FSID] were particularly interested to try unravel the past and I was keen to try to look ahead rather than dwell on past problems. I think we came to a reasonable compromise. Certainly when looking back they revealed some aggression over the way Liverpool in general had handled the problem. It is quite clear that they regard Dick as quite excellent and that all the problems have been imposed on him! I felt it would be quite unprofitable at this stage to do a character assassination on Dick and tried to emphasise his good points whenever I could!'

8.2   Professor Orme then set out for Professor Foster's benefit the answers that he had given to questions raised by FSID as to the future of the Unit. The answers were in general supportive of research in the short term but non-committal in the medium- to long-term. His letter closed,

> 'They are concerned about the attitude to the Foundation support for Peter Pharoah and I hope I was able to reassure them there.
>
> Overall the meeting ended on a positive note but I shall be interested in the feedback from Professor Cooke to whom I shall send a copy of this letter.'

9.   'No Human Tissues' – No *'raison d'etre'* for Professor van Velzen

9.1   Meanwhile Professor Foster was considering the future for Professor van Velzen and wrote to the University Registrar, Mr Carr, on 28 February 1995. He enclosed his letter of 27 February 1995 including Professor van Velzen's effective 'job plan' but he also dealt with general policy factors of common concern for the University and FSID. Referring to the re-shuffle of Professor van Velzen's service work he said,

> 'Whilst not involving the University directly, any change in the diagnostic activities within the Department of Pathology would indirectly, but significantly, affect the University, particularly if Alder Hey Children's Hospital and the Liverpool Women's Hospital NHS Trust chose to take their work away from the Department. This would leave Professor van Velzen with no human tissues for his research or academic activities, and therefore, no *raison d'etre* [purpose justifying his existence] within the University.'

10. First Written Warning?

10.1 Professor Foster also made it clear in the above letter of 28 February 1995 that he did not at that stage want to institute disciplinary proceedings against Professor van Velzen but rather he was,

> 'Mindful of the fact that Professor van Velzen should remain as unfettered as possible in order to have the maximum freedom to develop his research and academic potential.'

10.2 However, while Professor Foster was not keen on disciplining him, Mr Carr endorsed the letter to the effect that he had spoken with Professor Orme,

> 'Agreed that he would talk to C Foster. Velzen in breach of contract in at least two areas, and guilty of neglect/failure to fulfil conditions of office and duties. Velzen to be seen and given a first written warning.'

There is no evidence at all to suggest that action followed this decision.

11. 'Paediatric Tissue Bank'

11.1 Human material as research material is a major theme in 1995. The next relevant document is a draft job description for the senior lecturer's post to be taken up by Dr Kokai dated 3 March 1995,

> 'The Department of Pathology
> a) General and Diagnostic:
> …A paediatric tissue bank has already been established and the appointee will be expected to maintain this in liaison with others, as appropriate.…
>
> b) Research:
> The University Department of Pathology has developed a strong initiative in basic and applied biomedical research which is well-funded and is founded on an enlarging central core of scientific expertise linked to the immediate availability of a wealth of clinical material, both paediatric and adult in origin. The Department houses the independently funded Cancer Tissue Bank Research Centre (CTBRC) which aims to be the well documented repository of locally-obtained cancer tissues, including information on tumour immunophenotypes and nucleic acid profiles. The appointed Senior Lecturer will be responsible for ensuring the safe collection and deposition of paediatric tissues (surgical and post mortem, neoplastic and non-neoplastic) in a tissue bank dedicated to the collection of paediatric tissues. Within the University Department are several

distinct lines of research linked by the application of common technologies. This strategy has resulted in strengthening the overall research initiative while maintaining an economy of methodologies, equipment, consumables etc. The appointed Senior Lecturer will be expected to develop an appropriate research programme into diseases affecting children. A close working relationship with the Cardiac Unit is expected in order to support work on cardiac morphology that is currently being undertaken.'

11.2 There was quite distinct and later discussion within this draft document of the heart collection in the ICH. The above passage cannot be construed, as some witnesses suggested, as referring simply to the heart collection. Here is a clear reference to a 'paediatric tissue bank' amounting to a 'wealth of clinical material' in the Department of Fetal and Infant Pathology. Indeed Dr Howard described it as 'priceless' at the University Review and in his evidence to the Inquiry.

12. Continued Access to Research Materials

12.1 FSID continued to be concerned to protect their original investment and Professor Orme had to write again on 28 March 1995 in an effort to reassure them. In particular he was at pains to discuss the number of ongoing research studies and the continued presence of Dr Howard, Dr Sibbons and the PhD students. He anticipated that the necessary facilities would be available either in the Myrtle Street laboratory or in the parent Department of Pathology. He continued on this theme,

> 'The researchers in the unit will have access to research material in two ways. The perinatal samples will be processed in the unit as they are at the moment. The samples from Alder Hey will come via the senior lecturer providing the service at Alder Hey. That individual will be expected to provide a close liaison with the Myrtle Street unit and to provide all research material. Indeed, I should expect that senior lecturer to be closely involved with research endeavours in the unit.'

12.2 In truth, the continued availability of research materials was the only thing left for the University to gain in maintaining the senior lecturer's post and links with Alder Hey. The post was to be committed in the first two of the remaining four years to the service at Alder Hey as against research.

13. The Service Level Agreement –
'Collection and Processing of Specimens'

13.1   Professor Foster had to handle the service side, so as to maintain links for the purposes of research samples, and Professor Orme was liaising with FSID on the same issue. Another document in the spring of 1995, drafted by Professor Foster, would attempt to reinforce that link. Whereas there had been no strict agreement between the University and Alder Hey drawn up by Professor Heath or Professor Harris when the Chair was first established, Professor Foster now drafted a Service Level Agreement to govern the relationship between the University and Alder Hey. One passage has particular and obvious significance,

> **'The Service – collection and processing of specimens**
> viii. Whenever submitted tissues are in excess of those required for diagnostic purposes, tissue samples may be made available for research purposes, if required. However, in this respect, ESTABLISHMENT OF THE CORRECT DIAGNOSIS WITH THE MINIMUM OF INTERFERENCE WILL BE THE PRIORITY and only after such materials have been secured will additional tissues be available for research, teaching or other purposes.
>
> ix. Any tissues taken for research, will be identified by one of the surgical pathologists recognised by the anatomical Pathology Laboratory … as providing the service to Alder Hey to be in excess of that required for diagnostic purposes. This may be the Senior Lecturer or, where appropriate, one of the trainee pathologists.
>
> x. Immediate responsibility to ensure that appropriate samples are taken for diagnostic purposes, and that a primary diagnosis is not jeopardised by the unauthorised taking of other samples, will be taken by the Senior Lecturer in Paediatric Pathology. The ultimate responsibility will rest with Professor Foster, Director of the Anatomical Pathology service.'

The capitals used are in the original text.

14. Backlog of 'Organs' at Myrtle Street –
Memo to Clinicians

14.1   Meanwhile Alder Hey and not just the University was considering how to deal with the backlog of material at Myrtle Street. On 24 April 1995 Professor Carty circulated a memo to the senior clinicians in the following terms,

'I have now obtained the full list of post mortems, in which the macro is complete but **the microscopic sections have not yet been done**.

I am trying to sort out the backlog. I understand, from talking to Professor Foster, that it is not unusual for histopathology to be omitted if the macroscopic examination provides the answer. However, I am aware that it is reasonable to retain the **organs** for subsequent histological analysis in certain cases.

With the impending changes in histopathology, I want to ascertain in which cases it is important either that the **organs** are retained for future analysis, or you are still awaiting important histopathology results. I do not wish to subject the unit to a deluge of backlog of work if this is not pertinent to the case. Could you therefore, please, see them to identify those cases in whom you want the histopathology carried out or whose **organs** you wish retained in case of future problems.

Please amend the list by adding your initials, a comment about retention of **organs**, or the request for it. I am sorry for troubling you with this but I am trying to tidy up the arrangements.'

Emphasis has been added for the general reader who will note the word 'organs' on four occasions, in the light of the introductory paragraph stating that the 'microscopic sections have not yet been done', i.e. the organs were still whole.

15.   'Organs' Repeated

15.1   On 25 April 1995 Professor Carty wrote a letter to Ms Rowland about a complaint of delay similar to the earlier complaints that dogged the fetal and perinatal service in 1990. In that letter, Professor Carty again used the word 'organs', twice, referring to the material awaiting histology.

16.   Re-circulation of the Memo

16.1   The memo of 24 April 1995 was circulated on about four occasions, the final circulation being as late as 28 September 1995. A copy of the memo was also sent to Professor Foster on 1 May 1995 with the following short covering letter,

'I thought you should have sight of this. I have told Henry [Meade] to go and try and sort out the problem and find out exactly what we need to transfer to what from the point of view of the NHS. Please can you put a hold on this until I get the NHS component on this sorted out.'

A copy of that letter was sent not only to Mr Meade but also to Ms Rowland.

17. Alder Hey Knowledge of 'Organs'

17.1   The clinicians at Alder Hey have varying degrees of recollection of the circulation of the memo and the long lists of cases in which post mortem histology had not been carried out. Some clinicians and departments, where deaths were more frequent, had a great deal more interest in the lists than others. Some have suggested that, with the circulation of the lists, they would have inferred that what remained at Myrtle Street were 'blocks' and 'slides' awaiting reporting. However, that inference is difficult to draw in the light of the use of the word 'organs' which has a precise meaning to a layman let alone a doctor. The use of the word 'organ' is specific and incapable of misinterpretation. The Concise Oxford English Dictionary, 8th Edition, current at the time of the memo gives the following definition,

> 'a usually self-contained part of an organism having a special vital function (*vocal organs; digestive organs*).'

17.2   If the usual method of sampling was to take blocks and sections, the use of the word 'organs' is highly significant and cannot be explained away as easily as saying that Professor Carty must have made a mistake. She knew what the word meant.

17.3   The inference suggested by clinicians is made even more difficult to draw for most of them since the basic nature of Professor van Velzen's research into SIDS was well known in the hospital, as it was at the University. The research involving stereological measurement of whole organs had been trumpeted over the very Sunday newspapers likely to be read by clinicians in early 1993, causing no little consternation at the time because of provisional results of research being published outside medical journals. It is entirely plausible for clinicians to deny that they knew of the precise and widespread nature of Professor van Velzen's protocol on organ retention; but the denial of knowledge of the collection at Myrtle Street can only be 'one of degree' and not of its essential nature. The repeated use of the word 'organs', in the context of the microscopic sections not yet done, makes the nature of the collection clear to all beyond any reasonable doubt. The lists of cases (sent out on four occasions because clinicians did not respond to earlier memos) where a preliminary report had been written but histology had not been attempted ran to over 350 children from late 1988 to early 1995, and these were all Alder Hey cases. The number took no account of the neonatal deaths in the other hospitals associated with the service of Professor van Velzen.

17.4   While Alder Hey as a whole did not know the precise extent of the organs retained at Myrtle Street, it did know as a collective group that a substantial number of organs must be there, collected over a substantial number of years in a substantial number of cases. Why was there no outcry?

17.5   The simple fact is that the retention of organs was commonplace over the country. Doctors had been brought up to expect it. The doctors at Alder Hey no more considered the validity of the collection at Myrtle Street than they did of the Heart Collection in the ICH. As will be discussed in Chapter 10 covering the Human Tissue Act 1961, the medical profession has exhibited a general ignorance of what the law requires and maintains a paternalistic attitude to the likely concerns of relatives. The attitude was that there were organs in every hospital. If Professor van Velzen had accumulated more than others it was not to them something to worry about unduly. If that was the attitude of doctors it is not surprising that hospital managers, including Ms Rowland in 1995, did not view the issue as one requiring radical change. One might have hoped that as lay people in a hospital setting, the managers could have seen more clearly the fundamental human issues, not having been steeped in the traditions of medical practice in recent years. Unfortunately no one saw just how terrible the position would appear to the outside world. Restricted vision is an inevitable consequence of a paternalistic attitude.

18.   Proposed Disposal of Specimens

18.1   Professor Carty spoke of her memo at the meeting of the Board of Clinical Directors on 22 June 1995 chaired by Dr Martin. The minute of the meeting reads,

> 'Post mortem reporting
>
> [Professor] Carty reported that she has re-circulated the list of outstanding post mortems. Arrangements for the transfer of Histopathology to Alder Hey will have to start soon, and the specimens not identified will have to be disposed of.'

18.2   At this point it is clear what Alder Hey envisaged. Organs were to be treated in one of two ways. If they remained clinically important and requiring histology, they were to be retained. Otherwise, there was to be disposal.

19. Difficulties with the Supply of Materials – Constraints from Outside the University

19.1   FSID remained concerned and Dr Chanter wrote to Professor Orme after a meeting on 8 June 1995. Some of her immediate concerns revolved around funding for Dr Sibbons and the University commitment to the PhD students for continuation of their work. Her third 'immediate concern' was,

> 'I understand that they are experiencing difficulties with the supply of materials although I do not have specific details.'

19.2   Professor Orme replied on 27 June 1995. Having dealt with the wider issues he answered the third immediate concern of Dr Chantler,

> 'I am aware that some of the constraints on the unit have been imposed from outside the University. I am in the process of investigating these with the individuals or bodies concerned. We remain committed to the unit and to the Ph.D students …
>
> I am happy to assure you that the necessary resources will be available for Dr Sibbons to work for the next two months and I shall be pursuing, with the NHS authorities, the issue of availability of resources in the longer term.'

19.3   No witness has helped us with any meaningful evidence as to the 'outside constraints' and the ongoing issue of 'resources'. The documents will have to speak for themselves and do so powerfully enough.

20. Visit to the Unit of Fetal and Infant Pathology

20.1   In the letter of 27 June 1995 referred to above Professor Orme also said,

> 'I have just seen Dr Howard and Dr Sibbons and they have expressed their anxieties to me about the facilities that are available. I have arranged for Professor Foster – who as Professor of Pathology and Clinical Director is in overall charge of the Fetal and Infant Pathology Unit, to visit the Unit with me on Thursday morning 29 June. Professor Foster only returns from holiday on Wednesday.'

20.2   Neither Professor Orme nor Professor Foster appears to remember the visit and both deny any appreciation of the true extent of the collection in the cellar. Dr Howard remembered a visit but, again, he did not remember the detail to any great extent. He believed it likely that he spoke of the research material and revealed the contents of the basement. Of the visit of Professors Orme and Foster in January it is easy to accept that the discussion was limited to financial matters, given the content of the documentation which then concerned financial audit. However, it is surprising that, in the thick of the FSID correspondence concerning research materials that summer, the visit did not reveal the true extent of the collection in the Myrtle Street laboratories.

21.   Continued Availability and Supply of Specimens

21.1   On 30 June 1995 Dr Chantler wrote to Dr Sibbons,

> 'I am pleased to report that the Council have agreed to a supplementary award … subject to; …
>
> The continued availability of all the resources including supply of specimens necessary for your work….
>
> Professor Orme is trying to ensure continuity of funding for you and we would very much wish to be kept informed of progress on this matter.'

Somebody, presumably Dr Sibbons, has written on the letter, 'Contact Chris Foster in Pathology'.

21.2   In mid-July 1995 Ms Rowland and Professor Carty met with Professor Foster to speak about 'a range of issues … as a matter of urgency'. The letter from Ms Rowland to Professor Foster after the meeting identified only one issue upon which they had spoken, the Service Level Agreement.

22.   Importance of Professor van Velzen for the Epidemiological Research of Professor Pharoah

22.1   On 22 July 1995 Dr Chantler at FSID wrote to Professor Orme,

> 'It remains very important to us that the pathological aspects of IUGR are focussed and links with epidemiological features are sought and I have asked Peter [Pharoah] to maintain these links to facilitate this.'

The letter also discussed the provision of technical support, access to routine equipment and reagents. FSID asked for a 'written brief of the immediate and longer term needs' to enable the Foundation to assess the position and determine 'viability'. Dr Chantler ended her letter,

> 'I do not think we can allow this level of uncertainty to continue as we do need assurance that the Foundation's investment will bring a return….'

22.2   On 26 July 1995 Lady Limerick at FSID wrote to Professor Pharoah following the opening of the new Unit. She said,

> 'As said in my opening words it is the emphasis on infant vulnerability and the collaboration between different disciplines – epidemiology, paediatric pathology, microbiology and genetics which encouraged the Foundation to award the grant to you in Liverpool and we have high expectations of the outcome.
>
> The visit was also an extremely useful occasion to see Professor Dick van Velzen and his colleagues on Myrtle Street. I hope very sincerely that their unique study of pathological specimens will be enabled to continue, since the value of their techniques and IUGR funding is inestimable.
>
> The FSID grant was on the understanding that a paediatric pathologist ie Dick van Velzen would be undertaking the post mortems on all unexpected infant deaths and the detailed IUGR data would be linked with yours. If this is no longer going to be the case, the FSID would expect to be informed in detail of any change in arrangement. The FSID Council (Trustees) are conscious of our large investment in your collaborative multidisciplinary unit and will need assurance that this is not likely to be jeopardised in any way by structural changes in pathology arrangements in Liverpool.'

23.   Professor Foster Acting Under Protest

23.1   Correspondence written by Professor Orme in late July 1995 reveals that Professor Foster was intimately involved in the discussions with regard to FSID and the continued research. Professor Foster was questioned about this and protested that he was acting under pressure from Professor Orme as Dean, and he himself as Head of Department had no academic interest at all in the material. By now he claimed to be utterly sick and tired of the Unit of Fetal and Infant Pathology.

24.   Hearts/Lungs from Coroner's Post Mortem Examinations

24.1   On 1 August 1995 Professor Carty wrote to Professor Foster in memo form, copied to Ms Rowland, Mr Meade, and Mrs Waring. The memo dealt with a lot of matters to do with staff uncertainty, general arrangements for Dr Kokai and the servicing of the Women's Hospitals Trust work. However, she also wrote the following,

'There is work accruing from the sorting of heart/lung specimens to be sent to Alder Hey. Some of these specimens are Coroner's specimens and I understand that Dick [van Velzen] wishes to retain these. This seems reasonable to me but perhaps you could comment upon it and advise me as to the transfer of these specimens once the Coroner's issues have been resolved, as it seems logical that these specimens should end up in the Heart Unit in Alder Hey.'

24.2 Clearly somebody, with the knowledge of Professor Carty, had been sorting through the containers to retrieve the heart/lung specimens. Equally clearly, she had been told and understood that some of the specimens were Coroner's specimens. There does not appear to have been any expressed recognition recorded at this stage of the dubious legal status of the material retained after the Coroner's post mortem process was over, but she asked Professor Foster for his advice.

24.3 Later in the autumn Professor Carty wrote to Mr Barter, HM Coroner, asking for permission to dispose of such material and Mr Barter gave his consent to disposal in the usual way. These issues are dealt with in Chapter 9 relating to the Coroner and it is sufficient here to appreciate that Alder Hey asked for permission to **dispose** and not for permission to **research**, which Mr Barter maintained that he would not have given and had no power to give.

25. FSID's Concern for Unrestricted Access to Research Materials

25.1 Dr Chantler wrote a short note to Professor Orme on 2 August 1995 expressing her dismay at the continuing problems and that she was to speak to Professor Foster. She wrote a faxed message to Professor Foster on 3 August 1995,

'Our main concerns relate to whether organisation is really in place to ensure smooth and unrestricted access to research materials for our researchers.'

She dealt with technical support, including equipment and processing reagents, in a separate section of the fax and hence 'research materials' in the above passage is highly likely to relate to 'human materials'. The memo closed in gloomy terms,

'Frankly we now feel that the research at Liverpool has and will continue to be compromised by recent changes and the Foundation's expectation of a new multidisciplinary unit embracing the pathology and epidemiology of IUGR is greatly endangered. We would like to be convinced otherwise.'

25.2 On 11 August 1995 Professor Orme wrote to Professor Foster enclosing copies of all his correspondence with FSID for Professor Foster's information.

26. Free Access to Myrtle Street

26.1 Perhaps because of the summer holidays the FSID research material correspondence appears to have died out until 9 November 1995, when Professor Carty wrote a relevant letter to Professor Foster expressing her concerns at,

> 'the free access, by numerous people, to Myrtle Street which has been solely used by research students since mid October.'

The context of that letter was concern at the loss of equipment and there was no reference to material. However, the letter provides a backdrop for what followed.

27. 'Very Sensitive Ethical Issues Around the Use of Human Tissue' – 'Objective to Safeguard the Trust's Position'

27.1 On 15 November 1995 Ms Rowland wrote to Professor Foster. In the opening paragraph she set out the background. Professor Carty had spoken with her. The Professor had had a 'difficulty because of her concern regarding the immediate location of some of the blocks'. Ms Rowland continued,

> 'You will be aware, more than me, of the very sensitive ethical issues around the use of human tissue. Helen's [Carty] prime objective was to safeguard the Trust's position with regard to these tissues; clearly this is the Trust's responsibility…. I understand that you have also spoken to her about the transfer of other blocks on which you wish to do research.
>
> *The Trust does not wish to hinder research but it must, in the first instance, ensure that we know why and where tissues are required before they are released.* I understand that Helen has indicated to you that you can have access to tissues providing we are appropriately informed. I am confident that we can resolve these issues.'

Emphasis has been added to the text to aid the analysis that will follow the next letter.

28. University 'Assurance' on the 'Appropriate Way Forward'

28.1   On the very next day 16 November 1995 Professor Carty wrote to Professor Foster,

'Following our conversation this morning, you and I agreed the following:-

1. That the movement of POTS [containing organs] to Alder Hey could proceed.

2. That those POTS which contained material which may be required by Alder Hey would move to Alder Hey.

3. That the heart and lungs in the appropriate cases would be removed and sent to the Cardiac Lab in Alder Hey [ICH].

4. *That the POTS relating to other post mortems, not required for further use in Alder Hey, would be left stored in Myrtle Street for you to use for research material, if required.*

You have assured me that this is the appropriate way forward to hand over tissue to you and that further responsibility for its use would be undertaken by you. I have therefore instructed Henry [Meade] accordingly, who will now make arrangements to proceed.'

Emphasis has again been added.

29. Analysis of the Correspondence Regarding Research Material

29.1   The correspondence taken on its own reveals a clear picture. In the spring of 1995 it was the policy at Alder Hey to identify those cases requiring clinical examination, notwithstanding the immense delay, and to dispose of all remaining organs. There were thus only two categories. This policy was incompatible with ongoing research. In the summer the researcher encountered 'constraints' which had to be taken up with the 'NHS authorities'. Inferences are not difficult to draw in the light of the clauses in the draft Service Level Agreement stressing that no research could be done until the clinical diagnosis had been established. This was precisely the position in relation to the ongoing research in 1995 until the clinicians had responded properly to Professor Carty's memo indicating which cases required post mortem histology. In the face of outside NHS constraints the researchers had no option but to contact FSID, which in turn contacted Professor Orme. He then prevailed over Professor Foster, who attempted to persuade Professor Carty to release the organs for research.

29.2　By the time of Ms Rowland's letter on 15 November 1995 Alder Hey appeared to have in mind three categories for the organs in the collection. The first category was the same as before, namely those cases requiring histology for clinical purposes. The second category was cases in which the University could tell Alder Hey *why* and *where* tissues were required, that is to say could justify a case for research. This category would certainly have included the hearts/lungs that had already been earmarked for the ICH collection. Ms Rowland issued a clear invitation to the University for it to justify the other cases wanted for the purposes of research. By implication there would be disposal of the third category, encompassing all that remained. However, following a meeting on the next morning the second and third categories were evidently merged, so that all materials not required for clinical purposes were to be left at the disposal of the University for research without further justification. Professor Carty stressed in writing that she been 'assured' by Professor Foster that it was 'appropriate' and the University had 'responsibility' thereafter.

30. Contrast the Analysis with the Recollection of Witnesses

30.1　No witness has agreed with the above interpretation of the documents. However, neither has any put forward an account of the events in 1995 that can remotely lie with them. Whether or not the detail of the above interpretation is correct in its entirety, the overall thrust of what happened in 1995 is apparent.

31. Finale on the Organ Collection

31.1　On 21 November 1995 there was a meeting in the Department of Pathology. Present were Ms Rowland, Professor Carty, Mr Meade and a member of the Finance Department. Minutes of the meeting were copied to the executive directors,

> '[Professor] Carty confirmed the arrangements for post mortem specimens; these will generally be stored here at Alder Hey. Hearts and lungs will go to Dr Audrey Smith and the remainder to Dr Howard.'

The minute speaks for itself and completes what happened with regard to the organs in 'the van Velzen Years'. Part 9 will deal with the research output and accuracy of reporting.

32. Disciplinary 'Inaction'

32.1   The final section of 'the van Velzen Years' deals with his ultimate departure from the University.

32.2   After receiving the job plan in the letter of 27 February 1995 Professor van Velzen took another unauthorised leave of absence. Up to now Professor Foster had 'played it by the book'. He had firm evidence upon which to bring disciplinary proceedings. Accordingly he wrote to Mr Carr describing Professor van Velzen's absence and complaining of his continued attempts to spend on a 'frozen' current account. He concluded his letter,

> 'Overall, I see no attempt on the part of Professor van Velzen to recognise his responsibilities implicit in holding a personal Chair in the University of Liverpool and in running his own unit within Pathology. As the Professor and Director of the Department of Pathology, I am now making a formal request to the University of Liverpool to begin disciplinary procedures against Professor van Velzen such that he can be in no doubt as to his contractual responsibilities to the University and, through the University, to the NHS Purchasers at the Women's Hospital – with which he holds a contract.'

32.3   There is no record of any disciplinary procedure ever having been started. For some reason the intention of Mr Carr to discipline in early March 1995, as endorsed on the earlier letter from Professor Foster, wavered. Even when Professor Foster, mindful of what was really required for disciplinary action, had the evidence and wanted to take that action the decision was not taken. The reader can speculate on the reasons as well as the Inquiry can. One particular pressure on Professor Orme in March 1995, as we have seen from the correspondence, was the need to maintain appearances and the research for FSID. There must have been others.

33. Professor van Velzen States his Intention to Leave

33.1   Professor van Velzen was hardly in Liverpool in 1995 and made no real clinical contribution. On 19 October 1995 Professor Orme wrote to Ms Rowland about cross-funding between the University and Alder Hey on wider issues, mentioning,

> 'particularly now that we are expecting Professor van Velzen to leave Liverpool.'

33.2   On 20 October 1995 Professor Foster wrote to Professor Orme,

> 'As you know, Professor van Velzen has now made it known to all and sundry
> that it is his intention to leave Liverpool in the near future. However, I have not
> received, in writing, his resignation nor have I been given an estimated date of
> his departure.'

Professor Foster went on to complain about the uncertainty and how Professor van Velzen
appeared to have 'relinquished all commitment and responsibility'. He concluded,

> 'From the dates and time I have given you, it appears likely that Professor van
> Velzen is liable to leave this University without giving the statutory three
> months' notice.
>
> I am now requesting the University to suspend payment of Professor van Velzen
> so that I may employ a *locum* on the liberated salary in order to provide the
> level of service expected by a number of different purchasers.'

33.3   On 24 October 1995 Professor Orme wrote to the High Commission of Canada,

> 'To whom it may concern
>
> Professor van Velzen has been Professor of Fetal and Infant Pathology at this
> University since 1989. He is very well trained in this discipline and has in
> addition considerable research and teaching interests.
>
> From what I have heard about the post in Canada, Professor van Velzen seems
> to me to be an ideal candidate for the post.'

33.4   Readers without academic and clinical experience should be careful in forming their
own conclusion as to the accuracy and quality of this reference. While the last sentence
might be debated depending upon Professor Orme's knowledge of the post in Canada,
the clipped reference would have highlighted in the proper circles that Professor van
Velzen was far from an ideal candidate.

34.   Frustration at the Stalemate –
Professor Foster Generates Pressure

34.1   Whether it was as a result of having to deal with the collection at Myrtle Street or the
clinical work, Professor Foster was becoming more and more angry at the stalemate.
He wanted to make plans for the future and to do so he needed the money backing
Professor van Velzen's salary. Only then could he fund and find a replacement. He was
also in contact with NHS Executive North West Regional Office in an effort to obtain
funds for a new consultant post in fetal and perinatal pathology. He devised a plan to

exert pressure on as many people as possible, either to provide him with funds or to support him in that venture. These skilful and well-motivated political manoeuvrings were in sharp contrast to what had preceded them.

34.2 Having involved Regional Office, on 22 November 1995, Professor Foster wrote an explicit, accurate and embarrassing letter to the Vice Chancellor, Professor Love, and copied it widely around Liverpool and the Regional Office. Shortly afterwards he wrote to the representatives of the Women's Hospitals Trust, again copying the letter widely, effectively inviting them to look elsewhere for their pathology services because he did not have the resources. It was never his serious intention that they did so, but he was generating as much pressure as he could on the University to get rid of Professor van Velzen, freeing up the monies, and on the Regional Office to provide funds for an additional perinatal consultant. There is weak hearsay as against direct evidence from a number of witnesses to the effect that a lump sum was paid to Professor van Velzen to induce him to leave. We have pursued this angle vigorously, particularly in the light of the letter to the Vice Chancellor which might be construed as an attempt to embarrass him into providing a lump sum.

34.3 Quite simply, there is no evidence of a payment to Professor van Velzen. While it is likely that Regional Office made available a lump sum in the region of £30,000 – £50,000 to support Professor Foster's reorganisation of pathology services, other than that there is no reliable indication of any money changing hands at this time. There is no need to read into the letter to the Vice Chancellor any deeper motive than was revealed within it and the previous letter of 20 October 1995 from Professor Foster to Professor Orme. The motive was simply to pressurise the University into freeing up Professor van Velzen's salary. The pressure succeeded. Professor van Velzen resigned on 5 December 1995, with effect from 31 December 1995, and by early 1996 Professor Foster had funding for an additional perinatal pathologist.

35. Epitaph to University Involvement in 'the van Velzen Years'

35.1 The reader has yet to see the letter of 22 November 1995 discussed at some length in the above section. This important letter, used at the time as a tool to generate pressure for reform and improvement of the service, is also an outstanding summary of what happened from the perspective of the University in 'the van Velzen years'. The letter reveals:

- the primary motive of Professor Foster in writing it,

'I am now asking you to suspend Professor van Velzen forthwith and
without payment. This action would clarify the chaotic situation that has
been allowed to persist … and release funding that will enable me to devise
an alternative and clinically-acceptable diagnostic pathology service….';

- the long-standing clinically-inadequate diagnostic service;

- the complete withdrawal of Professor van Velzen from diagnostic and academic work
  in 1995;

- the repeated failure of the University Administration to discipline Professor van
  Velzen on the several opportunities which became available between 1992 and 1995.
  In evidence before us Professor Foster was 'clinical' in his criticism of the Review in
  1993. He asked rhetorically what was the point of carrying out a Review if nothing
  came out of it and a job plan was not then devised and enforced;

- the very real requirements of University research departments for fetal, perinatal and
  paediatric human tissues. These requirements provide a backdrop to this Inquiry and
  the FSID correspondence in 1995 described above;

- the continued refusal of the University to comprehend its contractual requirements or
  at least its failure to appreciate the responsibilities inherent in providing an accurate,
  reliable and timely diagnosis to clinicians and their patients. Time and again
  University witnesses acknowledged a moral if not legal responsibility but time and
  again they retreated to a theoretical standpoint, maintaining that it was simply up to
  Alder Hey to take responsibility for service requirements and nothing to do with
  them. In contrast Professor Foster did not shirk responsibility;

- the original failure of the University to accept the authoritative and informed opinion
  of Professors Wigglesworth and Risdon in 1987;

- the studied inactivity of members of the University resulting in the vandalism of
  what might have become 'a flagship' unit within the country;

- the onus of contributory negligence on the University in allowing the scenario to
  develop. Professor Orme did finally acknowledge in evidence before us that the
  University played a contributory role in the sorry saga of the van Velzen years.

35.2   The letter is now set out in its entirety as an effective summary and fitting epitaph to University involvement,

'Dear Vice Chancellor,
Re: Professor D. van Velzen

As the Clinical Director of Pathology at the Royal Liverpool and Broadgreen University Hospital (NHS) Trust, I am writing to you, directly and candidly, so that you will be left in no doubt whatsoever as to the grave and detrimental effects now being inflicted by a senior member of the University Academic staff on Perinatal and Paediatric Pathology services in the Liverpool, Merseyside and North West region. I enclose copies of my correspondence dating back to December 1994 which have already been communicated to senior members of the University administration and who, even at that time were well aware of the significant and serious problems surrounding the activities and conduct of Professor van Velzen.

I am now asking you to suspend Professor van Velzen forthwith, and without pay. This action would clarify the chaotic situation that has been allowed to persist surrounding Professor van Velzen's activities, and release funding that will enable me to devise an alternative and clinically-acceptable diagnostic pathology service before this work, and the associated teaching and research resources, are transferred to Pathology Departments in Manchester, Leeds, Bristol or elsewhere.

For many months, and certainly before I was appointed to the Chair of Pathology at the University of Liverpool, Professor van Velzen has not been providing a clinically-adequate diagnostic Perinatal/Paediatric pathology service to the satisfaction of the purchasers at Alder Hey Children's Hospital, at Unit III of the Liverpool Women's Hospital or at the Countess of Chester Hospital. He continues to flout, without redress by any of the affected parties, the authority of the University, despite earlier verbal and written warnings.

Several months ago, Professor van Velzen announced that he is shortly to leave Liverpool to take-up a position in Halifax, Nova Scotia. However, he has neither communicated his intention in writing, nor has he submitted his resignation to myself (as Professor and Director of Pathology), to the Dean of the Faculty of Medicine or to the Personnel Department in the University. Conversely, for the past several months, and since Professor van Velzen announced that he was about to leave the University, he has withdrawn completely from the provision of any Perinatal/Paediatric diagnostic service and has failed to fulfil those academic activities for which he has been scheduled. Furthermore, he has neither requested leave from the diagnostic service or from the University department, nor has he had the courtesy to indicate his intended absence to his colleagues, or to make alternative arrangements to give those lectures and tutorials to which he had agreed in the earlier part of this year. In summary, Professor van Velzen is providing neither the diagnostic service nor fulfilling his academic obligations for which he is contracted.

It might have been possible for me to have continued 'carrying' Professor van Velzen's absence from the diagnostic service for the next several weeks but for two events: (1) Dr. George Kokai, the recently-appointed Senior Lecturer informed me by FAX, only yesterday, that he will not be able to take-up his post on 1 December as planned. It is now unlikely that he will be available before January 15, 1996, at the earliest. (2) The contract for Dr. June Khine, Senior Registrar in this Department, presently funded on short-term soft money by the University, is due to terminate, without renewal by the end of December. Presently, this junior doctor is (quite inappropriately) carrying a workload widely recognised to require a minimum of three pathologists of Consultant/Senior Lecturer grade, together with one Senior Registrar. As you will deduce, the continued absence of Professor van Velzen, together with the imminent departure of Dr Khine, will shortly leave no trained Perinatal/Paediatric pathologist in Liverpool/Merseyside. Under these circumstances, and without the resource presently occupied by Professor van Velzen, I have no alternative but to close-down Perinatal/Paediatric pathology in Liverpool University and transfer the diagnostic service elsewhere.

Repeated failure by the University administration to discipline Professor van Velzen, on the several opportunities which became available during the past three years, has directly contributed to the current situation in which all diagnostic Paediatric and Perinatal pathology is about to be transferred from this Department of Pathology in Liverpool to providers in other parts of the country. The precise relocation of the services will now depend upon the requirements of the individual purchasers (Alder Hey Children's Hospital, Liverpool Women's Hospital etc.). However, you should be aware that after these services have been transferred it is extremely unlikely that diagnostic Perinatal/Paediatric pathology will be returned to the University of Liverpool within the foreseeable future. The implications of the transfer will extend far beyond the obvious provision of a diagnostic pathology service to purchasers such as Alder Hey Children's Hospital, Unit III at the Women's Hospital, the Countess of Chester Hospital, Whiston Hospital, Ormskirk Hospital or to the numerous general practitioners who currently refer material to this Department for specialist opinion. The consequences of the transfer will include the following: (1.) All specialist perinatal and paediatric autopsies, now performed in the expanding sub-Department of Forensic Pathology at the University, will be transferred out of the North West Region to Forensic units at Leeds, Sheffield or Cardiff. (2.) Postgraduate students and other researchers within the University of Liverpool who require fetal, perinatal or paediatric tissues for their studies will no longer be able to obtain those tissues locally – and so much current research activity will terminate rapidly. (3.) Loss of diagnostic and research activities will be accompanied by an immediate and significant decline in the revenue currently brought to this Department of Pathology and to the University of Liverpool. (4.) Medical students in this University will no longer have direct access to Perinatal/Paediatric pathology as part of their curricular studies – with an obvious impact in terms of the adequacy of their training. (5.) The Royal College of Pathologists is likely to require its trainees to spend a component of their training outside this Region – in a location where they will have access to Perinatal/Paediatric pathology – thus making the Liverpool/Merseyside training scheme significantly less attractive to prospective trainee pathologists.

Unfortunately, it appears that the University of Liverpool persists in its unwillingness to tackle the long-standing problem of Professor van Velzen. Either there is a continued refusal to comprehend the contractual requirements of competitive purchasing within the National Health Service or an abject failure to appreciate the responsibilities inherent in providing accurate reliable and timely diagnoses to clinicians and to their patients.

The original failure by members of the University Academic or Administrative staff to accept the authoritative and informed opinion of Professors Wigglesworth and Risdon, following their review in 1987/88, coupled together with studied inactivity by members of the University, has resulted in the vandalism of what might otherwise have become a 'flagship' unit within this country – and capable of achieving the very highest standards of diagnostic and academic Perinatal/Paediatric pathology. Currently there remains a unique opportunity to build an outstanding and comprehensive Paediatric and Perinatal Pathology service within the Liverpool and Merseyside region, and centred upon Liverpool University. When established, this unit would attract a wide range of materials for second opinion as well as stimulating and enhancing the academic reputation of this University in this field. If this unit fails to develop for the reasons stated here, then the University of Liverpool should accept the onus of contributory negligence in allowing the scenario to develop.

I look forward to your comments. In due course, I will be pleased to discuss this matter with you.'

The van Velzen Years: Part 9

An Evaluation of the Research and Clinical Work of Professor van Velzen

Research

1.   General Background

1.1   Professor van Velzen was responsible primarily to the Trust in respect of his clinical work and to the University in respect of his research and academic commitments. Some members of the Selection Committee in 1988 expressed concern at his previous track record in research. As a new professorial appointment, Professor van Velzen was acutely conscious of the need to perform at a high level in research. However, there were no established resources other than the FSID grant and his early efforts did not create much impact. By the time Professor Orme visited the Vice-Chancellor in February 1993 he reported that FSID was unhappy about Professor van Velzen's 'science'. The research was discussed in negative terms during the visit but little did they know at the time how 'unhappy' our findings would be. Professor van Velzen's research output was to be one of the concerns addressed by the University Review in June 1993.

2.   Professor Johnson's View

2.1   In 1993 Professor Johnson was the Deputy Dean with special responsibility for research. He collated evidence of research output, publications, theses and research grants. When he gave evidence to the Review Committee he stated his concerns that Professor van Velzen was working at an isolated site. There was confusion about how he fitted into established departmental lines of reporting for research output and research grant expenditure. Nevertheless, on the whole his evidence was positive, indicating that, while Professor van Velzen started slowly in terms of peer-reviewed publications, there had been a considerable increase in research activity and output in the preceding 12 months. Professor Johnson subsequently confirmed to the Inquiry that the improvement continued following the Review, saying in his witness statement,

> 'Professor van Velzen continued to publish at a high level in 1994 and 1995, continuing to get papers into internationally recognised peer-reviewed journals, and so the twelve-month improvement that I had identified did seem to continue. There would be no criticism of Professor van Velzen in terms of research paper output between 1993 to 1995 as they were externally reviewed.'

3.   Professor Cooke's View

3.1   Professor Cooke, Professor of Neonatal Medicine, was Chairman of the Grants and Scientific Advisory Committee of FSID and was well placed to assess the quality of Professor van Velzen's research contributions. His assessment of the research at the University Review in 1993 was limited to just two sentences in his letter of 20 May 1993,

> 'The research output of the Unit has been largely from Dr Howard and his research associates. I am unclear as to Professor van Velzen's contributions in this area.'

Just as the clipped reference of Professor Orme for Professor van Velzen to the Canadian High Commissioner (see 'The van Velzen Years' Part 8, paragraph 33.3) highlighted concern, so this clipped assessment indicated a dim view of the research, as Professor Neilson who chaired the University Review conceded in evidence. This view, if correct, cannot be reconciled with that of Professor Johnson unless Professor Johnson had been taken in by Professor van Velzen's propaganda.

4.   The Analysis

4.1   We have considered carefully the research output of Professor van Velzen's Unit. It is necessary to examine the fundamental hypothesis underlying much of the work to assess its quality.

5.   The SIDS-IUGR Hypothesis

5.1   The purpose of the research was to investigate the mechanism involved in two poorly understood groups of deaths. These were late fetal deaths (normally formed stillbirths) and unexplained infant deaths (Sudden Infant Death Syndrome – SIDS). The theory which Professor van Velzen wished to explore was a connection between such deaths and intrauterine growth retardation (IUGR). Both he and Dr Vyvyan Howard were interested in the developmental period and in particular the theme of 'imprinting'. The suggestion, in very basic terms, was that there are 'windows of opportunity' in development which also constitute 'windows of vulnerability'. Growth-retarded fetus affected in those windows can suffer permanent deficits. The hypothesis is that babies who suffer from IUGR have greater potential than babies with normal growth development to experience subsequent problems. Professor van Velzen and Dr Howard wished to investigate whether an IUGR baby was more likely to die from SIDS than a normal birth-weight baby.

6.   Dr Howard's View

6.1   There was nothing particularly new about the theory although, as explained in Part 2, paragraph 4 of 'The van Velzen Years' Professor van Velzen had the dual advantage of Dr Howard's specific expertise in the field of stereology and abundant research material. It was the technique of stereology which Professor van Velzen and Dr Howard applied consistently to their hypothesis and this was behind much of the research work generated by the Unit. Dr Howard gave evidence to the Inquiry that his collaboration with Professor van Velzen was 'very productive' and felt that the research had put down valuable markers for the future. In his witness statement he said,

> 'The point I am trying to make is that there was a rationale behind what we did in research areas and the focus was to find out what permanent damage growth retardation can do to the body. I think we have achieved steps along the way towards improving the situation for those individuals in that position.'

7.   SIDS – a Diagnosis of Exclusion after Thorough Investigation

7.1   Any evaluation of research in the most difficult field of SIDS depends upon the selection of true SIDS cases to form the basis of the research. SIDS is a diagnosis reached by the exclusion of all other causes of death, such as malformation or infection. A definition of SIDS was set out in full in several of the papers and theses produced by Professor van Velzen's Unit. A typical definition is that set out in the PhD thesis prepared by Dr Darren Beech in 1997 – 'A stereological investigation of the development of the respiratory and renal systems of victims of Sudden Infant Death Syndrome' (1997). Dr Beech described SIDS as,

> 'the sudden death of an infant under one year of age which remains unexplained after a thorough case investigation, including performance of a complete autopsy, examinations of the death scene and review of the clinical history'.

8.   'Post Mortem Histology Still Not Possible …' – the Research Legacy

8.1   Here Professor van Velzen's dereliction of his clinical duties impacts directly on the validity of his research. He reached the diagnosis of SIDS in cases where there had been no thorough 'examination of the death scene' or a full 'review of the clinical history', but most importantly he consistently failed to perform 'a complete autopsy'.

As Parts 1–8 of 'The van Velzen Years' show, Professor van Velzen only rarely carried out clinical histology after post mortem examination over the entire period 1988–1995. Quite simply, without histology the SIDS diagnosis cannot be reliable.

9. Domino Effect – 'All Fall Down'

9.1 Researchers, relying on Professor van Velzen himself to identify SIDS cases, were misinformed as to the diagnostic basis used for case selection and the conclusions drawn from their research cannot be relied upon. The methodology described in various papers states that all paediatric post mortem examinations had been performed with histology, microbiology and virology, but this is now obviously not the case. We make no criticism of the individual researchers, who were entitled to assume that they were considering appropriate cases. However, Professor van Velzen knew full well the crucial importance of histology in SIDS cases. In his oral evidence to the Solicitor to the Inquiry he was asked about the clinical implications of his failure to undertake routine histology following post mortem examination. He said,

> 'It is unacceptable. It is like operating on a patient and not waking him up from anaesthesia or taking out his kidney and not closing his skin. It is not proper medical practice. When you do a post mortem you do that for a purpose. That is (a) to assess whether the treatment was carried out properly (b) whether the diagnosis for which somebody has been treated was correct and (c) whether or not any unexpected complications have arisen. None of these things were effectively done ... . As a result of that, errors in clinical practice would not be corrected, *parents would never be given the true final cause of death*, people would not become aware of pitfalls in diagnosis, medical mistakes would never be reviewed and proper advice to parents about the risk to their next offspring would never be given properly. That is why it is unacceptable.' [**emphasis added**].

9.2 Professor van Velzen's general comment is all the more relevant in cases where SIDS is a possible diagnosis of last resort. It cannot be made without histological analysis to rule out all other potential causes.

9.3 Dr Howard acknowledged in his oral evidence to the Inquiry that CESDI Studies have found that 20% of sudden infant deaths were subsequently explained (Fleming P, Bacon C, Blair P and Berry P J (eds) 2000. *Sudden Unexpected Deaths in Infancy: The CESDI SUDI Studies 1993-96*. HMSO London). Professor P J Berry, Professor of Paediatric Pathology, as part of the CESDI SUDI Studies has shown that histological examination of tissue provides the most useful information to distinguish between unexplained and explained deaths.

9.4 The 'SIDS' cases were improperly authenticated. Thereby the group upon which the research is based is invalid.

10. 'Normals' – the Problem Compounded

10.1   The studies are also reliant upon comparison with non-SIDS cases. These 'normal' or 'control' groups differed in definition from publication to publication depending upon which organ was being studied. The absence of histology in the 'control' cases raises similar doubt about the validity of the 'control' group. An example is the paper Beech D J, Sibbons P D, Howard C V and van Velzen D. 1999. *Renal Development – Expressed as Glomerular Number – in Victims of Sudden Infant Death Syndrome*. The 'control' group included cases with less than precise causes of death such as 'vomit inhalation', 'hypoxic infarction' and 'birth asphyxia'. In the absence of full diagnostic histological examination the 'control' groups are invalid.

11. Lists of Papers

11.1   In September 1999 Professor Johnson, who was by then Dean, asked Dr Howard to prepare a paper summarising the research undertaken by Professor van Velzen's Unit. Dr Howard summarised in less than three pages the nature of the work undertaken, and provided a list of 49 'published papers and abstracts'. At the end of this chapter we set out the list. Only 14 of those publications were full, peer-reviewed publications (numbers 3, 17, 21, 22, 28, 30, 31, 33, 34, 35, 36, 37, 41, and 43). Four of those peer-reviewed publications have no connection with the IUGR/SIDS work (numbers 30, 33, 35 and 36). Their clinical context is well defined, the methodology clear and justified and they amount to high quality papers published in appropriate journals. The remaining work is fundamentally flawed by reason of the lack of 'post mortem histology'.

11.2   If we ignore the peer-reviewed publications we are left with little, even overlooking the fundamental flaw. Some of the papers essentially repeat the research in the peer-reviewed papers. Others consider stereological techniques as applied to the SIDS work. Others still are abstracts for presentation at conferences. Others are yet to be published.

11.3   The hope of parents and of the Inquiry that the wholescale retention of organs between 1988 and 1995 might at least have led to valuable progressive research is unfortunately dashed. We recognise that this comes as a great disappointment.

12. Organs Used for Research – Precise Demarcation Impossible

12.1   We are unable to state exactly what organs have been subject to research. Dr Howard confirmed that specific work was undertaken on the brain (neocortex, cerebellum, corpus callosum and brain stem), phrenic nerve, kidney, lung, diaphragm, ileum and colon.

12.2   We were provided with a list of 154 post mortem cases sampled for morphometric studies. When they are checked against an Alder Hey database of retained organs and against the post mortem reports themselves, it is clear that diagnostic histology had not been done in the majority of those cases, even in the SIDS cases. In two cases included in the research list there is no post mortem report of any sort on file. It is also clear, from comparison of the 'materials' and 'methods' sections in the various publications, that far more cases have in fact been sampled than is suggested by the data supplied to us. This conclusion is reinforced by an examination of the retained organs themselves undertaken by the Inquiry's clinical expert and Panel Member, Dr Keeling. Organs, or parts of organs, used in the studies were missing, as anticipated, from the containers; but in other cases *additional* samples from other organs had clearly been taken. In some containers, organs which were expected, based on the post mortem reports and Professor van Velzen's practice, were absent. This suggests that they have been taken from the containers and used for research.

12.3   There are no proper records detailing the organs or tissue used for research. This raises serious questions about the control of access to the material. We were told specifically by Dr Howard,

> 'To my knowledge there has been no sampling of organs from the pots since Professor van Velzen left the lab in 1995. The pots have been revisited for the returning of tissue and maintaining formalin levels.'

12.4   That evidence is clearly incorrect. On 9 November 1995 Professor Carty wrote to Professor Foster expressing concern that there had been 'free access' to Myrtle Street by research students since mid-October. Expensive equipment had gone missing and there had been no proper supervision. In Chapter 3 we explained how it was clear to Alder Hey in September 1999 from the location and condition of the containers that they had been accessed since 1995. Formalin levels had not been maintained. We began the Inquiry hoping to find high quality research, only to be frustrated; additionally we have been unable to account for organs as we had set out to do.

Clinical Work

Throughout our report we have highlighted examples of poor clinical practice on the part of Professor van Velzen and in particular the failure of post mortem histology. In Chapter 4 we explained how in the cases of Christopher and Kathryn he brazenly overrode the parents' limited consent, removing multiple organs for examination. Our most shocking finding, however, is the deliberate and total fabrication of some post mortem reports.

13. Weights of Individual Organs When Undissected

13.1   In February and September 2000 Dr Keeling inspected the contents of 140 containers at Alder Hey. During the period June to August 2000, an independent pathologist, Dr Gordan Vujanic, also inspected the contents of all containers still held at Alder Hey when re-cataloguing the remains. Those inspections revealed the remains of 20 cases where the internal organs of the chest and abdominal cavities still *remain attached to each other and unopened*. It inevitably follows that references in reports in those cases to the weights and the internal structure, or cut surfaces, of individual organs are fabricated. In 12 of those 20 cases there are full post mortem reports on file which purport to include all organ weights and detailed descriptions of the internal structure of organs or their cut surfaces. The reports can be nothing other than fabrication. In seven other cases some organ weights are given, cut surfaces described or similar. In the last case there does not appear to be any completed post mortem report at all.

14. Society Cannot Tolerate Such Conduct – Trust Destroyed

14.1   When Professor van Velzen attended the Inquiry to give oral evidence a sample number of the cases was specifically put to him for comment. He admitted fabricating reports and suggested that there might be 'eight or ten' such cases. The evidence shows that this was an underestimate and we have highlighted 20 cases as representing extreme fabrication. These reports are essentially fiction. Society cannot tolerate such conduct. It imperils the health of families involved. It destroys the basic trust between the medical profession and society at large and that between the pathologist and clinical colleagues.

14.2   Fabrication is not confined to these 20 cases as inspections of the containers reveal considerable numbers of intact organs. In the post mortem reports the internal features of organs such as the lungs, kidneys or adrenals, are routinely described. This suggests to clinicians that a more thorough examination has been performed than was actually the case.

15. Unaltered Template

15.1   Professor van Velzen's practice was to use a computerised template for speed and uniformity of presentation. An unwanted by-product is that the reports were excessively long, repetitious and often included detail not specifically relevant to the individual case. Errors were introduced because of careless use of the template. In one, a report makes reference to the spleen on two occasions but the baby had a complex cardiac malformation in the absence of the spleen. In another, the appearance of a prostate (male) gland was reported although the deceased child was female and could not have had a prostate. Errors introduced by the template even extended to confusion over the identity of the pathologist, when one name appears on the front sheet and two names (or a different name) at the end of the report. Some post mortem reports prepared by Professor van Velzen are incorrectly attributed to Dr Khine.

16. Delay in Examination

16.1   If there is any one theme over and above the absence of histology running through Professor van Velzen's work, then it is delay. Delay occurred in the actual examination of the body following death, in the preparation and issue of the initial report and, most noticeably, in the performance of histology if ever undertaken. An analysis of 356 post mortem reports reveals unacceptable delay in the performance of the initial post mortem examination,

Time from death to post mortem examination	
Same day	46
Next day	145
2 days	59
3 days	46
4 days	38
5 days	11
6 days	5
7 days	2
8 days	2
17 days	1
18 days	1
Total	**356**

16.2   While the majority of post mortem examinations were performed within three days
of death more than 15% were performed four days or more after death. This is an
excessive period which may invalidate microbiological culture tests and result in poor
preservation of tissue if samples are to be submitted for histological examination.

17.   Delay in Provisional Reporting

17.1   Clinicians gave evidence that they had difficulty in obtaining even a provisional report
after the post mortem examination had been performed. Unfortunately on most reports
there was no date of issue, many were not even signed. We have been able to access
computer records at Alder Hey and to establish when Professor van Velzen first entered
the reports on to the computer. Analysis confirms that delays of several months were
common and delays in excess of one year were identified. Even these delays pale into
insignificance compared with the delay in producing final reports. Despite frequent
complaints by clinicians, the results of histological examination were only occasionally
included in post mortem reports. The inevitable consequence is that there have been
failures to identify infection in perinatal deaths and to assess organ maturity against
gestational age. Other specific diagnoses must have been missed. Histological
examination of the heart and lungs was rarely done in cases of congenital heart disease,
implying that the presence and degree of pulmonary hypertension has not been
recorded. The extent of myocardial ischaemia is likely to have been under-estimated.
The brain was rarely examined even when the clinical history, or the appearance of
the brain, suggested that cerebral pathological abnormality was likely and might
have contributed to death.

18.   Examination of Fetus – Appalling Delay

18.1   Fetus received by Professor van Velzen's Unit following termination of pregnancy
for fetal abnormality remained unexamined for several years. Many have never
been examined. In one case the report had to be completed by Professor van Velzen's
successor, following complaint, no later than ten years after the termination had been
performed.

18.2   When termination of pregnancy is undertaken because of fetal abnormality it is
obviously important for the family to know exactly what is found. It is vital for genetic
counselling that the fetus is carefully evaluated and minor abnormalities which might
contribute to a 'syndrome diagnosis' are identified. This can lead to the evaluation of
risk in future pregnancy and may assist in indicating different methods of surveillance
during future pregnancy. The obstetrician has an equally important interest, as the fetal

examination at post mortem forms part of the clinical audit of pre-natal diagnostic investigation against which quality of performance can be gauged and future mistakes avoided. What we have found in the course of this Inquiry is little short of appalling.

18.3   The consequence of Professor van Velzen's delayed, incomplete and falsified reports is that clinicians were not in a position to have informed discussions with parents about events leading to the death of their children. Parents are naturally anxious to have detailed information and if clinicians are unable to answer their questions it leads to mistrust of the medical profession. Without a full post mortem examination, genetic counselling can be imprecise at best and inaccurate at worst.

19.   Conclusion – Never Again

19.1   There can be no doubt that Professor van Velzen failed parents and doctors at every level. Organs were retained so that parents unwittingly buried 'shells' of their children, causing immense distress when discovered. The failure to perform histology means that the research undertaken by Professor van Velzen's Unit is fundamentally flawed. His failure to report promptly, comprehensively and honestly means that parents were given inaccurate and incomplete information about the deaths of their loved ones and were denied proper genetic counselling. We have no hesitation whatsoever in recommending that Professor van Velzen's activities be investigated by the General Medical Council (GMC) as a matter of urgency. In our opinion he should not be allowed to practice again in the United Kingdom or anywhere else.

20.   Previous Reprimand in Nova Scotia

20.1   The GMC is already acquainted with Professor van Velzen. On 7 May 1999 he formally consented to the issue of a written reprimand imposed by the Investigation Committee of the College of Physicians and Surgeons of Nova Scotia, Canada. A copy of the letter of reprimand was sent to the GMC. We note that by signing the letter Professor van Velzen accepted that he had fallen below acceptable standards of care in examining hearts by probing instead of by actual dissection and by examining placentae by palpation and bisection. Despite his experiences in Liverpool Professor van Velzen has proved himself incapable of reform. He further accepted that he had predicted histological findings in post mortem reports before examinations had been performed and that this was inappropriate. The echoes from Liverpool resound.

21. Organs in Storage in Canada

21.1 We must refer to more recent events in Canada. On 18 September 2000 the Canadian Police seized 13 boxes of what appeared to be internal organs. They had been contacted by staff at a storage company who were removing items stored by Professor van Velzen on leaving Canada in 1998. The contracted period for storage in the warehouse had expired and the large wooden crate, which contained the boxes, had been turned over to auction.

21.2 Testing of the organs revealed that in 12 of the boxes were animal organs and in the last box were human organs. The Canadian Police believe that they relate to two young children but do not link them to children in the United Kingdom. Professor van Velzen's legal representatives also have indicated that the organs do not originate from the United Kingdom. However, a number of original medical records relating to children at Alder Hey were discovered, some dating back to the 1970s.

22. Report to the Director of Public Prosecutions

22.1 In view of our findings and the possibility of theft of original medical records from Alder Hey we will deliver a copy of our Report to the Director of Public Prosecutions.

References

Published papers and abstracts

1. Ansari T, Beech D J, Howard C V, van Velzen D and Sibbons P D. 1999. Developmental delay or arrest *in utero* and possible postnatal consequences. *Fetomaternal Control of Pregnancy*. Havemeyer Foundation Workshop Monograph.

2. Ansari T, Howard C V, van Velzen D and Antunes S. 1995. A rapid embedding free method for estimating the total number of neurons and glial cells in the neocortex using the optical fractionator. *Proceedings of the 9th International Congress for Stereology*. ISBN 87 984765 1 3.

3. Ansari T, Howard C V, Yan L, MacMillan A, Pahal N, Hinchliffe S A, Beech D, Beddoes L, Friedman K, Sibbons P D and van Velzen D. 1995. A stereological assessment of IUGR in relation to the brain, the phrenic nerve, the kidneys and the lungs. *European Journal of Morphology*. 33, #4, 294–298.

4. Ansari T, Rossi M L and Sibbons P. 1998. Analysis of cardiovascular and respiratory nuclei in sudden infant death syndrome (SIDS) infants. *Pediatric Pulmonology*. 26, #6, 444.

5. Ansari T, Sibbons P, Rossi M, Broome J and van Velzen D. 1999. Investigation of axonal tracts within the central nervous system in Sudden Infant Death Syndrome (SIDS) infants. *Pediatric Research*. 45, #5:2, 82.

6. Ansari T, Sibbons P D, Howard C V and van Velzen D. 1999. Morphometric analysis of the phrenic nerve and diaphragm in sudden infant death syndrome (SIDS). *Pediatric Research*. 45, #5:2, 83.

7. Ansari T, Sibbons P D, Howard C V and van Velzen D. 1998. Stereological analysis of the neocortex & phrenic nerve in Sudden Infant Death Syndrome (SIDS) & control cases. Total neuronal number, mean neuronal nuclear volume & total myelinated axon number. *Journal of Pathology*. 184, #SS, A14.

8. Ansari T, Sibbons P D, Howard C V and van Velzen D. 1999. Stereological analysis of the neocortex with respect to total neuronal number and mean nuclear volume in sudden infant death syndrome (SIDS). *Pediatric Research*. 45, #5:2, 84.

9. Ansari T, Sibbons P D, Pahal N, Howard C V and van Velzen D. 1996. Fibre Type imbalance in the diaphragm of SIDS cases. *Pediatric Pulmonology*. 22, #6, 427.

10. Ansari T, Yan L, Howard C V, Sibbons P D, MacMillan A and van Velzen D. 1995. A stereological study estimating the total number of neurons in postnatally compromised humans and SIDS infants from 3 weeks to 1 year. *Proceedings of the 9th International Congress for Stereology*. ISBN 87 984765 1 3.

11.   Ansari T, Yan L, Howard C V, Sibbons P D, MacMillan A and van Velzen D. 1995. A stereological study investigating the total number of neocortical neurons in postnatally compromised humans and SIDS cases. *Pediatric Pulmonology.* 20, #5, 345.

12.   Ansari T, Yan L, Howard C V, Sibbons P D and van Velzen D. 1995. Total neuron number in the neocortex of SIDS infants, related to birth weight. *Pediatric Pulmonology.* 20, #5, 345.

13.   Ansari T, Yan L, Sibbons P D, Howard C V and van Velzen D. 1996. A stereological study estimating total neocortical numerical cellularity in SIDS and compromised infants. *Journal of Pathology.* 179, #SS.A26.

14.   Ansari T, Yan L, Sibbons P D, Howard C V and van Velzen D. 1996. A stereological study estimating total neocortical numerical cellularity in SIDS and compromised infants. *The Journal of Pathology.* 179, #SS, 32A.

15.   Beech D J, Sibbons P D, Howard C V and van Velzen D. 1998. A stereological investigation of lung and kidney development in victims of Sudden Infant Death Syndrome. *Journal of Pathology.* 184, #SS, A14.

16.   Beech D J, Ansari T I, Sibbons P D, Simmons K, Lloyd C, Pahal N, Howard C V and van Velzen D. 1996. A multi-organ analysis of IUGR and SIDS cases. *Pediatric Pulmonology.* 22, #6, 428.

17.   Beech D J, Howard C V, Reed M G, Sibbons P D and van Velzen D. 1999. Unbiased and efficient estimation of the total number of terminal bronchiolar duct endings in lung: a modified physical dissector. *Journal of Microscopy.* Accepted.

18.   Beech D J, Sibbons P D, Howard C V and van Velzen D. 1998. A stereological investigation of lung and kidney development in victims of sudden infant death syndrome. *Journal of Pathology.* 184, #SS, A14.

19.   Beech D J, Sibbons P D, Howard C V and van Velzen D. 1995. Absolute terminal bronchiolar duct number in lungs in SIDS and IUGR. *Impact of Antenatal and Postnatal Environmental Factors in Infant Outcome.* ISBN 0 9527125 04.

20.   Beech D J, Sibbons P D, Howard C V and van Velzen D. 1994. Lobe volume, absolute terminal bronchiolar duct number and gas exchange surface area in lungs of SIDS and IUGR. *The Journal of Pathology.* 172, #SS, 54.

21.   Beech D J, Sibbons P D, Howard C V and van Velzen D. 1999. Lung development – expressed as terminal bronchiolar duct ending number and gas exchange surface area – in victims of Sudden Infant Death Syndrome. *Pediatric Pulmonology.* Submitted.

22.   Beech D J, Sibbons P D, Howard C V and van Velzen D. 1999. Renal development – expressed as glomerular number – in victims of Sudden Infant Death Syndrome. *Pediatric and Development Pathology.* Submitted.

23. Beech D J, Sibbons P D, Howard C V and van Velzen D. 1995. SIDS-specific reduction in number of terminal bronchiolar ducts/kg bodyweight using stereological techniques. *The Journal of Pathology*. 176, #SS, 5A.

24. Beech D J, Sibbons P D, Howard C V and van Velzen D. 1995. SIDS-specific reduction in number of terminal bronchiolar ducts/kg bodyweight using stereological techniques. *Pediatric Pulmonology*. 20, #5, 345.

25. Beech D J, Sibbons P D, Howard C V and van Velzen D. 1993. Stereological assessment of lung gas exchange surface area in SIDS & IUGR. *Pediatric Pulmonology*. 16, #6, 388.

26. Beech D J, Sibbons P D, Howard C V and van Velzen D. 1993. Stereological estimation of absolute terminal duct number in SIDS & IUGR. *Pediatric Pulmonology*. 16, #6, 388.

27. Beech D J, Sibbons P D, Howard C V and van Velzen D. 1995. Stereological estimation of absolute terminal duct number in SIDS and IUGR. *Proceedings of the 9th International Congress for Stereology*. ISBN 87 984765 1 3.

28. Beech D J, Sibbons P D, Howard C V and van Velzen D. 1999. Terminal bronchiolar duct ending number does not increase post-natally in normal infants. *Early Human Development*. Submitted.

29. Beech D J, Sibbons P D, Lloyd C, Howard C V and van Velzen D. 1996. Lung and kidney development in Intra-Uterine Growth Retardation and Sudden Infant Death Syndrome – 3 dimensional analyses. *Pediatric Pulmonology*. 22, #6, 427.

30. Hinchliffe S A, Chan Y F, Jones H, Chan N, Kreezy A and van Velzen D. 1992. Renal hypoplasia and postnatally acquired cortical loss in children with vesicoureteral reflux. *Pediatric Nephrology*. 6, #5, 439–444.

31. Hinchliffe S A, Howard C V, Lynch M R J, Sargent P H, Judd B A and van Velzen D. 1993. Renal development arrest in sudden-infant-death-syndrome. *Pediatric pathology*. 13, #3, 333–343.

32. Hinchliffe S A, Howard C V and van Velzen D. 1995. Maternal smoking and blood-pressure in 7.5 to 8 year-old offspring. *Archives of Disease in Childhood*. 73, #4, 378.

33. Hinchliffe S A, Kreezy A, Ciftci A O, Chan Y F, Judd B A and van Velzen D. 1994. Focal and segmental glomerulosclerosis in children with reflux nephropathy. *Pediatric Pathology*. 14, #2, 327–338.

34. Hinchliffe S A, Lynch M R J, Sargent P H, Howard C V and van Velzen D. 1992. The effect of intrauterine growth-retardation on the development of renal nephrons. *British Journal of Obstetrics and Gynaecology*. 99, #4, 296–301.

35.   Hinchliffe S A, Sargent P H, Chan Y F, van Velzen D, Howard C V, Hutton J L and Rushton D I. 1992. Medullary ray glomerular counting as a method of assessment of human nephrogenesis. *Pathology Research and Practice*. 188, #6, 775–782.

36.   Hinchliffe S A, Sargent P H, Howard C V, Chan Y F and van Velzen D. 1991. Human intrauterine renal growth expressed in absolute number of glomeruli assessed by the dissector method and Cavalieri principle. *Laboratory Investigation*. 64, #6, 777–784.

37.   Howard C V, van Velzen D, Sibbons P, Ansari T, Li Y and Pahal N. 1995. Unbiased stereological measurements using conventional light-microscopy, applied to the study of human intrauterine growth-retardation. *Zoological Studies*. 34, #S1, 109–110.

38.   Howard C V, van Velzen D, Sibbons P D, Ansari T, Yan L and Pahal N. 1995. Generalised hypoplastic organ maturation in human intra uterine growth retardation. The first syndrome to be uncovered by design based stereology. *Proceedings of the 9th International Congress for Stereology*. ISBN 87 984765 1 3.

39.   Khine M M, Sibbons P D, Howard C V, McGill F and van Velzen D. 1994. Gestational-age dependence of regional proliferation in fetal kidneys – an immunocytochemical study. *Pediatric Research*. 35, #2, 269.

40.   Pahal N, Ansari T, Howard C V, Sibbons P D and van Velzen D. 1995. Fibre type imbalance in the diaphragm of SIDS patients related to IUGR. *Pediatric Pulmonology*. 20, #5, 346.

41.   Ricketts S A, Sibbons P D, Howard C V and van Velzen D. 1998. Bacterial translocation in pre-necrotizing enterocolitis (NEC) intestinal mucosa assessed by confocal laser scanning microscopy. *Journal of Cellular Pathology*. 3, #1, 17–26.

42.   Sibbons P D, Ansari T, Beech D J, Pahal N, Howard C V and van Velzen D. 1997. Micro-anatomical defects in kidneys, lungs, brain, phrenic nerve and diaphragm, in SIDS infants – a stereological study. *Pediatric Pulmonology*. 24, #6, 448.

43.   Sibbons P D, Ricketts S A and van Velzen D. 1996. Sub-clinical NEC in a group of infants dying from other, unrelated causes – a histopathological study. *Journal of Cellular Pathology*. 1, 153–160.

MSc Thesis

44.   Li Y. 1995. *Investigation of the cellular stabilisation of neurons and glial cells in human neocortex during normal ontogeny*. Brunel University, Uxbridge.

PhD Thesis

45.   Ansari T I. 1998. *Stereological analysis of SIDS-linked micro-anatomical anomalies in specific regions of the brain, phrenic nerve and diaphragm.* The University of Liverpool, Liverpool.

46.   Beech D J. 1997. *A stereological investigation of the development of the respiratory and renal systems of victims of Sudden Infant Death Syndrome.* Brunel University, Uxbridge.

47.   Hinchliffe S A. 1993. *The Pathogenesis of Developmental and Acquired Renal Abnormalities in Paediatric Refluxive and Obstructive Disease.* Erasmus University, Rotterdam.

48.   Oguz E O. 1999. *The maturation of the human cerebellum in normal and low birthweight infants. A stereological study.* The University of Liverpool, Liverpool.

49.   Pahal N K. 1996. *A morphometric study of the phrenic nerve and diaphragm during late gestational and neonatal development.* Liverpool John Moores University, Liverpool.

The van Velzen Years: Part 10

Recommendations

1. Recommendations

1.1   The following recommendations arise out of the mistakes in the 'van Velzen Years' and are essential to avoid their repetition in the event of the coming of another Professor van Velzen. The recommendations are evidence-based in the sense that they are straightforward safeguards based on our analysis of the actual mistakes made by both Alder Hey and the University. Many of the mistakes are of a type that must be frequent but do not in the usual course of events lead to disaster. They are nevertheless better avoided.

1.2   Our recommendations are also evidence-based in a different sense. The themes in the recommendations formed the basis of the actual questioning during the course of the Inquiry. They have been tested not just by us in our deliberations but also gauged against the reaction of witnesses to the potential criticisms raised. Very few witnesses had any difficulty in seeing the force of the points and most were comfortable to concede what should have been the tests governing the behaviour of them and others involved. The difficulty came not in terms of the concept but when people found on reflection that they had not lived up to the sentiments expressed. Mutual trust between universities and hospitals could have avoided the worst excesses of Professor van Velzen. All witnesses agreed that such trust is essential for the future.

2. Relationship Between Universities and Trusts

2.1   Whatever the underlying contractual position, the relationship between Universities and Trusts, in respect of individuals and departments with dual clinical and academic functions, shall be one of the utmost good faith in both directions.

2.2   The duty of utmost good faith shall require either party to disclose to the other any substantial matter relating to the performance of the individual or department, whether clinical or academic.

2.3   Where there is any doubt as to whether a matter is of a substantial nature, if it relates to patient care the doubt shall always be resolved in favour of disclosure.

2.4   The appointment of clinical academics shall be approached with fair representation on each side reflecting the proposed split between clinical and academic sessions.

2.5   The appointment of external advisors shall be approached on the basis that they are truly external, if not strictly independent in a legal sense. There is no point having external advisers as 'window dressing' for a fixed internal view. Where they or representatives of the Royal Colleges give advice, proper weight shall be given to that advice. In giving advice, external advisers shall bear in mind the paramount requirement of patient care where there is a conflict of interest.

2.6   A single job description for clinical academics shall be drawn up jointly to represent a fair and realistic expectation of the work envisaged by both parties.

2.7   There shall be a joint procedure for disciplinary action against an individual perceived to be failing. It shall contain provision for immediate suspension from patient care as a minimum, irrespective of academic requirements and positions.

2.8   There shall be formal annual appraisal of an individual by both parties. They shall share their information in line with the duty of utmost good faith in order to draw up a joint statement of aims in the following 12 months against which the next appraisal is to be judged.

2.9   Where there is disagreement each party shall reconsider bearing in mind that patient care is of paramount importance. In the event of continued disagreement an arbitrator may be appointed, but in any case the Trust shall take immediate steps to secure proper patient care.

2.10   The relationship between Universities and funding bodies shall be of the utmost good faith and similar considerations shall apply.

3. New Ventures

3.1 Where a new venture, such as the establishment of a Chair or department, is contemplated, both parties where appropriate shall consider in detail the aims and resources available and draw up a realistic business plan before any final commitment is made. As in all these matters, if patient care is to be included in the venture, patient care shall be paramount in its consideration.

3.2 There shall be close performance management of any new venture in its early stages and appropriate steps taken to modify the business plan as required.

3.3 Any substantial alteration in an existing venture shall be treated as if a new venture.

4. Audit

4.1 Where there is good reason to believe that an individual or department may be failing and affecting patient care, it shall be the duty of the Trust with the co-operation of the university, and if appropriate on a joint basis, to investigate. Investigation shall continue until the problems are identified or it is found that in reality no problem exists. Where appropriate, independent outside assistance shall be obtained.

4.2 Where problems are identified a plan, jointly where necessary, shall be drawn up to resolve them as soon as possible.

4.3 If no solution is found after all diligent attempts, the parties should keep records of their attempts and the reasons why they have failed, such records to be lodged by way of report to the relevant NHS Executive Regional Office.

5. Management Standards

5.1 No clinician shall be appointed to a position of managerial authority in a hospital without having relevant clinical experience for the position.

5.2 No clinician should take effective control of a management position until trained in all necessary management techniques and in any relevant legal requirements.

5.3 No clinician shall be asked to take on responsibilities that impair the ability to carry out patient care to the appropriate standard.

5.4   Hospital managers shall be of a suitable background and calibre for the role expected of them, provided with all necessary training (including continued education) and themselves regularly appraised for the quality of their performance.

5.5   Hospital managers without medical qualification shall seek medical advice on matters requiring it. If there is doubt as to the need for advice on any matter relating to patient care, the doubt shall be resolved by seeking advice.

5.6   While hospital managers will usually seek medical advice from the medical director or clinical directors in the first instance, if any substantial doubt remains they shall seek advice from independent specialist medical advisers or the Royal Colleges, whether directly or through their regional advisers.

        Other issues arising out of facts in 'The van Velzen Years' have their own separate chapters. Recommendations in respect of those issues appear at the conclusion of those chapters.

Chapter 9. The Coroner

Contents

1. Introduction

1.1 Post mortem examinations can be carried out under two different legal powers. The most commonly used nationally is that under the jurisdiction of the Coroner (Coroner's post mortem examination or CPM). The other power lies under the Human Tissue Act 1961 (hospital post mortem examination or HPM) and will be covered in Chapter 10. In an HPM the surviving relatives should decide whether it takes place. In a CPM it is the Coroner who decides and the surviving relatives have no right to object. A CPM is required by law in certain circumstances.

1.2 Coroners are appointed and paid by local authorities. They are accountable to the Courts for their decisions by way of judicial review. They are also answerable to the Home Office and to the Lord Chancellor's Department for their conduct and administration.

2. Deaths Requiring an Inquest

2.1 Coroners must hold an inquest where there is reasonable cause to suspect that the death reported was:

- unnatural;

- due to violence;

- sudden and of unknown cause;

- in certain other circumstances not directly relevant to this Inquiry.

2.2 Where Coroners must hold an inquest they are also empowered to request a post mortem examination.

3. Function of the Inquest – the Scope of the Proceedings

3.1 The function of an Inquest is to determine certain facts:

- the identity of the deceased;

- the cause of death;

- the circumstances surrounding the death and its cause.

3.2   Inquests can help allay rumour or suspicion, draw attention to the existence of circumstances which if unremedied might lead to further deaths, advance medical knowledge and preserve the legal interests of the deceased person's family. It is not, however, the function of an inquest to establish either criminal or civil liability.

4.   Deaths Reportable to Coroners

4.1   Coroners must be informed in the case of a death:

- of any person not attended during his last illness by a registered medical practitioner;

- for which a certificate of cause of death cannot be obtained;

- occurring in circumstances where the deceased was seen neither after death nor within 14 days before death by the certifying doctor;

- the cause of which appears unknown;

- which is unnatural, suspicious or related to trauma;

- during an operation or before recovery from the effects of an anaesthetic;

- related to industrial diseases or industrial poisoning.

5.   Decisions Open to the Coroner

5.1   Following notification of a death, the Coroner may decide that:

- the circumstances require neither a post mortem examination nor an inquest and inform the Registrar of Births and Deaths accordingly – the Pink Form A Procedure;

- a post mortem examination is required. The Coroner makes the decision and may override the wishes of the surviving relatives. After the examination the Coroner may decide that an inquest is unnecessary if satisfied that the death was due to natural causes, in which case the cause of death identified by the examination will be notified by way of the Pink Form B Procedure;

- an inquest is required with or without a post mortem examination.

6. Coroner's Limited Right to Possession of the Body and Retention of Body Parts

6.1   Where a death has been referred to the Coroner, until an inquest has been held or the Coroner has decided no inquest is necessary, the Coroner has the right to possession of the body. This overrides the right of any other person until his duties have been completed.

6.2   Under Rule 36 of the Coroner's Rules 1984 the Coroner has the right to possession of a body only to carry out the function of the Coroner.

> 'The proceedings and evidence at an inquest shall be directed solely to ascertaining the following matters, namely:
>
> - who the deceased was;
>
> - how, when and where the deceased came by his death;
>
> - the particulars for the time being required by the Registration Act to be registered concerning the death.
>
> Neither the Coroner nor the Jury shall express any opinion on any other matter.'

6.3   There is no power to possess the body for research, medical education or therapeutic purposes under the Coroner's jurisdiction, which is a narrow one.

6.4   Rule 9 of the Coroner's Rules 1984 governs the circumstances in which body parts may be retained on behalf of the Coroner.

> 'A person making a post mortem examination shall make provision, so far as possible, for the preservation of material which in his opinion bears upon the cause of death for such period as the Coroner thinks fit.'

6.5   Again there is no power to preserve body parts for research, medical education or therapeutic purposes. Preservation is only allowed of material bearing on the cause of death. Once the process is completed, while it can be appreciated that in some cases it would be appropriate to preserve material for further examination of experts in a civil case, it is difficult to see how a Coroner could validly think it fit to preserve large quantities of material any longer.

7.   Background to our Inquiry

7.1   Our Inquiry began at a time when the new HM Coroner for Liverpool, Mr Andre Rebello, was opening inquests into cases many years old which did not appear originally to have been properly investigated. Some surviving relatives were alleging that they had felt pressured into agreeing to an HPM on the basis that if they did not agree there would be a CPM anyway. There appeared to be a general ignorance among surviving relatives of the Coroner's process and some claimed not to have understood the cause of death. In the light of what was emerging from the van Velzen years (see Chapter 8), we were interested to see if Professor van Velzen's practice with regard to CPM had differed from that at HPM and whether there had been compliance within the limited scope of the Coroner's process. If there had been failures we were interested to see how the previous HM Coroner for Liverpool, Mr Roy Barter, had reacted.

Pressure on Parents, Using Mention of CPM, to Consent to HPM

8.   Parents' Account

8.1   A number of parents gave evidence to the Inquiry to the following effect. When they were asked to 'consent' to an HPM they were put under pressure by references to a CPM. They were made to feel that a CPM would be carried out anyway and so there was little point in objecting to an HPM.

8.2   The mother of Samantha gave us a graphic example of the pressure she felt. Samantha had two operations and died within 48 hours of the second. The death was, therefore, clearly reportable to the Coroner and a CPM was in the end performed, finding the cause of death as cardiac and liver failure, due to chromosomal abnormality syndrome, congenital cardiovascular malformation and malformation of the liver. Samantha's mother, however, was asked to 'consent' to an HPM within five to ten minutes of Samantha's death. She protested that Samantha had been through enough and she would not consent to an HPM. At this point the treating clinician said that if she objected there would be a CPM anyway. Despite this pressure she continued in her objection. The CPM was appropriate but the pressure and reference to a HPM were not.

8.3   The mother of Simone reported a similar experience. Simone suffered from a congenital heart defect. She underwent surgery at 10 and 16 months of age. Following the later operation her condition deteriorated and she died three days after the operation. Her death was not reported to the Coroner and this case constitutes one of those now formally opened by Mr Rebello ten years on. Simone's mother said in evidence to us that Mr Franks, Consultant Cardiothoracic Surgeon, made it clear that if she did not sign the post mortem consent form then he would ask for a CPM. She told the Inquiry,

> 'He came in and placed a piece of paper in front of me and said, 'Can you sign that?' I said, 'What is it?' He said, 'It is for a post mortem.' I said, 'You do not need one. You have been working on her for over 6 hours. You know what she has died of. Leave her alone. You have done enough.' He said, 'If you do not sign it, I am going to get it done anyway. I will get the Coroner to get it done.' Basically, he was adamant that he was going to get that consent form signed.'

Simone's mother reluctantly signed the form.

9. Clinicians' Account

9.1 Mr Franks disputed in his evidence that he made any reference to a CPM, saying in his witness statement dated 7 June 2000,

> 'I deny categorically that the threat of a Coroner's post mortem was ever used by me as a stick to 'persuade' parents to consent to a hospital post mortem. I have never done that and would regard that conduct as completely unacceptable.'

9.2 Other clinicians, against whom the parents made no complaint, maintained that they never applied pressure in this way. Dr Arnold, Consultant Paediatric Cardiologist, said in his witness statement dated 19 June 2000,

> 'I believe that the circumstances in which the Coroner should be notified of the death of a child are quite straightforward and I have never used the 'threat' of a Coroner's post mortem as a stick to get parents to consent to a hospital post mortem. Indeed, I have never leaned on parents in obtaining their consent to a hospital post mortem: usually one can tell right away whether parents are likely to agree or not.'

9.3   Dr Peart, Consultant Paediatric Cardiologist, expressed a similar view.

> 'I have never held the threat of a Coroner's post mortem over parents' heads if they did not agree to a hospital post mortem. In my view a Coroner's post mortem would be undertaken for two reasons, firstly where there was a legal request – usually in the situation of a death either on the operating table or within 24 hours of surgery – and secondly where the clinician had no idea as to why the child had died, for instance where the clinician was unable to sign a death certificate giving a cause of death. Outwith those situations, if I wanted a post mortem then my role was to discuss it with the parents. If the parents did not agree, then a post mortem would not take place.'

9.4   Dr Ratcliffe, Consultant in Paediatric Intensive Care, said in her witness statement,

> 'I have always been clear about the distinction between the legal requirement for a Coroner's post mortem and a hospital post mortem ... I would be very clear during my discussions with families that a post mortem examination was not required by the Coroner for legal reasons and that I was in a position to sign a death certificate.... I can confirm therefore that I have never used a Coroner's post mortem as a threat to obtain consent to a hospital post mortem, and indeed I have no knowledge of this happening at Alder Hey, although I am aware that it did take place at institutions where I have worked previously.'

9.5   The final sentiment, that it was known to happen but not at Alder Hey, was also apparent from discussion at the Clinicians' Seminar, arranged by the Inquiry and which took place at Alder Hey on 23 May 2000. There was again anecdotal evidence of the practice but individual clinicians denied that they had followed it. There are no grounds at all for suspecting that Dr Ratcliffe's own evidence was not entirely honest on the point.

10.   Coroner's Officer

10.1   Further anecdotal evidence of the practice came from DC Carl Thompson who served as a Coroner's Officer in the Liverpool Office from 1992 to 2000. In his witness statement dated 30 June 2000 he said he was aware that doctors sometimes approached families to obtain consent for an HPM, telling the family that a death certificate would be issued at a later stage. He considered it to be unacceptable practice and explained that in cases not reportable to the Coroner a death certificate should be presented to the family before consent for any HPM was requested. In this way parents could object to an HPM and yet still hold a death certificate. He was not specifically aware of this unacceptable practice at Alder Hey.

11. Conclusion – 'A Clouded View of What is Required'

11.1 We are satisfied, having weighed the evidence carefully, that pressure was sometimes applied at Alder Hey in mentioning a CPM at a time when parents were considering whether or not to object to an HPM. The parents' evidence was compelling and supported in part at least by the evidence of clinicians and the Coroner's Officer. They were aware of such a practice generally, although not admitting it at Alder Hey, and we regard this as substantial if not complete corroboration of the parents. We find that Mr Franks had a mistaken view of what was required in the reporting of deaths to the Coroner and our reasons are to be found below.

11.2 A clouded view of what the Coroner's jurisdiction requires of clinicians has emerged generally in the course of our Inquiry. We have indicated in Chapter 10 how surprised we were to find the ignorance of the medical profession of the Human Tissue Act 1961. There was a similar confusion and lack of precision in the mind of clinicians as to when a death is strictly reportable to the Coroner. Dr Marco Pozzi, Consultant Cardiothoracic Surgeon, said in his witness statement,

> 'I have never been given a document setting out the particular circumstances in which I have a legal obligation to report a death to the Coroner. Even now, all I know is if a child dies in theatre or does not wake up from anaesthesia, I have to report it to the Coroner.'

11.3 Professor van Velzen himself, having undertaken numerous CPMs, appears to have had a genuine misapprehension of what was required of him and what material he could retain. Of course what he in fact did went well beyond any genuine misapprehension, but he said in his preliminary evidence to the Solicitor to the Inquiry,

> 'I was never fully instructed about how to go about Coroner's post mortems.'

11.4 There is nothing wrong with obtaining an HPM 'consent' under the Human Tissue Act 1961 to the retention of material beyond the Coroner's process for research, medical education or therapeutic purposes so long as the Coroner is notified and agrees. There is nothing wrong with returning to parents to ask for an HPM if the Coroner declines jurisdiction or decides not to carry out a CPM. What is unacceptable is for relatives to feel pressured into 'consenting' to HPM by reason of the suggestion of a CPM.

Systems and Procedures

We were interested to find out if there are cases where CPMs should have been performed but were not. We explored carefully the Coroner's systems and procedures.

12. Cases of 'Despair'

12.1   DC Thompson has extensive experience as a Coroner's Officer. Before his appointment in Liverpool in 1992, he spent six years as a Coroner's Officer in the Wirral. He explained that when there had been a death at Alder Hey, which was reportable to the Coroner, the usual procedure was for the senior doctor concerned, in his recollection invariably a consultant, to telephone the office to report the death. As the Coroner's Officer he then completed *pro forma* Form 97, which records basic information regarding the death. If the death followed an operation, the reporting doctor explained its nature. The doctor outlined what the operation involved, the probability of survival and the medical background of the child. Often the doctor indicated that he was happy to sign a death certificate and that the operation had really been one of 'despair', meaning that the child would probably have died anyway and the family had no concerns regarding the treatment.

12.2   DC Thompson's practice in cases of 'despair', acting on instructions from the Coroner, was to indicate to the reporting doctor that there was no need for any CPM and that a death certificate could be issued. He said,

> 'That, however, was dependent upon my being satisfied that there was nothing in the circumstances reported to me that was of concern. If there was anything at all which was reported with which I was unhappy, then I would insist that a Coroner's post mortem would have to be carried out.'

13. The Problem

13.1   How was DC Thompson to be 'satisfied' that there was nothing 'of concern' in the report to him? He was completely reliant on the accuracy of the information given to him by the reporting doctor. He had no training, no particular medical knowledge and yet he was required to make a 'judicial' decision concerning the performance of a post mortem examination. He was required to make no positive inquiry of the surviving relatives themselves to see if they had any concerns about the treatment. That they had not, he took completely on trust from the reporting doctor.

13.2   If satisfied DC Thompson then completed a Pink Form A, which the Coroner himself had to sign. This form was confirmation that a death had been reported but no post mortem examination performed. The reporting doctor was asked to initial the medical certificate of death. The Registrar of Births Marriages and Deaths then knew that the death had been reported to the Coroner. The Registrar agreed to the issue of the death certificate and expected Pink Form A from the Coroner's office in due course.

14. Clinicians' Knowledge and Use of the Practice

14.1 The above practice was not unique to Liverpool and was well known to the clinicians at Alder Hey. Both Dr Pozzi and Dr Peart were well aware of it, Dr Peart stating,

> 'I am not aware of circumstances where a Coroner's post mortem has been used as a threat to induce consent to a hospital post mortem but I am aware that there were circumstances where the Coroner waived his right to a post mortem.'

15. Mr Franks' Memory

15.1 Mr Franks' memory of exactly what the practice involved differed, slightly but significantly, from that of DC Thompson. He remembers that the Coroner only authorised the issue of a death certificate without a CPM in the following circumstances:

- when the doctor was able to write a death certificate;

- when there was 'no problem or discontent on the part of the relatives';

- *and* there was going to be an HPM in any event.

15.2 Mr Franks said he did not have such a discussion with the Coroner's Officer

> '… unless I was sure that I had a formal consent to post mortem because otherwise there could be a change of mind…. My usual practice was therefore to speak to the Coroner if I was in any doubt as to the circumstances regarding my duty to report but then I would have left it to the Coroner to decide whether there should be a Coroner's post mortem. His questions however, were usually the same, "Could you write a death certificate and would there be a post mortem examination giving the opportunity to modify the death certificate?" If the answers to those questions were in the affirmative then the Coroner would generally say that the death did not need to be formally reported but he would *see the post mortem report and file it* on that basis'. [emphasis added]

16. Contrast DC Thompson

16.1 DC Thompson's recollection is different. He is clear that in making the decision to perform a CPM he never offered the reporting doctor the opportunity of performing an HPM instead, only for a copy of the report to be sent to the Coroner.

16.2   We prefer DC Thompson's evidence. Mr Franks seems to have a mistaken view of the
role of the Coroner and the rules governing the Coroner's procedures. It is illogical, in
the case of a reportable death, for a Coroner to state that a CPM is unnecessary, but that
an HPM should be performed. It is not surprising that, despite looking, we have found
no evidence of HPM reports being sent to the Coroner. Mr Franks' evidence is
confused. Whether he was sure that a death should be reported is not the issue. The real
question, to be addressed by the Coroner, is whether a CPM should be performed, the
death having been formally reported. There is the clear potential for mistake, or even
abuse, in the procedure designed to provide the information upon which the decision
is to be made.

17.   Views of Clinicians

17.1   At the Clinicians' Seminar one consultant expressed his confidence in the Coroner's
Officers, but Dr Pozzi disagreed in his evidence.

> 'The communication has been with an Officer who, from my point of view, had
> very little understanding of what the problem was and who seemed to have
> difficulty spelling the name of the pathologist. We could tell these people just
> about what we wanted and we could decide almost whether or not we wanted
> a Coroner's post mortem report by putting the emphasis on the severity of the
> disease and their happiness to produce a cause of death.'

17.2   Dr Pozzi exposed the lack of transparency of the system and his views were echoed in
those of Dr Ratcliffe. She said,

> 'I now accept that on the face of things, that system is not transparent in that
> if the reporting doctor wished to put a history in terms such as to persuade
> the Coroner's Officer that a post mortem was not necessary, then due to the
> Coroner's Officer's lack of knowledge there would be the potential for that to
> happen. This problem is exemplified by the fact that in many cases I would be
> telephoning to report the death to the Coroner and yet I would not have been
> directly involved with all the treatment. For example, I would not have been
> party to cardiac surgery, yet would have often dealt with that patient in intensive
> care and may not have had any knowledge of any untoward events in theatre.
> Having said that, I have no evidence of the system having been abused in
> this way.'

17.3   In relation to Dr Ratcliffe and Dr Pozzi there is no issue as to their honesty or any
suggestion of any abuse of the trust placed in them. We found them to be caring
clinicians and open in their approach.

18. Conclusion

18.1   DC Thompson himself recognised the problem.

> 'I personally was aware of the inherent dangers of taking at face value what had been said to me by the reporting doctor and authorising the issue of the death certificate without a Coroner's post mortem. However, it was clear to me that this way of dealing with things was how Mr Barter wanted us to proceed.'

18.2   Failure to carry out a CPM in cases where such an examination should be performed leads to lack of proper scrutiny of medical practice. Transparency and openness are lost.

The Coroner's Non-delegable Duties

19.   Rule 4 – 'Ready' at all Times

19.1   We have outlined in the previous section how the Coroner's Officer regularly decided whether a post mortem examination should be carried out. Under Rule 4 of the Coroner's Rules 1984,

> 'A Coroner shall at all times hold himself ready to undertake either by himself or by his deputy or assistant deputy any duties in connection with inquests and post mortem examinations.'

19.2   This imposes a personal duty on the Coroner, and both Rules 5 and 6, which deal with the arrangements for post mortem examination, are specific in referring to the Coroner as the one directing or requesting the examination. The wording of the Rules clearly lays the responsibility on the Coroner personally, and not on his Officer, of taking decisions regarding the authorisation of a post mortem examination.

20.   Role of Coroner's Officer

20.1   The standard text, *Jervis on Coroners*, states,

> 'The Officer is not the Coroner, and he must never appear to assume more than transitory responsibility for what is being done, ordered or arranged. He must report to, and receive instructions from, the Coroner, though he may know from experience the likely sequence of events in certain fairly common and well-defined circumstances.'

21. Pink Forms Revisited – the Coroner's Decision

21.1 While the Coroner did in fact sign the Pink Form A personally, this amounted to little safeguard when the Officer was the one in direct communication with the clinician. DC Thompson said that on occasions Mr Barter asked for more information before signing the Pink Form A but he had never ultimately refused to sign one. The present Coroner for Liverpool, Mr Rebello, supervises the officers much more closely. DC Thompson said,

> 'The practice to which I have referred above however, whereby I am able to authorise the issue of a death certificate without the necessity for a Coroner's post mortem subject to being satisfied with the information given to me by the reporting doctor, is a practice which continues. The difference now is that my contact with the Coroner is much closer. Mr Rebello personally authorises all post mortems whereas Mr Barter was more remote than that. Provided that there were no queries he was more than happy for post mortems to be authorised on his behalf and he did not expect to be consulted all the time. Now, however, I am obliged to check matters with Mr Rebello. I am no longer able to agree that no Coroner's post mortem should be performed without specifically referring to Mr Rebello first. Previously the only effective control was that ultimately Mr Barter would sign the pink form A in each case.'

22. Stacks of Pre-signed Forms

22.1 Improper delegation of his duty by Mr Barter led to other undesirable practices. We obtained evidence that there were stacks of pre-signed blank Pink Form B (authorising issue of death certificate where no inquest was ordered) and Form Cert E (releasing the body for cremation). Mr Barter explained that he wished to help grieving families in any way he could, particularly by issuing promptly those documents enabling funeral arrangements to proceed. Pink Form B and Form Cert E were pre-signed to avoid delays. Pink Form A was not pre-signed, as in such cases the death was registered on the basis of the cause of death given by the medical practitioner and not on the contents of Form A which simply confirmed the Coroner had no further interest in the death. The upshot of having these pre-signed forms was that Coroner's Officers were able to take decisions whether to hold an inquest or not without being obliged first to refer to Mr Barter.

23. Training of Coroner's Officers – Misplaced Confidence

23.1 The lack of personal control of the previous Coroner is all the more concerning because of a similar lack of training in Coroner's Officers generally. DC Thompson maintained that he had received no formal training. Essentially he learnt the job through sitting next to one of the other Coroner's Officers. In oral evidence Mr Barter suggested that the decision whether to carry out a CPM was basically a simple administrative decision. He considered that an experienced Coroner's Officer was perfectly competent to know when a post mortem examination was needed and said he had every confidence in his senior Coroner's Officers. However, he accepted that ultimately he was responsible for the decisions reached, that there was no written instruction or training of Coroner's Officers and the job was learned 'hands on'.

24. Conclusion

24.1 In our view it is quite wrong to suggest that the decision whether to carry out a Coroner's post mortem is 'a simple administrative decision'. The decision is one to be taken by the Coroner personally, after all proper enquiries. No doubt the Coroner's Officers can assist, but it is not their decision to take.

Further Illustrations

Sean

25.1 Sean was born in 1996. He had been diagnosed as suffering from a congenital heart defect (double outlet right ventricle, hypoplastic left ventricle with hypoplastic aortic arch). He underwent a repair of the aortic arch a week after birth and at 15 months a Fontain procedure. He died on the operating table during this second surgery. Before the operation Sean's parents were told differing prospects of success – 80 per cent but then 50 per cent. His father gave us clear evidence that after death he was approached by the surgeon, Mr Franks, for consent for an HPM which he gave, limited to the heart and lungs,

> 'I specified that Sean's heart only be looked at, because I figured that because he died during open heart surgery, that was the reason for his death.... We were stunned he had died, and we wanted to know why he had died, and that is what we thought we were consenting to, to help the hospital and to help ourselves to discover why.'

The Royal Liverpool Children's Inquiry

25.2   Precisely why Mr Franks asked for an HPM is a matter of some speculation when it was so obviously wrong. A CPM was clearly indicated because Sean had died during surgery but the parents did not then know this. Sean's mother said,

> 'I did not even realise that a Coroner could and should have done the post mortem.... Mr Franks should have stepped back and said, "I am very sorry, but at this point I do have to hand over to the Coroner", for want of a better phrase.'

25.3   His father said,

> 'I do recall Mr Franks saying to me words to the effect that, 'you can have a Coroner's post mortem if you want, but obviously we know why he died, so we will just do a hospital one because it will be quicker'. They are not his words, but that was the general tone.'

25.4   Mr Franks said, in a supplementary statement dealing specifically with Sean, that the death had been reported to the Coroner, who had been happy for a death certificate to be issued subject to the performance of an HPM. We have established that the death was reported to the Coroner on the following day. The Coroner's officer completed the Form 97A,

> 'Elective admission to correct complex congenital heart condition (high risk but essential to preserve life). Surgery commenced 09:00 21/10. Baby died on table at 20:00 same day. Natural causes, family happy to accept certificate.'

25.5   There is no evidence of any HPM report having being sent to the Coroner. A Pink Form A was issued, confirming that a death certificate could be issued without a post mortem examination, and the cause of death was recorded as 1(a) heart failure and 1(b) complex congenital heart disease.

26.   Conclusion

26.1   This is as clear a case as any where a CPM should have been performed. On the basis of the actual death certificate the Registrar of Births and Deaths was not even aware that there had been surgery, let alone that death had been on the operating table. The comment on Form 97A, 'high risk but essential to preserve life', might well be correct; but it begs the question whether Sean had the quality of surgery and care that is owed to us all, even a critically ill baby. Only a CPM independent of the hospital could have provided open and transparent evidence upon which to decide whether to hold an inquest.

26.2   The parents gave evidence in their initial questionnaire,

> 'Had we truly understood the situation as to the events around Sean's death we now know that we would not have signed any consent form, nor allowed anyone else at Alder Hey to touch him, and also most significantly we would have wanted the Coroner to be involved as Sean died during an operation.'

26.3   Sean's parents understandably feel that the sole reason for the HPM was to enable the hospital to retain Sean's heart for the collection at the ICH. We now know that Professor van Velzen made no distinction between CPMs and HPMs, so that the parents' concern on this score is unlikely to be accurate. However, this sort of suspicion is precisely what comes out of secrecy and disregard of proper procedure. The present Coroner is now investigating and an inquest is expected soon.

Sarah

27.1   Sarah was born in 1991 and died at the age of 5 weeks following surgery on the previous day. The death was correctly reported to the Coroner, but Form 97A reveals only the scrappiest manuscript note. It records simply that an operation for transposition of the great arteries had been performed and that Sarah had died at 0300 the following day. The cause of death was recorded as 1(a) heart failure and 1(b) transposition of great vessels and coarctation, with a note 'PHos' (apparently 'per hospital').

27.2   Even though a death certificate could be issued without post mortem examination, an HPM was performed. Mr Franks, the surgeon involved, commented specifically on the case and suggested that a CPM was carried out, but there is no copy of any post mortem report on the Coroner's original file, and the post mortem report copied to us indicates clearly that Professor van Velzen performed an HPM. When Sarah's parents gave oral evidence to the Inquiry her father rightly questioned how it could be that the Coroner did not request a post mortem examination when Sarah had died within hours of surgery.

28. Conclusion

28.1   As with Sean, an HPM was carried out when it was indicated on behalf of the Coroner that there was no need for a CPM. Had the parents objected to an HPM, there would have been no investigation at all into the death. This would have been highly unsatisfactory. In each case, as with many others, a CPM was surely indicated.

Information for Parents

29.   Information Irrespective of 'Consent'

29.1   While as a matter of law consent to a CPM is not required, nevertheless surviving relatives should be informed of the purpose of the procedure, what it involves and, most importantly, the findings and conclusions. We found little evidence of any detailed discussion in the case of CPM. The general experience of parents was that they were told it had to be performed and that 'this was the law'. Inevitably those 'discussions' often took place at the most difficult of times, immediately after the death and when parents were most vulnerable. Some clinicians limited 'discussion' of a CPM to a bare minimum precisely because 'consent' was not required. This reflects the difficulties of some clinicians in discussing post mortem examinations generally.

Gareth

30.1   Gareth, who died following surgery for a congenital heart defect in 1993, is a typical case where the parents were given inadequate information. They gave evidence to us of Mr Franks' explanation that a CPM was required.

> 'He came out saying something along the lines of, 'You know there is going to have to be a post mortem', basically saying we did not have any choice in the matter, no option. I think we appreciated that ourselves, from our own knowledge, but at no time did he come out and explain the post mortem procedure, or why it was necessary. We were not really given any time to consider it.... We were just told, 'it is going to happen.'

30.2   The lack of proper explanation led the parents to suspect something had gone wrong with the treatment. That was not the case and the upset and suspicion could easily have been avoided.

31. Clinicians 'Slightly Defensive' When Coroner Involved

31.1   Clinicians generally felt that they had to be more circumspect in cases where the Coroner was involved. Dr Arnold, Consultant Paediatric Cardiologist, said in his witness statement dated 19 June 2000,

> 'In relation to Coroner's post mortems I would confess that I had always felt our attitude in this regard has been slightly defensive in terms of being very careful in relation to what is said to parents given that a Coroner's inquiry is underway, particularly when an inquest is being arranged. With the benefits of hindsight I do not think that that was helpful, and there should be more liaison between clinicians and the Coroner.'

31.2   Circumspection in discussing the presumptive cause of death before a CPM is easily to be understood, but there is no reason why a full explanation of the procedure and the reason for the examination cannot be given. Dr Ratcliffe agreed. She made no distinction in the way she worked with parents in a CPM or an HPM. She explained to parents that a CPM was required by law in certain circumstances and was explicit as to what the examination involved. We received written evidence from some parents who appreciated this explicit but sympathetic approach and they had specific praise for Dr Ratcliffe.

32. Examples of Poor Communication

32.1   In some cases there was practically no communication. The mother of Lindsay, who died in 1991, did not know that a CPM had been performed until she attended the funeral parlour. The mother of Craig, who died in 1986, was told of the need for a CPM, but the subsequent report suggested that when the discussion took place the examination had already been performed. The parents of Philip, who died in 1989, knew that as a result of their son's death there would be some investigation, but understood this to be 'an internal inquiry'. They did not appreciate that a CPM had been performed, even when the treating clinician came to see them to discuss Philip's death some six to eight weeks later.

33. Conclusion

33.1   If parents want a full discussion of what is involved in the Coroner's process, they should have it. Some parents, however, do not want to go into such detail. We appreciate that it is upsetting. Whereas Parliament has given the surviving relatives the responsibility for making the decision to have an HPM and they have to be told upsetting information to inform their decision, no such considerations apply to CPM. It is wrong to force them to listen to the detail if they do not want to hear it. Sympathetic enquiry can be made of what they want to know and the information suited to their wishes.

33.2   While there is no statutory requirement, good practice clearly dictates that surviving relatives be told the results of a CPM as soon as is reasonably practicable, and in writing if requested. Results of examinations have not been communicated as a matter of routine in all past cases. Lindsay's mother did not receive the report until she requested a copy in November 1999, more than eight years on. There was no system at Alder Hey or at the Coroner's Office to ensure that parents who wished to do so received copies of reports in an appropriate setting. Given the basic human need for grieving parents to understand the cause of death of their child, it was wrong not to have ensured proper counselling of parents in the light of the reports. If parents have to 'endure' post mortem examination irrespective of consent in the case of CPM, then the least society can do in return is to communicate and counsel properly to help them understand and, in so doing, to help in the process of grieving.

The Use of Organs Retained at CPM for Research

34.   The Extent of the Power to Retain Material at CPM

34.1   We have already set out the basic extent of the power in the above description. Section 11(5)(b)(i) and (ii) of the Coroner's Act 1988 defines precisely the extent of the Coroner's jurisdiction which is to determine who the deceased was, how, where and when he came by his death, and no more.

34.2   Paragraph 6 of 'Practice Notes for Coroners', a document issued by the Coroners' Society of England and Wales and approved by Council of the Society on 19 November 1998 states,

> 'It is long recognised that the Coroner's ability to direct that an examination be made is limited to the purposes laid down in the Coroners Act 1988, viz, to establish a cause of death and how that cause of death arose. Although a post mortem may offer the opportunity for wider research or investigation, the Coroner has no power to authorise any such extension to the examination to be made, and those wishing to avail themselves of this opportunity will have to resort to consent under the Anatomy Act 1984 or Human Tissue Act 1961, obtaining appropriate consent in each case.'

34.3   The Coroner therefore has no power to direct or request the removal of tissue or organs for any purpose other than to establish the cause of death. Mr Barter himself confirmed that this was his understanding too. His pathologists had his authority to remove and examine only those organs which they felt necessary to identify the cause of death. He had never been asked permission for the retention of organs for the purpose of teaching or research. If he had, he would have refused, he had no power to grant the request. If a family were to have said they had no objection to the use of organs for research, then he would not have been concerned. It would have been a matter for the hospital and the family to resolve directly. He concluded,

> 'It is clear … that the pathologist's authority to remove organs is only to establish the cause of death, and that authority would be breached if entire organs were being preserved and being kept in a collection without my knowledge or authority. It would appear from what knowledge I have that what was done was in breach of Coroner's rules.'

We concur in this statement of principle and the conclusion.

34.4   The Department of Health Circular, HC (77)28, gives further guidance at paragraph 7,

> 'The provisions relating to the removal of tissue for therapeutic use and for medical education and research apply when a post mortem examination is ordered by a Coroner as they apply to any other post mortem examination, save that their removal requires also the consent of the Coroner.'

35.   Conclusion

35.1   If there is an intention to remove tissue/organs over and above what is necessary to identify the cause of death, then the consent of the Coroner and of the parents is required at the outset of the CPM. If there is an intention to use the material legitimately removed to identify the cause of death later for research or educational purposes, that consent is also better obtained at the outset.

35.2   Rule 9 of the Coroner's Rules 1984 can be conveniently restated at this point,

> 'A person making a post mortem examination shall make provision, so far as possible, for the preservation of material which in his opinion bears upon the cause of death for such period as the Coroner thinks fit.'

35.3   There is no evidence that Mr Barter ever made a decision under Rule 9 so as to indicate the disposal of such 'material'. As a result, hearts continued to be delivered to and stored at the ICH after the Coroner's process was over and without the 'consent' of the parents under the Human Tissue Act 1961. This continued even after Dr Ibrahim wrote to Mr Barter in 1988 pointing out the position (see Chapter 8, Part 1, paragraph 24.2).

36.   Research

36.1   There is no doubt that research was carried out on organs retained at CPM. Dr Gould identified in his report of the internal inquiry at Alder Hey (paragraph 9.2) that organs had been taken for research from at least 63 CPMs. In only one of those cases had there been any diagnostic histology. Mr Dearlove, an experienced MLSO within the Department of Pathology at Alder Hey, said that for the purposes of research there was no distinction made between tissue or organs removed at CPM and HPM. Professor van Velzen conceded this himself. He had no qualms in undertaking research on organs even if they had not been clinically reported. He argued that the decision to retain was not originally made to further opportunities for research, but the wholesale removal of organs was to carry out thorough routine reporting of histology,

> 'Most organs that we took as a whole, we took as a whole for routine reporting need.... Whether or not we wanted to do research from those later is relatively immaterial.'

36.2   We have already rejected Professor van Velzen's contention in our detailed findings in Part 2 of 'The van Velzen Years'. The nature of the fundamental flaw in the research has been exposed in Part 9. However, one aspect of the research material is particularly relevant to organs obtained at CPM. A research paper was rejected for lack of 'control' cases, or cases of death in 'normal' children as judged in the context of the paper. Professor van Velzen said,

> 'So we then added the very few kidneys that we had from children who had died in *car accidents* and it was only in that period that we *started collecting those as a whole.*' [emphasis added]

36.3   This is a specific example of the use of organs from CPM for the furtherance of research. We reject as extraordinary the alternative explanation put forward by Professor van Velzen, that he needed to take all the internal organs following a car accident to see if there was any underlying health problems that had made the child 'vulnerable to having an accident'! These were the clearest instances of organ retention well beyond what was required to establish the cause of death at CPM.

36.4   Both Professor van Velzen and Dr Howard apparently believed that it was legitimate to undertake research on organs taken at CPM without the need for further HPM 'consent'. Both conveniently ignored that the initial removal and retention of organs was in excess of that required to identify the cause of death. Moreover, diagnostic histology following the examination was never undertaken in the vast majority of cases. Professor van Velzen explained in interview with the Solicitor to the Inquiry that, once research had been undertaken on an organ, the material would be returned to the containers and a note made confirming what had been done. He said this would ensure the information was available 'as and when' diagnostic histology was undertaken. When he attended the Inquiry in Liverpool, Counsel to the Inquiry pressed the point,

> 'How can you square doing limited histology for your research purposes using stereology, using considerable technical time, consumables, manpower and skills.... how can you do that on the one hand and yet have parents not knowing the real cause of death of their children, and waiting for weeks and months?'

36.5   Professor van Velzen's response was,

> 'I can only say that what we did was in that sense inexcusable, but that we were driven by the requirement to perform, as formulated by the Dean, to have research output and that in the balance of things, we made this judgment call. Looking back on it, it was unwise.'

36.6   The response is as relevant to all organ retention as it was to CPM retention and 'unwise' is a clear understatement.

Post Mortem by Independent Pathologist

37.   CPM

37.1   Under Rule 6 (1)(c) of the Coroner's Rules 1984 it is stated, in simplified form,

> 'In considering what legally qualified medical practitioner shall be directed or requested by the Coroner to make a post mortem examination, the Coroner shall have regard to the following consideration:
>
> • if the deceased died in a hospital, the Coroner should not direct or request a pathologist on the staff of, or associated with, that hospital to make a post mortem examination if:
>
>   – that pathologist does not desire to make the examination, or
>
>   – the conduct of any member of the hospital staff is likely to be called in question, or

    –   any relative of the deceased asks the Coroner that the examination be not made by such a pathologist …

unless the obtaining of another pathologist with suitable qualifications and experience would cause the examination to be unduly delayed.'

37.2   There is no evidence that Mr Barter had Rule 6 (1)(c) at the forefront of his mind. Quite rightly he wished to ensure that an expert in paediatric pathology investigated the death of any child, but he seemed unconcerned that Professor van Velzen was routinely reporting on deaths at his own hospital. He emphasised the point of theory that the pathologist performing the post mortem examination would be 'wholly independent' in the sense of someone instructed by him and owing a duty to him as Coroner. Of course, if that were the only consideration there would be no need for the Rule.

37.3   In the ordinary course of events Mr Barter may well have felt entitled to rely upon Professor van Velzen's independence, expertise and integrity. However, time has shown this assumption to be unsafe. Mr Barter was not to know it initially, but the real problem surrounding the application of Rule 6 (1)(c) arose out of his reliance on the Coroner's Officer to authorise CPMs. There is no evidence that the Coroner's Officers were trained to consider Rule 6 (1)(c). In practice they did not and, as the duty to authorise and arrange CPMs had been delegated to them by Mr Barter, there was therefore no proper application of Rule 6 (1)(c).

38.   HPM/CPM Interface

38.1   The lack of true independence was even more evident in at least three cases of HPM where Professor van Velzen undertook the examination and the child had been under the care of his partner, a consultant haematologist at Alder Hey. He should have declined as his independence was compromised.

38.2   Further questions arise with regard to transparency as a result of the practice prevailing in 'cardiac' deaths, whether at HPM or CPM. There is inevitable overlap between HPM and CPM in the light of our earlier findings and the practices of Mr Barter and Mr Franks. Dr Audrey Smith, Honorary Research Fellow at the University worked in the ICH. She had originally been appointed as a technician in 1966 but her expertise increased so that that her work on the heart collection became recognised both nationally and internationally. The usual practice at Alder Hey was to examine the heart following post mortem examination through Dr Smith in conjunction with the cardiac surgeon(s), rather than through the pathologist himself who, at best, prepared a brief report on the macroscopic findings. Essentially, therefore, the pathologist provided the heart 'unopened' for further examination. Dr Smith was eminently well qualified to undertake a 'morphological' examination but she was not a pathologist. In any cardiac case it was essential not just to carry out a morphological examination but also to marry up the pathological findings of the heart with those in relation to the other organs and systems. This wider pathological examination was not performed as a matter of routine in the van Velzen years, nor could it have been without routine histological examination. Again, transparency and openness in cardiac deaths were sacrificed.

Preliminary Reports – Inaccurate Causes of Death?

39. The Parents' Position, as Exemplified by Professor van Velzen

39.1 Many parents stated in written and oral evidence that they found it difficult to accept that the Coroner could have been unaware for so long that post mortem histology was not being completed. When the Solicitor to the Inquiry asked Professor van Velzen if he had made the lack of histology explicit to Mr Barter he replied by asking rhetorically, 'But how much more explicit do I need to get?' He continued that each report was clearly headed as a 'preliminary' rather than a 'final' report. However, those 'preliminary' reports were so long and complex that recipients, including Mr Barter and even clinicians, appear to have accepted them as if final reports. At the very least clinicians often took the view that the reports contained sufficient information to enable them to counsel parents properly, although the approach was a practical compromise, as against theoretically proper, in the absence of histology.

40. The Coroner's View

40.1 Mr Barter gave evidence that histology was only ever indicated in a relatively small proportion of cases and it was only in those cases that he expected histology to be done. He said that Professor van Velzen had completed histology on all those cases where histology was awaited.

41. Professor van Velzen's Weakness

41.1 It is certainly relevant to note that Professor van Velzen was given every opportunity in his oral evidence to allege that he had specifically told Mr Barter that post mortem reports were not being completed because of the failure to perform histology, but he singularly drew back from making such an allegation when pressed.

42. Resolution

42.1 In order to resolve whether Mr Barter knew, or should have known, that the reports were essentially incomplete, we again scrutinised the Coroner's procedures. DC Thompson explained that once a CPM had been performed the pathologist telephoned and gave the cause of death. While he was aware that part of the post mortem process might entail histology, he did not inquire of the pathologist whether histology was to be done. This issue lay with the pathologist. If the pathologist made no mention of histology he simply arranged for the death certificate to be issued. When the post mortem report arrived he checked that the cause of death was in accordance with that given over the telephone and if so he simply filed the report. Nobody actually read the report in any detail and the practice was merely to look at the name and the cause of death as a cross check. Dr Khine indicated in evidence that the Coroner's Officer might ask if histology was to be performed, but Mr Barter stated that the duty lay with the pathologist to draw this matter to the attention of the Officer.

42.2 If Professor van Velzen did not tell the Coroner's Officer that he intended to do histology then the Coroner did not expect histology to be performed and accordingly did not chase him for it. According to the evidence of DC Thompson the report itself was only scrutinised if the death was to be the subject of an inquest. Even if it was made clear on the face of the report that histology was awaited this fact was probably not appreciated as the system ran in practice. This effective disregard for the actual content of the report must be condemned. What was the purpose of a detailed, even if incomplete, report if it was not to be read in full? Inevitably some cases where histology was to be performed were not noted as such. We examined Coroner's files where the 'tick box' for histology was not completed, implying that this was not to be performed, and yet supplementary histology reports were in fact provided.

42.3 There was also another way in which the failure to perform histology might escape scrutiny. The correct procedure, if the pathologist indicated that histology was to be done, was for Pink Form B to be completed. A death certificate could then be issued and Pink Form B sent to the Registrar. Eventually the Office of Population Census and Surveys sent a form to the Coroner's office, for completion by the pathologist, to indicate whether, once histology had been performed, the cause of death had changed. It should then have been the pathologist's duty to complete that information, albeit the form when completed would have to be signed by the Coroner. However, there was no system in place to chase histology in such circumstances, let alone to obtain the information from the pathologist. Indeed, from Mr Barter's point of view, a cause of death had been established and a death by natural causes recorded. The only further involvement on his part was through his administrative staff, who processed the financial aspects and should have expected a claim in due course from the pathologist to cover the cost of histology. The staff did not chase the pathologist for histology, but merely checked when a financial claim was submitted that histology had indeed been done.

42.4   Our inspection of the Coroner's files did not support Mr Barter's claim in evidence that in *all those cases where histology was awaited* histology was in fact done. We identified cases where promised histology did not materialise and where the form from the Office of Population Census and Surveys still remains on the file to this day, many years later. In one such case the cause of death given in the post mortem report was 'myopathy', but it was noted that 'possible causes such as septicaemia or metabolic disease are under investigation'. Despite this clear indication that the cause of death was not a final one there was no further correspondence or documentation on file.

43.   Conclusion

43.1   There can be no other conclusion than that there was no proper system for clarifying the cases in which histology was required, or what tissues or organs would be preserved for examination and for pursuing that histology from the pathologist.

Coroner's Knowledge of Incomplete Histology

While Mr Barter did not have effective systems there is some evidence that at various times the problems with the performance of histology did come specifically to his attention.

44.   Coroner 'Extremely Patient'

44.1   The manuscript notes made for the University Review on 1 June 1993 record Professor Carty as confirming that there was no routine post mortem histology service. She specifically referred to one case where the Coroner 'would not issue a death certificate until he had a histology report' and notes that in that case there had been a delay of several months before it had been produced. In her written report for the Review, dated 26 May 1993, Professor Carty referred to this case and wrote that 'the Coroner had been extremely patient'. There is no direct evidence but Mr Barter may have been put on notice at this stage of the problem regarding the provision of histology.

45. 'Unprocessed Tissue' Remaining

45.1   In November 1995 Professor Carty wrote to Mr Barter (see below) referring specifically to 'unprocessed tissue' from Coroner's post mortems. The use of the phrase 'unprocessed tissue' is significant. If causes of death had already been attributed (as they had) Mr Barter must surely have appreciated that, for there to be 'unprocessed tissue' in such circumstances, meant that tissue over and above that required to identify the cause of death must have been taken in breach of the Coroner's Rules. Alternatively, histology had not been carried out as envisaged, in support of the above analysis. Mr Barter did not raise the point with Professor Carty, nor did he then chase the histology. Instead, his response through his Coroner's Officer was to indicate that in each of the cases in question death by natural causes had been confirmed and so there was no need for the histology.

The Importance of Histology

46.   Differing Perceptions

46.1   The former and present Coroners have different perceptions of the importance of histology. Mr Barter said,

> 'In my view histology can do no more than fine tune the cause of death. It might more particularly specify the cause of death under 1(a), (b), or (c), but in 30 years' experience I never had a case where what was initially reported as a natural death turned out to be an unnatural death following performance of histology.'

46.2   Mr Rebello stated in contrast,

> 'The microscopic findings on histology are an important check on the macroscopic findings to assist in making the report complete and I am therefore surprised that the reports were not finalised properly.'

47.   The Importance in SIDS Cases

47.1   The importance of histology in SIDS cases cannot be understated and has been considered at some length already in Part 9 of Chapter 8. Professor van Velzen accepted in evidence that a true diagnosis of SIDS can only be made once histology has been undertaken, the diagnosis being one of exclusion. Dr Davidson, the present Medical

Director at Alder Hey, stated that if there had been no histology in a SIDS case then 'I'd hope the Coroner wouldn't be happy in that situation, because I wouldn't be.' Dr Davidson is, of course, medically qualified and Mr Barter is not. Nevertheless the point is clear.

48. A SIDS Illustration

48.1 After a CPM following Katy's death in 1990 the cause was formally registered as SIDS. However, the parents did not accept it. The mother had been up all night with Katy. She had been coughing, was off her feeds and was basically unwell. Common sense suggested that SIDS was unlikely to be a true cause of death.

48.2 Katy's parents did their utmost to have the death certificate changed and even met with Dr Heaf, Consultant Paediatrician, Mr Butler, the Chief Executive, and Professor van Velzen. These efforts were eventually successful and the death certificate was altered to record the cause of death as 'bronchospastic syndrome'. It is extraordinary that histology was not performed bearing in mind the significance of the clinical history and this failure effectively invalidated the whole post mortem procedure.

49. Conclusion

49.1 On several occasions SIDS was accepted by the Coroner as a proper cause of death despite the lack of histology. It exemplifies the Coroner's lack of medical knowledge in a relatively routine matter. In failing to insist on histology Mr Barter must have recorded an inaccurate cause in a number of cases.

Coroner's Knowledge of Widespread Organ Retention?

'The news that there had been widespread retention of organs came as a complete shock to me. I had no idea what had been kept, and did not know that the Myrtle Street basement even existed.' (Mr Barter, witness statement, 18 May 2000.)

50.   The Documentary Evidence

50.1   Despite Mr Barter's clearly stated position we have noted that over the years various letters were sent to him which might have prompted him to make enquiries to a greater or lesser extent.

51.   Dr Ibrahim's Letter

51.1   On 16 February 1988 the locum Consultant Histopathologist, Dr Ibrahim, wrote to him enclosing 'a copy of the new Anatomy Regulations 1988'. The letter has been set out in Part 1 of 'The van Velzen Years' but is worthy of repetition,

> 'The current practice regarding heart (heart/lung) specimens from Coroner's autopsies is to study them histologically and then to discuss them at regular sessions with cardiac surgeons and physicians. In fact, most of these specimens from both Coroner's and Hospital autopsies over the last 35 years have been properly preserved and filed with the relevant data. In the light of the new Anatomy Regulations, I am not sure if the authority for possession of these specimens has been sought from the relatives of the deceased. I therefore wonder if it is possible to ask the relative for such a consent. If a consent is withheld then we have to dispose of the specimen properly after we have studied it microscopically.'

51.2   Dr Ibrahim asked for Mr Barter's advice, but the files disclosed to the Inquiry do not contain a copy of any response. Dr Ibrahim recalled hearing nothing further. Mr Barter denied having received the letter, which was correctly addressed.

51.3   Dr Ibrahim's letter, if received by Mr Barter, can only have alerted him to the existence of the heart collection. It also highlighted the possibility that the heart and lung specimens might have been preserved without appropriate consent in Coroner's cases. At the very least, the letter should have rung alarm bells and prompted further enquiry by Mr Barter.

52. Ownership of Post Mortem Tissue – 1994

52.1 Other correspondence with Mr Barter included a letter again considered in 'The van Velzen Years' (see Part 7, paragraph 9.1). On 9 May 1994 Margery Clark, who was by then working in the legal department but had previously been Professor van Velzen's personal assistant, wrote to Mr Barter seeking clarification on the ownership of 'post mortem tissue'. She wrote,

> 'We should be grateful if you could give a definitive ruling on the legal ownership of such tissue once the post mortem examination and all subsequent tests have been completed. Do you retain authority for its disposal (or otherwise) at your discretion or, in law, does this revert back to the next of kin of the deceased? Usually this tissue is ultimately disposed of by the hospital where the patient was treated or by the pathologist who performed the post mortem examination. We have not experienced any problems in the past over this issue, but the potential is always there, and for this reason we are anxious to establish the correct position in this respect.'

52.2 Mr Barter replied on 13 June 1994,

> 'I do not know a definitive answer to the question raised in your letter. It is often necessary for a pathologist to retain possession of tissue samples etc for some time after the autopsy, either because they may be needed for further examination or because some person properly interested in the death wishes to have his own examination carried out. Having said that, I think that any tissue that remains after all necessary examinations have been carried out belongs to the person entitled to possession of the body. In over 25 years' experience I have never had a legal representative ask for the return of such material, and I cannot visualise any circumstances in which it would be likely.'

52.3 Readers will have formed their own conclusion of the correspondence around this time and later in 1995. There is nothing on the face of the letters exchanged so far as Mr Barter is concerned to tell him of wholescale organ retention.

53. Disposal of Tissue – 1995

53.1 The final piece of relevant correspondence consists in a letter from Professor Carty to Mr Barter and a response from DI Whalley, Coroner's Officer, on behalf of Mr Barter. In her letter of 22 November 1995 Professor Carty wrote,

'There are a number of Coroner case post mortem tissues in the laboratory which have not been processed, list attached, and we would like to transfer the heart and lungs of these post mortems, many of whom were cardiac patients, to a museum in the Institute of Child Health, here at Alder Hey, which specialises in the teaching of cardiac surgeons. The remainder of the unprocessed tissue would remain at the Myrtle Street laboratory and would be the responsibility of Professor C Foster at the Royal Liverpool University Hospital. We are informed that none of the tissues are required for medico legal or forensic purposes. I would be grateful if you could let us know, as soon as possible, if this is acceptable to you and could you also let us know if there are any other procedures which we should follow.'

53.2   The significance of the phrase 'unprocessed tissue' has been considered above and should again have alerted Mr Barter to the failure to provide histology reports. In fact, the list referred to by Professor Carty was returned under cover of a letter from DI Whalley dated 28 November 1995. He advised that there was only one Coroner's case which was subject to inquest and where the post mortem had not revealed a natural cause of death. In the remaining cases …

'the Coroner has no objection to the tissue being disposed of in accordance with your normal procedures.'

54.   Conclusion

54.1   Professor Carty's letter did not refer specifically to 'organs' other than the heart and lungs, and no inference can be drawn that Mr Barter knew from this letter of the true contents of the containers at Myrtle Street. Specific reference was made to the heart and lung collection, just as in Dr Ibrahim's letter of 16 February 1988. To this extent he was put on specific notice of the retention of heart and lungs. Mr Barter said that he was unaware of the general organ retention at Myrtle Street and the weight of evidence on this specific point cannot cause us to disbelieve him. Furthermore, there is no evidence in the light of Professor Carty's letter, to suggest that he would or should have known, that whole organs were retained at Myrtle Street awaiting histology. If Mr Barter had applied his mind to it he would have been entitled to assume that the appropriate blocks had been taken.

Recommendations

We believe that the irregularities and difficulties revealed by our Inquiry in Liverpool point to one conclusion only. The Coroner's system, in which a legally qualified person makes decisions requiring medical expertise with little or no independent advice, will always be liable to error. Where 'unnatural death' and death following operative treatment are to be considered, specialist medical knowledge is more important than legal knowledge. Our Terms of Reference, however, are not to consider the Coroner's jurisdiction further than to make recommendations within the existing system.

55. Recommendations for Clinicians

- The Department of Health, the Royal Colleges and medical schools shall instruct members of the medical profession in the precise terms and provisions of the Coroner's Act 1988 and in particular the circumstances in which it is obligatory to report cases to the Coroner.

- Clinicians shall give the following basic information to the next of kin when a Coroner's post mortem examination is to be performed.

  - The nature of the examination, including the need to open the body and to remove and weigh organs.

  - The need for samples and possible retention of organs.

- Clinicians wishing to retain organs or samples after the end of the Coroner's process for the purposes currently allowed under the Human Tissue Act 1961 shall follow the Recommendations in Chapter 10.

- Clinicians shall not mention to the next of kin the possibility of an examination under the Coroner's jurisdiction unless the death is reportable to the Coroner.

- Clinicians requesting a hospital post mortem examination after the Coroner has declined to authorise an examination shall make it clear to the next of kin that there is no compulsion remaining for such an examination.

- Clinicians shall explain the contents and implications of a Coroner's post mortem report to the next of kin as if the examination had been carried out as a hospital post mortem examination on their own recommendation.

56. Recommendations for Coroners

- The Coroners' Society shall instruct Coroners that:

  - in the proper exercise of their judicial discretion, the decision to order a post mortem examination is not to be delegated to Coroner's Officers and Deputy Coroners must be available at all times;

  - organs are not to be retained unless relevant to establishing the cause of death and only when specified by the pathologist in writing.

- The Home Office and the Coroners' Society shall ensure all necessary medical education for Coroners.

- The Home Office and the Coroners' Society shall ensure all necessary training of Coroner's Officers and ancillary staff.

- Coroners shall be introduced, their function and procedures explained and the next of kin invited to express any specific concerns and requests.

- If a decision is made to authorise a post mortem examination Coroners shall ensure that the next of kin are advised of:

  - the reasons for authorising the post mortem examination;

  - their right to ask the Coroner that the examination be carried out by a pathologist independent of the hospital in which the deceased died;

  - the place and time of the examination and the identity of the pathologist;

  - the nature of the examination, including the need to open the body and to remove and weigh organs;

  - the need for samples and possible retention of organs;

  - their option to delay the funeral, while the pathologist fixes and examines any organs, to enable the return of the organs to the body for burial or cremation;

  - their option for a funeral without the return of the organs, in which case they shall be invited to consent to respectful disposal by the Coroner;

  - their option to make their own arrangements for respectful disposal of the organs.

- If a decision is made not to authorise a post mortem examination, Coroners shall notify the next of kin of that decision and give sufficient reasons for the decision.

- Coroners shall ensure the expeditious examination and recording of samples and organs.

- Coroners shall establish efficient systems for securing final post mortem reports following histological examination.

- Coroners shall ensure that all existing retained organs, tissue, blocks, slides, photographs and X-rays are specified within any preliminary and final post mortem reports.

57. Recommendations for Pathologists

- The Royal College of Pathologists shall instruct all practising histopathologists that they shall not retain samples and organs beyond those reasonably incidental to establishing the cause of death unless there is also written consent properly obtained under the Human Tissue Act 1961.

Chapter 10. Human Tissue Act

Contents

1.   Background

1.1   The Human Tissue Act 1961 came into force on 27 September 1961, two months after it received Royal Assent. It is central to the deliberations of this Inquiry and covers hospital post mortem examinations as against those under the jurisdiction of the Coroner.

1.2   The purpose of the Act was to provide for:

● the use of parts of bodies of deceased persons for therapeutic purposes and purposes of medical education and research;

● the circumstances in which post mortem examinations may be carried out;

● the permission for the cremation of bodies removed for anatomical examination.

2. The Relevant Provisions to Make Post Mortem Examination Lawful

2.1 Our Inquiry is restricted to matters relating to babies and children. However, the following analysis covers those provisions within the Act that concern the questions parents must be asked before a hospital post mortem examination or the use of body parts of babies and children is lawful. In order to concentrate on what is essential, unnecessary phrases are removed and some uncontroversial aids to interpretation inserted to make the meaning clear.

3. Phrases Extracted from Section 1(2)

3.1 There are a number of phrases to be extracted from **section 1(2)** to show the test to be applied. If, but only if, the test is satisfied the removal and retention of tissue is made lawful by virtue of **section 1(3)**.

- The person lawfully in possession of the body of a deceased person [for our purposes the doctor or other person designated on behalf of the hospital] …

- may authorise the removal of any part from the body for use for therapeutic purposes or for purposes of medical education or research **if** [indicating a *condition* or that what follows must be satisfied] …

- **having made** [indicating a *condition precedent* or that he must do it first] **such reasonable enquiry as may be practicable …**

- **he has no reason to believe** that … any surviving relative of the deceased objects to the body being so dealt with.

3.2 The remaining subsections within **section 1** are not relevant to this analysis but can be seen in the Act itself.

3.3 **Section 2** deals with a 'hospital' post mortem examination where there is no intention to retain tissue for therapeutic purposes, medical education or research. In this situation the examination is for the purpose of establishing or confirming the causes of death, or of investigating the existence or nature of abnormal conditions. Then the person in lawful possession of the body has to satisfy the same conditions but with a hospital post mortem as the purpose, as against the purposes of therapy, medical education and research covered in **section 1(2)**.

3.4 The Act does not contain any criminal sanction for breach of its provisions. Neither does it support a civil claim in respect of breach.

4. Background to the Act – the Parliamentary Debate

4.1 In the Second Reading of the Bill on 20 December 1960 the Parliamentary Secretary to the Minister of Health Miss Edith Pitt said,

> 'It is important that the dissemination of knowledge and the progress of research should be encouraged. The study and, if need be, the retention of parts of the body are essential for this purpose. The Bill removes whatever doubt there may be as to the legality of this at the present time so long as the conditions in the Bill are complied with.'

4.2 Speaking of the Corneal Grafting Act 1952, which was repealed by the Human Tissue Act 1961, Miss Pitt went on to say,

> 'The Minister advised them [medical practitioners] strongly not to rely on the power given in the Corneal Grafting Act to remove eyes in the absence of any known objection, but, wherever relatives were available, to seek their consent. *It is proposed to recommend hospital authorities to adopt the same procedure of obtaining the consent of relatives where they are available in relation to the removal of any part of the body as authorised by this [Human Tissue] Bill.*' [Emphasis added.]

4.3 Later Miss Pitt said,

> 'The provisions in the Bill relating to the removal and use of parts of the body have the wholehearted support of leading members of the medical profession.'

4.4 During the debate Mr Kenneth Robinson MP reminisced about an approach he had received some time earlier from certain members of the medical profession concerning the difficulty of obtaining sufficient corneas for the purposes of corneal grafting. He spoke to the then Minister of Health about whether there was anything he could do by way of publicity and Parliamentary questioning. Following consultation the reply was,

> 'For heaven's sake do not raise this matter. Corneal grafting is going on but the moment we give it any publicity there will be religious objections and the whole matter may come to an end. So please leave it alone.'

4.5 The Human Tissue Bill was drafted in order to address in part the mischief of the secretive way in which matters had been handled previously.

4.6   Lord Balniel MP said during the debate,

> 'This is an important Bill because it touches on some of the most deeply felt
> instincts of man; instincts that say that the human body, once life has been
> extinguished from it, should be treated with the utmost dignity and respect, and
> that pending interment or cremation, it should be left in peace. These instincts
> are felt by most persons whatever religious – or indeed, irreligious – beliefs
> they may have.
>
> I confess that I shared those instincts when I first read the Bill. Knowing some
> of the consequences that will flow from it I read it with a certain amount of
> emotional disquiet. On the other hand if one tries to throw away untenable
> prejudices and to look at the matter objectively there is something infinitely
> wonderful in the thought that the advance of medical science now allows men
> to use the tissues and organs from a dead body in order to bring health and
> happiness to the living and in particular to those who, because of misfortune or
> disease are deprived of the good health that most of us enjoy.
>
> To my mind there is something infinitely wonderful in the thought that this
> advance that we are now legalising enables medical science to create something
> approaching the immortality of the living cell, because the living cell will now
> be transferred, and can be transferred from generation to generation, bringing
> with it new health.'

4.7   The controls introduced in the Human Tissue Act 1961 were to allay these deeply felt
       and instinctive fears expressed so cogently but with perfect balance by Lord Balniel.

4.8   In the second reading of the Bill the Minister of Health, Mr J Enoch Powell, dealt with
       the meaning of the phrase 'any surviving relative'. He said,

> 'If he [the Honourable Member] looks at the context he will see that the
> reference is to having 'no reason' after 'reasonable enquiry' 'to believe' that
> 'any surviving relative' objects. In that context I have deliberately left the term
> 'any surviving relative' undefined so that if a relative makes it known, or *if
> there is reason to believe, that there is objection, it shall not be necessary nicely
> to enquire into the degree* of consanguinity; because *I am convinced that far
> more harm can be done to the cause which the House has at heart tonight by a
> single case in which a strongly held scruple is overridden than perhaps a
> temporary loss of opportunity due to the width in which this clause has been
> drawn.* So I say it is quite deliberately left at large that anyone who can claim
> to be a relative may be able to express an objection under Clause 1(2)'.
> [Emphasis added.]

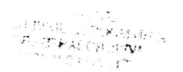

5.   The Evidence before the Inquiry

5.1   We have had the benefit of lengthy and detailed evidence from parents. We have also heard from numerous doctors, clinical academics including those currently in charge of undergraduate medical training and a Professor of Bio-Ethics.

6.   The Attitude of the Parents who Gave Evidence

6.1   It was the common experience of the parents that they had been given little or no information as to what would happen to their babies and children or their organs and tissue, during and following the post mortem examination. The most common experience was that they were *not* told that the heart would be taken for the Heart Collection in the Institute of Child Health at Alder Hey, or that the brain also would be removed and retained for fixation prior to examination so that they would bury the body without the brain. No parent had understood that every organ in the body would be taken during the van Velzen years and that they would only bury the 'shell' of their child.

6.2   Many parents from whom we heard expressed a desire at the time of the death of their baby or child to donate organs to save the life of another child. Many parents, had they been approached properly, with transparency and openness at the time, would have been prepared to discuss the use of organs and tissue from their deceased baby or child for therapeutic, medical education and research purposes. In retrospect fewer would have been willing for their child's heart or brain to be retained in a collection. However, had they been treated at the outset with transparency and openness they may have given it serious consideration. The parents' evidence is now highly coloured by their experiences surrounding the issue of organ retention, and the retention and handling of the heart and brain in particular provoke the most emotion. Those experiences remain an overriding impediment to their retrospective consideration of whether they would have agreed to the use of the heart or brain for medical education, research purposes and in particular as part of a collection.

6.3   Nevertheless several parents expressed the view that, properly approached at the time, they would have given serious consideration to the use of organs and tissue, including the heart and brain from their deceased baby or child. To illustrate this we refer to those parents who carried organ donor cards and several older children who had expressed the wish to carry organ donor cards. Sadly, the attitude of the medical profession, as it has affected parents of children involved in this Inquiry, has resulted in some of them destroying their cards. They cannot comprehend how the medical profession could conceal the retention of organs and tissue from them by omission.

7. The Evidence of the Medical Profession

7.1   There was no real factual dispute between the medical profession and the parents. There was no evidence from the doctors that they made enquiries beyond the next of kin as a matter of routine. We heard evidence from one younger consultant who explained to parents about the removal of the brain for the purpose of fixation and what would happen in general terms at the post mortem examination. None of the others went anywhere near as far. We heard no evidence from any doctor that parents were ever told that they would be burying the body without the brain or heart. It was conceded that no mention had been made of retaining hearts for the Heart Collection. The doctors themselves were ignorant of Professor van Velzen's practice of removing all the organs for fixation, so they could not have explained this to the parents. In reality, none would have begun to attempt an explanation of such an unjustifiable practice.

7.2   We were surprised at the general ignorance of the medical profession concerning the provisions of the Human Tissue Act 1961. No doctor could remember having read it before preparing to give evidence to the Inquiry. This included the University-based clinical doctors in charge of, and active in, the Institute of Child Health at Alder Hey. It also included the very people who ran, and often collected for, the Heart Collection. None had any training in the legal requirements at undergraduate level and nor did they receive training in their various clinical training posts. Most had seen a senior consultant deal with parents on the issue of post mortem examination in the course of their careers. Some, however, had not even had that experience and had devised their own approach. All had as their starting point an overwhelming desire not to upset the parents further than they thought necessary at their time of grief. This should be contrasted with the parents' overwhelming view that the worst had already happened, the death of their child, and that they could not have been more upset. They might have objected in their grief but they correctly considered that was their right. From doctors' evidence the implication was they did not want to tell the parents the details precisely because they did not want to face the parents' likely objections. Understanding the medical benefits, the medical profession was naturally keen that post mortem examinations were carried out.

8. The Real Issues

8.1   The medical profession has recently and publicly admitted what has been called a 'paternalistic' approach in the past to the issue of the enquiry into the parents' objection to post mortem examination. It claims this was done with the best motives of the profession and asserts that times have changed, so that there is now a new climate requiring openness, frankness and transparency of approach. Whereas in the past the attitude has been to spare the feelings of parents by not giving them full information, it is now proposed that fully informed consent should be the standard to be applied in future.

8.2   The issues before us, having set out our findings of fact, are to see whether the Human Tissue Act 1961 has been complied with in the past and to see whether there should be recommendations for changes in the Act, notwithstanding the present position of the medical profession.

9.   The Analysis

9.1   The Human Tissue Act 1961 was drawn up against a backdrop of advice from the Minister for medical practitioners to obtain the 'consent' of relatives, where available, in relation to the removal of eyes for corneal grafting. There is no indication in the debate of any intention to relax that advice after the Act came into force, there is rather an indication of the intention to enforce it.

9.2   The Minister clearly believed that he was recommending a test with the safeguard that it was a high threshold for the doctor or designated person to climb in order to say that he had *no reason to believe* in objection. He expressly stated this in the debate at the Second Reading of the Bill in relation to the degree of consanguinity to be required. *No reason to believe* in the objection of *any surviving relative* meant precisely that. If there was to be a dispute as to the closeness of the relationship the doctor was not to attempt to resolve it. He could no longer say that he had *no reason to believe* in an objection. There was no suggestion, however that a doctor had to enquire as a matter of routine beyond the next of kin if they did not object.

9.3   The Minister clearly recognized the harm that would be done if even one strongly held objection were overridden by the medical profession.

9.4   The concept of the high threshold before a doctor can have *no reason to believe* is just as relevant to the existence of an objection at all as it is to the closeness of the surviving relative. While the section introduces the condition precedent of making *such reasonable enquiry as may be practicable* that condition can conveniently be put on one side for a moment to consider the main thrust of the section. We can have a reason to believe that someone might object to something without ever asking that person or even knowing that person. The context will often suffice. For instance, we can be overwhelmingly confident that there would be objection to a burglary without ever asking or identifying the householder. The context of the matters under consideration in this Inquiry makes it clear that the starting point of the medical practitioner can only be he *has* reason to believe that there might be objection. We can remember the instinctive response of Lord Balneil quoted from the Parliamentary debate. In fairness, no doctor contended otherwise during the Inquiry.

9.5 Whether or not the Statute puts the express burden on the doctor to make reasonable enquiry, as it does in fact, the *only* way a doctor can overcome the obvious starting point that there *might* be objection is to ask. Indeed many doctors who gave evidence to the Inquiry conceded in questioning the lack of detail given by them to parents when making enquiry on the basis that if they were told they would be upset and object! That thought process in itself would suffice to render a breach of the section, subject to whatever protection is afforded to the doctor who claims to have made reasonable enquiry, which is considered below. The doctor simply could not state that he had *no reason to believe* in objection. Again in fairness, when it was put to the doctors in these terms in evidence at the Inquiry they did not contend otherwise but recognized the force of the position.

9.6 It is now convenient to return to the *condition precedent* in the section *having made such reasonable enquiry as may be practicable*. Many doctors in evidence stated that it was a difficult exercise to tell the parents the detail of a post mortem examination and that organs would be retained. The paternalistic approach of the medical profession to spare the parents further grief has already been stated. The question is whether this approach to the enquiry of parents can lead to the medical profession reacting along the following lines,

> 'We do not want to upset the parents unnecessarily. A *reasonable enquiry is not an upsetting enquiry*. We will tell what we can without upsetting them unduly and if at this point they do not object we can then say we have complied with the Act. After all we have made a reasonable enquiry and that suffices to comply with the condition precedent and thereby to negate the starting point of having reason to believe that the parents might object.'

9.7 This reaction is based upon the evidence of the medical profession to the Inquiry. Is such a formulation a proper one under the Human Tissue Act 1961?

9.8 Just as the concept of *no belief in objection* depended on the context, what is or is not a *reasonable enquiry* must also depend on the context. Nobody could contend that it is *not practicable* to make a detailed enquiry in the setting of the issues before this Inquiry, unless in the context that the next of kin were incapable of being traced or contacted. Conversely it would not usually be practicable to enquire of all surviving relatives even if they could be traced or contacted. The issue of relevance for the next of kin is the *reasonableness* of the enquiry. The context in which to judge the reasonableness or otherwise of the enquiry can only be whether or not the doctor can truly say, after the enquiry, he has no reason to believe in objection.

9.9   It stands to reason that if the very issues, known to the doctor but not known to the parents, that may provoke them to object are not raised in the enquiry, the enquiry is fundamentally flawed and therefore *unreasonable*. The question 'Do you object?' cannot be answered in a vacuum. The context of the question is vital to the obtaining of a meaningful answer. The question is incapable of meaningful answer by parents ignorant of the procedures involved. If the answer lacks meaning, how can the doctor dismiss the starting point that he has reason to believe in objection?

9.10   It is a sad fact of life that many important decisions have to be made when we are upset, under pressure or otherwise, when we would wish to turn away. Parliament, in the Human Tissue Act 1961, expressly cast the fundamental decision regarding objection to post mortem examination and tissue retention on to the surviving relatives. As Professor Harris, Professor of Bio-Ethics at the University of Manchester, said in evidence, the parents were wronged if their consent was not obtained or they were not given enough information to provide competent consent.

9.11   It was not the intention of the Act to leave the essential decision to the doctors, with an exercise in window-dressing under the guise of reasonable enquiry of relatives. Such a construction would offend the clear language and intent of the Act. In any event we are impressed by the reasoning within the Polkinghorne Report at paragraph 6.2 on the issue of informed consent as long ago as 1989. We have slightly adapted the following quotation from that report to substitute 'child/organs' for 'fetus' but otherwise leaving the meaning unaltered.

> 'Discussion of consent has been affected by the consideration that a 'mother' may be distressed if she has to consider too closely the possibility of her child/organs being used for 'medical education or research purposes'. The Peel Committee had this in mind when reaching the form of words in their Code at Paragraph 3(ii) that there should be no known objection on the part of parents. We regard this as insufficient. We are conscious of the need to avoid distress but are even more strongly opposed to formulations which disguise the reality of what is to take place. Distress will be caused to the mother if she later feels that she did not know what was going to happen to her 'child/organs'.

> We recommend that positive explicit consent should be obtained from mothers to the use of the child/organs. We see the process of consent as requiring the mother to be counselled and given all the information in a form that is 'comprehensible to enable her to make a proper judgement of whether or not to allow the child/organs to be used for 'medical or research purposes ....'

> While we also would wish to avoid needless upset, the immediate upset at the time of the enquiry has to be balanced by that to be caused in later years if parents eventually discover what has happened, as this Inquiry all too poignantly demonstrates.'

9.12 We are fortified in our view because even the rationale of the 'paternalistic' attitude is put forward in hindsight. There is no evidence that the medical profession ever attempted to construe the Act and came to the decision that the construction now put forward on their behalf is correct. Even now, we are told, these matters are not dealt with at any stage of the process of medical education and training, despite the experience of Mr Kenneth Robinson MP expressed in the debate. However it did not appear that the doctors individually were unable to grasp the wording and requirements of the Act under questioning. When taken through the Statute most acknowledged the difficulties in reconciling the 'paternalistic' attitude with the wording of the Act.

9.13 The concessions of the doctors went even further. It was acknowledged as a mistake that parents had not been told their child's heart would be removed and placed in the Heart Collection at the Institute of Child Health, Alder Hey. It would no doubt have been upsetting to explain this to a grieving parent. However once the concession is made, and rightly so, that parents should have been asked about the retention of hearts, the 'paternalistic' attitude cannot be sustained as a explanation for what has occurred. The fact is that the medical profession did not properly consider the Human Tissue Act 1961 in the first place.

9.14 Leaving aside the Heart Collection and the strict terms of the Act, what occurred in the van Velzen years cannot go unmentioned at this point. The comment does not relate to the actual processes in which individual doctors made their enquiries of parents under the Act, because they did not know what would happen. However the enormity of what has happened in the eyes of parents can be summed up in the following question put to a number of witnesses,

> 'Would any parent not have objected if told that every organ of their child would be taken and in most cases left untouched for years, without even an attempt at clinical histological examination?'

10. Conclusions

- While the wording of the Human Tissue Act 1961 differs from the concept of *informed consent*, in practical terms there had to be informed consent for the next of kin at least for there to have been compliance with the Act in the overwhelming majority of cases.

- There has been a general failure to comply with the terms of the Human Tissue Act 1961 with regard to the enquiries that should made of parents to see if they objected to post mortem examination and retention of organs.

- The medical need for information and samples from post mortem examination is clear. There is no present justification for shifting the burden of the decision away from surviving relatives to the medical profession.

- The medical profession has recently introduced new consent forms and thereby, whether intentionally or otherwise, an additional test before post mortem examination can be carried out. There are consent forms at Alder Hey which specifically provide for the consent of the 'next of kin', in line with previous practice of making enquiries of the closest relatives. However, the legal test remains that of 'lack of objection in any surviving relative'. There is now effectively a two-tier test without foundation in law.

- The concept of 'informed consent' is only workable with an ascertained class narrower than that of all surviving relatives. The *Concise Oxford English Dictionary* defines 'next of kin' as 'a person's closest living relative or relatives'. There may be more than one person who qualifies as 'next of kin'. Such a class is workable in the context of informed consent. The actual definition of next of kin to be used in this context is a matter for the legislative draftsman.

- It is possible to continue to apply a test of 'informed consent of next of kin' on top of an underlying test of 'no known objection' in the wider class of surviving relatives. However, we regard the importance of post mortem examination to the next of kin and medical science to be such that if all those who qualify as next of kin provide fully informed consent, any objections of wider surviving relatives should no longer prevail. In terms of previous practice all surviving relatives were not asked as a matter of course. If the next of kin did not object the doctor no doubt concluded that he could satisfy the test of no belief in objection *after such reasonable enquiry was practicable*. It is unworkable to enquire of all surviving relatives to see if they object and still more to get their fully informed consent. In practice the next of kin are in the best position to be in contact with the wider group and to take their wishes into account in forming their own fully informed consent or refusal. We strongly recommend drawing a certain line between the next of kin and all remaining relatives.

- All reasonably practicable steps should be taken to trace the next of kin. Where there is more than one next of kin it may not be reasonably practicable to trace each of them. We regard it as sufficient for post mortem examination to be carried out if all traced next of kin give fully informed consent and there is no known objection on the part of the remaining next of kin.

- The evidence before this Inquiry strongly suggests that the sensitive painting of a full and balanced picture can overcome an instinctive reaction on the part of the next of kin to refuse consent. There will be sufficient numbers of post mortem examinations and samples available for the purposes of medical advancement. The full picture includes the benefits to them in knowing the cause of death and any complicating or hereditary conditions and the potential benefits to medical science flowing from the examination. It also includes necessary detail of the post mortem process and the organs and/or samples to be retained. Where relatives nevertheless refuse their consent, they must be respected in that decision.

- We recognise that our conclusions and the recommendations that follow differ from those expressed in the Interim Report of the Bristol Royal Infirmary Inquiry. We have striven to form our own conclusions on this and on all matters before us. Our Inquiry was set up specifically to consider the issues covered in this chapter. We have had the considerable benefit of far more evidence, tailored to the issue and subjected to detailed questioning, than has previously been possible.

11. Recommendations

11.1   We respectfully recommend that:

- The Department of Health, the Royal Colleges and medical schools shall instruct members of the medical profession in the precise terms and provisions of the Human Tissue Act 1961, on the basis of our analysis, and the need for strict compliance.

- The Human Tissue Act 1961 shall be amended to provide a test of fully informed consent for the lawful post mortem examination and retention of parts of the bodies of deceased persons. While we have concluded that there has been little difference between 'lack of objection' and 'informed consent' in practical terms for the next of kin, it is important that the law and future practice are brought into line and updated.

- The class of persons relevant to the obtaining of fully informed consent shall be defined as the 'next of kin'.

- The class of 'any surviving relative' shall no longer be relevant to post mortem examination.

- There shall be a programme of health education for the public relevant to the medical need for continued post mortem examination and access to organs and samples for therapeutic, educational and research purposes.

- The Department of Health, the Royal Colleges and medical schools shall provide training for all those involved in obtaining fully informed consent.

- The Human Tissue Act 1961 shall be amended to impose a criminal penalty by way of fine for breach of its provisions in order to encourage future compliance.

- Guidelines relating to the requirements of the Human Tissue Act 1961 and the obtaining of fully informed consent shall be drawn up and provision made for breach to result in disciplinary proceedings which could lead to suspension, dismissal or financial penalty.

- The Human Rights Act 1998 makes provision for an effective remedy other than in criminal proceedings. If breaches of the Human Tissue Act 1961 amount to breaches of the Human Rights Act 1998 consideration shall be given to incorporating a financial remedy with the Human Tissue Act 1961 itself. If necessary, reference should be made to the Law Commission.

Chapter 11. Consent

Contents

1.   Consent to Post Mortem Examination of Children

1.1   In the preceding chapter we concluded that fully informed consent is required and nothing less. Fully informed consent must be freely given without imposition of pressure. It is the application of basic principles of respect for the person, their welfare and wishes.

1.2   Comprehensive information is required to obtain a valid consent. Parents must be informed of the identity of each organ to be retained and the purpose for which it is to be used. Dr Peart, a Consultant Paediatric Cardiologist at Alder Hey, accepts that consent forms must be specific about every organ to be retained. Blanket consent is inadequate for organs but is worthy of further consideration with regard to the retention of small tissue samples for diagnostic purposes, medical education and research.

1.3   Fully informed consent means that a person must have all the information required to form a final decision. It is not enough for clinicians to tell the next of kin that they would like to examine the body after death and this might involve taking some tissue. The next of kin need to understand what is involved in a post mortem examination, including a description of whole body systems, removal of the brain and the steps necessary to remove various organs, no matter how distasteful the giving of this information might be to the clinician concerned.

1.4   Paternalism is defined in the *Concise Oxford Dictionary* as follows,

'the policy of restricting the freedom and responsibilities of one's dependants in their supposed best interest'

1.5   We accept that for some clinicians it might be unpleasant to provide the detailed information necessary to obtain consent. However, their responsibility cannot be avoided. A practical test for the clinician in considering whether he has given full information is to question whether any significant detail not mentioned could have led to a different decision by the next of kin. If so then the test for fully informed consent will not have been met.

1.6   The issue of consent arises at a time of extreme grief. Nevertheless, a post mortem examination should be completed as soon as possible to obtain the best clinical results. It is not possible to allow sufficient time to assuage grief. Therefore, consent must be discussed with sensitivity, openness and the necessary detail to enable clinicians to discharge their duty.

1.7   Clinicians agree that they are best placed to obtain fully informed consent. With proper training, they should be able to communicate effectively and sympathetically with the necessary medical knowledge to inform the next of kin. They must understand the value and process of post mortem examination in the clinical setting and also what it means for relatives. We regard it as best clinical practice for clinicians to work closely with pathologists who can assist in determining which organs should be retained for the relevant purposes. They can also assist parents in providing detail relating to the cause of death.

1.8   The general public should be educated to understand how human tissue is stored and archived as an ongoing resource for the general benefit of society. For example, the general population benefits from a better understanding of disease and more effective treatment becomes available. The annual influenza epidemic is better managed now than ever before. Researchers are able to access archives to study a previous particular strain of influenza virus and can therefore improve preventative treatment when that strain reappears in any particular year.

1.9   If the Liverpool experience represents general practice there must be substantial archives of human material at various locations around the country, most of which have been obtained unlawfully. We cannot undo the wrongs perpetrated in obtaining that material, but can now consider what should happen in the future. In relation to retained organs or tissue it is the right of surviving relatives to request respectful disposal, and they must be given that opportunity. If relatives do not demand respectful disposal, this material may be of great value to society, if it is used for research and education in the future.

2.   Consent Forms in the Future

2.1   We have considered a number of consent forms for hospital post mortem examination. Until recently all Alder Hey consent forms referred solely to 'tissue' and not 'organs'. The parents are keen to use the terms which are defined by the *Concise Oxford Dictionary* as follows,

> 'Tissue: A collection of cells specialised to perform a particular function.
>
> Organ: A part of the body composed of more than one tissue that forms
> a structural unit responsible for a particular function.'

2.2   We have also considered a model consent form contained in the publication by the Royal College of Pathologists in March 2000 entitled 'Guidelines for the Retention of Tissues and Organs at Post Mortem Examination'. The model is formal and complex.

2.3   None of the forms we have seen provide the basis for clinicians to obtain fully informed consent and properly to set out and record the decision. Clear informal language is essential. It appears to us that the more official the form, the less efficient it is in practice. Understanding, particularly in grief, is vital. We suggest a new approach.

3.   New Approach to Consent

3.1   A more flexible yet formal document is required, setting out all the options clearly. It should be used nationally. The document should be in a question and answer format capable of covering the needs of any individual case. It should be completed jointly by the clinician, a bereavement adviser and the next of kin. We have heard evidence that the specialist cardiac liaison nurses at Alder Hey have successfully taken up a role supporting parents and clinicians in the obtaining of consent. It works well and clinicians, as much as the parents, value the support that this system provides. This role should be performed in a wider context by bereavement advisers and we recommend that it is adopted nationally.

3.2   The form will be longer than the existing form. This will allow the questions to be drawn up more sensitively and to cover all areas necessary for fully informed consent. It should include any instruction from the next of kin for final disposal of organs or tissue. The next of kin should be provided with a copy of the document which should be signed by the clinician, bereavement adviser and next of kin. Later sections of the same form could deal with other matters related to the death, with which the bereavement adviser can assist. This written record will ensure that clinicians discharge their responsibility to provide all necessary information to the next of kin. The next of kin can then discharge the responsibility placed upon them by the Human Tissue Act 1961 to make an informed decision.

3.3   Once the consent form is signed we favour the next of kin relinquishing further control. This relinquishment is to be subject to the next of kin having the right to specify how, following completion of the purpose for which it was retained, the material should be disposed of respectfully. This is to include their specified religious requirements. We have already stated that the intended use of any organ to be retained must be explained fully to the next of kin. A more liberal attitude should be considered with regard to the retention and use of tissue, particularly in the form of wax blocks and slides. These are of invaluable benefit for research and teaching. They may also be an important resource for families who may seek access to archived material for the benefit of their family and future generations.

3.4   Retained tissue is an invaluable asset for diagnostic as well as research purposes. Once fully informed consent has been obtained for its retention and use, the hospital's undertaking to use it and dispose of the remainder respectfully should be enough. Were it otherwise we would have a situation where clinicians/researchers/teachers would have a difficult obstacle course to negotiate. This could involve repeated requests to parents for additional consent as the original research developed and diversified or as new interests arose. The consent to retain tissue should be general, to permit use within ethically approved research projects so long as it is treated respectfully throughout, including its ultimate disposal.

3.5   We set out below an illustration of the content of the consent form we envisage. The list is for discussion purposes and is not prescriptive.

4.   National Health Service Hospital Post Mortem Consent Form for Children

4.1   **Section 1**

Patient Details:

- Name of hospital
- Name of child
- Address
- Date of birth
- Date of death
- Place of death
- Next of kin
- Relationship to child
- Address
- Hospital consultant

- Contact number
- Hospital reference number
- Telephone/fax numbers
- General practitioner
- Address
- Telephone/fax numbers
- Allocated bereavement adviser
- Date of appointment
- Telephone/fax numbers

4.2 **Section 2**

Purpose of hospital post mortem examination to establish:

- Cause of death
- Effects of surgery
- Effects of treatment
- Accuracy of diagnosis

4.3 **Section 3**

Post mortem examination may extend to:

- The whole body
- The chest and abdomen
- Access restricted to a surgical incision
- Small samples from specified organs

4.4 **Section 4**

Consent:

- Consent to full post mortem examination
- Consent can be limited to specified organs
- Consent can be refused

4.5 **Section 5**

Purposes for retaining organs:

- Diagnostic
- Therapeutic
- Medical education
- Research

4.6 **Section 6**

Purposes for retaining tissue:

- Diagnostic
- Therapeutic
- Medical education
- Research
- To enable organs to remain in the body
- To enable organs to be returned to the body for the funeral

4.7   **Section 7**

A request for consent to retention of organs or tissue *following completion* of the Coroner's process should be made *before* the Coroner's post mortem examination is carried out. There should be no distinction in the consent process between organ retention following completion of the Coronial process and a hospital post mortem examination

4.8   **Section 8**

Retention – individual attitudes to the body following death must be identified, acknowledged and respected

Identify, explain and discuss with next of kin:

* Each organ to be retained

* Purpose of retention

* Confirmation that retained organ(s) will only be used for purpose consented to by next of kin

* Whether organs to be examined will be returned to body prior to funeral – if not:

    – How long the funeral would have to be postponed to complete examination before organs can be returned to body

    – Whether next of kin wish to postpone the funeral or not

    – Certificate to confirm organs returned to body prior to funeral to be issued to next of kin

    – Organs retained beyond funeral will be identified and accompanied by signed consent form throughout use for relevant purpose

    – Tissue samples and purpose for retention

    – Whether tissue may be used for therapeutic, medical education or research purposes following diagnostic use

    – Whether next of kin consent to retention of organ or tissue:

    ○ In a collection

    ○ In an archive

    ○ As microscopic samples

    ○ Date when, place where and by whom ethical approval granted if purpose of retention for research

○ Whether organ or tissue can be retained without limit of time for medical education and research so long as it is handled respectfully

○ Next of kin have right to give instruction for respectful disposal following completion of purpose for which organ or tissue retained

4.9 **Section 9**

Signatures:

- Next of kin for post mortem examination

- Countersignature of clinician, bereavement adviser or other witness as appropriate

- Date, time and place of signing of consent

We have tried to set out the matters that the clinician must consider in order to obtain fully informed consent from the next kin. The standard is high but achievable given openness, frankness and honesty between clinician and next of kin. We feel that this process can be assisted by the availability of a bereavement adviser, particularly as the next of kin is likely to be suffering a grief reaction. The function of the bereavement adviser is considered in the next chapter.

5. Recommendations

5.1 We respectfully recommend that:

- Following examination of the retained organs or tissue, there should be a meeting between the clinician and parents and referral for genetic counselling or other specialist advice if appropriate.

- Once fully informed consent is obtained for research purposes, the researchers are entitled to remain in possession of the material retained while research continues. We recommend this extends to accessing archives and DNA analysis. All research remains subject to ethics committee approval.

- Local ethics committees be given a supervisory role to police approved research.

Chapter 12. Bereavement Adviser

Contents

1.   Background

1.1   In the late 1980s and early 1990s cardiac social workers provided a 24-hour on call service in the Alder Hey Cardiac Department and would sit with bereaved parents and talk to them. Clinicians would often take their lead from the cardiac social workers in terms of when the parents were able to cope with being given the necessary information following their child's death. The system worked very well and in the mid-1990s the cardiac social workers were replaced by cardiac liaison nurses. The service now is equally as good as the system it replaced.

1.2   There is always a cardiac liaison nurse available for consultation at Alder Hey. There is also a community-based cardiac liaison nurse supported by the British Heart Foundation who is available to speak to parents at any time.

1.3   In evidence the parents identified the need for this type of service. It should not be restricted to the cardiac department, but should be generally available. In his Interim Guidance on Post Mortem Examination issued on 1 March 2000 the Chief Medical Officer indicated that all NHS Hospital Trusts should designate a named individual in a Trust who will be available to provide support and information to families of the deceased where post mortem examination may be required, whether this is requested by a hospital doctor or the Coroner. This person should be trained in the management of bereavement. We feel that a bereavement adviser would be the person to discharge this role.

1.4   Parents must be involved in decision-making as well as in requesting and accepting support. The aim is to assist them in the difficult period following death. Their individual feelings and needs must be identified and respected. Their paramount need is for accurate, consistent, co-ordinated information. Choices available to parents should be fully explained, with all the necessary information provided. They must be given time together and time with their child. Time must also be available to make practical arrangements. They must be treated with respect and dignity at all times.

1.5   The bereavement adviser should not be judgmental in dealing with parents. Parents must be supplied with clear, factual, unbiased information. Confusion must be avoided. Parents may need help with thinking what they want to ask and even asking their clinician questions. No subject should be avoided and they must be treated with honesty even if the truth is painful. Their confidentiality must be respected at all times. The bereavement adviser should try and ensure that parents are dealt with on equal terms by the clinician and other professionals and time must be made available to meet the parents' needs.

1.6   It should be understood that grief can be expressed differently in different cultures. The nature of grief is personal and private. In a hospital, which often appears impersonal and public, there should be a private place where the bereavement adviser and parents can meet and have time together or alone. Parents must have time, space and support to relive, think and talk about what has happened to them.

1.7   The training of a bereavement adviser should include the appropriate use of language, the need to provide individual attention and to anticipate the requirements of bereaved relatives.

1.8   They must have a full understanding of post mortem procedures and the issue of consent. This will include identifying and distinguishing between a Coroner's and hospital post mortem examinations. They should be able to obtain information from clinicians and pathologists about the identification of organs to be retained and whether or not they will be retained beyond the funeral. Training must include why certain organs have to be 'fixed' before examination and the length of time necessary to 'fix' and examine a particular organ.

1.9   The bereavement adviser must be able to advise on all aspects of the funeral including return of organs to the body following post mortem examination, or identification of organs, tissue, blocks, slides, X-rays and photographs retained beyond the funeral. An awareness of all funeral procedures, religious requirements and the purpose of memorial services is necessary.

1.10   There will be a psychological component in bereavement advisers' training, relating to sensitive and respectful communication as well as gentle treatment of stressful topics such as consent to post mortem procedure. They will require liaison skills in order to discuss matters with clinicians, Coroners and other professionals.

1.11   The bereavement adviser should try to involve the pathologist more openly with clinicians and parents. The pathologist will be of particular assistance with regard to explaining why organs are retained and what purposes, including therapeutic, medical education and research, are served by retention of organs or tissue.

1.12 Parents should be given every opportunity to express their wishes about the eventual disposal of organs. A bereavement adviser can facilitate this. Parents' wishes must be respected. The need for respect cannot be overstated.

1.13 Every hospital should have a bereavement adviser. A dedicated office should be provided and include a private sitting area for parents or surviving relatives.

2. Recommendations

2.1 We have considered the evidence and recommend that the functions of a bereavement adviser include:

- Explaining the circumstances of death, identifying when, where and who was present.

- Arranging and attending a meeting for relatives with anyone who was present at the death if requested.

- Encouraging a meeting between relatives and the treating clinician to explain the clinical circumstances of death and if requested arranging and attending the meeting.

- Ensuring that relatives have a full explanation of the reasons for post mortem examination including therapeutic, medical education and research.

- Explaining the need for consent to carry out a hospital post mortem examination (HPM) and the retention of organs.

- Explaining that consent is necessary for the retention of organs following a Coroner's post mortem examination (CPM) and that the consent must be obtained before the CPM is undertaken.

- Ensuring relatives have sufficient time, privacy and support to reflect upon the request for consent to an HPM or the retention of organs following a CPM or an HPM.

- Ascertaining whether the clinician will attend post mortem examination.

- Facilitating meetings between parents, clinician and pathologist as appropriate.

- Noting discussions between relatives, clinicians and pathologists and providing a copy to each party involved.

- Developing and using information packs for relatives on all aspects of death in hospital.

- Assisting relatives in the following practical matters:

  - collecting the deceased's personal belongings and arranging return to relatives;

  - ensuring provision of certificate of death and the formal notice;

  - explaining the procedure to register the death;

  - providing support in attending the registry office if requested;

  - arranging contact with funeral director;

  - arranging contact with hospital chaplain and/or local priest as required;

  - contacting the Coroner's office as appropriate;

  - offering to attend if contact with police necessary;

  - ensuring that the General Practitioner is informed;

  - ensuring that schools are informed as appropriate (including the schools of siblings);

  - assisting the relatives in informing other persons, including other relatives, friends and employers, of the death and its consequences;

  - assisting the relatives in dealing with the Benefits Agency, insurance company, housing matters;

  - assisting the relatives to place announcements in newspapers if wished.

- Discussing counselling or long-term support needs with relatives, including the needs of wider family members and making contact with appropriate counselling/support agencies if requested.

- Ensuring that relatives are aware of the full range of counselling/support resources available including those external to the hospital and bringing these matters to the attention of the relatives.

- Accessing translation/interpreting services including services for people with hearing or visual impairment and providing appropriate written/taped information.

- Assisting with any other individual problem presented by relatives in consequence of death.

- Undertaking general liaison duties.

2.2   We intend this list to be illustrative rather than prescriptive. There must be recognised training courses for bereavement advisers. Qualification should be certificated, perhaps at a National Vocational Qualification level. Annual assessment and appraisal should be routine and the role should be performance managed. Continuing education and training is essential. The bereavement adviser should work closely with the hospital management, clinicians, the Coroner and the full range of non-medical services including counsellors and other non-medical professionals. There will of course be relatives who do not wish to avail themselves of the services of a bereavement adviser. Nevertheless the service should be offered to everyone as should the facility to return to the bereavement adviser in the event of their services having been declined in the first instance.

2.3   The distinction between a cardiac liaison nurse and the bereavement adviser is that the nurse has the advantage of contact with the parents in the period prior to death. We suggest that some aspect of the bereavement adviser's multi-factorial function will bring them into contact with the parents before the death of their child.

2.4   We have been heartened at the support for the concept of bereavement adviser from parents and clinicians. We commend the concept for development and implementation.

Chapter 13. Human Rights

Contents

The purpose of this chapter is to identify those human rights which might have a bearing on the issue of organ retention at Alder Hey and the University of Liverpool. We are not required by our Terms of Reference to adjudicate upon whether or not the matters under consideration constitute a breach of any Article under the European Convention on Human Rights or of the Human Rights Act 1998. The Act does not apply retrospectively. This chapter is for information purposes only.

1.   Background

1.1   The European Convention on Human Rights was created in the aftermath of the Second World War. The UK Government was heavily involved in the drafting of the Convention and was the first to ratify it in 1951. Since 1966 the UK Government has accepted the right of individuals to petition the Strasbourg Commission and Court in respect of alleged breaches of the Convention. A significant development has been the passing of the Human Rights Act 1998, which came into force in England on 2 October 2000 and incorporated the Convention into domestic law. The Convention had already been implemented, in part, in Scotland following Scottish devolution. Now, domestic courts must take the Convention into account whether or not it is put to them in argument by either party.

2. Human Rights Act 1998

2.1 The Human Rights Act 1998 preserves the sovereignty of Parliament to the extent that where there is a head-on conflict between UK legislation and the Convention, no court will be able to declare the legislation void. The highest courts, however, will be able to make a Declaration of Incompatibility with the Convention, which may result in amending legislation. Section 4(5) of the Human Rights Act 1998 provides that the relevant courts are:

- the House of Lords;

- the Judicial Committee of the Privy Council;

- the Courts-Martial Appeal Court;

- in Scotland the High Court of Judiciary sitting otherwise than as a trial court or the Court of Session; and

- in England and Wales or Northern Ireland the High Court or the Court of Appeal.

2.2 In addition Parliament, when enacting a statute, will have to consider whether there is any contravention of the European Convention on Human Rights. Section 19 of the Human Rights Act 1998 requires a Minister of the Crown in charge of any Bill, before its second reading, to make a statement that the provisions of the legislation are compatible with the Convention or specifically that the Minister cannot make such a statement.

2.3 It is unlikely that there is conflict between the Convention and domestic legislation with regard to the subject matter of this Inquiry. The duties of the Courts to take the Convention into account in determining cases involving the duties of public authorities are relevant and should be noted. In particular:

- section 6 of the Human Rights Act declares that it is unlawful for a public authority to act in a way incompatible with a Convention right;

- section 7 permits any person who is or would be a victim of an unlawful act to bring proceedings against the authority in the appropriate Court or Tribunal (determined by regulations);

- proceedings must normally be brought within one year;

- nothing in the Act creates criminal liability;

- the Courts may grant damages in an appropriate case;

- there can be little doubt that an NHS Trust and a Health Authority qualify as public authorities under the Act even if also carrying out private functions since section 6 (3) defines 'public authority' as including 'any person certain of whose functions are functions of a public nature'.

2.4 However under section 6 (5) a person is not a public authority in relation to a particular act by virtue only of section 6 (3) (b) if the nature of the act is private. It may be that employment decisions might be regarded as purely private following a similar argument to that in *R v East Berkshire HA ex parte Walsh* (1985) QB 152. It is unlikely that decisions about the treatment of NHS patients would be regarded as private because the obligations of Trusts, Health Authorities and the Secretary of State for Health are imposed by statute. The Convention is unlikely to be relevant in circumstances concerning private medicine since that rests on contractual rather than statutory obligations.

2.5 There is little doubt that a university has functions of a public nature, as well as private functions. University functions such as sharing employees with the Trust, as for instance when a senior lecturer in a department of medicine devotes 5/11ths of his time to academic work and 6/11ths of his time to clinical practice within the Trust, may well result in a finding that the University's actions are deemed to be public in nature. However, determination of this issue is not for this Inquiry.

2.6 Courts and Tribunals are also themselves public authorities and must therefore take account of the Convention in deciding disputes, whether or not these are with public authorities or with private individuals.

2.7 The European Commission and Court have developed important principles in their jurisprudence. Two are the 'margin of appreciation' and the 'proportionality' doctrines. The margin of appreciation principle gives a range of discretion to public authorities to make laws for their own states while respecting the principles of the Convention. 'Proportionality' allows Member States to exercise this discretion but only to the extent that it is necessary to do so to achieve their intended purpose. A balance must be struck between the rights of individuals and the general welfare of others and of the community. Thus, in an abortion case the right to life, argued on behalf of the fetus, was balanced against the rights of the mother – (*Paton v UK* (1980) 19 DR 244). In a case involving the killing of a gunman and his hostage in a failed rescue attempt, the Court determined that the degree of force used was proportionate to the danger of the situation (*Andronicou v Cyprus* (1998) 25 EHRR 491).

Potentially Relevant Articles

3. Article 3 – 'Prohibition of Torture'

3.1 *'No one shall be subject to torture or to inhuman or degrading treatment or punishment.'*

The argument here is that the treatment of parents has been inhuman or degrading. The Human Rights Court has held that ill treatment must attain a minimum level of severity if it is to fall within the scope of Article 3 (*Ireland v UK* (1978) 2 EHRR 25 para 162). Corporal punishment of prisoners has been held to be degrading (*Tyrer v UK* (1978) 2 EHRR 1). Since the purpose of the Article is primarily to outlaw torture it is doubtful whether it should be applied in the present circumstances although it is arguable that mental anguish alone if sufficiently severe could fall within the Article. However, the Commission is considering whether a victim of rape, cross-examined personally for long periods by the defendant in a criminal trial, was degraded and humiliated by the process. Article 3 might have some application in cases concerning rationing of healthcare if palliative treatment is withheld. Article 3 has been invoked to challenge the refusal to supply pain-relieving therapy to a severely mentally handicapped woman. Here, a settlement was reached. The area for examination is whether the complaints of the parents summarised in Chapter 2 and resulting in the need to have two, three or even four funerals constituted inhuman treatment, namely treatment that causes immense physical and mental suffering. This is a matter to be determined elsewhere.

4. Article 8 – 'Right to Respect for Private and Family Life'

4.1 *'Everyone has the right to respect for his private and family life, his home and his correspondence.'*

It may be argued that the funeral and burial or cremation of a member of one's family is one of the most important and sensitive parts of family life, and that to invade a family's privacy at such a time by withholding part of the deceased's body without consent is a denial of respect. There is, however, a balancing provision in Article 8 (2): 'There shall be no interference by a public authority with the exercise of this right except such as is in accordance with the law and is necessary in a democratic society … for the protection of health or morals, or for the protection of the rights and freedoms of others.' The argument is that the promotion of medical education and research is in the long term for the protection of health for all.

4.2   It is our view that organ retention, without establishing lack of objection or obtaining informed consent following a Coroner's or hospital post mortem examination, was in breach of the provisions of the Human Tissue Act 1961 and thus not in 'accordance with the law.' This matter is analysed in Chapter 10. We are also of the view that without establishing lack of objection or obtaining informed consent the medical profession had no authority to retain the organs following the conclusion of the Coroner's process. Similarly, the medical profession had no right to carry out a hospital post mortem or retain organs without establishing lack of objection or obtaining fully informed consent.

4.3   There is a strong argument that burial/cremation of a child relates to a fundamental aspect of family life for the surviving family. The counter-argument is that it is not a fundamental aspect covered by Article 8 such as the right to live together and that the right to bury/cremate a child is something families do together but the question is whether it relates to 'family life'. This is not a matter for us to determine.

5.   Article 9 – 'Freedom of Thought, Conscience and Religion'

5.1   *'Everyone has a right to freedom of thought, conscience and religion.'*

        There is a balancing exercise in Article 9(2): 'Freedom to manifest one's religion or beliefs shall be subject only to such limitations as are prescribed by law and are necessary in a democratic society in the interests of public safety, for the protection of public order, health or morals, or for the protection of the rights and freedoms of others.'

5.2   It is arguable that where the parents' religious beliefs dictate that a body be buried or cremated as a whole it would be a breach of their freedom of religion to deny this, unless there was some important health reason such as the spread of infection. It may be regarded as especially contrary to their human rights to flout their religious customs without their knowledge or consent. The purpose of this Article is to permit the relevant freedoms subject to the limitations as prescribed by law under Article 9 (2) or necessity as there defined. However, although there has been a breach of the Human Tissue Act 1961, none of the relevant necessities in a democratic society appear to apply.

6.   Article 10 – 'Freedom of Expression'

6.1   *'Everyone has the right to freedom of expression. This right includes freedom to hold opinions and to receive and impart information and ideas without interference by public authority and regardless of frontiers.'*

There are limits on this right set out in Article 10 (2). This article does not appear to impose a positive duty on a public authority, and in particular a doctor, to tell a person/patient anything. It appears to be outside the scope of any matter arising from this Inquiry.

7.   Article 13 – 'Right to an Effective Remedy'

7.1   This is not included among the Convention rights which are to be given effect in the domestic law under the Human Rights Act (see schedule 1). This is because the passage of the Act itself is regarded as meeting the requirement for a right to an effective remedy. The right overlaps with other Articles, particularly Article 6 (right to a fair trial). It has been held by the European Court that Article 13 does not oblige Member States to implement the Convention in domestic law in any particular manner (*Swedish Engine Drivers Union v Sweden* (1976) 1 EHRR 617).

There may be an argument that the inadequacies of the Human Tissue Act 1961 which provided for no sanction for breach were a contravention of Article 13. We recommend at the conclusion of Chapter 10 that the Human Tissue Act be criminalised by way of financial penalty for breach and consideration be given to the creation of a civil right of action.

8.   Article 14 – 'Prohibition of Discrimination'

8.1   This is not a free-standing right. It provides that the enjoyment of the rights and freedoms set out in the Convention shall be secured without discrimination on any ground such as sex, race, colour, language, religion, political or other opinion, national or social origin, association with a national minority, property, birth or other status.

8.2   Discrimination goes to the status of those visiting or staying at the hospital not whether they as a group have been discriminated against. Parents have not been discriminated against. In fact we find they have been treated the same. The question is whether there have been primary breaches of other Articles.

8.3   In order to bring a complaint it must be shown that one of the other Articles applies. Article 14 does not stand alone. The question for consideration would be whether there would be any evidence that parents were discriminated against on one of the grounds set out in Article 14, in respect of their rights under other Articles.

9.   Conclusion

9.1   The Human Rights Act came into force in October 2000. Interpretation of its provisions is in its infancy. There is much to be decided as to the scope and application of the Act. It is for the courts, following detailed public argument as against the context of this confidential Inquiry, to develop the application of the Articles and the foundation for the future interpretation of the relevant law as well as making appropriate declarations for Parliament to consider.

Chapter 14. Parents' Evidence

The strength of the parents' evidence is such that the only way to do it justice is to set out faithful summaries. Wherever possible we have endeavoured to use the parents' own language in the narrative. We have adopted the simple strategy of introducing each summary with the child's first name, age and year of death. We do this as a mark of respect and also as a permanent memory of their involvement in and contribution to the Inquiry, while preserving the anonymity of their family. On occasions the word stillbirth has been used by parents but not always in the strict legal sense.

We commend the summaries to all who read them for their compelling content, understandable and reasonable expression of emotion, consistency of response and identification of recurrent concerns.

Contents

Marie	6½ months
Alexandra	Stillborn
Sarah	5 weeks
Laura	Stillborn
Kenneth	5 weeks
David	2½ months
Tony	11 days
Kirsten	4 months
Lindsay	7 months
Jordan	Stillborn
Lisa	Stillborn
James	1 day
Katy	15½ months
Lee	18½ months
Samantha	1 month
Kathleen	18 months
Anthony	3 years 10 months
Claire	14 years 11 months
Sam	18 months
Philip	5 years 3 months
Nicola	13 years 5 months
Robert	21 months
William	Stillborn
Paul & Gemma	8 months & 6 days
Christopher	Stillborn
Ryan	19 days
Nicholas	11 months
Katy	5 months

Written Evidence 434

Name of Child	Age
Karl	11 days
Andrew	11 months
Christopher	5½ years
Stephen	Stillborn
Charlie	13 years
Scott	9 months
Jason	14 days
Katy	12 days
Philip	7 months

Oral/Written Evidence Relating to the Cerebellum Collection 440

Name of Child	Age
Craig	3 years 5 months
Jessica	2 months
Kayleigh	4½ months
Dean	2½ months

Oral Evidence

Craig – 10 Days

Craig was born with congenital heart disease. He died while undergoing heart surgery at Alder Hey Hospital in 1986. His parents were told by telephone that he had died at 6.45pm.

In late 1999 they discovered that the medical records and post mortem report recorded the time of death as 7.50pm. Immediately prior to death his parents offered to donate his liver and kidneys if Craig died. They were told that his condition was too poor for his organs to be of use.

Shortly after they were told about his death his parents rang the hospital to make arrangements to see him. The nurse was insistent that they did not visit because it would be very upsetting and that they should leave it for a day or two.

They visited the hospital two days later and were told that a Coroner's post mortem would have to be carried out as a matter of procedure. When they saw the post mortem report in 1999 they discovered that post mortem examination had in fact been carried out on the previous day without their knowledge. They were never seen by the paediatric cardiologist or surgeon following Craig's death.

They received a letter from the paediatric cardiologist explaining the death but were not told that his heart and lungs had been retained. They were devastated to learn of this in 1999. They thought that they had buried their son intact.

In retrospect they would not have given consent for retention of the heart and lungs in a collection. They would have postponed the funeral to permit tissue sampling from the heart and lungs. They offered to donate organs to save the life of another child.

On learning of the organ retention in late 1999 they contacted Alder Hey who refused to answer even the most basic question and were told that the medical records had gone astray. His mother said that if the surgeon or paediatric cardiologist had told her of the benefit to medical science and to other children of keeping the heart and lungs in a collection in order to advance medical science, she would have considered donation but only after discussing it with her husband.

The question of genetic counselling following his death was never addressed. His parents expected an interview following death to explain the cause of death. It did not happen. They were never provided with a copy of the post mortem report at the time.

In 1999 they were provided with the post mortem report but it was not explained to them. After their initial contact with Alder Hey they had to wait three days for information about retention of the heart and lungs.

They express the need for the secrecy to end now and for the truth to come out. They wonder whether experimental surgery was carried out on their child. They did not know how seriously ill Craig was when surgery was carried out. Had they known they would not have consented to it.

They do not expect medical research to stop. They do not know how much truth will emerge at the Inquiry from Alder Hey. It is their view that there will be a lot of people with very loose memories stating that they cannot remember events so far back.

They want changes in the culture within the departments they dealt with. They feel they were entitled to full knowledge of what was being done to their son at the time of death and not so long after the event.

Sean – 15½ Months

Sean was born with congenital heart disease. He died while undergoing heart surgery at Alder Hey Hospital in 1997. His parents had been told that the chance of successful surgery was 80 per cent. Twelve hours after death the cardiac surgeon told them that they could have a Coroner's post mortem examination but that a hospital post mortem examination would be quicker. They had no opportunity to take independent advice nor time for reflection. The consent form was marked 'limited to heart and lungs only'. Apparently the death had been reported to the Coroner but a hospital post mortem examination was carried out.

His parents expressed to us a primal need to protect Sean even in death. They thought that tissue was a microscopic sample of an organ. Had they been told that the heart and lungs would be removed at post mortem and retained after burial they would have forbidden post mortem examination.

Their treating clinician met with them to discuss the post mortem report but merely stated that Sean's heart could not cope with the operation. There was no proper explanation.

They felt a sense of revulsion on discovering that the heart had been retained. They felt betrayed because the cardiac surgeon and paediatrician had not told them that the heart and lungs were to be removed and retained. It is their view that they would still have been ignorant of the retention but for Professor Anderson's evidence at the Bristol Inquiry.

In memory of Sean and to reflect the outstanding treatment in life he had received from Alder Hey, family friends and work colleagues raised £2,000 for Alder Hey. Shortly after this charitable effort they were informed by Alder Hey that Sean's heart and lungs had been retained. This was late 1999.

On initial contact Alder Hey made a mistake as to Sean's name. It took weeks of telephone calls to secure the release of his heart. Without seeking permission from his parents and immediately before return of the heart and lungs the hospital sampled them. The parents felt betrayed by retention and last minute sampling. In consequence they question whether it was Sean's heart which was returned to them. They regard Alder Hey's handling of the organ retention issue as unprofessional. They are concerned that as Sean died in surgery there should have been a Coroner's instead of a hospital post mortem.

On the issue of organ retention they cannot accept that the Chief Executive and management knew nothing about it. They should have done if they were proper managers. The parents said it was appalling that the hospital should blame loss of income from charitable donations upon the issue of organ retention.

On the evening prior to surgery they were given a very detailed explanation of what the surgery would involve. They expected but were denied the same detailed explanation of what a post mortem examination involved. They also want to know why at post mortem samples were taken from the thyroid, oesophagus and trachea.

They identify the need for proper management procedures, fully informed consent and the need for truth. They say an upheaval is needed in all these areas to prevent the Alder Hey experience occurring again.

Philip – 3 Months

Philip was one of twins. He died in his pram in 1988 apparently from Sudden Infant Death Syndrome. His body was taken to hospital and removed from his parents by a nurse. They were not told where the body was held for four days. During this time a Coroner's post mortem was carried out without their knowledge. All the organs including the heart and brain were removed and retained without parental consent.

A nurse at Alder Hey eventually told them that Philip's body was in the mortuary at Alder Hey. His twin was being investigated at Alder Hey for signs or symptoms of any condition which might cause him to die in similar circumstances.

When the family saw Philip in the mortuary the post mortem had caused his features to drop to the back of his head. Mother described his appearance as horrible. This was the first time that the family had seen him since he had been taken from them on admission to hospital. Neither his father nor his mother had been offered any time with Philip before he was taken from them.

Subsequently at a Foundation of Infant Deaths Conference they met Professor van Velzen who had carried out the post mortem examination. He said that Philip's organs were normal and there was no explanation for his death. He said 'it was rather like buying a light bulb and the shop testing it before taking it home yet when the bulb was fitted at home it failed'!

Philip's twin was detained in hospital on and off for three months and underwent very extensive, distressing tests. In the end there was no obvious conclusion to the tests and his parents took him home.

His parents discovered that Philip's organs had been retained in December 1999. Initially they were told of partial retention. They were then told of the full extent of the retention, from brain to reproductive organs, and were shocked. A second burial took place in January 2000. It had always been their desire to bury their child intact.

They feel that they were told lies by Alder Hey in December 1999. This has left them with concerns about whether Philip's organs have been used for pharmaceutical research and whether his eyes were removed. They were incredulous at retention of his reproductive organs and this in itself raised the incidence of suspicion.

Their overriding concern is why the organs were retained. If some useful research had been carried out it might have comforted them. They regard storage without research as totally futile.

They feel that they were treated cruelly in not being given time to grieve in Philip's company shortly after death. They feel deceived about the organ retention issue. They were distressed on discovering the extent of the retention 11 years after the event.

They have done their best to protect themselves and their children from the consequences of their loss. Their view is that to be left ignorant of the retention and then finding out about it 11 years later is too cruel in all the circumstances and no parent should go through that.

They feel that the hospital should have talked them through every stage of bereavement including post mortem examination. They would have wanted to know the basic post mortem procedure and this might have alerted them to the possibility of retention. They feel they might have been able to prevent it.

Sisters: Claire – 7 Days
               Heather – 2 Days

Claire was born with congenital heart disease. She died in theatre at the Royal Liverpool Children's Hospital in 1982. Her parents were told that there was no need for them to attend the hospital immediately. They were told to wait until Monday for the paper work to be completed to secure release of Claire's body. There was no mention of a post mortem examination. They did not see Claire for eight days.

They contacted Alder Hey Hospital on 18 October 1999 and discovered that Claire's heart and lungs had been retained. It took 11 weeks 3 days for them to be provided with legible medical notes relating to Claire. They then discovered, 17 years after the event, that there had been a Coroner's post mortem examination! They are still awaiting a copy of the post mortem report.

They first saw the death certificate in early 2000. They feel guilty for showing blind faith in everything they were told by the doctors. They were referred for genetic counselling by their General Practitioner.

The parents are left with the feeling that after Claire died the only thing that was wanted of them by the medical profession was to come over to conclude the paper work.

Heather was born like her sister Claire with congenital heart disease. She died in theatre at the Royal Liverpool Children's Hospital in 1984. The cardiac surgeon reported the death to the Coroner and a Coroner's post mortem was carried out. After the death of Heather the parents felt they were treated as though they did not exist.

When she became pregnant with Heather her mother expressed concerns over Claire's death to the doctors but they thought she was overreacting. They said that she had no need to worry. Claire was the last time and it was not going to happen again. They seemed dismissive about the chances of Heather being born with congenital heart disease.

They discovered in October 1999 that Heather's heart had been retained. There had been no discussion with the cardiac surgeon of the possibility of retention or the benefits of medical research or teaching.

They wanted an explanation from the doctors as to the death of both daughters. The parents were merely told that the post mortem examinations confirmed the causes of death but the reports themselves were not explained to them.

They feel that Alder Hey has handled the issue insensitively. They discovered the fact of organ retention on 18 October 1999. Their link worker left in December 1999 and thereafter every contact was beset with the problem of having to explain the whole situation with regard to both daughters to a new person. They feel that Alder Hey should have set up a special unit to deal with enquiries. They should have been invited to sit down and see everything concerning their daughters. They could have taken decisions there and then instead of having to deal with the stress of repeated enquiries. They were stunned that at the time of the death of each daughter they were not told that the hearts would be removed and retained in a collection.

Until recently both parents had carried organ donor cards for many years. They would have donated their daughters' organs to another child. They would have seriously considered the organs being used for research but they were never asked. The right to decide the fate of their daughters' bodies was taken away from them. After the death of Heather her parents were even more inclined to agree to their daughter's heart being used for medical research and teaching purposes.

They should have been told what was involved in the post mortem examination. If they had known that organs were removed they would have ensured that they were replaced in the body before burial, or used or disposed of in accordance with their wishes. They were denied the opportunity of asking what the organs would be used for, where they were to be taken and what the final outcome would be.

The parents fully accept that the medical profession will never discover anything in the future without research. They remain uneasy as to whether other organs were retained. This is fuelled by Alder Hey's inability to confirm anything to them.

They were prepared, in 1999, if they had been reassured by Alder Hey, to have allowed their daughters' organs to have remained at the hospital for medical research and teaching purposes.

They did not discover that Heather's heart was in the heart collection at Alder Hey until they gave evidence at the Inquiry. Had they been told that their children's hearts were being used for teaching purposes they would have allowed them to stay there. Alder Hey were not prepared to give this type of information. The parents cannot now decide whether to bury the hearts or leave them where they are.

They are concerned that the hospital took away their basic right of making a choice. They want to know who took the decisions to keep the organs without consent, why they did it, what the organs have been used for and what the purpose was.

They say that the Coroner should have been more alert to what was going on at Alder Hey. They did not even know the Coroner was involved with Claire. They had no contact with the Coroner at all. They think it should be up to the Coroner's office to make sure the parents are fully aware of what is going on.

Kathryn – 15 Years

Kathryn developed Hodgkin's disease and died at Alder Hey Hospital in 1993. Because of the extent of her condition she had undergone a bone marrow transplant. Her parents are concerned as to whether she died from complications arising from 'Beam' chemotherapy, which they subsequently discovered to be an experimental treatment for a 15-year-old.

Less than one hour after her death the clinician asked for permission for a post mortem examination. They were told that small tissue samples only would be taken through a restricted incision from the lung, liver and kidney. They consented to a limited post mortem examination. This failed to isolate any causative organism for infection causing or contributing to Kathryn's death.

Shortly after Kathryn's death her parents signed a handwritten consent form which read as follows:

> 'We the parents of Kathryn give permission for removal of tissue for diagnostic and other purposes other than transplantation.'

In a letter dated 27 September 1993 from the consultant haematologist to the parents' general practitioner there is reference to permission having been granted for a limited post mortem.

Prior to her death, Kathryn had been deteriorating under her chemotherapy regime for 7½ weeks. On 19, 20, 22 and 23 August 1993 Kathryn and her parents requested that she be allowed home but this was refused. Her parents feel that had she been allowed home she would not have been stripped of her organs and she would have been buried with respect and dignity.

On 8 December 1999, her parents were informed by Alder Hey that Kathryn's heart, chest and abdomen had been retained. On 20 December 1999 they received a letter from Ms Hilary Rowland, Chief Executive at Alder Hey, indicating that the heart, lung, liver, spleen and kidneys had been retained. In the post mortem report Professor van Velzen said that only a small mid-sternal incision approach was made with splitting of the caudal sternum. Only the upper organs and the lower aspects of the chest organs were brought in to view and inspected. The remainder of the assessment was done on palpation. Only organ biopsies were taken. This was a fiction confirmed by the list of organs described by Ms Rowland in her letter of 20 December 1999.

When matters came to light on 8 December 1999 the parents had to wait 13 weeks for Kathryn's clinical notes. They make the point that they did not consent to the 'Beam' treatment nor the sampling of organs beyond the lung, liver and kidney. They did not know she had been buried without her lungs, liver, kidney, heart and spleen. They remain concerned that other organs may have been retained. They do not trust the management at Alder Hey.

Their view is that parents are generous when a child dies. Even now they want to make things better. They do not want others to go through what they have been through. People should be given as much information as possible to make informed decisions, whether it is life or death. There is a need to respect human beings, their wishes, and all human beings should be treated with dignity. Society owes the truth to the children who have died. They have been lied to on several occasions not only by Professor van Velzen but also by management. Parents feel that they have been deceived and treated with insensitivity. They cannot trust anything the hospital says.

Gareth – 2 Months

Gareth was born with congenital heart disease and referred to Alder Hey where he died in 1993 following major heart surgery. The clinicians had advised the parents that the surgery had an 80 per cent chance of success. Shortly after death the cardiac surgeon told the parents that there had to be a post mortem examination.

In describing the failed surgery the surgeon was angry, incredulous at failure, blunt and insensitive. He upset the parents by referring to the need for an Inquest. The paediatric cardiologist was insensitive when he said words to the effect – 'Do not worry. You can have another baby.' The parents' overriding concern with Gareth was that he died despite the cardiac surgeon describing the operation as a complete technical success.

They telephoned the Alder Hey help line in the first week of October 1999 and it was confirmed on 8 October 1999 that Gareth's organs had been retained. At first it was only the heart and then later heart and organs and finally heart and lungs. Alder Hey would not answer questions raised by the parents about what use had been made of the organs. In a letter dated 21 January 2000 Ms Rowland wrote to the parents stating that the hospital did accept that many parents felt misled and did not fully understand that their child's organs had been retained. She did not answer the question whether the organs had been used for research purposes.

The parents were taken through the post mortem report by their general practitioner. The report indicates that the post mortem examination was carried out ten minutes after death. This is likely to be yet another mistake. If it is not a mistake then the post mortem was carried out before the parents had had the chance to say goodbye to Gareth.

The parents found Ms Rowland's letter dated 21 January 2000 incredibly insensitive. They never remotely anticipated organ retention. It was never broached with them and they had not signed a consent form. They had difficulty obtaining information from Alder Hey. A second burial was only possible in December 1999 because Gareth's father intervened to secure the organ release documentation. Even so the time scale was too tight and caused unnecessary distress. It had been a fight to secure release of the organs.

They described the handling as appalling, incompetent and insensitive. Even after discovering retention of their son's heart and lungs without their knowledge or consent they would have considered leaving the organs with Alder Hey had they been useful for research/training purposes. Alder Hey would not answer their questions with regard to use of the organs and therefore they reclaimed them for burial.

In her letter dated 21 January 2000 Ms Rowland admitted that the heart and lungs had been used for research/training. Prior to giving this information Alder Hey had commented in the Daily Post (11.12.1999) that hearts had been kept for extensive research and had been used regularly for teaching and by consultants. The parents feel that they have been treated with complete lack of respect. Had this information been conveyed to them earlier then the second funeral would not have been necessary because they would have allowed the organs to remain with Alder Hey for research.

They are grateful that the hospital is attempting to put something right. There is an opportunity to improve the chances of survival for children born with congenital heart disease. Parents should consider leaving organs for research purposes. If the reasons are sympathetically explained they feel many parents would agree.

In their case they would have preferred Gareth's body to be buried intact but if the case for retention had been put forward properly they would have seriously considered it. Alder Hey has failed to answer their questions as to what the organs have been used for.

For the future the parents want a situation where it is clear in whose power the body rests so that if the hospital wants organs it has no option but to go back to that person for their consent. There is a need for doctors to be honest and open about things. More time is needed at the point of death with appropriate counselling and sufficient opportunity to consider what has happened and what the arrangements should be for the future. They would prefer all the arrangements they discuss to be in a legislative framework.

Ross – 5 Months

Ross was born prematurely at 27 weeks and died in 1990 at Liverpool Maternity Hospital. The cause of death was cardio-respiratory arrest consequent upon chronic lung disease. His parents consented to a post mortem examination to determine the cause of death if it would help other children who had the same disease. No steps were taken to explain the consent form to them. Because of their distress they describe signing it 'blind'. They realised that samples would be taken from organs in the post mortem procedure but understood that to mean a small piece of tissue for microscopic examination.

They were never told that whole organs would be removed and retained. The question of retention of organs was never mentioned. They thought they had buried their son intact whereas in fact they buried a husk. They insist on the need for fully informed consent and the right to bury a body intact unless express consent is obtained for retention of organs.

In early November 1999 his parents were informed that all Ross' organs had been removed and retained. His mother was employed as a nurse by Alder Hey and she was expected to continue working. She was offered neither counselling nor medical treatment. Her husband's employer provided counselling and appropriate leave of absence. In short they looked after their own which Alder Hey did not.

In November 1999 the whole of Ross' organs were returned by Alder Hey and buried. As they interred the organs they discovered that the casket bore the inscription for a child of 4 years 2 months yet Ross was only 5 months old when he died. This caused additional unnecessary grief and anguish.

His parents were angry that there was never any discussion following death of the desire or intention to retain organs. Had they been asked for retention of the heart and lungs to investigate and research chronic lung disease they would have agreed. His parents at death asked Alder Hey if they wanted the heart or other organs to use for the benefit of other children. They would have agreed to the heart entering the heart collection for medical research and teaching purposes at the time.

Had the hospital wanted other organs and explained the need fully they would have discussed the matter in depth. They would have welcomed counselling following the death of Ross. That person could have helped them understand the consent form they signed. As it was they felt pressurised by the circumstances.

His parents knew that body parts were removed for weighing at post mortem examination and that tissue samples would be taken for microscopic examination but they assumed that the body parts would be returned for burial. Nobody told them to the contrary. As to donation of the heart and lungs the parents said it was not a problem because they believed it was helping and it was their contribution to help other children with similar problems to Ross. They said that they were great ones for research and everything else. There was never a problem. Had the hospital turned round and said that it wanted to take the heart for research purposes or for teaching students or whatever the parents would have agreed.

They feel deceived and cheated at the way removal and retention took place without their knowledge. Alder Hey lost the opportunity of benefiting others from Ross' death. It appears that Alder Hey were not even aware that a nurse was involved in the issue of organ removal and retention until somebody brought it up at a meeting several months after the event. This seems to reflect the insensitive and unprofessional way Alder Hey had handled the issue.

Thomas – 3 Months

Thomas was born with a congenital cardiac defect which had been diagnosed before birth. Following birth he was transferred to Alder Hey where he underwent major heart surgery and died in 1992 in the intensive care unit. The cardiac surgeon requested a post mortem examination which was refused by the parents. They were told it would help other children in similar cases and they agreed. They were then asked whether organs could be retained after post mortem examination. They replied 'Absolutely not, no way'.

When his father was asked to sign the consent form for post mortem examination he was asked again if organs could be retained. Before signing the consent form he asked whether he was consenting to organ retention and the doctor said he was not. His parents did not consent to retention of the heart. They regarded tissue removal as being unrelated to organ retention.

The funeral took place four days after death and his parents thought that Thomas was cremated intact. On the basis that Alder Hey had done everything possible to save Thomas' life his parents sponsored a raffle and raised £250 for Alder Hey. They were not offered counselling by Alder Hey. They received genetic counselling from another hospital.

His parents contacted Alder Hey about organ retention in September 1999. It took three telephone calls before organ retention was admitted. His parents described the way they were treated by Alder Hey as very bad, dishonest and patronising. They feel they have been lied to on several occasions. They feel betrayed, let down and angry.

They eventually received a letter of apology from Alder Hey. It was addressed to their deceased son Thomas. This caused further upset. They asked, but were never told, where the heart had been kept for more than seven years. Had their wishes at post mortem examination been complied with there would have been no need for a second funeral in December 1999.

They were told by Alder Hey that most parents were trying to rebuild their lives and were getting on with it. The parents feel that Thomas was butchered and are furious. The post mortem consent form was altered after father had signed it in that 'heart only' was included. This was at a time when both parents had refused anything other than sampling of tissue so that Thomas would be cremated intact. They say that on the issue of post mortem examination Alder Hey acted contrary to their consent. They were lied to and deceived.

Michael – 4½ Months

Michael was born with congenital heart disease. He died nine days after major heart surgery at Alder Hey in 1989. His parents had been told there was very little risk at surgery. They were told of his death by Mr Roy Barter, HM Coroner of Liverpool. The purpose of his call was to inform them that a Coroner's post mortem examination was to be carried out. They were told by Alder Hey when the post mortem examination would be carried out after which the body would be available for the funeral. They received a telephone call of condolence from the treating clinician but no mention was made of organ retention.

They discovered the fact of organ retention on 11 October 1999 and were told that the heart, brain, chest and abdomen had been retained. They were told that Alder Hey would pay for the second funeral and the Co-operative funeral directors would be retained. The hospital wanted a disposal decision immediately. His parents requested more information from Alder Hey. They were asked whether they really wanted to know and what difference would it make. They were treated with indifference.

Twenty-four days after their first request they were told that the brain, heart, lungs, liver, spleen, kidneys and intestine had been retained. There was no mention of the thymus, pancreas or adrenal glands. In one of the post mortem reports, however, these were recorded as retained but have not been located. They discovered that there were two post mortem reports, each with a different cause of death. The first provided by Professor van Velzen was incomplete. The Coroner appears to have acted upon an incomplete post mortem examination report and not chased the completed report.

They have received no apology from Alder Hey. The hospital seems to have been reluctant to give information as well as being defensive and insensitive.

His parents' aim has been to try to restore faith and confidence in Alder Hey. In fact they feel that the hospital has treated PITY II and the parents generally as enemies. Michael's parents feel an intense need to know what happened. They have asked to speak to Mrs Karen England, the senior laboratory technician working with Professor van Velzen in 1989. They were told such contact was inappropriate. Ms Hilary Rowland, Chief Executive at Alder Hey confirmed that Mrs England was a key figure and this was possibly the reason why it was inappropriate for her to be seen by the parents.

His parents describe a catalogue of errors, disasters, misinformation, insensitivity, long delays, missing medical notes and post mortem reports on the part of Alder Hey. No explanation has been provided as to why there are two post mortem reports.

They were told by the clinician that it was Professor van Velzen's decision to retain the heart and other organs to allow further studies so that a more accurate cause of death could be established. They were told by Professor van Velzen that the Coroner never questioned the fact that the post mortem reports were preliminary. The parents gave no consent, either before or after the post mortem examination, for the removal of tissue or organs.

Any parent receiving the body of their loved one back for cremation or burial should have the confidence that the body is intact. They would have agreed to microscopic examination of tissue from the body so long as the body was intact for funeral purposes. In failing to do this the hospital deprived the parents of choice. Their views were never taken into consideration.

They also complain that the hospital restricted the supply of information to the link worker who then passed on limited information to them on the basis that they were being told everything, only to find out that the information was incomplete. Eleven years after Michael's death they remain in a state of anguish and turmoil.

Jake – 2 Months

Jake was born with congenital heart disease. He underwent treatment at Alder Hey and Great Ormond Street. He died in 1998. His parents have great admiration for the help and treatment received from Alder Hey during Jake's life and in particular from the intensivists.

His parents wanted to know precisely why Jake had died. They were told that there could be a limited post mortem. They signed a consent form limited to chest only. They understood that only the heart and lungs would be examined and this was written in bold on the consent form. Tissue was to be taken for microscopic examination. They were told that the body would be returned intact.

They were not told that the heart and lungs would be retained. A leaflet was supplied to them which stated that tissue samples would be taken and nothing was said about organ retention. His parents had already offered to donate Jake's organs but this had been declined on medical grounds. They assumed that the heart and lungs would be removed for examination, tissue taken and the organs returned to the body for burial.

During Jake's life they had the utmost admiration for the doctors, nurses and staff on the intensive care unit at Alder Hey. They told us that to this day they would still support Alder Hey and refer any of their other children with a serious illness. It was only after Jake died that things went wrong and were not properly explained. Retention of organs has caused them distress.

In September or October 1999 they rang Alder Hey to enquire whether Jake's heart had been retained. They had to wait for three weeks before retention was confirmed. In February 2000 they were informed that the lungs had also been retained. There was a second funeral in March 2000 which caused immense distress. They buried the casket containing the heart and lungs on top of the coffin which they had laid to rest 18 months earlier. It was particularly difficult for them when the casket was lowered on top of the coffin. They cannot describe their precise emotions.

In life they were told everything about Jake's treatment. In death they should have been told everything about post mortem examination. They had a right to know.

There should have been better and quicker communication about organ retention. There should have been a proper inventory of what was retained. There should not have been a three month gap between discovering that the heart had been retained and subsequently that the lungs had also been retained. They have not had an explanation from Alder Hey. They were offered counselling but declined because theirs is a strong family.

A proper explanation as to what post mortem examination involved and of the need for removal and retention of organs would have resulted in consent. In addition they would probably have consented to the heart being examined and retained in the heart collection.

They hoped that what was actively requested at post mortem examination was to further their own and the clinician's knowledge. They were both willing to consider organ retention if only someone had bothered to ask them openly and frankly. Post mortem consent forms need to be clearer.

They told us 'Jake nearly died a couple of times over a couple of weekends. Where else do you get the actual doctors and nurses crying with you! That is how close and how caring they were. They were actually heartfelt with us.'

They are saddened that the concealment of organ retention has threatened their appreciation and admiration of all that was done to save Jake's life.

Georgina – 3 Days

Georgina was born with a congenital heart disease. She died in theatre in 1995. Her parents were told quite bluntly that a Coroner's post mortem was required as a matter of law and that one reason was to make sure surgeons were performing properly. Their complaint is that the matter was dealt with arrogantly and that there was a lack of communication about the reason why a Coroner's post mortem was necessary.

They asked whether any organ would be useful for donation. Their offer was refused. They asked whether the heart would be needed for future reference and were told that the hospital did not retain organs for future study. Nobody told them why Georgina was a 'cardiac' baby. Her mother thought they might have needed organs to research the illness more thoroughly. The parents would have considered organ donation to another child or for medical research so that Georgina's life was not useless.

They were told to register the birth in Manchester and the death in Liverpool. Later they discovered both could have been dealt with in Liverpool.

They discovered the issue of organ retention in mid-October 1999. They contacted Alder Hey and asked if Georgina's heart had been retained. Three days later they were told that Alder Hey was having problems finding out. The following Monday they were told that Alder Hey did not have Georgina's heart. Her parents asked if they had anything else. Alder Hey told them that there was something else but they were not too sure what it was. Alder Hey telephoned three days later and said that they had still not heard. This message was repeated the following day. Following the intervening weekend they were told that the brain had been retained and it had not been examined.

Her parents requested the post mortem examination report. Alder Hey was reluctant to provide it. Subsequently they obtained one report of six pages and a second report of 16 pages. Each was carried out by a different pathologist. No explanation has been provided.

They never received an apology. They have lost trust in Alder Hey and feel that there has been a cover-up. They were invited to the hospital to ask questions but no apology or answers as to why the brain had been retained were given. They asked to see a brain surgeon but were told none was available. At the hospital they were told that it had done nothing wrong and everything was in the interests of furthering scientific development.

A letter from the Chief Executive Ms Rowland failed to answer the question as to why the brain was retained when Georgina had died from a heart defect. Ms Rowland was unable to answer the question about what information had been gathered from examination of the brain at post mortem. Similarly she was unable to answer what subsequent information and research was gathered from the brain and if no research had been done why it had been retained.

The parents feel that the hospital has lied and tried to justify its actions. Having been told by the cardiac surgeon that Georgina's heart was too badly damaged to be retained they are distressed that they were not told that other organs and in particular the brain might be retained.

They had a distressing second burial on New Year's Eve 1999. Their overriding view is that the hospital has just covered up and that it never had any intention of ever telling them of the retention of the brain until the revelation at the Bristol Inquiry. Alder Hey confirmed in writing that they have retained the brain but they will not put in writing that they have not retained anything else.

Delay in receiving information of brain retention, the distress of the second funeral and the realisation that they had not buried their daughter whole in 1995 has had a profound effect upon the family.

However, throughout it all her mother says that when she closes her eyes tight her baby comes through with blond hair, chubby legs and cheeks and bright blue eyes. The smell of her when she held her and the feelings when she was born all rush through her. Nobody can destroy that but Alder Hey's handling of organ retention has come very close.

Marie – 6½ Months

Marie died in 1962. The delayed diagnosis was of congenital heart defect. Prior to death her parents' general practitioner had told them that he did not want anything more to do with them because they were complaining to him on a daily basis about Marie's allegedly declining health. He told them to take her to hospital and he rang the hospital to tell them they were coming. At the hospital they were kept waiting and eventually a house officer came and asked them if they were the couple who did not want their child. They were staggered at the general practitioner's representation to the hospital. The house officer rang the GP and confirmed that Marie was extremely ill.

Marie remained in hospital for three months and died quite suddenly. On the evening of her death her parents had been sent home by the hospital to rest. They were then told by a policeman, who came to their house, that they were required back at the hospital. They sat in an office and waited for someone to tell them what had happened. While looking over the desk mother saw Marie's death certificate. She went straight to Marie's room but was not allowed to hold her.

Her parents would not have given consent to the taking of organs for medical research or teaching but they would have considered organ donation to save the life of another child. They did not sign a post mortem consent form.

In 1973 Marie's mother trained as a nurse and worked at the hospital where she was allocated to the same ward on which Marie died. She told her tutor who said that she either got on with it or went home and that would be the end of her training. She thinks the tutor did her a favour in helping her get over the problem!

She rang Alder Hey to enquire about organ retention on 2 February 2000 and was told on the 13 February that Marie's heart and lungs had been retained and subsequently this was altered to heart only. She was physically and mentally devastated when she realised that she had not buried Marie intact.

She is concerned that the medical profession should be stopped from walking over the rights of patients and their families. She complains of the long-winded release procedure for the second burial which occurred in April 2000. Her faith in the medical profession has been rocked. The second funeral caused her to rake over memories of losing Marie in the first place.

She commends the co-ordinator Ms Betsy Fitzgerald who gave her the bad news in a very humane and helpful way. She could not have been told in a nicer way and would have picked Betsy if anyone had to tell her such bad news. However, she was not offered counselling facilities by Alder Hey.

She feels a compelling need that the medical profession should be open and that families and relatives should be given full information about post mortem examination. Her general practitioner explained the post mortem report to her in 1962 and she found this to be helpful.

Alexandra – Stillborn

Alexandra was stillborn in 1995. Her parents agreed to a hospital post mortem in order to establish the cause of death. They were provided with a leaflet describing post mortem procedure. They were not told that organs would be retained, neither were they told that they had a right to object. They were informed that only tissue samples for microscopic examination would be taken and that anything removed would be put back and the body buried complete. They were told that the post mortem results would be available within six weeks of the stillbirth. Later they were told that the results would not in fact be ready within six weeks because Professor van Velzen who had conducted the post mortem examination was out of the country on a project in Canada.

Subsequently they contacted the Health Authority who told them that Dr Khine had actually performed the post mortem examination. They asked the Chief Executive to investigate and were told that it was an unexplained stillbirth and that the gross pathology was normal. The matter was investigated by the relevant clinical director who was not a pathologist and could not provide the answers the parents wanted. They asked for a copy of the post mortem report.

They were told that there was a placental report which was provided. They were told that part of the delay in dictating the report was due to the necessity to compare the organs removed with normal standards.

In December 1999 they could not escape the national news of the organ retention issue at Alder Hey. They realised that Alexandra was probably involved. Twelve days after contacting Alder Hey they were told that Alexandra's heart and other organs were retained. They requested return of the organs and a funeral as soon as possible before Christmas. Alder Hey refused. A second funeral was held in January 2000. This would not have been possible had the family's funeral director not intervened to force the issue of return of the retained organs with Alder Hey.

After the second funeral they received an unsigned post mortem report which at one time it was alleged that Professor van Velzen had carried out. Later they were informed that it had been carried out by a different pathologist.

More particularly the recorded weight of the child examined was 950 grams whereas Alexandra weighed 4kg. However, the remainder of the weights of individual organs appear appropriate.

Their overall view of the handling of the news was that every step of the way they had hassle and had to battle just to have returned that which should never have been taken in the first place. They rang Alder Hey yet again and spoke to Ms Therese Harvey, the Human Resources Director, and the first thing she asked them was whether they were contacting a solicitor. The parents replied that they would if they did not get the answers they required. They explained to Ms Harvey exactly what they wanted but never heard from her again.

They feel that Alder Hey has consistently refused to answer questions relating to why organs were retained, why they were not informed of the retention, why they have had to contact Alder Hey and why it took so long for a definitive answer after the initial inquiry.

Alder Hey did not keep to deadlines nor keep in contact with parents. They did not have people available to answer calls. They felt that Alder Hey put up brick walls and tried to pass the buck to the Chester hospital and the crematorium where the second funeral was to take place. Alder Hey should have met the parents and admitted that they were unable to answer all the questions. Alder Hey should have been honest and replied promptly to all the parents' requests. The parents say that they have been treated arrogantly, without sympathy or compassion. They feel that there has been a total disregard of the respect to which their dead child was entitled. Their trust has been betrayed, they have been deceived and their child desecrated. They remain angry.

Alexandra's mother said she wanted to talk about the emotion involved because she knew that to people not involved it must seem incomprehensible why anybody could get so upset about a dead person's organs because at the end of the day they are dead. Nothing more could happen to them and the organs would be disposed of anyway so what does it matter that they have been taken away even without consent.

Had she been asked at the time for consent to organ retention she may well have agreed. The question is why is she so emotional about it? She accepts the logic of the argument and has repeatedly gone over it in her mind since discovering the fact of organ retention in an effort to try and cope with the situation. Nevertheless she finds the emotion overpowering and it controls her daily life.

She is emotional for several reasons. The first is the deceit involved. She did not know what had happened to her daughter or that she had been desecrated. Alexandra had been stripped bare of everything and somebody believed they had the right to do it and to return her apparently complete for funeral purposes but in fact without her internal organs. For five years she believed Alexandra was intact and at rest.

The second reason for her emotion is the feeling of immense betrayal by Alder Hey. She believed that the hospital owed a duty of care to her daughter and that they had breached that duty.

The third and most compelling reason for her emotion as a parent is that she would have done anything and everything in her power to protect her child. That was what she was there to do even more so in death because it was only thing she could do for her child at that stage. She had put her trust in the doctors, the midwives, the clinicians, the pathologists that they would respect her child and that they would deal with her in the way one would wish to deal with a dead person. They did not, they desecrated her. She feels let down. There was only one thing she could do and that was to protect her in death and she did not do it and she has to live with that. Alexandra's parents thought they did the right thing in consenting to post mortem examination and now they know they did not.

Sarah – 5 Weeks

Sarah was born at Preston with congenital heart disease. She died within 24 hours of major cardiac surgery at Alder Hey in 1992. Her parents were given excellent prospects of success for surgery and cannot understand what went wrong. They are concerned about the surgical performance in the cardiac department. There should have been a Coroner's post mortem examination. In fact the cardiac surgeon informed them of the death six hours after the event and told them that there would be a hospital post mortem to find out what went wrong. Her parents have no recollection of signing a consent form but Alder Hey has recently produced a consent form signed by the father. They asked if the hospital wanted them to donate any of Sarah's organs and this was declined. They think they should have been told precisely why there was to be a post mortem examination, where it was to be carried out and what it involved.

They are of the view that Alder Hey is trying to blame Professor van Velzen for what has in fact been going on for a very long time. They cannot understand why their child died after the second major cardiac procedure and why it was necessary to harvest all the organs from the brain to the pelvis. They were not told that any organs would be retained. They were pleased for what had been done for them at Alder Hey and invited donations instead of flowers for the funeral and raised £400 for the hospital.

They contacted Alder Hey about organ retention in late 1999. Two weeks later they were told that there had been a full retention of organs. They have never been told the reason for organ retention. Ultimately they want a return of the organs but not until this Inquiry has reported.

They make the point that having offered to donate organs it is very difficult for them to understand why Alder Hey would want to keep them after that. They would have discussed retention of the heart in the heart collection and would probably have said yes if they had they been fully informed as to the reasons.

They have lost their faith in the medical profession. They thought that they had buried their child intact. Their lives have been devastated by the disclosure of organ retention. They cannot believe their daughter is involved in such an horrific scandal. They cannot understand why the Coroner was not informed about the death of their daughter within 24 hours of the second major cardiac procedure which she underwent.

Laura – Stillborn

Laura was stillborn in 1993. Her mother was not told that a hospital post mortem examination would be carried out at Alder Hey. She told the funeral director to collect the body from the hospital where Laura had been left, and she thought her baby had been buried intact.

There had been a discussion about organ donation and a nurse said that her eyes could be handy but there was no mention of post mortem examination. Three minutes after the stillbirth she was asked to sign a consent form but could not recall that she had signed it and did not know what she had signed. In any event she told a nurse to leave her baby alone.

In October 1999 Laura's mother contacted Alder Hey and was told that the heart and stomach had been retained. A second funeral took place in November 1999. Shortly before the second funeral the undertaker informed her that the release form from Alder Hey referred to many more organs including the heart, brain, lungs, liver, spleen, kidneys and intestine. Prior to the second funeral mother made many calls to Alder Hey which were not returned. She did not receive full information as to what precisely was retained.

The whole event caused her eldest son to become very upset and he refused to go to school. He saw a counsellor. He was obsessed with cutting pictures of Professor van Velzen out of the newspaper.

Mother wanted to know where the organs had been kept and whether they had been used for research. She received uninformative letters from Alder Hey, the envelopes of which were open. Samples had been taken from the returned organs without consent.

She feels someone independent should have been with her when the original consent form was signed. She needed help with understanding the document and the process of bereavement.

She complains that Alder Hey have dealt with her insensitively. How does she know all the organs retained have been returned? She would have considered transplantation from her child to another child but not the retention of organs for medical research or teaching purposes. She wants to find out why the organs were retained. She feels sick about the organs having been kept for no purpose.

On 12 May 2000 she rang Alder Hey and asked whether she had buried her daughter with her eyes and was told 'you will never know'. She said that if she dug her up she would find out. She was told, 'go on then but you still would not find out'. She has still not been told whether or not the eyes were removed and retained. She feels guilty that she let her daughter down in death by letting the pathologist 'butcher' her.

Kenneth – 5 Weeks

Kenneth died in 1987. Post mortem examination was carried out at Chester. He was cremated. His mother was told by the Coroner that he died because his heart defect was worse than the scan had shown.

In December 1999 his mother contacted Alder Hey and two weeks later was told that the heart only had been retained. She had difficulty obtaining details. She was concerned that other organs might have been retained. She was told again that it was the heart only but she wanted written confirmation.

She has subsequently seen a letter from the paediatrician at Chester to the paediatric cardiologist at Liverpool offering Kenneth's heart either to be sent to or collected by Liverpool. This letter is dated 8 April 1987 but mother was not told. The hospital at Chester has apologised for heart retention and said that it should never have happened. It amounted to a secret interchange of organs between hospitals.

The family has been bitter at the discovery of heart retention. They remain concerned about the cause of death. They have in fact been told of three different causes of death on three different occasions namely heart defect, cot death and virus. His mother is very distrustful of the medical profession. Her grief has been exacerbated by the discovery of heart retention. She feels she has been lied to by Chester Hospital as well as Alder Hey. She would never have consented to retention. She was asked if samples could be taken from the heart before it was returned but said no. She had been threatened that unless she consented the heart would not be returned.

Her eldest son has become distressed at the issue of heart retention.

Kenneth's mother remains concerned as to the cause of death. She feels she should have been told what a post mortem examination involved. She would have liked an independent bereavement adviser to have been present at the time. Had the hospital asked to examine the heart she would have held the funeral back until it was completed.

She says that the memory of her child has been ruined by living under the illusion that he was buried intact when in fact he was missing his heart. She cannot even look at pictures of him now because she just sees him in a different way.

David – 2½ Months

David was born with liver disease and died in 1987 at Alder Hey. His parents refused a hospital post mortem because he had been through enough in life and was like a 'pin cushion'. They were persuaded to sign a post mortem consent form on the basis that only microscopic samples of the liver, rather like a biopsy, would be taken. The purpose would be to find out the precise cause of death. The only content of the post mortem report which they were informed of was that David died of acute liver failure. He had been awaiting a liver transplant.

They would have considered donation of his organs to another child to save that child's life. They would not have consented to removal of organs for medical research and teaching purposes.

They had been led to believe that organ retention only related to the period 1988 to 1995 whilst Professor van Velzen was in post. They did not expect to be told on 3 December 1999 that any of David's organs had been retained. They thought that they had buried him whole. They were told that samples had been taken and there were incomplete post mortem reports. Post mortem histology had been carried out and reported upon in David's case by November 1988! They were told that the heart was removed for research yet there is no record of nor data relating to research work.

Alder Hey has failed to answer the parents' questions satisfactorily. They were told by Ms Harvey that the brain had probably been removed and clinically disposed of. Ms Harvey then told them on 1 February 2000 that block samples had been taken from the brain, kidney, heart and bowel. His parents cannot understand why the brain and heart were retained if the cause of death was liver failure.

On 8 March 2000 they were told by the treating clinician that it was likely that the liver had been retained and was in the deep freeze at Alder Hey. They were then told on 10 April 2000 that there was no evidence of retention of the brain. The information they have received from Alder Hey has been conflicting and unsatisfactory in every respect.

They say that in life the care of David at Alder Hey from the staff and doctors was marvellous. When they were told by Alder Hey through their solicitor that there was no evidence of retention of the liver and brain they could not understand this because there is reference in the post mortem report to the brain being fixed in formalin. This could not have been done prior to burial!

The parents feel that they should have been told what the post mortem examination involved. They were given full details of his treatment in life. It might have alerted them to the possibility of organ retention. Certainly they would have asked whether organs removed for examination would be returned to the body before burial. They would have liked an independent person to advise them on bereavement and the issues immediately following death.

They see this as further protection against organ retention. The last piece of information they received in April 2000 from the treating clinician is that he did not know why the heart and brain were retained.

His parents say that in the circumstances they are never going to be able to lay David to rest now. They have already been told that his brain and liver have been clinically disposed of. His father feels guilty that he signed the consent form for the post mortem examination.

Tony – 11 Days

Tony died in 1994. His precise cause of death is still under investigation. After he was admitted to Alder Hey his parents were put in a side room and told the nurse and doctors that they did not want a post mortem examination. They were told that there had to be a Coroner's post mortem examination. The difference between a Coroner's and a hospital post mortem examination was not explained to them. They asked the clinicians to promise to put everything back as it was. The hospital said that they would only take slivers of tissue for examination. They were also reassured by the nurses that Tony would be put back together again intact after post mortem examination.

When they rang Alder Hey in late 1999 to enquire if any organs had been retained they were told the following day that there had been retention. They asked what had been taken and the reply was 'everything basically'. A list was reeled off to them including brain, heart and chest and whatever. On the Friday prior to the second cremation his mother asked for a guarantee that the returned organs belonged to Tony. They had also been promised that no samples would be taken prior to release of the retained organs. His mother told the hospital that they had stolen the organs and she wanted a 100 per cent guarantee that Tony's were not being retained, to which the hospital said 'alright you have got a 100 per cent guarantee' after previously refusing to give such a guarantee.

His parents feel that Tony was not given the rights he was entitled to at his first cremation. This rendered it a sham. Faith in the hospital and clinicians has been lost. Had they been asked the parents would have waited for two months to find the proper answer as to why Tony died provided they put him all back together again ready for his funeral.

When Alder Hey were giving them information about organ retention they felt that when they asked too many questions Alder Hey became very sharp and rude. They feel it would have been better if Alder Hey had offered to come to them to talk to them about the problem. The parents say that if Alder Hey wanted organs because another child was dying they might have considered it. However they are appalled at the hospital taking everything without telling them particularly as they had insisted upon everything being put back prior to the funeral.

They have an overriding impression that everything will be swept under the carpet and blame will not be properly apportioned.

Kirsten – 4 Months

Kirsten died on her first day in intensive care in 1991. It was described as a cot death. A Coroner's post mortem examination was carried out. There was no explanation given to her mother about what was involved in a Coroner's post mortem examination or the difference between a Coroner's and a hospital post mortem examination.

She implored the hospital to treat Kirsten as a baby and not an object and to put everything back which they removed for examination. The hospital told her that they were always gentle and compassionate. She never thought it was legally possible to retain organs without permission or knowledge. She thought she had cremated Kirsten complete. In fact six months after Kirsten's death she received counselling during the course of which she was told that nothing was retained following post mortem examination, not even tissue. At one stage she even saw Professor van Velzen and he said he always treated babies gently.

After post mortem examination the parents were allowed to see Kirsten. Her swollen appearance shocked her mother so much that she gave instructions for the coffin to be closed rather than left open.

Kirsten's mother contacted Alder Hey in September 1999. She was made to feel that on death she had no rights over her baby's body. There were weeks of telephone calls and then one Sunday she was told that the heart and brain had been retained. She nearly vomited. The following day she was told to choose between return and cremation of the retained organs or to leave them with the hospital for research or to commit the organs to a mass communal burial.

She was greatly offended by the second alternative, namely retaining the organs for research, when the organs had remained untouched and not examined in the eight years following death. She never received an apology or an explanation for what had happened.

Later she received another letter stating that there were other organs. She was drip-fed information because it was felt that giving all the news at once would be too distressing for her to receive. She did not see the post mortem examination report until late 1999.

The mother says that the way she was treated at Alder Hey has destroyed her heart, soul and memory. She needs answers to ensure that her baby is given the respect she deserves. It might have been more acceptable if the hospital had said the research on the retained organs had saved the lives of other children.

She cannot contemplate that her baby's organs have been stored and not touched for eight years. She feels violated. Her daughter was butchered. She was let down, betrayed and lied to. She poses the question, 'would they have done it to one of their own?'

Learning of the retention has been a complete nightmare. She should not have been given bad news over the telephone but face to face. She should not have been told by a nurse 'try not to look at it emotionally it is just tissue'. Her request for group counselling should have been granted.

Lindsay – 7 Months

Lindsay was born with congenital heart disease and was a Down's Syndrome child. She died eight days after cardiac surgery in 1991. A Coroner's post mortem examination was carried out shortly after death. Her mother did not discover that a post mortem examination had been carried out until the day before the funeral.

Lindsay's death itself involved her parents making a decision on medical advice to switch off the life support machine which had sustained life following surgery. After death her mother offered to donate Lindsay's organs but this was declined. Her mother was not provided with counselling. Even when she discovered that there had been a post mortem examination she thought that the body would have been opened and all the organs examined would have been returned. She did not even consider the prospect of retention of organs.

Had microscopic examination of the organs been necessary she would have delayed the funeral until that had been completed. She would have been willing for her daughter's organs to have been used for transplantation as well as medical research. She would have considered Lindsay's heart being used in the Alder Hey heart collection. None of these matters were discussed with her other than refusal of donation because of Lindsay's condition.

She discovered the fact of organ retention in October 1999. It took eight days for Alder Hey to confirm that the brain, heart, lungs and abdominal organs had been retained. She received a written apology but no explanation has ever been given as to why the organs were taken and kept. She asked repeatedly for an explanation and to date there has been none.

She feels that she did not properly lay her daughter to rest and only buried a shell. The second burial took place in November 1999 and re-opened grief from the first burial. At the second burial the original coffin had to be exhumed to accommodate the small casket containing the returned organs. It was extremely distressing for the family.

She feels her daughter has not been treated with the respect she deserved in death. She feels guilty that having loved her daughter so dearly in life she let her down when she needed her most, namely in allowing her organs to be retained without consent. Overall she feels let down, disgusted, angry, upset and betrayed.

Having regard to the delay, apology and lack of explanation as to why the organs were retained despite repeated requests for an explanation, unbelievably Alder Hey rang Lindsay's mother in August 2000 as she returned home from work to tell her that Lindsay's cerebellum (part of the brain) had also been retained. At the time of the call she was with her other young children and became distressed. She feels she should not have been given this information without the support of a friend or relative at the very least. The correct method of communication was face to face.

She has been given no reasonable explanation as to why the cerebellum was retained. She is now considering whether to have a third funeral. She feels more devastated this time than on the initial return of the organs because she thought she had reburied Lindsay to render her intact.

Jordan – Stillborn

Jordan was stillborn in 1994. His parents were told that it was important to discover why he had died particularly as it was their first child and there might be genetic considerations.

His parents refused a post mortem examination at first. They said that Jordan had been through enough already. They were reassured by a nurse and social worker that the organs would not be used for medical science. They were told that if they consented to a hospital post mortem examination to establish the cause of death everything would be put back. They had a short time to discuss matters with a social worker and were persuaded to sign the consent form for the removal of tissue. They were told the result of the post mortem examination by the gynaecologist.

They contacted Alder Hey on 13 October 1999 to enquire whether any of Jordan's organs had been retained. They received a reply on 27 October 1999 telling them that every organ had been kept. They felt despair and anguish. They thought they lived in a civilised, caring society and trusted doctors. Although they were offered counselling at Alder Hey they wanted independent counselling away from the hospital but this was not provided.

They cannot face asking Alder Hey for the return of the organs to bury them and this matter is being looked into by their solicitor. They are anxious to have a second burial but are fearful of the consequences.

At the original burial they thought they were putting their child to rest. They thought he was complete and that he had a nice funeral and burial.

They now feel that they signed the consent because they were under pressure and lied to. Their child lost his dignity and was treated like a piece of meat in a butcher's shop. They feel let down. They feel that their child's dignity was taken away when his organs were retained. Had they been told at the time it was necessary microscopically to examine the organs they would have delayed the funeral until this had taken place. If they had been given full information they would have considered donating organs to save the life of another child.

They feel guilty that they did not protect their child in death and did not prevent all his organs being removed at post mortem examination. Both parents are unwell as a result of discovering the fact of organ retention.

Lisa – Stillborn

Lisa was stillborn in 1985. On return to the ward after delivery her mother was tired and confused and had received pethidine for pain relief. She was told that a hospital post mortem would be routine procedure to discover the cause of death. Confused and distressed she signed the consent form. She was not told she could object. She would have liked a counsellor present at the time to help her with the bereavement and its consequences. She was not told that organs would be removed and retained at post mortem examination.

The post mortem examination itself was carried out at Alder Hey. Lisa's mother has only recently discovered this fact. She was not told the result of the post mortem examination.

In October 1999 she rang Alder Hey enquiring whether Lisa's organs had been retained. Two weeks later she was told that they had not. She feels she should have received more sympathy and understanding and a quicker response. She should have been given more detail.

On 11 March 2000 she was told that Lisa's heart had been retained. She feels it will be a long time before she can ever trust Alder Hey again. She is hoping to arrange a second burial. She thought she had buried Lisa intact. The second burial will cause great distress in the family.

Discovery of the retention of Lisa's heart has had a bad effect on the eldest child who has gone to pieces. Sooner or later the other children will discover that they had a sister who was stillborn. Their mother is fearful that they will react in the same way as her eldest child.

Lisa's mother feels that her daughter came into the world whole and should have been buried whole. She feels guilty for not preventing the heart being removed and retained. Her major concern now is how she can arrange to unite the heart with the body which was buried in a public grave. She is receiving assistance from her solicitor and has the support of this Inquiry.

James – 1 Day

James was born in 1990 with complex congenital heart disease. He died in theatre the next day. His parents knew that everything possible was done for him. They were 'totally dashed' by his death.

Following his death his father was asked in the hospital corridor to sign a consent form for post mortem examination by the cardiac surgeon. No understanding of the plight of the parents was shown. He recollects that he was in no fit state to read what he signed. He trusted the surgeon and signed the form. He felt that James had been through enough in his short life and that he did not want a post mortem to be carried out.

The surgeon told him that he needed to have a post mortem so he could make sure he had done everything right and it could help him improve in future. James' father only agreed to sign the consent form because he wanted to do something to help another child. Nobody told him what a post mortem examination involved nor that organs would be retained. He was not told that it was to be a Coroner's post mortem or what that meant. In fact it was a Coroner's post mortem examination and a consent form was not necessary. James' parents now feel that it was always known that it was to be a Coroner's post mortem and they were asked to sign the consent form so that organs could be retained for other purposes. They would never have agreed to the retention of their son's organs.

After reading of the organ retention scandal in a national newspaper their first thought was that it could not happen to their son. They contacted Alder Hey and had to wait for four or five days to be told that James' heart and some organs had been retained. When they pressed for further details they were told that the lungs, brain and abdominal organs had also been retained. Later they were told that his intestines, liver and kidneys had also been retained.

In November 1999 all James' organs were returned. A second funeral service and burial took place. The organs were placed in a casket next to the coffin. It was very distressing.

They then learnt that tissue samples had been taken from the organs before they were returned without their consent. They had been informed that it was unlikely that further examination of the samples would be completed. They are still waiting for the return of the tissue samples so that the histology report can be completed.

They describe the way they have been treated by Alder Hey as the epitome of arrogance. They would have appreciated being told where things had gone wrong and then been offered some emotional support.

They thought that they had done everything they could as parents for James and now are left with a tremendous feeling of guilt. A religious ceremony was held and they felt that they had laid James to rest in a dignified way at the first funeral. To them, burying only part of James has made a mockery of it all.

They want to know why this practice went on for so long. Why did it happen and why have so many parents been put through such distress? They still require a full explanation of the post mortem report and remain doubtful as to whether they have even now buried all their son's organs.

Katy – 15½ Months

Katy was born with immunodeficiency syndrome. She died in 1990. Her parents know that Alder Hey did everything they could to try and save her and they want to pay tribute to Katy's doctor Dr David Heaf, 'the best doctor they have ever met'. They think of Alder Hey as a caring and professional hospital. They are now deeply saddened for the doctors and nurses who work so hard to save lives.

Katy's parents agreed to post mortem examination to try and help other children like their daughter. A nurse explained what would happen at post mortem and assured them that Katy's body would be treated with dignity and respect. They felt the pressure of time was upon them to make an immediate decision. They should have been told the full facts from the outset. Katy's parents would never have agreed to organ retention.

They found out about organ retention at Alder Hey from a radio programme. They were informed that Katy's heart, brain, some of her intestine and her ovaries had been retained. The post mortem report does not reveal that organs were retained. The report does not state that the post mortem was incomplete. By not giving Katy's parents full information Alder Hey gave themselves the opportunity to retain her organs without parental consent. They knew that her parents would say no. Her parents understand the need for the study of organs.

The sad result is that the first funeral was not a proper funeral. They were just burying part of her. They can find no words to explain their view on the second funeral. People feel sick at what they have had to do. Normal society did not know what to do when the scandal broke. It was unthinkable to people. They are further outraged that samples were taken without consent before the organs were returned.

Her parents want to know who knew that organs were retained?

They want to know who authorised that the organs be taken. They want to know what the justification was to do it. They want to know if any of Katy's organs assisted in research into immune deficiencies or were used for any other purpose.

They are left unsure as to whether they have buried the correct organs at the second funeral.

Lee – 18½ Months

Lee died unexpectedly in 1989. His mother knew that staff at the hospital did all they could to resuscitate her son. She thanked them for all they had done. She now feels it was all a front.

She was told that a Coroner's post mortem examination would be done. She was also told that it was to find out why he died as he was such a healthy child. She accepted the need for post mortem examination. She needed to know the reasons why her son had died. She was never asked if organs could be retained. She might have considered donating organs had she been asked.

The Coroner's Office informed Lee's mother that her son had died of Sudden Infant Death Syndrome (cot death).

The first funeral was a full Requiem Mass. His mother feels that her son did not have a decent funeral. Because of Lee's changed appearance following post mortem examination the coffin had to be closed. The first funeral was very hard to get through. There was a lot of anger at the second funeral. It was a smaller funeral by Lee's graveside.

She learnt of the organ retention scandal from a newspaper and the television news. She then phoned Alder Hey. The next day she was told that her son's heart had been retained. She was later told that her son's brain and all other internal organs had been retained. She was given no explanation as to why organs had been retained.

She knows that her son's post mortem report is incomplete. The report states that further tests need to be done to determine the cause of death. These have not been done. She does not know for certain why her son died.

Lee's mother wants to put right the wrong and make sure this never happens again. She feels cheated and let down. All the trust she had for the hospital has gone.

Samantha – 1 Month

Samantha was born with congenital heart disease. She died in 1997. She had undergone cardiac surgery on three occasions in the three weeks preceding her death. Five to ten minutes after her death her parents were asked to consent to a hospital post mortem and refused. They were told that it was necessary and the death was then reported to the Coroner who asked for a post mortem examination.

Her parents' attitude was that in her short life Samantha had gone through enough. They also asked the nurse to keep the Sacred Heart medallion with Samantha but this was not done.

Their clinician attended the post mortem examination. They were never told why it was necessary. They assumed a small amount of tissue had been taken at the post mortem examination but otherwise that when they buried Samantha they had buried her in her entirety.

They also raised the question of the second consent form to surgery which referred to tissue being taken in the event of death. The meaning of 'tissue' was not defined by the cardiac surgeon who said that the second form was a new form and he was surprised that it had come into use so quickly.

The Coroner told the parents that the post mortem report was too upsetting for them to read and sent it to their general practitioner. Alder Hey denied that they had received the report from the Coroner despite numerous telephone calls from the parents. The Coroner said they had. In fact Alder Hey subsequently went through the results of the post mortem examination with them and the clinician was most sympathetic and understanding and told them everything.

They discovered on 14 December 1999 that Samantha's heart had been retained. They remain concerned that they have not been told the full extent of organ retention. They have concerns about the possibility of the brain and lungs being retained. They feel that it is very clinical to obtain consent to a post mortem examination within five to ten minutes of death at a time when the parents are grief stricken. They feel that up to 24 hours should elapse before the post mortem is requested.

They want the following points answered.

- Parents should be told why a post mortem examination is necessary.

- Twenty-four hours should be given to parents to grieve before consent is requested for a post mortem examination.

- Parents should be told what rights they have if they refuse a hospital post mortem examination.

- There should be a clinical summary from the hospital before the matter is reported to the Coroner.

- It is necessary to define the terms 'tissue' and 'organ'.

- Parents should be told if anything is to be taken from their child, what it is and why it is to be retained.

- Parents should be told what organs have been retained beyond burial and why.

- Parents should be fully informed as to the wording of the operation consent form.

- Nothing should be removed from a child's body without the consent of both parents in writing and on the basis that the parents have been fully informed as to what they are consenting to.

Kathleen – 18 Months

Kathleen was born with congenital heart disease. She died at Alder Hey in 1991. The cardiac surgeon had discussed post mortem examination before Kathleen died. There was a discussion about organ donation to save another life. Her parents agreed to donation of the corneas and the pulmonary valve. After death her mother consented to post mortem examination but her father did not know that it was going to happen. He took her death very hard. Neither parent knew that Kathleen would be opened up and organs retained. They would not have consented had they known.

It is their view that Alder Hey should remain what it always was 'a fantastic hospital with a fantastic staff and hopefully it will continue with its excellent work'. The medical interest shown in Kathleen was prodigious in life but no doctor came to see or speak or discuss the death with them. They were not informed of the post mortem results. They repeatedly wrote to Alder Hey for a meeting with the doctor and finally one took place in Preston which lasted for ten minutes. It had taken eight months to arrange the appointment.

They were invited to contact Alder Hey in October 1999. Their daughter's name was wrongly spelled. This caused distress. They were informed that a number of organs had been retained and subsequently that fragments of bone and muscle had also been retained. They asked for the medical notes. When they received them they were badly copied. Information came to them in dribs and drabs.

On 9 May they were devastated to hear that their daughter's tongue had been retained and father protested silently outside Alder Hey. Her parents complained that Alder Hey did not follow the requirements of the Human Tissue Act and retained organs illegally. They were devastated to find that they had not buried their daughter whole. This involved a breach of trust and exploitation of a beloved daughter's beautiful body.

They describe the hospital as having stolen their daughter's body which was 'as white as driven snow. It was reduced to skin and bone by predators and it must never happen again'.

Their view is that those involved should be severely and publicly censored. They remain disgusted, damaged and devastated by what has happened. They describe the way they were informed about the organ retention on an ever increasing basis as 'abysmal'. They made repeated calls during which they could have been told the truth. They complain about repeated provision of incomplete information.

They have a host of questions left unanswered by Alder Hey, the NHS Executive – North West Regional Office and the Government.

Anthony – 3 Years 10 Months

Anthony was born with congenital heart disease. He died in 1996 within 24 hours of major heart surgery. The first major procedure had been carried out in 1996 and the cardiac surgeon told the family it had been a complete success. It was not and had to be reversed.

About five hours after death his parents were asked to consent to a hospital post mortem examination to help others and find out why the surgery had been unsuccessful. They were not asked if they had any questions. They consented to help others. They were never told that there would be organ retention. His parents had not slept and were in a state of distress when the question of consenting to post mortem examination was raised.

In late September 1999 they contacted Alder Hey and although they were treated professionally they always felt that certain information was being withheld. The hospital was evasive in certain areas. However their link worker was honest and extremely helpful. At first they were told that the heart had not been taken. They asked for a copy of the post mortem report. As an afterthought they asked what tissue samples had been taken and to their surprise were told brain, stomach, one kidney and one lung.

They then contacted the treating clinician who told them that the heart had been taken as well. They received a letter stating that the heart and other organs had been taken but they have not received a list in confirmation. They question the cause of death being heart failure. They feel that there were other potential causes of death including surgical damage to the liver. Anthony's medical records were drip fed to them. They received new information each time they received a section of the records. They were told that the heart had been retained at the request of the cardiac surgeon who attended the post mortem examination. They were told that other organs had been sampled. These organs were returned.

His parents feel that there should have been a Coroner's post mortem because the death was within 24 hours of surgery. They feel that they should have been told what was involved in a post mortem examination. They would never have consented to the retention of organs. They wanted the body to be buried intact but would have delayed the funeral to allow examination of organs which needed to be fixed (see Chapter 5, paragraph 4.8). They feel that a bereavement adviser should have been present to help them with the issues of consent and the consequences of death.

They were shocked to find out that the cardiac surgeon who was responsible for taking care of Anthony in life and during surgery was also the person who requested removal of the heart without telling them that this would happen. He must have known that it would be retained.

They want the law to be changed to render it illegal to retain organs without proper parental consent. Medical research must not be carried out at the expense of innocent children. It is their view that there should be a criminal penalty for unauthorised organ retention.

They had an interview with the paediatric pathologist Dr George Kokai and found him to be honest but another member of Alder Hey was present and prevented him from answering certain questions put to him by the parents which he was willing to answer. Alder Hey did everything possible to stop Anthony's father opening the casket containing the retained organs to find out what precisely was there.

His father feels that Anthony was the bravest person he had ever met. He had immense inner strength to tolerate his condition and surgery. He is proud to have been his father.

His parents now know that his heart went to the heart collection at the Institute of Child Health. They also know that his other organs were transferred out of the hospital to the University but would like to know where they went, for what purpose and whether they were ever used for research. They have not had any answers to these questions.

Claire – 14 Years 11 Months

Claire died in 1988. She died from a paracetamol overdose. There was a Coroner's post mortem and an inquest. Her parents thought they had buried their daughter's remains intact. They were not told what was involved in a post mortem examination. Neither were they told the difference between a Coroner's and a hospital post mortem examination. They were not told that organs would be retained. However, they say their treatment at Alder Hey at the time of loss was extremely sensitive and sympathetic.

In October 1999 they responded to a letter from Alder Hey suggesting they call the help line. They are angry at the deceit, grotesqueness and obscenity of removing without their knowledge or consent their daughter's brain, heart and lungs. The cause of death was a formality. Although the person dealing with them from Alder Hey was very pleasant and helpful nevertheless the whole attitude was defensive and unco-operative. It appeared to be a damage limitation exercise. They requested the return of the organs which were subsequently cremated.

This is an unusual case. The usual attempt at justification for organ retention is not applicable. It cannot have been to assist research into infant mortality because Claire was almost 15 years of age when she died. It cannot have been to assist research into congenital heart disease because her heart was strong and healthy. There cannot be any justification for stockpiling organs awaiting final post mortem reports. Her parents have not been given any explanation as to why Claire's organs were retained. They were not given the reason for post mortem examination being carried out.

Her father says that he thinks everybody has a right to lay the dead to rest. It is a critical right because it is part of the grieving and healing process. It is doubly important with the loss of a child because that in itself is an obscenity of nature. Nobody expects to survive their own children. It is a long and very painful grieving and healing process. It cost him his marriage, his career prospects and a heart attack. To be pushed back into the situation 12 years on is unforgivable.

The treating clinician said that whether you tell somebody that the brain has been retained depends on whether, in the clinician's view, telling them would cause unnecessary trauma. He admitted he knew that hearts were systematically retained but was not aware of retention of other organs.

Claire's father says there is a whole moral issue around the basic right of somebody being able to bury their dead in a dignified and complete way. This right must be defended and protected. He thinks the common perception of the word 'organ' involves the entire organ, and tissue by definition means part of that organ and probably a fairly small part of that organ. This definition should be incorporated in the Human Tissue Act 1961.

Sam – 18 Months

Sam was born with congenital heart disease. He died in surgery in 1990 at Alder Hey. A Coroner's post mortem examination was carried out. The post mortem examination procedure was not explained to his parents. The distinction between a Coroner's and a hospital post mortem was not explained. They feel that they should have been allowed more time to come to terms with their grief before post mortem examination was discussed. They also feel that their objections to post mortem examination should have been considered even though it was a Coroner's post mortem.

The surgery had been delayed for almost 12 months because of unavailability of intensive care beds. There were several last minute cancellations. They are left wondering whether this delay contributed to Sam's death. They had been allowed to hold Sam in their arms after he died for two hours. They then wanted to hold him again after the post mortem examination. When they went to see him in the Chapel of Rest at Alder Hey mortuary his hair was pink and standing up and blood was oozing from his scalp and nose. They were so distressed that they ran out of the mortuary.

They reported the situation to Alder Hey who denied it. The matter was subsequently verified by the social worker who had been with them and subsequently Alder Hey apologised. They wrote letters about the delay in surgery to the Department of Health and Social Services, to their MP and anyone else who would listen. They complain that when the post mortem issue was raised with them no mention of organ retention was made.

They received news of organ retention in January 2000. Eventually they were told that there had been a full retention. They demanded immediate return and a second funeral was held in April 2000.

They feel let down and deliberately misled. They were not told the facts and procedures they were entitled to know. The impression given by Alder Hey was that an individual's identity ends at post mortem examination if not death. They describe Alder Hey's handling of the issue as appalling with denial of knowledge. They tried to fix blame solely upon one person, Professor van Velzen. However, the immediate representative of Alder Hey who dealt with them was very helpful and available, open and honest but only so far as permitted by management at Alder Hey.

They say it would have been nice to have been asked about donating organs and leaving the heart for the heart collection. They would have considered the matter seriously had they been approached properly. Everyone should be told what is involved in a post mortem examination. They feel that they protected their child in life but in death when he needed their protection more than ever, they feel guilty that they let him down in allowing or permitting organ retention.

They feel that the meaning of tissue and organ is very clear. It is their view that an organ is the whole organ and tissue is a thin slice of organ usually for examination. They were told precisely what was involved in the major cardiac surgery their son underwent. They should have had similar full information about post mortem examination, organ retention and the results of post mortem examination. Alder Hey should have divulged the news about organ retention and been totally transparent and honest from the outset.

Philip – 5 Years 3 Months

Philip was born with a congenital heart defect known as Noonan's Syndrome. He died in 1989. He never regained consciousness from an operation to correct the heart defect. He had very bravely undergone a lot of treatment in his short life. His parents know that the clinical teams did all they could to save their son's life and are grateful.

A Coroner's post mortem was carried out two days after his death. Nobody told them that a post mortem examination was to be carried out. They should have been told what, if any, organs would be retained. They should have been informed of the result of the post mortem examination. They were fully informed of the details of all the operations their son had to go through. They consented to these operations. They should have had extended to them the same fullness of information at death as in life.

If everything had been explained to them they would have agreed to organ donation. As nothing was explained the hospital denied themselves the opportunity of organ donation to save the life of another child. The parents have no objection to research. They understand why there was interest in their son's heart and lungs. They do not understand why his other organs were removed and retained.

His parents first heard of the organ retention on the radio on 21 September 1999. His mother rang the hospital the following day. Two days later she was told that they had his heart. On Saturday 9 October 1999 they received a letter from the hospital informing them that they also had his chest organs, abdomen, brain, lungs and 'other organs'. There was no-one at the hospital to help them until the following Monday. They still do not know what 'other organs' means. They are still waiting for written confirmation of the organs that were returned to them.

The first funeral was a Catholic burial. The Church was packed with friends, family and work colleagues. Their son should have been buried intact. His body was desecrated.

The second funeral was very low key. Seven people attended. Their eldest son could not face a second funeral. They feel cheated that the first funeral was indecent. They were not sure what they were burying at the second funeral.

They are suffering from social exclusion as friends and family do not know how to handle seeing them. They want someone to be held responsible for what has happened. They want a change in the law. Parents must be fully informed about what is to happen to their children immediately upon death.

Nicola – 13 Years 5 Months

Nicola suffered from epilepsy. She died in 1989 of septicaemia at Alder Hey. Nicola had been in hospital many times and her parents held the hospital and its staff in the highest regard. Their daughter had always had wonderful treatment.

Nicola's clinician told her parents that as she had died suddenly a post mortem examination would have to be carried out. Her parents were very distraught. They could not bear the thought of their daughter being disfigured or cut in any way. They understood why a post mortem examination had to be carried out although they did not fully understand what it involved. They should have been told at the time.

They said that under no circumstances were any organs to be taken. They were given a personal assurance by the clinician that nothing like that would happen. They were assured that any procedures would be unnoticeable and the brain would be examined and replaced. They were misled about the extent of the post mortem examination. They would not have agreed to organ donation. It was very important to them that their daughter be buried intact.

When the news first broke in September 1999 they did not think it involved them. They had been given assurances by their daughter's doctor that no organs would be removed or retained. They received a letter from Alder Hey inviting them to contact the hospital if they wanted to check if they were involved. They were then told on the telephone that 'basically they had taken everything'.

At the second funeral they did not realise how big the casket would be. The second burial brought back all their pain and suffering. They are uncertain if they will ever know if things have been put right.

They think they should have been seen personally by Alder Hey not contacted by letter or telephone. They have a right to know everything relating to their daughter's death. They have a right to control what happens to their daughter's organs after her death. She was their daughter. Sending a letter to tell them the distressing news is too impersonal. Anyone can send a letter. It is not the same as seeing someone face to face. They used to think Alder Hey was absolutely wonderful and feel that there has been a breach of trust. They feel let down by all involved and always will.

Nicola's parents want to know why it was done. It appears someone was a collector. Parents must be given the fullest of information about what is going on with their children. They feel really badly let down. Their daughter was abused and treated like a piece of meat. They feel guilty that their daughter's organs were removed without their knowledge.

Robert – 21 Months

Robert was born with a congenital heart defect. He underwent a high-risk operation and died three weeks later in 1989. He was in his mother's arms when he died.

Nothing was said to the parents about post mortem examination. The cause of death was renal failure due to septicaemia. The Coroner did not accept this cause of death and ordered a post mortem examination. The Coroner informed Robert's mother that he had ordered a post mortem examination and explained why it was necessary. The cause of death on the death certificate was changed to cardiac failure. Robert was then placed in the Chapel of Rest where his mother noticed that he looked very odd.

Nobody asked her if organs could be retained. She might have allowed them to take the heart but only if it would have been used to help other children.

His mother learnt of organ retention from the newspaper and on television in the Autumn of 1999. She knew her son had had his post mortem examination at Alder Hey but did not contact the hospital. She would rather not have gone over the threshold and made enquiries. She then received a letter from Alder Hey in October 1999. They informed her that she might be involved in the matter. She then felt that she had to telephone Alder Hey to find out. After a few days she was told that they did have her son's chest, abdominal organs and heart. She was absolutely devastated. She had not wanted to know. She would have rather made the decision herself to know or not to know.

She feels that it is her fault that she buried her son without his organs. She understood that the organs would be put back when the post mortem was completed. She would have allowed them to keep his heart to try to save future lives. She would not have agreed to organ donation. She understood that all her son's organs were damaged. She thought she had done all she could to protect him in life and in death. She now feels guilty, angry and inadequate as a mother. She could not bring herself to attend the second funeral. Her son's organs were laid with his ashes in his grave.

She wants there to be clear guidelines for the pathologists, to include what they can and cannot do. Parents should be told everything that is going on.

William – Stillborn

William was stillborn in 1989. His mother was told that there would need to be a post mortem examination. Prior to birth she was told her baby had spina bifida. She wanted a post mortem examination to confirm that he would have been born with spina bifida. It was the reason why she had her pregnancy terminated. She needed to know whether she was right to have consented to the termination. She has had a terrible feeling of guilt throughout. She has never been offered counselling to help her cope with her loss.

The hospital told her that they would arrange the burial. They told her he would be buried in the hospital grounds. Mother believed the hospital would bury him respectfully. She thought that they would tell her where her baby was buried so she could visit him. After the midwife's visits to mother she asked to see her baby as he had not yet been buried. She spoke with Professor van Velzen. She was told it would be too distressing for her to see her child. He told her that he had been put in solution and he would not look the same. She understood that she did not have any rights in the matter.

William's mother asked the hospital for two years for the results of post mortem examination without success. She heard of organ retention in September 1999. She thought it did not apply to her as her baby was not born at Alder Hey. She called the hospital to find out the results of her baby's post mortem examination. In November 1999 she went to see her gynaecologist to be told what she thought would be the results of the post mortem examination.

Instead she was told that her baby was still in solution in a jar. She was then informed that post mortem examination had only been carried out that same week. It was confirmed that the baby had spina bifida. The doctor read the post mortem report to her. She was distressed to learn that the first post mortem report was 11½ years after William's stillbirth.

She would never have agreed to organ donation for research. He was such a small baby. She just wanted to lay him to rest. Mother finally buried William in March 2000. She wants to know why this happened to her baby. Steps must be taken to make sure that it never happens again.

Brother and Sister: Paul – 8 Months
Gemma – 6 Days

Paul was born with a hole in his heart. Following cardiac surgery he died in 1984. Nobody mentioned to his parents the need for a post mortem examination. They received details of the post mortem report from their general practitioner two months later.

Gemma died in 1986. She was found to have a heart murmur. Her mother thinks that if the hospital had acted more quickly her daughter's life would have been saved. Again nobody mentioned that a post mortem examination would be carried out.

She learnt of the organ retention scandal from her sister who had contacted Alder Hey. She was informed the next day that Gemma's heart had been retained. The following day, she was also told that Paul's heart had been retained.

Her wishes and feelings were totally disregarded and her opinions ignored. She should have been informed step by step of the proceedings following each bereavement.

Organ retention is something which requires parental consent. It should not be a 'free for all pick and mix'. If she had been asked if they could keep the hearts to save the lives of other children she would have given them with her blessing. She would also have agreed to organ donation. It is hard to be told your child has died. You are devastated. If some good can come out of it and help other families then she supports that, if it is done properly with full parental consent.

She does not understand how an infant's body can be returned to the parents and for them not be told that organs have been retained. She regards the retention of her children's organs as theft. Gross incompetence has been demonstrated and the situation has been spiralling out of control. She has no confidence that the post mortem examinations carried out on Paul and Gemma are complete. She wants those responsible for doing this to her children barred from practising medicine again. It should not stop at the pathologists themselves. It includes anybody who has had anything to do with denying her rights and more particularly the rights of her dead children.

Christopher – Stillborn

Christopher was born prematurely stillborn in 1987. His mother never saw her baby. He was taken away from her at birth. His parents do not know why their baby died. At the time they were told that the hospital would bury the baby. The hospital insisted that the baby be buried in hospital grounds. They were told that it would be a dignified ceremony. They asked if they could see their son buried. They were told it would not be possible and that seeing the burial grounds would only further upset them.

They were told to have another child. The parents had no control over what was to happen to Christopher. They wanted to bury him themselves. They are a Catholic family and burial is important to them. To bury their child intact is part of their religious belief. They wanted to name their child and did not get the chance.

They were told that their baby would be sent for post mortem examination to Alder Hey to find out why he had died. They agreed to slivers of organ being taken to find out why Christopher had died. They were told that examination of the slivers did not reveal an obvious cause of death.

His mother heard of the organ retention scandal in the autumn of 1999. She did not associate it with her baby. She realised later that she might be involved. After numerous attempts to contact Alder Hey she went to see a solicitor for help. She then found that her baby had been sent to the University from Alder Hey without her knowledge or consent. Christopher had never been buried. His parents never gave authority for anyone to keep their child neither did they authorise anyone to retain his organs. They wanted to find out why their son had died. They would have agreed to organ donation to save the life of another child.

They eventually buried their baby in March 2000 almost 13 years after his death. They were then told that their son's pancreas had been retained together with a small piece of duodenum and gastrointestinal tissue. They do not know why or where their child has been stored for 13 years. They believe every parent has the right to their own child. Whether they want to give the organs to help another child, whether they want to give the organs for research or whether they just want to take the baby and bury it themselves is a matter for them.

They want to know why this happened. They want to know what was gained from the organs being taken and stored.

Ryan – 19 Days

Ryan was born with congenital heart disease. He died following open-heart surgery in 1995 at Alder Hey. Immediately after surgery the cardiac surgeon said that the procedure had seemed to be a success but nevertheless Ryan died shortly afterwards.

Some hours later the cardiac surgeon asked Ryan's parents to consent to a hospital post mortem examination. Mother replied that her son had been cut up and mauled enough. She was told that there would be no more cuts because his chest was already open following surgery. For one hour the cardiac surgeon tried to persuade them by playing on their heartstrings despite their continuing refusal of consent.

They did not understand the consent form. They thought they were being asked for microscopic samples from the heart and lungs only. They were told that the heart and lungs would be put back into the body following examination. They were further told it would be as though he had never been touched. They could not understand this because they had already been given the death certificate two hours before being asked for their consent and found it very confusing.

They received news of the organ retention issue in mid-September 1999. They feel that the way they were treated was a fiasco. They felt that there was an attitude of non-co-operation with parents. They asked for information. They were told that someone would ring back. No one did. Mother told Alder Hey that she alone should be contacted about what organs had been retained because her husband was too distressed. She gave them her home and work numbers. She and her husband work at the same establishment. After seven days Alder Hey rang work specifically asking for the husband. Fortunately mother was able to intercept the call and could not believe that Alder Hey had made such a mistake.

Eventually after being told that the heart, lungs and abdominal organs had been retained, Alder Hey rang them every other day pressing for a decision as to whether or not they wanted the organs to be returned, donated for medical research or sympathetically disposed of. The parents were having difficulty making their mind up and felt unnecessarily pressured just as they had been on the issue of consent to a post mortem examination by the cardiac surgeon.

They were never offered counselling. They were informed that counselling was available for siblings only. They are devastated by what has happened. Husband blames mother for having signed the consent to surgery. Mother blames husband for signing the consent for post mortem examination. Husband is in denial and mother is depressed. Their marriage is threatened. They feel that Alder Hey should have come out to them rather than dealing with matters over the telephone. They remain concerned as to the accuracy of details relating to retention of organs and will never trust Alder Hey again.

They thought they had buried their son whole. They would have donated his organs to save the life of another child. They would not have consented to donation of the heart to the heart collection. Mother has not been able to return to the same church where her son was buried because she is too upset. His parents would have been greatly assisted by counsellors coming to the home because they need counselling and they did not know how to explain to their 10-year-old son what happened in order that he might understand thoroughly.

They feel that Alder Hey used the word 'tissue' when it suited them, and if they were looking to have an organ from a child and put it into another child that would be organ donation but because the organs have been retained for medical research purposes they are then classed as tissue samples. Mother is unhappy at this false distinction. Tissue should be regarded as small pieces of an organ and the meaning of organ is obvious.

Nicholas – 11 Months

Nicholas was born with congenital heart disease. After several major cardiac procedures he died at Alder Hey in 1990. The doctor asked his parents what they felt about a post mortem examination. They said 'no way, leave him alone, he has been through enough. He is like a road map already'. They refused a request for a hospital post mortem. Shortly afterwards the doctor returned and said it was out of his hands as the Coroner had ordered a Coroner's post mortem examination. They were left in the room. No-one else came to see them and they left when they wanted to.

The post mortem procedure had not been explained to them. There had been no suggestion of organ retention. They had no bereavement advice. They were left to their own devices. They are extremely concerned that the hospital ignored their wishes without explanation as to why a Coroner's post mortem was necessary.

In mid-September 1999 they telephoned Alder Hey to enquire whether they were involved in the organ retention issue. The next day they were told that Nicholas' heart had been retained. They asked if any other organs had been retained. They were told that a check would be made. Two days later they were told that there were no other organs retained. Two weeks later they received a letter from a clinician at Alder Hey. He reeled off that the heart, lungs, liver, kidneys, spleen, pancreas and brain had been retained as though it was a shopping list. The parents were devastated.

Following the death of Nicholas they went back to the hospital and saw the treating consultant. After discussion the consultant said he would have another look at the heart. The parents said 'are you saying that we have buried him without his heart?' 'No' replied the doctor 'I can assure you everything after a post mortem goes back.' The consultant explained that he really wanted to look again at his reports. The parents, even now, remain concerned over the treatment they received from the cardiac surgeon. This is being investigated elsewhere.

In May 2000 they received an even fuller list of the retained organs which referred to heart, spleen, kidney, adrenals, bladder, reproductive organs, diaphragm, trachea, larynx, oesophagus, stomach, intestines, lymph nodes, thyroid, pancreas, part of the brain, part of the liver and fragments of tongue, bone and muscle.

On 16 June they received further information to the effect that a rib had been retained and a clavicle in two parts. Their distress has increased with each piece of news relating to further details of what organs were retained. Their sleep is disturbed and their relationship is threatened. They are receiving treatment for depression. Their children are having bereavement counselling at school. They feel that in their case there should be an inquest.

Mother says that each time she has asked why organs have been retained she has asked about research and has been told that no research has been carried out. She needs to know why the organs were retained.

They were offended when they were told that Alder Hey did not need to tell them about organ retention. They were told that the organs could quite easily have been disposed of in the middle of the night. Several parents were told of this possibility which they found unimpressive. They remain appalled at the way Alder Hey has taken so long to tell them the full nature and extent of the organ retention, in all a period of nine months.

Katy – 5 Months

Katy was an identical twin who died in 1990 from what was eventually diagnosed as bronchospastic syndrome. Her parents know that the clinical teams tried everything they could to save their daughter.

She was transferred to Alder Hey for a Coroner's post mortem examination. Nobody told them that their daughter had been taken to Alder Hey and they were not told that a post mortem examination would be carried out. They were not asked whether they wished to donate organs. They would not have agreed.

They wanted to bury their daughter whole in accordance with their religious beliefs. They discovered that a post mortem examination had been carried out when they were told that they could collect the death certificate. They feel betrayed because they were never consulted.

Katy's brain, heart, lungs, liver and intestine were retained. They were told over three stages that organs had been retained. They still do not know if all their daughter's organs have been returned. The first funeral was a full Catholic Mass. They thought they had buried their daughter whole. They thought they had put their daughter to rest. They did not know they had buried only the shell of their daughter. They have had to inform their four children of the death of their sister. The second funeral was more horrific than the first. The parents had to try to console their distraught children. The children are finding it very hard to understand what has happened and why. They hope they have now buried their daughter so she can finally rest in peace.

They want to know why this was allowed to happen. Why did the medical profession support it? How many years has this gone on for and how many people are involved? They now know they have only a preliminary post mortem. They know that samples were taken and have not been reported upon. They have still not received a complete post mortem report. They have been left in a great state of uncertainty against a background of mistrust.

Written Evidence

Karl – 11 Days

Karl was born with congenital heart disease. He died in 1972 at Myrtle Street Hospital. Two weeks later his parents were informed by letter that a post mortem examination had been carried out and were given the results. When Karl died his mother was insistent that there should be no post mortem examination. He had suffered enough and was entitled to rest in peace. His father had to explain to Karl's mother that he had tried hard but unsuccessfully to resist the clinicians relentless pressure on him to sign the consent to a post mortem examination. He described it as emotional blackmail. He signed on condition that his wife never found out. When she did there was great distress and the marriage was imperilled. Karl's mother believes that this has been the cause of her grieving today. Her feelings and opinions as a mother should have been respected. Karl's father believes even today that she has not fully forgiven him. Both parents thought that they had buried Karl whole.

In September 1999 a link worker at Alder Hey rang Karl's parents informing them that his heart had been retained. Three weeks later they had a letter stating that his lungs had also been retained. For 27 years his heart and lungs had been stored in a jar of formalin on a shelf. In their nightmares his parents could not imagine this happening.

Some time before 5 November 1999, when Karl's organs were buried, the organs were cut and examined microscopically. Tissue samples were taken although the original excuse given for retention was that the organs were to be used for teaching purposes only. Karl's parents believe it was ethically and legally wrong to take samples in 1999 without consent. They are not against medical research. Their faith in the medical profession has plummeted. Parents must be made fully aware of the consequences of consenting to a post mortem.

Andrew – 11 Months

Andrew died at Alder Hey in 1980. He had been transferred from another hospital with breathing problems. His mother was told by telephone that he had died from Sudden Infant Death Syndrome and that a post mortem examination would be necessary to confirm the diagnosis. She begged them not to cut her baby up but was told she had no choice. She asked if everything would be put back in its right place and was told 'yes'. She was not in a fit state to question anyone. Someone rang Andrew's mother at home to give her the post mortem results but she was in hospital suffering from shock. His grandmother took the message. His mother does not know why the post mortem was done. She says no one knows how parents feel. She felt lost and alone when Andrew died. His heart was kept on a shelf for 19 years. When she visited his grave she never thought she would be burying the rest of him 19 years later.

On 4 October 1999 an Alder Hey link worker rang Andrew's mother and told her that his heart had been retained. She felt like a zombie. The grief was the worst she had felt since Andrew died. The only communication with Alder Hey has been when she telephoned them. They never give a straight answer to questions. They never return her calls.

Mrs Karen England, Acting Director of Operations at Alder Hey, sat with Andrew's mother at the hospital and told her how upset she (Karen England) was at what had happened. Andrew's mother did not believe her. His mother found everyone she spoke to untruthful, uncaring and frightened because the issue of organ retention was now public. The only thing Alder Hey appeared concerned about was for Andrew's mother to hurry with the funeral arrangements. Later she was told that his kidneys, adrenal glands and thymus were also retained. His mother was not told about this until after she had buried his heart so they still remain at Alder Hey along with 36 other 'samples'.

For 19 years Andrew's mother believed that the cause of death was Sudden Infant Death Syndrome. She has now discovered that he had two heart attacks on the day he died. She was never told this. She has no trust in anyone. Alder Hey took it all. This must never happen to anyone again.

Christopher – 5½ Years

Christopher was born with congenital heart disease and died in 1988 while undergoing surgery. His parents were told that a post mortem examination would have to be done as Christopher had died on the operating table. They begged that he was not cut any more. They wanted to take him home and bury him. The clinician and ward sister promised that everything taken from Christopher would be returned to his body. He would be treated with the utmost respect.

His parents had no idea that his organs would be removed and retained. They understand why a post mortem was necessary but not why his brain was removed. His parents feel extremely let down by the clinician for not being honest with them.

His parents contacted Alder Hey in September 1999. They were told about Christopher's organs in stages and feel that this was not the correct way to do it. The first phone call told them that his heart and brain had been retained. Later they were told that his lungs had also been kept. The hospital link worker did his best in the circumstances.

Under no circumstances would Christopher's parents then or now have given permission to retain any part of their much loved son. They feel totally betrayed by the clinician. The post mortem report states that his spleen, kidneys, pancreas, liver, heart, lungs and brain were removed and weighed. It is hard to believe that the hospital retained only the brain, heart and lungs and put the other organs back into his body.

After Christopher's death and during the post mortem process his parents were assured he would be cared for. Christopher was as precious in death as he was in life. His parents can never forgive or erase the memory of what happened to him following his death.

Stephen – Stillborn

Stephen was stillborn in 1990. No one spoke to his mother about a post mortem examination. She does not remember giving consent. When she had her post-natal check the locum consultant obstetrician informed her that a post mortem had taken place. Stephen had died from a form of cot death in the womb.

Stephen's parents wanted to know the cause of his death. If they had been told that tiny samples of tissue were needed for research they would have given permission. They would not have agreed to the retention of whole organs. To take all Stephen's organs from his body and store them for almost ten years without establishing the definitive cause of death is unacceptable. His parents buried him ten years ago as a shell. It is like grave-robbing before being put in the grave. His body has been mutilated.

In mid-October 1999 Stephen's mother telephoned Alder Hey. A couple of days later someone from Alder Hey rang to say that his heart and other organs had been retained. Later Stephen's parents went to see a consultant from the maternity hospital to ask exactly what organs had been kept. The consultant said 'You really do not want to know!' On numerous occasions his parents have asked for a detailed list of organs retained. All they have been told is heart, brain, chest and abdominal organs. What does 'chest and abdominal organs' consist of? No-one will tell them exactly.

Alder Hey's handling of the situation has been atrocious. Nobody knows what anyone else is doing. Stephen's parents feel totally let down.

Charlie – 13 Years

Charlie died at Alder Hey in 1990, having been in hospital for many weeks. During this time his mother lived and slept at the hospital. When he died she agreed to a post mortem examination. His mother believed that this would make sense of his suffering and would assist research in finding an effective treatment or cure. A nurse told her that tissue samples would be taken, all the organs replaced and incisions hidden. Charlie would look normal. No-one was with his mother when she signed the consent form 30 minutes after his death.

Three months later one of Charlie's clinicians rang his mother to confirm the cause of his death. Six years after this his mother contacted another of Charlie's clinicians to ask for the post mortem results. He did not send her a copy of the report, saying that it was detailed and technical, but he did outline the major findings. These were characteristic of that particular disease. He did not refer to any microscopic examination or to the retention of any organs.

Charlie's mother is bitter and angry. Her trust was abused and she is having to relive her grief. She has nightmares and terrible memories of Charlie's last hours. If told the truth about the post mortem process she could have made an informed choice and not been shocked and horrified ten years later.

In October 1999 Alder Hey wrote to Charlie's mother saying that his organs might have been retained. Two weeks later she had a telephone call from Alder Hey to say that Charlie's heart, respiratory organs, abdomen and brain had been kept. She had buried an empty body. His mother was told that a dead body belongs to no-one, but it was her responsibility to dispose of the parts. A letter was to be sent outlining her options. Despite numerous telephone calls no letter was received.

In February 2000 Alder Hey wrote asking for consent to samples being taken before the organs were released. It appears that no research was done following the initial retention. Charlie's mother felt betrayed. She was horrified and refused this new request. Alder Hey would not abuse her son's remains again. When Charlie died his mother was relieved that his suffering was over. The disclosure of organ retention has opened wounds she thought long healed. She has feelings of loss, guilt and anger. Charlie was abused by an arrogant system that failed to protect the interests of those it is meant to serve.

Scott – 9 Months

Scott was born with congenital heart problems and died at Alder Hey in 1990 following surgery. His clinician told his parents that a post mortem examination would be performed as standard procedure. It was to make sure that no hospital procedure had gone wrong. The post mortem was carried out a day later than expected. Scott's parents were told to walk round Liverpool and come back later for the death certificate. His mother was distressed as she was then five months pregnant. She never thought that organs could ever be removed and retained without consent from the next of kin. Scott's parents assumed that his body would be returned to them complete.

In 1999 a social worker from Alder Hey telephoned Scott's mother at home. She was in the middle of a christening party for her younger daughter. His mother describes the way Alder Hey handled matters as like going back to Hell again. His brain, heart, lungs, liver, kidneys, bowel and lower stomach have been retained. She doubts they will all be returned.

A further concern is the parents' question about whether Scott's heart was sent to another hospital for research and if so, was it returned. So far their enquiries have not produced a conclusive answer.

Jason – 14 Days

Jason was born with congenital heart disease and died at Alder Hey following surgery in 1994.

Immediately after his death his parents were advised that a post mortem examination would determine the exact cause of his death and might help future children. It was not compulsory but would help the hospital modify future surgical procedures. His skull would be opened, but he would look no different except for stitches at the back of his head. Samples of tissue would be taken. His father agreed provided nothing major would be retained, by which he meant organs. He was categorically reassured about this.

Several weeks later his parents saw the surgeon and were told that Jason had died from heart failure resulting from a blood infection. They were advised not to read the post mortem report as it was technical and might be distressing. The surgeon did not tell them that organs had been removed and retained. Jason's father believes that they were deliberately misinformed about the post mortem. A cynical, exploitative exercise was carried out in order to obtain their consent by the back door. The intention was to stockpile organs without parents' knowledge. Jason's organs have still not been used for research. His father is disgusted.

In November 1999 his parents received a letter from Alder Hey saying that his organs might have been retained. In December this was confirmed. His parents describe the way in which Alder Hey has handled the situation since the news first broke as damage limitation and crocodile tears. They have now seen his medical records which contain much more information about his death than they were told by the surgeon. His parents were just palmed off.

Katy – 12 Days

Katy was born with serious heart problems. She died at Alder Hey following cardiac surgery in 1995.

The surgeon told Katy's parents that a post mortem examination would have to be performed. He said that the Coroner would prefer a full post mortem, but in the circumstances would accept a partial post mortem involving the heart and lungs only. Only minimal disturbance would be caused to her body. Her parents did not want her body disfigured any more and agreed to a partial post mortem. They now feel let down because the surgeon did not explain what was going to happen. Three months after Katy's death her parents were told that she died of a heart defect.

On 5 October 1999 her parents received an unsigned letter from Alder Hey saying the hospital had 'carefully examined all our records' but it could not give them any definite information about Katy's organs. Two weeks later they were told that her heart and lungs had been retained. Her parents were told they would be sent forms requesting information necessary for the internal inquiry. The results of the inquiry would be sent to them before publication. The forms were never sent. Her parents were not contacted during the inquiry nor were they sent a copy of the inquiry report.

Her parents now fear that much malpractice will be brushed under the carpet and those responsible never held to account.

Philip – 7 Months

Philip was born with congenital heart disease and died in 1996 at Alder Hey. The clinician told his parents that a post mortem examination was necessary as he had died shortly after surgery. His parents were told they could have an independent or hospital post mortem done. They were happy with Philip's care and so chose a hospital post mortem. They thought they had put all of Philip's body to rest.

His parents rang Alder Hey when the news broke of organ retention. First Philip's clinician rang back and then a link worker to confirm that his organs had been retained. His parents cannot understand why the clinician took the trouble to give them detailed explanations of his care and treatment while he was alive, but when he died told them so little. His parents would have willingly donated his organs or agreed to his heart being kept for education and research. All Alder Hey had to do was ask. Instead his parents are disgusted. They feel robbed and cheated.

Oral/Written Evidence Relating to the Cerebellum Collection

Craig – 3 Years 5 Months

Craig was born with congenital heart disease. In 1995 he collapsed at nursery school. He was taken to the Royal Liverpool University Hospital where he was pronounced dead. His parents were told that a post mortem examination would be necessary. The post mortem procedure was not explained. His parents were informed by a telephone call from the Coroner's office that he had died of myocardial ischaemia.

They were not told that this was a preliminary finding only as the organs had not yet been examined microscopically. Because Craig had previously had a heart 'switch' operation his parents thought only his heart and lungs would be examined. They assumed that the death certificate would state the actual cause of death not an educated guess. His mother feels deceived and cheated. His body was stolen and abused.

In January 2000 his parents were contacted by Alder Hey, firstly to say that Craig's organs were not at the hospital, and secondly that there had been a mistake and his brain, liver, heart, lungs and kidneys had been retained. His parents found this quite sickening. Later the help line link worker rang to ask if they would consent to samples being taken. Then they were told that samples had probably been taken at the post mortem examination in 1995.

Eventually Alder Hey sent Craig's organs to the undertaker. They were not in a casket but 'an awful white box', roughly put together, painted and in a shoddy state. The box showed no respect for either Craig or his parents. The undertaker gave Craig's parents a proper casket free of charge. The Alder Hey box was fitted into this. Craig's father complained to Alder Hey and was referred to Mrs Karen England, Acting Director of Operations, who was neither apologetic nor concerned. Her whole attitude was one of complete indifference.

Craig's parents are still very angry.

In August 2000 an Alder Hey link worker telephoned Craig's mother with the news that his cerebellum had also been retained. She advised Craig's mother to sit down as the news was distressing but did not ask if she was alone. A third funeral was mentioned but Craig's mother put the telephone down. In a further telephone call she was asked about her plans for a funeral and whether she had spoken to her solicitor. She was invited to meet with the Serious Incident Project Board (SIPB) Director, Mrs Kate Jackson, but still had not had a letter confirming retention nearly a month after the first telephone call.

Essentially the parents are burying Craig in little bits and pieces. Alder Hey do not understand the anguish caused to siblings. His twin brother is still too young to understand fully. Grief is a very difficult emotion for them to live with as adults let alone for a child. His parents are now living with this new grief. Craig was a beautiful little boy who was violated and abused and deserves justice.

Jessica – 2 Months

Jessica was born with congenital heart disease. She died in August 1991. A Coroner's post mortem examination was carried out. Her parents originally contacted Alder Hey in December 1999 about organ retention. Three days later they were told by telephone that Jessica's chest organs, abdominal, partial heart and brain had been retained. They were shocked and distressed. They asked for a full list of organs and were told it was very upsetting and did they really want it. They were then told that the heart, brain, lungs, liver, spleen, kidney, intestines, reproductive organs and pancreas had been retained. A second funeral took place in February 2000. Thereafter they thought they would only have to wait for the report from this Inquiry.

In August 2000 they were advised by a co-ordinator of PITY II to telephone Alder Hey to check whether Jessica was involved in the cerebellum collection. On 16 August 2000 they were told by Alder Hey on the telephone that Jessica's cerebellum had in fact been retained. They were immediately asked whether they had any plans for a third funeral. They asked for time to consider. They also asked if there were any wax blocks or slides in relation to Jessica. They were told that Alder Hey could categorically state that there were no more retained organs, bone or tissue. They were told that the cerebellum had been used for a PhD study. They were not told how the cerebellum came to be at Myrtle Street when the post mortem examination had been carried out at Alder Hey.

They describe Alder Hey's handling of the whole issue of organ retention as disgraceful. They are highly critical of the failure to provide correct information in relation to retained organs. They say that their marriage is threatened, as are family relationships.

Kayleigh – 4½ Months

Kayleigh was born with congenital heart disease and died at Alder Hey in December 1990.

On 5 October 1999 Kayleigh's parents received a letter from Alder Hey saying that her organs might have been retained. This was confirmed by telephone at the end of October. Her parents had not known that she had undergone a post mortem examination. They understand why post mortems are done, but they had not given their consent. They do not understand why all her organs were removed. They feel let down. Their daughter was let down and shown no dignity. The attitude of Alder Hey in handling the news of organ retention has been unbelievably uncaring and unsympathetic.

In November 1999 the family grave had to be reopened for Kayleigh's second funeral. The dignity and respect of the first funeral had been undermined. Her mother feels guilty that she was not able to protect her daughter in death as she had done in life. Now the family faces a third funeral.

Kayleigh's mother is a member of the Serious Incident Project Board. She was not invited to a Board meeting on 7 August 2000. No reason was given. However, Kayleigh was involved in the cerebellum collection. Alder Hey telephoned at about 12 noon on 13 August 2000 and spoke to her mother. They did not enquire whether she was alone. Alder Hey stated that they had Kayleigh's brain stem and immediately enquired whether or not her mother wanted to proceed by way of a third funeral. The caller must have heard Kayleigh's mother's children in the background. She said she was far too upset to discuss funerals and that she would ring back later in the week.

Kayleigh's mother drove immediately to Alder Hey to speak to Mrs Kate Jackson, Director of the Special Incident Project Board. Mrs Jackson explained that containers of organs were transferred from Myrtle Street to Alder Hey. One of them belonged to Kayleigh and had been identified by post mortem number. Mrs Jackson said that the cerebellum had been passed by Professor van Velzen to a PhD research student. The thesis was not available. Kayleigh's mother said that she wanted all Kayleigh's blocks and tissue samples returned with the cerebellum. They would have a third funeral and wanted to bury the cerebellum with the wax blocks. Mrs Jackson said that she did not intend to return the wax blocks until at least ten years had expired from death during which time medical records had to be preserved. Alder Hey were awaiting advice from the Secretary of State. This contradicts what has been said to other parents.

The distress caused by the cerebellum collection has to be understood in the context of a meeting Kayleigh's parents had in May 2000 with Ms Therese Harvey, Director of Human Resources at Alder Hey and Dr Ian Peart, Consultant Paediatric Cardiologist, about the extended list of organs. They asked whether any experiments or research had been carried out on Kayleigh while she was alive or dead. Dr Peart stated categorically that no experiments whatsoever had been carried out on Kayleigh. They feel this is directly contradicted by Mrs Jackson's explanation relating to the PhD student.

They are left with the impression that Kayleigh's organs have been scattered round various premises like a jigsaw. They feel that all they appeared to have buried was her eyes, her skin and some bones. They feel worse now than they did about the organ retention issue in 1999. Their home life has been affected and their children have been adversely affected. They have refused to proceed with the third funeral until the wax blocks are supplied to them. The University has refused to meet with Kayleigh's parents until after this Inquiry has reported.

Dean – 2½ Months

Dean died in 1994. His post mortem examination was carried out by Alder Hey. His parents first heard of the organ retention issue on television news. They rang the Alder Hey help line and were told that he was not involved. This was confirmed in a letter from Alder Hey dated 12 October 1999 signed by the Chief Executive at Alder Hey, Ms Hilary Rowland.

However, in August 2000 they re-contacted the help line and were told that Dean was involved in the cerebellum collection and Alder Hey had supplied wrong information in October 1999. They were then told that the original organs retained included half the heart, full brain, liver, spleen, pancreas, tonsils, both lungs, tongue, part bladder, trachea, some glands, bone tissue, skin, testicles, kidney, diaphragm, intestine and sinuses. They were devastated that Dean had been stripped of all internal organs.

He was a suspected cot death. There had been a Coroner's post mortem. He had been taken to Fazakerley Hospital. They were not told that he had been transferred to Alder Hey for post mortem examination until they turned up to view his body. They had specifically told Fazakerley that they did not want any organs to be taken even for the purpose of donation. They were reassured that no organs would be retained and only small samples would be taken from them.

They feel bitter towards Alder Hey not only because of the issue of retention but also the misinformation which they lived with from October 1999 to August 2000. They feel guilty that they did not protect Dean in death. They now want assurances from Alder Hey that all the organs have been returned to them before they carry out a second funeral.

Chapter 15. Epilogue

1.   We set out to discover how so many parents were induced into thinking that they were burying their children intact when in fact the large majority were buried without their vital organs. In our search we discovered the long-standing widespread practice of organ retention without consent. The practice arose from a sense of paternalism on the part of the medical profession which served to conceal retention in the supposed best interest of the parents. Such practice was misconceived and was bound to cause upset and distress when, inevitably, it came to light.

2.   We believe that the Liverpool experience is a considerable exaggeration of the national picture because of the exceptional practice of Professor van Velzen in the wholesale systematic retention of organs between 1988 and 1995. The large store of organs at Myrtle Street remained largely unused for medical education or research purposes throughout this period.

3.   The problem was compounded by the inept handling of the return of organs for burial or cremation by Alder Hey following disclosure of the heart collection at the ICH in September 1999. The result is that some parents are contemplating third or fourth funerals because their child's organs have been returned piecemeal. Whatever system there has been for return, the task has been made even more difficult by late disclosure of various collections of organs by Alder Hey and the University.

4.   A further aggravating feature has been Professor van Velzen's behaviour, including exaggeration, falsification of accounts involving both financial and human resources, fabrication of post mortem reports and a failure to provide the essential service of histology. He did not even fulfil his clinical contract at Alder Hey. He has imperilled future generations by fabricating post mortem reports and not reporting histology, thereby depriving parents of the opportunity of seeking genetic advice when appropriate. His conduct will be reported to the General Medical Council and the Director of Public Prosecutions. He must never practise again.

5.   Managerial inadequacy indulged Professor van Velzen's aberrant behaviour. Alder Hey and the University must now consider whether disciplinary action is appropriate in light of our findings.

6.   We have striven to unravel the history of events in order to provide an answer to the multitude of questions raised by the parents. Some will be answered in full. Some will be answered in part. Many will receive inadequate answers or on occasions no answer at all. The hope is that our trawl through the evidence over many months has provided as much by way of explanation as possible. The reader can draw his or her own conclusion from our close analysis of the evidence.

7.   The parents have been a source of inspiration and focus throughout. They are entitled to consider the facts as we have laid them out. We have told the story exactly as we have found it without interpretative slant, mitigation or modification. We realise that this might be upsetting for many readers but we have faithfully discharged our duty to report on the evidence, of which there is a daunting volume.

8.   Many retained organs have been returned for burial or cremation but many have not been reclaimed. There will always be parents who do not want to know, as well as parents awaiting the outcome of this Report before deciding what to do. The parents have a right to dispose of the organs and tissue respectfully. They also have a right to leave them for research.

9.   Tissue and organs which have been archived are an invaluable asset for medical research. Children who have survived serious illness or disease may well have benefited as a result. Some parents may wish to ensure continuing research as the best resolution hoping that retention of their children's organs will not have been in vain. The simple proposition is that for therapeutic, medical education and research purposes human tissue is an essential requirement. The ultimate control should be a proper system of fully informed consent. The evidence indicates that many parents will readily consent to retention for these purposes, if sensitively approached with openness, honesty and transparency. Whether that would extend to organs being retained in collections is a matter of personal choice but an open and honest approach to the obtaining of consent will have its own reward for the medical profession which must consign paternalism to the annals of history.

10.   We commend this Report to parents as representing our best effort to establish the truth. We encourage reconciliation with Alder Hey which continues to provide a medical service of distinction and renown for sick children. Alder Hey and the University should learn from their many errors and mistakes which we have identified. A full and humble apology from both would be an excellent starting point. A cathedral service or a memorial at Alder Hey or other act of reconciliation might be appropriate.

11.   The abiding message must be that the distress and grief suffered by the parents should be channelled into rebuilding and obtaining strength from the fact that so many people contributed to the Inquiry despite the risk of personal criticism. The whole process has been assisted by the willingness of Alder Hey and the University to disclose documents, even those with obvious damning content. Their co-operation has not come without individual cost.

12.   We are conscious that our Report will bring further pain and distress to parents who must live with the knowledge of what happened to their children after death. They have done everything in their power to ensure that never again will children's organs be retained without fully informed consent. We have made strong recommendations to that effect. Safe in that knowledge, may they direct their feelings towards the everlasting memory of their beloved children in life.

Chronology

1900	Construction of 'Myrtle Street' began.
1902	Construction of 'Myrtle Street' completed.
1946	National Health Service Act 1946.
1948	Heart collection (now stored at ICH) commenced.
1950s	Collection of children's body parts (now stored at ICH) commenced by Dr Ralph Latham, Lecturer in Oral Anatomy.
1951	European Convention on Human Rights ratified by UK Government.
1955	Fetal collection (now stored at ICH) commenced.
1961	Human Tissue Act 1961.
1966	Greenwood Trust Funding allows for employment of Dr Audrey Smith as research technician at ICH.
April 1968	Professor Donald Heath appointed Head of Liverpool University Department of Pathology.
November 1968	Mr Roy Barter appointed HM Coroner for Liverpool.
April 1970	Mr Henry Meade appointed Chief Medical Laboratory Scientific Officer (MLSO) at Alder Hey.
December 1970	Dr Latham leaves Liverpool.
1973/1974	Research on the children's body part collection ceases.
April 1974	Wholesale NHS re-organisation, Liverpool Area Health Authority becomes responsible for Alder Hey.
October 1974	Professor Frank Harris appointed Professor of Child Health and Head of Department.
1975	'Myrtle Street' leased to Liverpool Area Health Authority.
April 1977	Mr Meade promoted to Senior Chief for Pathology at Alder Hey.
1978	'Myrtle Street' leased to Mersey Regional Health Authority.

July 1978	Mrs Karen England appointed MLSO.
October 1979	Dr Smith awarded MPhil.
April 1982	Liverpool District Health Authority assumes responsibility for Alder Hey.
1984	Coroner's Rules 1984.
September 1985	Professor Harris appointed Dean of the Faculty of Medicine at University of Liverpool.
1986	ICH opened at Alder Hey.
January 1986	Ms Gwen Connell appointed research technician at ICH.
April 1986	Professor Graeme Davies appointed University Vice Chancellor.
May 1986	Miss Sheila Malone appointed Alder Hey Unit General Manager.
September 1986	Dr Jean-Marie Bouton retires from Alder Hey as Consultant Pathologist.
November 1986	Dr Salih Ibrahim appointed locum Consultant Pathologist at Alder Hey.
November 1986	Foundation for the Study of Infant Deaths (FSID) request University proposals for converting vacant consultant's post in paediatric pathology at Alder Hey into a 'Chair'.
March 1987	FSID offer University £250,000 over five years to fund supporting staff for the Chair.
July 1987	Mrs England becomes Acting Chief MLSO at Alder Hey.
August 1987	Professor Jonathan Wigglesworth resigns as external assessor to Selection Committee for the Chair having expressed concerns over the provision of the clinical service.
September 1987	Mrs Elizabeth Clapham appointed MLSO.
October 1987	Professor Wigglesworth and Professor Anthony Risdon write to Alder Hey, concerned that a satisfactory histopathology service will not be possible on a part-time basis.
November 1987	Job description for the Chair published.
December 1987	Dr Anthony Barson, prospective applicant for the Chair, expresses major concern at the University's short-term use of charitable monies and failure to consider the long-term development of the clinical service.

1988	Anatomy Regulations 1988.
1988	Coroner's Act 1988.
February 1988	Dr Smith writes to Professor Harris regarding the need to obtain proper consent for research; Dr Ibrahim writes to Mr Barter about the absence of consent for the heart collection.
April 1988	Selection Committee appoints Professor van Velzen Chair of Fetal and Infant Pathology.
June 1988	Mrs England appointed Chief MSLO permanently.
July 1988	Professor Richard Cooke appointed Professor of Neonatal Medicine.
August 1988	Dr Ibrahim leaves Liverpool.
August 1988	Professor Harris retires as Dean, to be replaced by Professor John Beazley.
September 1988	Professor Dick van Velzen takes up post: Mrs Margery Clark is employed as his personal assistant.
November 1988	Dr Peter Simpson appointed Regional Medical Officer for Mersey Regional Health Authority.
1989	Alder Centre established.
1989	Heart collection transferred from Myrtle Street Children's Hospital to ICH.
January 1989	Ms Fiona McGill appointed MLSO.
July 1989	Polkinghorne Report.
Summer 1989	Professor van Velzen's unit moves from Alder Hey to 'Myrtle Street'.
August 1989	Professor van Velzen writes to Dr Simpson identifying the lack of financial provision for the fetal and placental service.
August 1989	Mr Roger Franks appointed Consultant Cardiothoracic Surgeon at Alder Hey.
November 1989	Dr Yuen-Fu Chan appointed Clinical Lecturer in Pathology at the University and Honorary Consultant Paediatric Pathologist at Alder Hey.
November 1989	Mr Pearse Butler appointed Project Manager at Alder Hey to facilitate the transition to Trust status.

December 1989	Professor van Velzen seeks additional technical resource (widely copied letter).
December 1989	Professor van Velzen produces five-year paper for regional paediatric, fetal, placental and perinatal pathology service.
December 1989	Professor Harris leaves Liverpool.
January 1990	Professor van Velzen continues quest for proper funding of the Regional Fetal Pathology Services.
January 1990	Professor David Lloyd becomes Acting Head of Department of Child Health at the University.
March 1990	Professor van Velzen writes to the University Vice Chancellor advising him of the lack of funding for the fetal and perinatal service.
April 1990	Mr James Birrell appointed Unit Financial Manager at Alder Hey.
April 1990	Dr Smith appointed Research Fellow at the University.
June 1990	First detailed letter of complaint to management from a family regarding Professor van Velzen's failure to finalise post mortem reports.
July 1990	Miss Malone retires as Unit General Manager.
January 1991	Professor Cooke appointed Head of Department of Child Health at the University.
February 1991	Mr Butler suggests proposals to Unit III for the provision of fetal pathology services.
March 1991	Professor van Velzen contributes to the second Alder Hey overall business plan: 'PM histology is still not possible, final PM reports are not delivered'.
March 1991	Mr Butler's capital programme for the early years of the Trust makes provision for the return of Professor van Velzen's unit to Alder Hey.
March 1991	Dr Chan leaves Liverpool.
April 1991	Royal Liverpool Children's Hospital and Community Services NHS Trust created (Alder Hey). Mr Butler Chief Executive, Mr Birrell Director of Finance, Dr John Martin Medical Director, Mr Peter Tallentire Director of Personnel and Mrs Patricia Hooton Director of Nursing.
June 1991	Professor Davies retires as University Vice Chancellor.
July 1991	Backlog of 240 fetus at Alder Hey noted.

August 1991	Terms agreed between Alder Hey and Unit III for the provision of fetal pathology services.
August 1991	Professor Beazley retires as Dean to be replaced by Professor Michael Orme.
August 1991	Mr Meade promoted to Service Manager of Pathology at Alder Hey.
September 1991	Mr Paul Eccles appointed MLSO.
October 1991	Dr Myat Mon Khine appointed Lecturer in Fetal and Infant Pathology at the University and Honorary Senior Registrar at Alder Hey.
October 1991	Dr Vyvyan Howard appointed Senior Lecturer in Anatomy at the University.
November 1991	Mr Butler asks Professor van Velzen for details of post mortem backlog following complaints by clinicians regarding Professor van Velzen's failure to finalise reports.
November 1991	Mr Jason Sweeney and Miss Louise Costi appointed Medical Laboratory Assistants (MLAs).
December 1991	Professor van Velzen's failings in respect of the fetal contract noted (only five post mortems performed).
1992	Professor Cooke becomes a member of the Grant Review Panel of FSID.
1992	Mill Road Hospital closes, the fetal collection (ICH) ceases.
January 1992	Dr David Isherwood appointed Clinical Director for Pathology at Alder Hey.
January 1992	Mrs Clark ceases her role as Professor van Velzen's personal assistant.
July 1992	Mr Butler and Mr Birrell visit Professor van Velzen, confirm the intention to move the unit back to Alder Hey and ask for details of staff.
August 1992	Professor van Velzen's document 'Fetal and Infant Pathology located at the Alder Hey site' claims research and NHS work is so interlinked it is impossible simply to move the clinical side back to Alder Hey. The document lists fictitious staff said to be working in the unit.
August 1992	Working Party set up by Liverpool Obstetrics and Gynaecology Services NHS Trust makes recommendations as to the sensitive disposal of fetal tissue.
September 1992	Professor Philip Love becomes University Vice Chancellor.
October 1992	Professor Ian Grierson appointed Professor of Ophthalmology at the University.

October 1992	Dr Marco Pozzi appointed Consultant Cardiac Surgeon at Alder Hey.
November 1992	Professor van Velzen falsely tells Mr Butler he has cleared the full backlog of fetus and placentae for 1991.
November 1992	Miss Roxanne McKay, Consultant Paediatric Cardiac Surgeon at Alder Hey resigns.
December 1992	University Working Party on pathology. The view is expressed that Professor van Velzen is not doing his six clinical sessions and must be made to do so.
1993	Flow of hearts to ICH from Professor van Velzen's unit dries up.
1993	Final research papers on the fetal collection (ICH).
1994	Professor Cooke becomes a member of the Scientific Advisory Committee at FSID.
Jan/Feb 1993	Increase in complaints to clinicians regarding Professor van Velzen's failure to finalise post mortem reports.
February 1993	Professor Orme visits the Vice Chancellor to report his unease with Professor van Velzen and says Mr Butler would like Professor van Velzen to go. He describes Professor van Velzen as 'articulate, plausible and streetwise' and someone who will not go without making a fuss.
March 1993	Faculty Board meeting ratifies Working Party on Pathology recommendation that funds for senior lecturer position be removed from Professor van Velzen's unit. He demands a review of the decision.
March 1993	Professor van Velzen and Mrs England's paper 'Re-establishment of Histopathology and Neuropathology Reporting of Post Mortem Service in RLCH Alder Hey NHS Trust' highlights the failure to perform histology which 'constitutes an incomplete and professionally and clinically speaking unsatisfactory if not unacceptable service'.
April 1993	Clinical Directorate restructured. Dr Isherwood retires as Clinical Director of Pathology, to be replaced by Professor Helen Carty as Clinical Director of Support Services (including Pathology).
April 1993	Professor van Velzen writes to Professor Carty: there is no 'delay' in PM histology, 'this hospital does not receive any PM histology'.
April 1993	Professor Heath retires as Head of University Department of Pathology, to be replaced as Acting Head by Dr Jim Burns.

May 1993	Contributions to the University Review set up following Professor van Velzen's demand. Professor Orme – history of service problems, recent improvement to previous poor research output; Professor Cooke – unclear as to Professor van Velzen's contributions to research; Professor Carty – concerns regarding failure to perform histology, finalise reports and unreliability; FSID – Professor van Velzen's commitment exemplary; Mr Stephen Walkinshaw – overall adequate service.
May 1993	Meetings of Clinical Directors assess Professor van Velzen and Mrs England's paper: Mr Butler to deal.
May 1993	FSID Scientific Advisory Committee discuss Centre award of £500,000 over five years to facilitate research into cot death.
May 1993	Mrs England becomes Service Manager of Cardiac and Intensive Care Directorate.
June 1993	University Review.
July 1993	Mr Butler tells Professor Orme that in view of the removal of funding for the senior lecturer for Professor van Velzen's unit, in breach of the original agreement, he may remove NHS funding for Professor van Velzen's post and create an NHS post in paediatric pathology.
August 1993	Professor Orme offers Mr Butler reinstatement of funding for five-year senior lecturer post for Professor van Velzen's unit.
September 1993	Mrs Jacqueline Waring becomes Chief MLSO. Containers holding retained organs at 'Myrtle Street' are moved to the basement.
September 1993	Professor John Ashton becomes Regional Medical Officer at Mersey Regional Health Authority.
September 1993	District Audit of Pathology Services confirms all clinicians felt the Alder Hey histology service had deteriorated over previous two years.
September 1993	FSID put out £500,000 research grant to competitive tender.
October 1993	Mr Birrell leaves his position as Director of Finance at Alder Hey.
October 1993	Professor Christopher Foster appointed Head of University Department of Pathology (to take up post in June 1994).
November 1993	Professor van Velzen suggests reinstitution of histology service through purchase of microtome and training of mortuary technicians.
November 1993	Mr Butler leaves Alder Hey.

December 1993	Mr Alan Sharples replaces Mr Birrell as Director of Finance.
December 1993	Ethical approval given for research project by Professor Grierson, Professor van Velzen and Mr Mark Birch using fetal and neonatal eyeballs.
December 1993	Ms Hilary Rowland appointed Chief Executive at Alder Hey.
February 1994	Professor Ronald Kaschula appointed locum consultant paediatric pathologist at Alder Hey.
February 1994	Business plan for pathology department at Alder Hey indicates PM histology is 'to be introduced'.
March 1994	Ms Rowland visits 'Myrtle Street'.
May 1994	Mrs Clark, now in the Legal Department, writes to Mr Barter seeking clarification of the ownership of 'post mortem tissue'.
May 1994	Professor Carty writes to Professor van Velzen referring to his having expressed concern regarding the 'utilisation of stored tissue and the potential pitfalls for the hospital'.
May 1994	Complaint by a mother made to Ms Rowland states Professor van Velzen exceeded consent when performing post mortem examination.
June 1994	Mr Barter responds to Mrs Clark regarding the ownership of post mortem tissue.
June 1994	Professor Foster takes up post of Head of University Department of Pathology, replacing Dr Burns.
July 1994	Ms Rowland responds to the complaint made in May 1994. She accepts Professor van Velzen's explanation and an opportunity to discipline is lost.
August 1994	University successful in obtaining £250,000 grant from FSID in multi-disciplinary application led by Professor Peter Pharaoh. Bristol University awarded similar sum.
August 1994	£110,000 Wellcome Trust grant awarded to Professor Grierson, Professor van Velzen and Mr Birch for their research project involving fetal and neonatal eyeballs.
October 1994	Dyson Report on pathology services in Merseyside delivered in draft: productivity in terms of reports and MLSO workload of prepared reports lowest in the region yet non-pay costs extremely high. Recommends internal review of histopathology department to clarify the breakdown between service and research workloads.

November 1994	Confidential memo from Mr Tallentire to Ms Rowland exploring procedure for disciplinary action against Professor van Velzen.
December 1994	Mr Tallentire leaves Alder Hey.
December 1994	Professor Kaschula leaves Alder Hey.
December 1994	Professor Foster, with Alder Hey's support, removes Professor van Velzen from any responsibility for Alder Hey work which is now to be covered by Dr Khine. Professor van Velzen is to do fetal and perinatal work and research only. When told he takes unauthorised leave.
1995	Liverpool Maternity Hospital and Liverpool Women's Hospital, Catherine Street, close.
1995	'Myrtle Street' leased to the University.
January 1995	Professor van Velzen's authority for further expenditure frozen after £68,000 deficit found on audit.
January 1995	FSID express concern (and are reassured by Professor Orme) at the Alder Hey reorganisation.
January 1995	Professor James Neilson tells Mr Alan Kosmin to provide evidence of ethical approval for his research project which involves the use of fetal and neonatal eyeballs.
February 1995	Professor Foster demands that Professor van Velzen clear the fetal, perinatal and placental post mortem backlog by mid-April.
February 1995	Professor Foster tells Professor van Velzen to stop any research project which does not have proper ethical approval; Professor Grierson orders the collection of eyes to stop.
February 1995	Ms Therese Harvey becomes Director of Human Resources at Alder Hey.
March 1995	Professor van Velzen alerts Professor Foster to the fetal collection (ICH) which he says has no Ethical Committee approval, parental consent or pathology supervision.
March 1995	Mr Sweeney (MLA) leaves 'Myrtle Street'.
March 1995	Draft job description for senior lecturer post refers to 'paediatric tissue bank'.

Spring 1995	Draft service level agreement drawn up by Professor Foster deals with the collection of tissue samples: 'establishment of the correct diagnosis with the minimum of interference will be the priority'.
April 1995	Professor Carty writes to senior clinicians with list of post mortems where histology has not been done seeking their instructions in relation to the retained 'organs'.
July 1995	Ms McGill (MLSO) leaves 'Myrtle Street'.
August 1995	Mr Eccles (MLSO) and Miss Costi (MLA) leave 'Myrtle Street'.
August 1995	Professor Carty writes to Ms Rowland and Professor Foster regarding the distribution of the heart and lung specimens at 'Myrtle Street'.
August 1995	Dr Khine appointed Consultant Paediatric Pathologist at Royal Liverpool University Hospital.
September 1995	Mrs Waring (Chief MLSO) leaves 'Myrtle Street'.
October 1995	Professor Orme provides 'reference' to Canadian High Commission for Professor van Velzen.
November 1995	Correspondence involving Professor Carty, Ms Rowland and Professor Foster regarding the transfer of containers and material on the decommissioning of 'Myrtle Street'. Specimens required by Alder Hey to be transferred there, hearts and lungs to ICH, specimens not required by Alder Hey to be left in 'Myrtle Street' as research material. Mr Barter's instructions sought in relation to 'unprocessed tissue' from CPMs.
November 1995	Professor Foster widely copies letter to Vice Chancellor referring to 'grave and detrimental effects' of Professor van Velzen's activities.
December 1995	Mrs England becomes Service Manager of Theatres Directorate and the Acting Service Manager of Directorate of Clinical Support Services.
December 1995	Professor van Velzen resigns and leaves Liverpool.
January 1996	Dr George Kokai appointed Honorary Consultant and Senior Lecturer in Paediatric Pathology.
March 1996	Regional Health Authorities abolished, NHS Executive Regional Offices established. Trust changes its name to Royal Liverpool Children's Hospital NHS Trust.
July 1996	Professor Orme retires as Dean, to be replaced by Professor Bernard Wood.

March 1997	Dr Martin retires as Medical Director of Alder Hey, to be replaced by Dr Campbell Davidson.
June 1997	Professor Wood retires as Dean, to be replaced by Professor Peter Johnson.
August 1998	Professor Carty retires as Clinical Director for Support Services.
November 1998	Practice Notes for Coroners issued by Coroner's Society.
February 1999	Mrs England becomes Acting Director of Operational Services.
June 1999	Mr Barter retires as HM Coroner for Liverpool, to be replaced by Mr Andre Rebello.
September 1999	Professor Robert Anderson gives evidence to the Bristol Inquiry, referring to Alder Hey's heart collection. Mrs England writes to the Bristol Inquiry confirming there was no discussion with parents about organ retention.
September 1999	Parents begin asking Alder Hey whether their children's hearts have been retained. Mrs England asked to manage the incident. Ms Rowland states that practice at Alder Hey has not differed from other hospitals.
September 1999	Mrs England tells Ms Rowland of the store of organs at 'Myrtle Street'. Ms Rowland writes to parents of children whose post mortem examinations had been performed at Alder Hey between 1988 and 1995 inviting them to ask for information.
October 1999	Organs held at 'Myrtle Street' and ICH catalogued by Alder Hey. Alder Hey issue press release: devastated so many organs stored without the knowledge of the hospital, its doctors or parents. Dr Stephen Gould appointed to provide internal inquiry report.
November 1999	Mr Meade leaves Alder Hey.
November 1999	PITY II established.
December 1999	Lord Hunt announces Inquiry, Panel appointed and convene.
December 1999	Professor Johnson is told of the fetal and children's body part collections (ICH).
December 1999	Dr Gould produces internal inquiry report.
January 2000	Parents become aware that Alder Hey are taking small samples of organs before returning them, without seeking consent.
February 2000	Chief Medical Officer's census returned by University and Alder Hey.

February 2000	Inquiry opens at Norwich House, Liverpool; draft procedures agreed by all parties.
February 2000	Secretary of State for Health issues directive that no further tissue should be destroyed.
March 2000	Stephen White's organs mistakenly destroyed by Alder Hey. Lord Hunt demands report and refers the case to the Inquiry. Mr Frank Taylor, Trust Chairman resigns, Mrs Judith Greensmith appointed as Chair. Ms Rowland steps down and Mr Anthony Bell appointed Acting Chief Executive. Mrs England steps down as Acting Director of Operational Services. Special Incident Project Board (SIPB) set up under leadership of Mrs Kate Jackson.
March 2000	Inquiry notified by University of 'fetal eye' collection.
May 2000	Inquiry's oral hearings commence. Clinicians' seminar held at Alder Hey.
June 2000	Alder Hey declare six-week moratorium on disclosure of information to parents about organ retention. Dr Gordan Vujanic undertakes a complete re-cataloguing exercise.
July 2000	Inquiry's oral hearings completed.
August 2000	Existence of cerebellum collection (146 cerebella) disclosed. Fifty-eight parents who have had second funerals are affected. Following re-cataloguing, Alder Hey can now say 62 parents previously told they were unaffected by organ retention are in fact involved. Alder Hey also say some organs will never be positively identified.
October 2000	Human Rights Act 1998 comes into force incorporating the Convention on Human Rights into domestic law.

Appendix 1. List of Representatives

Parties and their Representatives before the Inquiry

Counsel to the Inquiry

Mr J James Rowley of 28 St John Street, Manchester

Solicitor to the Inquiry

Mr Stephen Jones of Pannone & Partners, Manchester

Parties	*Representatives*
Royal Liverpool Children's NHS Trust (Alder Hey)	Miss Sally Smith QC and Mr Owain Thomas, instructed by Mr Allan Mowat of Hill Dickinson, Liverpool
University of Liverpool	Robert Francis QC and Mr John Benson, instructed by Mr James Pinsent of DLA, Liverpool
NHS Executive North West	Miss Melanie Isherwood, Davies Arnold Cooper of Manchester
PITY II	Mr Iain Goldrein QC and Mr Scott Donovan, instructed by Mr Ian Cohen of Goodmans, Liverpool
Other Parents	Mr Peter Skelton, instructed by Mr Robin Makin of E. Rex Makin & Co, Liverpool
Professor Helen Carty	Mr Peter Fitzpatrick of Theodore Goddards, London
Mr Henry Meade	Mr David Jacks of Weightmans, Manchester
Professor Cooke Professor Lloyd Dr Khine Dr Martin	Mr Michael Ryan of Ryan Solicitors, Cheadle Hulme
Professor Harris	Mr Kaiser Nazir instructed by Mr Geoffrey Daunt of Beechcroft Wansborough, Leeds

Appendix 2. Issues Document

Development of Main Issues

Issues are to be referred to by Issue Section Number followed by grid reference e.g.1.B.2.

1.   Parents' Concerns

2.   Hospital Post-Mortem Examinations

3.   Coroner's Post-Mortem Examinations

4.   Actual Use of Retained Tissue

5.   Pathological Issues

6.   Laboratory Procedures

7.   Laboratory Resources

8.   Management Systems and Intervention

9.   Legal Framework

10.   Recommendations

1. Parents' Concerns

A	B	C	
See later sections for a detailed exposition of many Issues concerning parents:	In particular, sections entitled: 2. Hospital Post-Mortem Examinations 3. Coroner's Post-Mortem Examinations 4. Actual Use of Retained Tissue are of particular interest to parents; but they are understandably keen to know the answers to all questions posed within this document.		**1**
In addition parents are concerned with the following Issues which highlight aspects of other Main Issues or do not fall neatly into any one of them.	Why were post-mortem examinations often carried out remote from the place of death?	Why were many parents not told that their child's body would be taken to Alder Hey for examination?	**2**
	Why was *tissue* in fact removed, retained or used for *medical purposes* so often outside the realms of parents' perception?		**3**
	Why were they given little or no explanation as to what was to happen at post-mortem?	Should parents be told in future what happens, or would this upset them unnecessarily? Why cannot parents be told what they need to know sympathetically but with reasonable detail so that they understand?	**4**
	Why did the Trust and University do nothing about the store of organs until the news was out by chance as a result of the Bristol Inquiry?	Why were the organs of their children left to languish in the Myrtle Street basement, often miles away from their original homes?	**5**
	Why wasn't the fact that parents have no choice or control in a Coroner's post-mortem made clear to them at the time in a sympathetic as against perfunctory fashion?	How could it be that, where there was no choice or control, organs were retained without any consultation at the end of the process of Coroner's post-mortems?	**6**
	Were some parents told that their child's organs would be buried in the Hospital grounds after the post-mortem?	If so, why?	**7**
	Why were parents allowed to think that they were burying a complete body when they were not?	Why have parents had to go through a second period of grief and mourning many years after the event?	**8**

A	B	C	
	Why was the Hospital unable to tell them what organs had been retained quickly and definitively?	Why were some parents told inaccurate information? Why have some had to go through a second burial or cremation only for further organs to be discovered and a third to be required?	9
	Why were sections taken from organs recently before their return without the knowledge or consent of parents?		10
	What was the procedure to ensure that parents were told the results of post-mortem?	If parents weren't told, why? Why was the result given often in perfunctory form?	11
	Why has the Hospital not been more supportive of parents in their second grief and in their need to know precisely what was done to their child's organs?	How can the Hospital now arrange speedily for definitive information to be given to them? Should counselling now be available for the parents on request or in all cases?	12

2. Hospital Post-Mortem Examinations

A	B	C	
What criteria were applied in determining whether a Hospital post-mortem should be carried out?	Who determined the criteria? From where were the criteria obtained? Who applied the criteria in any case?	Provide documents.	**1**
What reasonable enquiry was actually made?	By whom? Of whom? When? Where?		**2**
	With what level of information and advice?	Did anyone explain that parents could object to a Hospital post-mortem ? Did anyone explain the difference between a post-mortem to identify cause of death only under Section 2 and a post-mortem to include the removal of body parts for *medical purposes* under Section 1.(2); and that lack of objection to the first was not incompatible with objection to the second? Did anyone explain that some or all organs would be removed from the body as a matter of course even if not to be retained but returned to the body? Did anyone explain what organs might be retained and the circumstances in which they might be retained? Did anyone explain as a matter of course that organs such as the heart and brain required to be fixed before sectioning, which could not be carried out within the usual time-scale of a funeral, that would therefore take place without those organs? Did anyone define the word tissue on the form and in what way? Did anyone explain what would happen to any organs removed after post-mortem in terms of research, education or therapy?	**3**

A	B	C	
	Was any written information given as a matter of course?	What?	**4**
	Was there any opportunity for advice or reflection?	For how long? From whom? What obtained? If not, were there matters going to reasonable practicability which militated in the circumstances against delay?	**5**
	What form(s) was used and what did it say?	Did parents actually read it? Did they, or ought they reasonably to have understood it properly? Was the form specifically explained to them? Why did the form not seek separate "consents" under Section 1.(2) and Section 2? How were parents to understand from a reading of the form that they might "consent " to one but not the other? Were there times when Hospital post-mortems were carried out without a signed form? Was a record sometimes made only in the clinical notes? Were there instances where no record was made at all?	**6**
	Did any parents actually object when asked?	If so, what happened then? Did anyone try to persuade them? Did the Hospital carry out any Hospital post-mortems in the face of parental objection? If so, which children?	**7**
	What rank of clinician actually obtained the "consents"? Was it delegated informally to non-medical staff?	What rank should have obtained the "consents"? If so, to whom and by whom?	**8**

A	B	C	
	How did the clinicians approach the task of obtaining the "consents"?	What training or instruction was given? When in terms of their career? By whom? Was there any continuing education or monitoring? Was there any strategy to allow for the grief and shock of relatives so as to provide for reliable/informed "consent"?	9

3. Coroner's Post-Mortems

A	B	C	
Did the Hospital authorities always report deaths to the Coroner that required to be reported under the Coroners' Act?	If not, why not? Why are inquests recently being opened into deaths many years ago if they were reported at the time?	Was there any pressure placed on parents to consent to a Hospital post-mortem in the case of deaths that ought properly to have been reported to the Coroner? If so, who applied such pressure and at whose behest?	1
What were the procedures adopted for communication between Hospital and Coroner?	In writing? Provide anonymous specimen documents to preserve confidentiality. With what detail did the Coroner give any instructions? Over the telephone?	How were these circulated in the Lab. so that all relevant people were aware of the Coroner's instructions? How did those in the Department know the content of any oral communication? What records were made of telephone conversations? Entries in the Day Books? Notes? Memo's? Provide specimens if available.	2
How did pathologists exercise their discretion over time as to which organs to remove and retain for examination, in answering the question as to how the victim died?	Did they exercise their discretion differently from a Hospital post-mortem when they had authority under Section 1.(2) for retention for *medical purposes*? Did different pathologists exercise their discretion differently, or the same pathologists differently at different times?	If so, how did the approach differ? If not, how is it to be reconciled with the narrow question *How?* to be answered in the context of a Coroner's post-mortem? If so, why?	3
How did the Coroner formally release the body?	What information did he have as to the preliminary results? Did he know what organs had in fact been retained at the time he released the body? Was any specific justification ever given, or asked for to retain whole, multi, and complete sets of organs?	How was it communicated? If in writing, provide specimens. By whom and to whom at the Coroner's Office? If so, how did he gain that understanding? Was the Coroner ever asked in practice to authorise the retention of organs for later testing after the release of the body? Was the Coroner ever asked to allow the use of organs taken at post-mortem as if obtained and retained for medical purposes under Section 1.(2)?	4

A	B	C	
Was the Coroner aware that large numbers of organs were being retained? Was he aware of the Myrtle Street basement and its use?	How? When? Through whom? Provide documents.	What did he do about it? Did he challenge the scope of retention as going beyond the ambit of a Coroner's post-mortem?	5
How was it that large numbers of even Coroner's examinations remained incomplete?	How should the procedures have concluded and within what time scale? What communication was there between the Hospital and the Coroner justifying the delay in and ultimately the failure in provision of final reports? What communication was there between the Coroner and the Hospital chasing and ultimately demanding final reports?	Provide any documents. Provide any documents.	6
What information was given to the parents with regard to Coroner's post-mortem examinations?	By the Coroner? By the Hospital?	Orally or in writing? Provide any documents. Were they told that organs might be retained for further testing after the release of the body? Were they told that organs would be widely removed even if only to be returned to the body for burial? Were they told that some organs required to be fixed and would not be available at the usual time for disposal of the body? Were they, if it be the case, told that the post-mortem would be carried out as if under Section 1.(2) and organs retained for research purposes? If not, why not? Why were parents not asked to give a parallel lack of objection or authorisation to keep organs after the process was over?	7
Did the Coroner ever give any directions or instructions for suitable and dignified disposal of organs retained after release of the body?	What? When? To whom? What happened to hearts and brains after fixing when the process was over?	Did the Hospital ever give any indication to the Coroner as to how it disposed of organs after release of the body? When, by whom and how?	8

A	B	C	
Did the Hospital ever seek directions from the Coroner as to disposal?	When? Through whom? Provide documentary evidence.	What response did the Coroner give? Provide documents.	9
Was there any procedure whereby the Coroner gave general advice, information and support to parents whose children were undergoing post-mortem?	What? When? By whom?	Orally? In writing? Provide any documents?	10
Were parents told as a matter of routine the result of Coroner's post-mortems?	By whom? By what means? In what detail? Were they given a copy of the post-mortem report?	If not, why not?	11

4. Actual Use of Retained Tissue (N.B. Over the entire period and not just 1988–1995)

A	B	C	
What *tissue* was actually used for research? (If answers cannot readily be given, what does this say of the procedures and record keeping?)	By whom?	If anyone outside the Trust or University: Under what terms (providing any documents here and in the following questions)?	1
	With what permission?	What documents or records exist to prove "permit to work"? Provide them.	2
	For precisely what research?	Was the research published? Where? Provide copies/ a bibliography. If not published, where are the notes and preliminary drafts/findings? Provide copies. Of what relevance and quality? If not, why not?	3
	Was there funding for research available from outside the Trust or University?	From whom? How much? Under what terms? Provide copies of any agreement or memoranda/correspondence.	4
What *tissue* was actually used for educational purposes? (ditto)	By whom? For whom? In what way(s)? Where?	If anyone outside the Trust or University, Under what terms? (ditto)	5
		Any "permits to work" or record of tissue leaving the laboratory? Provide any documents.	6
What *tissue* was actually used for *therapeutic* purposes? (ditto)	Precisely what purposes? With what authority or permission? When?	Documents/"permits to work"? Provide.	7

A	B	C	
	Was any use made of *tissue* for therapy by anyone outside the Trust or University?	By whom? In what circumstances? How? Under what terms? Provide any agreements or memoranda.	**8**
Has *tissue* not been used at all or not over long periods?	Why not? Why continue to keep it? Why take it in the first place?		**9**
Has any *tissue* been disposed of?	By whom? When? By what method? What records are there?		**10**
	Has any *tissue* been disposed of by way of gift or other transfer to a third party?	To whom and when? For what purpose? For what, if any, remuneration? Under what terms? Provide any agreement or memoranda.	**11**

5. Pathological Issues

A	B	C	
Professor van Veltzen	Who was responsible for advertising the new post?		1
	What response was there to the advertisement?	What was the number of applicants? What was the quality of applicants? Who were any other applicants?	
	What procedure was there for the appointment?	How did it work out in practice?	
	Who took the decision to appoint?	What consultation was there and co-operation between the University and the Trust on the appointment? Was there any dissent? Provide documentary evidence of the procedures, events, deliberations and decisions.	
	To whom was he answerable at both Trust (clinical work) and University (research etc.)?	What did they do? What records are there of communication, providing them?	2
	Who, at both Trust and University, were responsible for implementation of the Review Committee's recommendations?	What steps were taken to monitor the new Department and Professor? By whom? With what result? What was done between 1988–1993 and then 1993–95? How were matters allowed to reach crisis point in 1993–95? How did the Trust and University interact on this crucial issue? Please provide all documents.	3

A	B	C	
	Were complaints made against Professor van Veltzen or the running and performance of the Department while he was in charge?	By whom? When? With what content? Provide documentary evidence where made in writing. Were the complaints acted upon? When? How? By whom? Any records? To whom were the complaints made and to whom passed on?	4
	Were complaints made to Professor van Veltzen?	By whom? When? With what content? Provide documentary evidence where made in writing. With what follow up? Provide all documentary evidence and in particular any evidence of: disciplinary proceedings, notes of interview, written warnings, notes of oral warnings, formal and informal advice, annual or other review.	5
	Were complaints made by Professor van Veltzen?	To whom? When? With what content? What follow up? Provide all documents over and above the complaints contained in previous lists.	6

A	B	C	
	What were the true circumstances surrounding the departure of Professor van Veltzen?	Who were the driving forces? When did the process of departure begin? What procedures were implemented? Why did it take so long? What steps were taken to obtain and then maintain a clinically acceptable pathology service once the problems were evident? Was any money paid over to Professor van Veltzen on his departure? If so, how much, by whom and for what purpose? Ultimately, what was the real reason for the departure and the lapse of the Chair?	7
	What informed Professor van Veltzen in his clinical decisions as to the need for the removal and retention of organs? Were there any criteria that he applied, and if so, what and from where did they emanate?	Why remove all organs including the brain and reproductive organs on so many occasions? Was it for research purposes only as against what was reasonably required to establish cause of death? Why such extensive removal and retention in Coroner's post-mortem examinations, and especially in infant road traffic cases? Why continue to remove and retain if there was little or no anticipated opportunity to carry out a detailed examination? How did Professor van Veltzen's practices compare with those of pathology staff before and after him at Liverpool and with prevailing reasonable professional standards in the UK?	8

A	B	C	
	What provision did Professor van Veltzen himself make for ensuring reliable/informed lack of objection in parents?	What considerations did he give to the form(s) in use? What training and advice did he give to clinical staff? Were the clinical staff who actually obtained signatures to the forms aware of his practices and the difficulties in the Department? What provision did he make for an explanation to parents of the difference between a post-mortem simply to establish cause of death and one with the retention of organs for medical purposes?	9
Other pathologists	Who was responsible for overseeing their performance?	What did they do? What changes were brought about at all relevant stages and why? What steps were taken to improve performance after Professor van Veltzen's departure? When and by whom?	10
	How did their clinical practices and performance compare with those of Professor van Veltzen?	Consider all the considerations set out above in relation to Professor van Veltzen himself. In precisely what ways did they differ? Why? Were there any resource constraints over time, so as to form a comparison? If so what constraints, explaining their application?	11

6. Laboratory Procedures

A	B	C	
What procedures were there in terms of Laboratory Day Books etc. for the keeping of an accurate record of precisely what *tissue* was removed, examined, retained and later used?	Itemise all documents that were part of any systems over time. Can access be given to the records for inspection?	How come there was such disarray in 1999 when the problems came to light in public if basic records had been kept to a decent standard?	1
How were clinicians notified of the results of post-mortem examinations?	If orally, by whom and generally where if not over the telephone? If in writing, in what form?	Preliminary reports? Letters? Final reports? Any late addenda following detailed histology?	2
What was the procedure for obtaining *tissue* for *medical purposes* at a later stage?	Was there any "permit to work" system? Was there a record in any Laboratory Day Book or its equivalent? Was there a record kept of the *medical purpose* to which *tissue* was put?	Can access be given for inspection of any such records?	3
Was any distinction made in procedure and practice in using organs retained under Coroner's post-mortems as against Hospital post-mortems?	What distinction? With what record keeping, so that it can be seen that the procedure worked? Were any "consents" obtained from either the Coroner or the parents to use *tissue* obtained after Coroner's post-mortems?		4
Was any distinction made in procedure as to clinical approaches to Coroner's as against Hospital post-mortems?	Did practice differ over time? Did all pathologists at any given time always follow the same practice?	If so, why and who?	5
What procedures were there for disposing of *tissue* including whole organs following post-mortem or subsequent use for *medical purposes*?	By whom? What method? What paperwork?	Did procedures change over time? Were any organs buried in the Hospital grounds as one parent on the Panorama programme suggested she had been told?	6
What were the procedures for fixing brains and hearts?	How long did it take? How was the procedure speeded up in cases of urgency? How often were brains and hearts examined without fixing?		7

7. Laboratory Resources

A	B	C	
What were the resources available on an annual basis in real terms over time?	How were such resources allocated within the Trust and Universities? Provide relevant documents. Who made the decisions? Provide documents going to all relevant decisions. Was there any procedure for challenge or appeal for further funds?	Once funding had been allocated, who made the decisions as to how it was spent and prioritised within the Department of Foetal and Infant Pathology? How were decisions as to allocation reached and by whom? Provide all relevant documents. Were any such challenges or appeals made? When, by whom and with what result? Provide all relevant documents.	1
How many qualified paediatric pathology staff were available at any given time, and in particular between 1988 and 1996?	Provide a detailed chronology of all staff, including Registrars on rotation from Broadgreen Hospital. How many hours per week over time were each providing, so as to reach a total number of clinical hours available at any given point (over the entire period and not just 1988–1996). Who was responsible for organising, disciplining and recruiting staff at any given time?	What were those concerned doing if not engaged in clinical duties? How many hours per week should have been provided if anyone was not in fact fulfilling their role properly? How does the provision of resources over time compare with any differing workload (see below)?	2
How many support staff were available to assist with clinical work and secretarial duties at any given time?	Who were they? What were their duties? What were their hours?	How does the provision and allocation of support staff as a resource differ over time and compare with the workload (see below)?	3
How many post-mortems were required each week – maximum, minimum, average?	How long did each stage take on average? By whom was each stage carried out? How did the workload differ over time over the whole period and not just 1988–1996?	Initial dissection, sectioning and macroscopic examination? Writing preliminary report? Preparation of tissue blocks? Histological examination? Any delayed examination, saying why delay was needed? Writing final report? Can a total number of hours for post-mortems required be seen from records or reliably estimated over time to see any trends?	4

A	B	C	
How many other procedures were required each week – maximum, minimum, average? How did the workload differ over time over the whole period and not just 1988–1996?	Surgical biopsies? Renal biopsies? Oncological biopsies? Frozen sections? Gastro-enterological biopsies? Pulmonary biopsies? Needle biopsies? Frozen sections?	How long did each take on average? How long was required for reporting? Can a total number of hours of such work be seen from records or reliably estimated over time to see any trends? Any others?	5

8. Management Systems and Intervention (N.B. Over the entire period and not just 1988–1995)

A	B	C	
What was the management hierarchy over the Department of Foetal and Infant Pathology?	Who? What responsibilities? What powers to act without higher authority? To whom, in turn, were they accountable in senior Trust and/or University management?	Provide any contractual documents/ memoranda going to the relationship between Trust and University.	1
How did the hierarchies of the Trust and Universities coexist?	What responsibilities did each side have? What responsibilities did they in fact share? How often did Trust and University management teams meet to deal with pathology issues?	What was the system for reporting and auditing?	2
	How did the management of the Department of Foetal and Infant Pathology and the wider Department of Pathology coexist?	How did they communicate? Memo's; minutes of meetings; formal correspondence (provide any documents). What communication was there in fact relevant to the issues in this Inquiry? Where did ultimate responsibility lie?	3
	Did the arrangements differ over time?	How? Why? Who?	4
How did clinicians and the Pathology Hierarchies interact?	Who were the key players at all relevant times? Who devised the systems for communication of post-mortem results within the Trust?	What were the systems? Who had responsibility for overseeing the systems in practice?	5

A	B	C	
What happened when post-mortems were not completed?	What did the clinicians do when they had no definitive post-mortem reports?	How did clinicians inform clinical management in the future when they did not have final post-mortem reports?	6
	What did the Coroner do when he had no definitive post-mortem reports?	Were any decisions taken in the management of subsequent pregnancies/child deaths that might have been avoided with a full post-mortem report?	
	What should each have done to rectify the situation?		
	How was any audit of performance carried out without completed post-mortems?	Who was responsible for the audit of clinical performance?	7
		What was the system?	
		Who complained and to whom? Documents.	
		What was the system for communication and meetings?	
		How did the Trust and University coexist on this vital issue?	
		What memo's, minutes and correspondence were there?	
Who was responsible for Estates management and in particular for the use of Myrtle Street?	What were the systems for the management of the premises?		8
	What inspections took place?	When?	
		By whom?	
		With what records?	
		With what communication to wider management of both Trust and University?	
	What happened in relation to the transfer of ownership of Myrtle Street and the movement of Infant Pathology to Alder Hey?	Who decided it?	9
		When?	
		For what reasons?	
		With what audit at the time?	
		With what records, meetings and communication?	

A	B	C	
What role did FSID have in relation to management systems and the payment of staff/provision of resources?	Who was responsible at FSID? What meetings did they attend? What was the system for communication with FSID? Who was the interface with FSID at the Trust and the University? When things began to go wrong, what communication took place?	What documentary evidence is there? Between whom? In what form? Complaint? Request for more money? With what content? Documents. With what result?	10
What did FSID get out of the relationship?	What agreement was there? Provide. Was any research carried under any agreement with them? At what times was such research carried out? How long did it take? How did it fit into the clinical timetable? Who was responsible for fitting the timetable of clinical work and research together?	What system did FSID have for monitoring any research carried out on their behalf or as a result of their funding? What did any such monitoring reveal? Provide the timetables/logs. to show how the system worked.	11

A	B	C	
What were the recommendations of Profs. Wigglesworth and Risdon, following their review in 1987/88?	How did Trust and University management set about implementing the recommendations? Who was responsible? Who actually oversaw the implementation of the recommendations?	Provide a copy of the review paper and minutes of subsequent meetings and decisions. What did they do? What systems did they have for monitoring the new set up? To whom did they answer? What was the method of communication? Memo's, minutes, correspondence, face to face meetings? Provide all documents. How did matters come to be left until in crisis in 1993–95?	**12**
	Was the move to Myrtle Street part and parcel of the outcome of the review?	If so, why was Myrtle Street chosen? Who, in practice, had rights of access to the premises themselves?	**13**
	How did the review committee come to be established in 1993?	What did it do? How did it communicate? With what records? Provide. What did they recommend? Provide report?	**14**
What role did Regional management play?	What were the layers of systems and procedures above those set out in answer to the above questions? In what circumstances was Regional management to be involved?	Was Regional management in fact involved or copied in to correspondence etc. on any issues? What did they do or advise at each stage? If the situation varied over time, and in particular between the Mersey Regional Health Authority and the NHS Executive North West, in what ways? Provide all documentary evidence.	**15**

9. Legal Framework To inquire into the extent to which the Human Tissue Act 1961 has been complied with.

A	B	C	
S.1.(1) – *request of the deceased that his body… be used after his death…*	This section is not relevant to an inquiry into *infant* deaths.	Interesting points as to the validity of such a request in older children may, but are unlikely to, arise in the course of this Inquiry.	1
S. 1.(2) – *removal of body parts for medical purposes – therapeutic purposes/medical education/research.*	S.1.(2)(a) is as unlikely to be relevant in the case of infant deaths as S.1.(1). In the case of S.1.(2)(b), although interesting points may emerge as to conflict between relatives and difficulty in tracing them, the overwhelming issue for the Inquiry relates to the question: *"did the Hospital Authorities, after such reasonable enquiry as was practicable, have no reason to believe that the parents objected to usage for medical purposes (as distinct from simple post-mortem examination)?"*	Is this question purely objective, or partly subjective and partly objective? Can one have the state of mind required under the Act, without having asked the parents and given them an explanation suitable to *all the relevant circumstances including the extent of removal and the usage intended?* Does *"such reasonable enquiry as may be practicable"* define the extent of information to be given as well as attempts required to trace relatives? How far should such an explanation have gone? When should it have been given? Should the word tissue have been defined for parents as encompassing whole organ removal? What issues fall within the ambit of practicability? Do considerations of geography, family composition, time, play a part and if so, to what degree? Are the terms *therapeutic purposes, medical education and research* appropriate in the context of current medical and legal thinking?	2

A	B	C	
S. 2 – Hospital post-mortem examinations.	Questions similar to those under S.1.(1)(b) are to be posed.	Did the Hospital after reasonable enquiry have no reason to believe that the parents objected to a post-mortem examination? How much detail is required of the reasonable enquiry? Should a hospital give parents information about the post-mortem process, including the chance/likelihood that whole organs might be removed and not returned to the body for burial? Can one have the required state of mind under the Act, without having told the parents to gauge their reaction?	3
Retention/disposal of tissue held at the conclusion of Coroner's post-mortem examinations.	What is the legal status of tissue after the Coroner's process is over? Does the Human Tissue Act 1961 reattach to the tissue once the Coroner's process is complete, such that reasonable enquiry of the parents etc. is required before the Hospital can act to retain or dispose of the tissue? Do the parents have a right to possession of such tissue for the purposes of disposal, notwithstanding the prior disposal of the body?	When, in this context, is the Coroner's process over, or deemed to be over? Could this realistically apply to whole organs only, or would the duty have to apply to *all tissue*? Do the Hospital Authorities have the right to retain or dispose of the tissue, already lawfully removed in the Coroner's process, outside the application of the Human Tissue Act 1961?	4

10. Recommendations

A	B	C	
Recommendations cannot really begin to be considered until all the evidence has been obtained and evaluated.			1
Nevertheless	The continued application of the Human Tissue Act 1961 in its current form, not requiring the *consent* of parents in respect of the removal etc. of *tissue*, a word itself full of ambiguity to the layman, will be in the forefront of the Panel's deliberations.	How can relatives be given sufficient information at a time of grief, without unnecessarily increasing grief, so as to provide the basis for reliable and informed consent?	2
	The Panel will consider how the need of medical science and clinicians for accurate post-mortem information can be balanced with the concerns of families for loved ones and the proper dignity to be accorded to human organs after burial of the body.		3
	Wider considerations of the common law, relating to property rights in human tissue and genetic research, are beyond the scope of this Inquiry.	Such considerations are unsuitable for consideration in a confidential setting, and are properly within the public as against private domain.	4
	In terms of recommendations for the future, the Panel will be interested in compliance with the fundamental concepts of *human rights*.		5
	As to religious considerations, recommendations are likely to be on the basis of respect for all positions within the context of human rights, and a detailed consideration of comparative religions is not anticipated.		6

Appendix 3. Parents' Questionnaire

The Royal
Liverpool
Children's
Inquiry

Parents' Preliminary
Written Evidence

Please return as soon as you are able to do so.

If, but only if, you wish to remain anonymous, please detach this front page and you
need not sign at the bottom.

Royal Liverpool Children's Inquiry

Parents' Preliminary Written Evidence

All evidence will be confidential for the use of the Inquiry only

Please give your answer in the space beside each question. If you do not have enough space for your answer, please carry on at the end on the "continuation sheet".

This form is split into 4 sections. **Everyone should try to fill in Sections 1 and 4.**

In addition, you should try to fill in **either Section 2 or Section 3.**

- Section 2 deals with "Hospital" post-mortem examinations. If you were asked by the Hospital to sign a form, then your child almost certainly had a "Hospital" post-mortem. If so, you should try to fill in Section 2 but not Section 3.

- Section 3 deals with "Coroner's" post-mortem examinations. If you had contact with the Coroner or the Coroner's Officer, your child almost certainly had a "Coroner's" post-mortem and you should try to fill in Section 3 and not Section 2.

- If you are still uncertain, try to fill in as many answers as you can in all sections. Do not worry if you are unsure. When we have obtained all the documents, if you have made a mistake we will write to you again with the important documents and you will have another chance to answer the questions.

Above all, we understand the trauma you were suffering and the pressures you were under at the time. If you can't remember, don't worry. Just do the best you can to tell us what you remember. We hope that you will be able to fill in the form without professional help; but if you need it you can get help from any of the following people.

1. If you are represented by solicitors, you can ask them for help.

2. You can always ask the Parents' Support Group for help.

3. You can get help from the Community Health Council.

4. Stephen Jones, the Solicitor to the Inquiry, will be pleased to help you or answer any general questions that you may have.

Section 1 – General Information
(This section applies to you)

1. Where did your child die?

Only answer the Questions 2–4 if you were not at the Hospital when you were first told that a post-mortem examination was to be carried out.

2. How were you told (e.g. telephone, message via another relative or other)?

3. Who told you (e.g. doctor, nurse or other, senior or junior, name if known)?

4. Can you remember what you were told at this time, and, if so, tell us what you remember and anything that you said?

5. Did anyone speak to you about the post-mortem examination generally?

If so:

6. Who was it (e.g. doctor, nurse, pathologist, Coroner, Coroner's Officer or other, young or old, senior or junior, name if known)?

7. Did anyone tell you where the post-mortem examination would take place, and if so where?

8. If not, where did you expect that it would take place?

9. Did they tell you why they wanted to do a post-mortem examination?

   If so:

10. What did they say?

11. Were you asked if you had any questions?

    If so:

12. Do you remember what you asked and what you were told? (Please tell us as much as you can remember.)

13. Were you given any written information?

    If so:

14. What sort of document was it?

15. What do you remember that it said?

Section 2 – Hospital Post-Mortem Examinations Only
(See page 1 for help in deciding if this section applies to you)

1. Were you given a chance to think about it or get advice before you gave any "consent"?

   If so:

2. How long did you have?

3. Did you get any advice?

   If so:

4. Who from?

5. What advice did they give you?

6. Did anyone explain to you that you could object to a Hospital post-mortem?

7. Did anyone tell you that you could **agree** to a Hospital post-mortem examination to look for the cause of death, but **object** to the retention of organs for "medical purposes" ("medical purposes" means for therapy, medical education or research)?

8. Did you read the form that you were asked to sign?

9. What did you say when you were asked to sign the form?

10. Did you understand the form so that you knew that there were **two types** of Hospital post-mortem, one which simply looked into the cause of death, and one which also gave permission for the retention of organs for "medical purposes"?

11. If you read the form, or anyone mentioned the word *tissue* to you, did they tell you what it meant?

12. If you gave it any thought, what did you think *tissue* meant?

13. Did anyone tell you that whole organs, such as the heart, would be removed from the body?

   If so:

14. What organs did they tell you about?

15. Did they say what would happen to the organs?

   If so:

16. What did they say would happen to them?

   If they did not tell you what would happen to them:

17. What did you think would happen to them when the post-mortem examination was over?

18. Where were you when you signed (e.g. ward, office, or other – please specify)?

19. Who was with you when you signed (e.g. friend, family member or other – please specify)?

20. How long after (or before) the death of your child were you asked to sign?

21. Did anyone tell you the result of the post-mortem?

    If so:

22. Who told you?

23. Where were you when you were told?

24. What did they tell you was the result?

25. Did anyone tell you that the result might not be final because the organs had not yet been examined under the microscope?

26. Do you now feel that you fully understood why a post-mortem examination was carried out? In your own words, tell us if you feel let down.

Section 3 – Coroner's Post-Mortems Only
(See page 1 for help in deciding if this section applies to you)

1. Did anyone contact you after you had first been told of the need for a post-mortem examination?

   If so:

2. Who contacted you (e.g. Coroner, Coroner's Officer, doctor, pathologist, other)?

3. What did they tell you and what did you tell them? (Tell us as much as you can remember.)

4. How long after you were first told that there would be a post-mortem were you told that the body was available for the funeral?

5. Did anyone tell you at that stage that the body might be returned to you for the funeral without all the organs? Did you realise that this was possible?

6.   Did anyone tell you that some organs took longer to examine fully than the usual time allowed between death and a funeral?

7.   Did the Hospital at that stage ask you to fill in a form to do with keeping any organs for "medical purposes" ("medical purposes" means for therapy, medical education or research)?

If they did, please fill in any questions in Section 2 that you can answer as well, to tell us what happened at that time.

8.   Did anyone tell you the result of the post-mortem examination?

     If so:

9.   Who told you?

10. Where were you when you were told?

11. What did they tell you was the result?

12. Did anyone tell you that the result might not be final because the organs had not yet been examined under the microscope?

13. Do you now feel that you fully understood why a post-mortem examination was carried out? In your own words, tell us if you feel let down.

Section 4 – Your feelings and comment on the handling of the news.
(This section is for you)

1. Do you feel that you were treated in a sensitive and sympathetic way at the time of the post-mortem examination?

2. If not, how do you feel you should have been treated?

3. How did you first find out that your child's organs had been retained (telephone call, letter or other)?

4. When did you find out?

5. If a letter, who wrote to you?

6. If a telephone call, who spoke to you?

If your child's organs have been returned for burial or cremation:

7. Did the Hospital tell you that samples had been taken at the time of the original post-mortem?

8. Were you told that samples would be taken prior to release?

If samples were taken prior to release:

9. Did the Hospital ask for your consent before those late samples were taken?

10. How do you feel about the handling of the situation by Alder Hey since the news broke?

11. Is there anything else at all that you want the Inquiry Panel to know?

Signed..   Date...........................

(Name in Capitals)...

(Please correct any errors in the details on the front page for our records)

Continuation sheet.

Appendix 4. List of Witnesses

Witness List (Excluding Parental Evidence)

In addition to 43 parents, whom we have not listed in order to preserve anonymity, the following individuals gave evidence to the Inquiry. In each instance, save where indicated, a formal statement was prepared on behalf of the witness by Stephen Jones, Solicitor to the Inquiry, following personal interview. Those witnesses marked with an asterisk also gave oral evidence to the Inquiry during the course of the hearings between 11 May and 14 July 2000.

DR ROBERT ARNOLD – Consultant Paediatric Cardiologist at Alder Hey since 1975.

PROFESSOR JOHN ASHTON – Regional Medical Officer for Mersey Regional Health Authority (and thereafter North West Regional Health Authority) from September 1993, now Regional Director of Public Health and Regional Medical Officer of North West NHS Executive.

ROBERT ATLAY – Consultant Gynaecologist since 1970, ex Chairman of Liverpool Obstetrics and Gynaecology Division, Medical Director of Liverpool Women's Hospital Trust, from April 1992 to July 2000.

*ROY BARTER – HM Coroner for Liverpool from 1 November 1968 to 30 June 1999.

PROFESSOR JOHN BEAZLEY – Dean of the Faculty of Medicine, University of Liverpool, from September 1988 to August 1991, also Professor of Obstetrics and Gynaecology.

*JAMES BIRRELL – Unit Finance Manager and thereafter Director of Finance at Alder Hey from 1990 to October 1993, now Regional Director of Finance and Performance Management, NHS Executive North West.

*PEARSE BUTLER – Project Manager at Alder Hey from November 1989 and Chief Executive of the Trust from 1 April 1991 to November 1993.

*PROFESSOR HELEN CARTY – Consultant Paediatric Radiologist at Alder Hey since 1975 and Professor of Paediatric Radiology at Liverpool University. Clinical Director of Support Services (Radiology, Pharmacy and Pathology) at Alder Hey from April 1993 to August 1998.

¹DR YUEN-FU CHAN – Honorary Senior Registrar and Lecturer in Fetal and Infant Pathology at Alder Hey from November 1989 to March 1991.

---

1 A statement was given to the Solicitor to the Inquiry over the telephone: Dr Chan now works in Australia.

ELIZABETH CLAPHAM – Medical Laboratory Scientific Officer (MLSO) at Alder Hey having commenced as a temporary junior MLSO in September 1987.

*MARGERY CLARK – Personal Assistant to Professor van Velzen at Alder Hey from September 1988 to January 1992, now Legal Claims Manager of the Trust.

*GWEN CONNELL – Grade E Research Technician at the University of Liverpool, working within the Institute of Child Health, having commenced on 1 January 1986.

*PROFESSOR RICHARD COOKE – Professor of Neonatal Medicine at the University of Liverpool since 1988, Head of the Department of Child Health since 1990.

LOUISE COSTI – Medical Laboratory Assistant at Alder Hey from November 1991 to August 1995.

*ROGER CUDMORE – Consultant Paediatric Surgeon at Alder Hey from May 1972 to August 1995. Health Authority representative on the Appointments Committee for the Chair of Fetal and Infant Pathology.

*DR CAMPBELL DAVIDSON – Consultant Paediatrician at Alder Hey since 1976, and Medical Director since 1 April 1997.

*PAUL DEARLOVE – MLSO at Alder Hey since March 1964 (initially as trainee).

*PAUL ECCLES – MLSO at Alder Hey since September 1991.

*KAREN ENGLAND – MLSO at Alder Hey from July 1978 (initially as trainee) to May 1993, Chief MLSO within the Histopathology Laboratory from 1987 to 1993, thereafter Service Manager in the Cardiac and Intensive Care Directorate from May 1993 to 1994. Thereafter Service Manager of the Theatre Directorate in addition to the Cardiac and Intensive Care Directorate and then acting Service Manager of the Directorate of Clinical Support Services until February 1999. Acting Director of Operational Services from February 1999 to March 2000.

SALLY FERGUSON – Acting Director of Nursing and Service Manager for Community and Mental Health at Alder Hey.

²FRED FOREMAN – Mortuary attendant at Fazakerley Hospital late 1960s/early 1970s.

*PROFESSOR CHRISTOPHER FOSTER – Professor of Pathology at the University of Liverpool and Clinical Director of Pathology at the Royal Liverpool and Broadgreen Hospitals NHS Trust since June 1994.

---

2 A statement was given to the Solicitor to the Inquiry over the telephone: a detailed telephone attendance note was prepared, but no formal statement.

[3]**FOUNDATION FOR THE STUDY OF INFANT DEATHS** – Provided the Grant of £250,000 to support the Chair of Fetal and Infant Pathology at the University of Liverpool in September 1988.

*****ROGER FRANKS** – Consultant Cardiothoracic surgeon at Alder Hey/Myrtle Street Hospital since 1989.

[4]**STEPHEN GOULD** – Consultant Paediatric Pathologist and author of the Internal Inquiry Report published in December 1999.

JUDITH GREENSMITH – Chairman of the Liverpool Health Authority since 1996 and seconded in March 2000 to fulfill the role of Chairman of the Trust.

[5]**PROFESSOR IAN GRIERSO**N – Professor of Ophthalmology at the University of Liverpool since October 1992.

*****PROFESSOR FRANK HARRIS** – Professor of Child Health and Head of the Department of Child Health at the University of Liverpool from October 1974 to December 1989, Dean of the Faculty of Medicine from September 1985 to August 1988.

*****THERESE HARVEY** – Director of Human Resources at Alder Hey since February 1995.

KEITH HAYNES – Unit General Manager of Unit III (the old Liverpool Women's Hospital, the Maternity Hospital, Oxford Street and Mill Road Hospital) from 1991 to 1993.

[6]**PETER HERRING** – Chief Executive of Liverpool Women's Hospital Trust from 1993 to 2000.

*****THOMAS HILL** – Pathology Technician (mortuary) at Alder Hey since 1991.

*****DR VYVYAN HOWARD** – Senior Lecturer in Anatomy at the University of Liverpool, based at Myrtle Street from 1991.

DR DAVID HUGHES – Consultant Paediatric Nephrologist at Alder Hey since August 1993, and present Chairman of the Medical Board.

DR SALIH IBRAHIM – Locum Pathologist at Alder Hey from November 1986 to August 1988.

*****DR DAVID ISHERWOOD** – Consultant Clinical Biochemist at Alder Hey since April 1979, Clinical Director of Pathology from January 1992 to March 1993.

---

3 A written submission together with documentation was provided to the Inquiry confirming the circumstances of the grant and the involvement of the Foundation thereafter.
4 Interviewed on an informal basis by the Chairman and Counsel to the Inquiry in the company of the Secretary to the Inquiry.
5 Interviewed by Counsel to the Inquiry.
6 Interviewed personally by the Secretary to the Inquiry: a formal attendance note was prepared but no statement.

*PROFESSOR PETER JOHNSON – Professor of Immunology at the University
of Liverpool since 1985 and Dean of the Faculty of Medicine since July 1997.

DR BRIAN JUDD – Consultant Paediatric Nephrologist at Alder Hey since February 1991.

PROFESSOR RONALD KASCHULA – Locum Pathologist at Alder Hey from February
1994 to December 1994.

⁷JOHN KENYON – Senior Pathology Technician (Mortuary) at Alder Hey from 1987 to 1995.

*DR MYAT MON KHINE – Honorary Senior Registrar and Lecturer in Fetal and Infant
Pathology at Alder Hey from October 1991 to August 1995, now Consultant Paediatric
Pathologist at Royal Liverpool University Hospital.

*DR GEORGE KOKAI – Honorary Consultant and Senior Lecturer in Paediatric Pathology
at Alder Hey from January 1996, now Consultant Paediatric Pathologist at Alder Hey.

⁸JAMES LEWIS – Clerk to HM Coroner for Liverpool since 1982.

*PROFESSOR DAVID LLOYD – Professor of Paediatric Surgery at the University of
Liverpool and Honorary Consultant Paediatric Surgeon at Alder Hey since August 1988.

*PROFESSOR PHILIP LOVE – Vice Chancellor of the University of Liverpool since
September 1992.

*SHEILA MALONE – Unit General Manager at Alder Hey from May 1986 to July 1990.

VALERIE MANDELSON – Manager (Senior Counsellor at Alder Hey Centre since 1992,
co-ordinated Family Support Team October to December 1999).

*DR JOHN MARTIN – Consultant Paediatrician and Oncologist from August 1967 to March
1997, Medical Director from 1 April 1991 to March 1997.

*DR HEATHER McDOWELL – Senior Registrar in Paediatric Oncology at Alder Hey from
November 1988 to January 1990, thereafter Consultant Paediatric Oncologist at Alder Hey
since July 1991. Chairperson of the Ethics Committee from 1992 to 1996.

DR IAN McFADYEN – Honorary Senior Research Fellow at the Department of Obstetrics
and Gynaecology, University of Liverpool, and Honorary Consultant Obstetrician and
Gynaecologist at Liverpool Women's Hospital. Formerly Medical Director of Liverpool
Obstetrics and Gynaecology NHS Trust from 1991 to 1993.

FIONA McGILL – MLSO at Alder Hey from January 1989 (initially as junior) to July 1995.

7 Interviewed on telephone by the Solicitor to the Inquiry. A detailed attendance note was prepared but
no formal statement.
8 Seen on an informal basis by the Solicitor to the Inquiry in the company of the present Coroner.
No formal statement taken, but made available relevant files to the Inquiry.

[9]**ROXANNE McKAY** – Consultant Paediatrician Cardiac Surgeon at Alder Hey until 1992.

[10]**HENRY MEADE** – Appointed Chief MLSO in Microbiology at Alder Hey in April 1970, Senior Chief for Pathology in 1977, thereafter appointed Service Manager of Pathology in 1991. Left the Trust in November 1999.

WENDY NATALE – Chief Officer of Liverpool Eastern Community Health Council.

*PROFESSOR JAMES NEILSON – Professor of Obstetrics and Gynaecology at the University of Liverpool and Honorary Consultant Obstetrician and Gynaecologist to the Liverpool Women's Hospital. Appointed Consultant Obstetrician and Gynaecologist to the Liverpool Women's Hospital in January 1993. Subsequently chaired the University Review into the Unit of Fetal and Infant Pathology which reported in June 1993.

LIAM NOLAN – Locum MLSO at Alder Hey since November 1999.

*PROFESSOR MICHAEL ORME – Dean of the Faculty of Medicine at the University of Liverpool from August 1991 to July 1996 and now Director of Education and Training for NHS Executive North West.

*DR IAN PEART – Consultant Paediatric Cardiologist at Alder Hey since August 1988.

[11]***MARCO POZZI** – Consultant Cardiac Surgeon at Alder Hey since October 1992.

*DR JANE RATCLIFFE – Consultant in Paediatric Intensive Care at Alder Hey since July 1991.

ANDRE REBELLO – HM Coroner for Liverpool since July 1999.

DR LEWIS ROSENBLOOM – Consultant Paediatric Neurologist at Alder Hey since 1971, also Training Programme Director in Paediatrics for Liverpool Health Authority.

*HILARY ROWLAND – Chief Executive at Alder Hey since December 1993 (now on extended leave).

MANDY RUSSELL – Play co-ordinator (senior manager), help line co-ordinator and then senior manager in the Incident Team from January to May 2000.

SUSAN RUTHERFORD – Director of Personnel at the University of Liverpool since March 1995.

*ALAN SHARPLES – Director of Finance and Information at Alder Hey since December 1993.

9 Interviewed via telephone by the Solicitor to the Inquiry: Ms McKay now works in Canada. A detailed attendance note was prepared but no formal statement.
10 Was invited to give oral evidence but a medical certificate was produced to the Inquiry's satisfaction sufficient to excuse attendance in person.
11 Interviewed by Counsel to the Inquiry.

*DR PETER SIMPSON – Regional Medical Officer for Mersey Regional Health Authority from 1988 to 1992.

*DR AUDREY SMITH – Honorary Research Fellow at the University of Liverpool, originally appointed as technician in the Department of Child Health in 1966.

JASON SWEENEY – Medical Laboratory Assistant from November 1991 to March 1995 at Alder Hey.

*PETER TALLENTIRE – Director of Personnel at Alder Hey from April 1991 to December 1994.

DC CARL THOMPSON – Coroner's Officer in the Liverpool Office from 1992 to 2000.

PROFESSOR ROBERT TINSTON – Regional General Manager of Mersey Regional Health Authority (and thereafter North West Regional Health Authority) from September 1993 to April 1996, now Regional Director of NHS Executive North West.

[12]***DR RICHARD VAN VELZEN** – Previously Professor of Fetal and Infant Pathology at the University of Liverpool from September 1988 to December 1995 and Honorary Consultant Paediatric Pathologist at Alder Hey from September 1988 to December 1994.

STEPHEN WALKINSHAW – Consultant in Fetal and Maternal Medicine at Liverpool Maternity Hospital and thereafter Liverpool Women's Hospital since October 1989.

[13]**JOHN WALSH** – Consultant Orthopaedic Surgeon at Alder Hey.

*JACQUELINE WARING – Chief MLSO at Alder Hey from September 1993 to September 1995.

PROFESSOR JONATHAN WIGGLESWORTH – Consultant Perinatal Pathologist and External Assessor to the Appointments Committee surrounding the Chair of Fetal and Infant Pathology prior to his resignation from that post.

12 The Solicitor to the Inquiry spent two days in the Netherlands interviewing Dr van Velzen. The interview was taped and the full transcript of that interview put in evidence rather than a formal statement prepared. Subsequently Dr van Velzen attended the Inquiry in Liverpool to give oral evidence.

13 Statement prepared by the Trust's solicitors at the request of the Inquiry.

The Inquiry was unable to take evidence from **Professor Donald Heath**, former Head of the Department of Pathology at the University of Liverpool until 1993, who had died in 1995. Medical evidence was supplied on behalf of **Dr Jean Marie Bouton**, previously Consultant Pathologist at Alder Hey until 1986, confirming that he was medically unfit to give evidence. The Inquiry also felt it inappropriate to interview **Professor John Hay**, formerly Professor of Child Health at the University of Liverpool and responsible for establishing the heart collection, and **Patricia Hooton**, Director of Nursing at Alder Hey since April 1991. The former was in his 90s and in poor health whilst the latter had been absent from work for a considerable time for health reasons. **Dr Ralph Latham**, formerly Lecturer in Oral Anatomy at the University of Liverpool and now resident in Canada, failed to co-operate with the Inquiry.

In addition a clinicians' seminar was held at Alder Hey Hospital on 23 May 2000 to facilitate obtaining evidence from as wide a group of doctors as possible.

Appendix 5. Salmon Letters

JJR/CJK/130300
13th March 2000

Dear

Giving evidence to Stephen Jones, the Solicitor to the Inquiry

The Chairman of Royal Liverpool Children's Inquiry has asked me to write to you in my position as Counsel to the Inquiry.

You will have heard of the Inquiry into the removal and retention of organs at Alder Hey. The Inquiry Panel would like to take written evidence from you. Stephen Jones, the Solicitor to the Inquiry, may have already made arrangements to see you through the Solicitors to the Trust or the University. If not, he will be in contact very shortly. Everyone hopes that you will be able to make yourself available and feel able to express yourself openly about what has happened. Before you give evidence I must explain a number of points to you.

Stephen Jones will ask you questions and take a statement of your evidence. In the interests of fairness and so that everyone may do their best, you may, and are encouraged, to have a solicitor of your choice present at the interview. I understand that the Solicitors to the Trust or University will offer their services to you. However if they do not or if you would like a different solicitor for a good reason, the Chairman is likely to offer you reasonable expenses in instructing someone else. It is a matter for you to consider now, and to contact Stephen Jones in advance if you want someone else. The solicitor will be present throughout and will be able to give you advice during the interview if you request it. If you do not want a solicitor present, that is perfectly acceptable as well.

I should also explain another important matter to you in the interest of fairness. Stephen Jones and all other members of the Inquiry Team will treat you with courtesy and consideration. The Inquiry is not a 'witch hunt'. The procedures adopted by the Chairman will ensure that you give your evidence in private and that the sources of all evidence will remain confidential. However, the Report will set out the Inquiry's findings based on that confidential evidence, and it is quite possible that some individuals will be mentioned in relation to those findings (as against in the giving of evidence itself). It is therefore appropriate for those who may have adverse comment made of them to have an opportunity to prepare properly and to say what they wish to justify their position. It is my duty to give you that opportunity. However, in an Inquiry of this nature where the Panel does not know in advance what the evidence will throw up, it is impossible for me to tell you now, specifically, if the Panel consider it likely that adverse comment may be made of you, and precisely on which matters.

In order to do the best in the circumstances, the Chairman has asked me to write to everyone, other than parents, who is invited to give evidence, in similar terms. You should not feel that because you receive this letter you are particularly likely to receive adverse comment. I enclose the draft of what the Panel presently perceives as the areas that it wishes to examine. Many of the Issues will not apply to you. However, you should consider in advance all areas on which you think you may be able to assist the Inquiry. When all the written evidence has been obtained, I can assure you that the Panel will consider it carefully. If it is likely that adverse comment may be made of you, the Panel will invite you to give oral evidence at a later date. Before that occasion I will write to you again and identify the areas where the Panel may be considering adverse comment and where your evidence may clash with that of others. This will enable you to meet any potential for criticism.

Please take this letter as it is intended. The Panel's sole aim is to establish what happened and to make recommendations to prevent recurrence. It is everyone's wish to re-establish Alder Hey and the University in their rightful positions of excellence.

Yours sincerely

J James Rowley
Counsel to the Inquiry

Our Ref: JR/BC/Velzen1206

12th June 2000

Dr R van Velzen

Dear Dr van Velzen

Detailed 'Salmon' letter

Thank you for giving such detailed evidence to Stephen Jones. I can see from the transcript, which I have studied with great interest, that you have had the opportunity to put your side of the affair. As I promised in my first letter to you, it is now my duty to warn you of the areas where there may be adverse criticism, insofar as it is possible to do so at this stage. I should emphasise that the Inquiry is still hearing evidence and has not made up its mind on anything. All that appears below simply has the status of 'allegation' or 'facts yet to be proved'; and the whole purpose of my writing to you and the Panel hearing your oral evidence next week is so that the Panel can form a truly balanced view of all the allegations and evidence. The list below is one-sided, in the sense that it sets out the allegations which do not reflect well on you; but I can assure you that everyone at the Inquiry has read your interview with Mr Jones and appreciated all the points that you make. But you will understand that, in the same way as the Panel has not yet fully made a decision in relation to the evidence of other witnesses and their allegations that impact upon you, it cannot simply accept at the moment the evidence which you give in your own favour and which adversely affects others. Similarly, this letter does not focus on allegations that can be made against the Hospital and University.

As you will appreciate, there is a large amount of evidence now before the Inquiry, much of which is relevant but some of which is peripheral. I hope to help you to focus your preparation not by setting out a long disjointed list of small points, but in identifying the areas and trends that you need to consider.

I can best put the majority of the allegations by building up in chronological order the points which the Trust and University are likely to urge upon the Panel. I am well aware of your position in relation to these points as I have already said.

You will appreciate the strictly confidential nature of the information and allegations contained in this letter. Apart from your legal adviser, if you have one, the content of this letter remains confidential to you and the Inquiry and should not be divulged to any other individual in any circumstances.

1.   Appointment

a)   …

b)   It is the perception of some that your appointment was a 'fix' engineered by Professors Harris and Emery.

2.   September 1988 – end 1989

a)   …

b)   At any rate, it was not long before you realised that there were no further resources to be had at Alder Hey and, to use your own phrase, you had to embark upon 'zero money' research.

c)   You were unable to generate any serious outside money over and above the FSID grant which was already allocated in terms of resource.

d)   Well before you raised resources as an issue with management, and in fact immediately upon your arrival in Liverpool, you began to collect whole/multi organs without completing histology and providing a final post mortem report.

e)   It is alleged that you never 'blocked' organs when carrying out the autopsy at Alder Hey, but preferred always to put whole organs into pots. Unblocked whole organs were an integral part of the research technique of stereology which you were intending to use. In any event it is alleged that your primary motive in retaining all organs intact in every case was not to carry out a full clinical histological examination, but rather to establish a 'tissue bank' for research, with a broad range of material to cover all the twists and turns that your research might take.

f)   The Inquiry has seen nothing in writing (and I repeat the invitation of Stephen Jones to provide your documents immediately to the Inquiry) which explicitly alleges that it was the management's decision to suspend post mortem histology until your paper in March 1993 sent to Mr Butler and Dr Martin. While there are documents complaining generally of resource difficulties, as you will see below, none alleges that it was a management decision before March 1993.

g)   The fact that you understood that Alder Hey had no more resources is alleged to militate against your position that tissue was only ever taken for purely clinical reasons. If resources were non-existent, why not take small specimens of the important organs only?

h) There was no standard international protocol dictating that every organ be taken whole and retained for histology, the body being buried as a shell. Again, the zero money/zero resource argument, it is said, militates to taking less material and carrying out fewer tests rather than taking entire sets of whole organs.

i) Your 'Five Year Vision' paper dated 13th December 1989, produced shortly after Mr Butler arrived as the shadow Chief Executive of the 'embryonic' Trust, significantly made no complaint with regard to your ability to carry out post mortem examinations and histology in particular. You made no complaint in that paper in relation to problems typing post mortem reports. Indeed you represented that you needed no further resources on that score.

j) The resources you sought in your 'Five Year Vision' paper in relation to fetal/stillborn work were given to you.

k) At the time of the 'Five Year Vision' paper dozens of post mortems were already incomplete and there were hundreds of pots of organs.

l) In relation to the typing/resource argument raised by you, it is said that you were an extremely fast typist, as good as your PA Margery Clark, and that after a short period when you used the typing pool, your post mortem report was essentially set up on a computer macro. In those circumstances it is alleged that you misrepresented the amount of time that you had to spend typing post mortem reports and that it was your own choice anyway.

m) By the end of 1989 Dr Chan had arrived and it is said that you were already putting upon him to carry out the clinical work to the detriment of his research work, such that you were able to devote the majority of your time to other matters.

n) Over the early years of your time in Liverpool, it is alleged that you sacrificed your clinical practice without permission in so far as the Trust were concerned in the amount of time you spent away from the Department including:

   (i) Days when you were in Holland with your family and with your SSZD commitment

   (ii) Days in Switzerland on work with Ciba Geigy

   (iii) Preparation for and attendance at Seminars and Conferences

   (iv) Preparation and attendance at FSID meetings

   (v) Meetings to do with the centralisation of pathology services in the Merseyside area

   (vi) Confocal

   (vii) …

   (viii) Corresponding with hospital and university authorities and attempting to raise funds.

The Panel fully understands your explanation as set out in your witness statement and that you claim to have had assurances from the University that all was in order. Nevertheless, it is alleged that you were not in fact providing a full six clinical sessions to the hospital on clinical work even in this early period.

3.   1990

a)   Your letter to Mr Butler on 17th January 1990 did not identify any so called management decision to suspend post mortem histology or even identify a specific case with regard to resources on that score. The inference is that there was no such genuine case.

b)   The complaint in the case of … in the summer of 1990 led to you being told by Sheila Malone to prioritise your work and yet it prompted nothing in writing, to the Inquiry's knowledge, blaming the 'management decision to suspend post mortem histology' or complaining about lack of resource on that score. It will be argued that there should be the same inference.

c)   Later on there are letters on file from clinicians, complaining, prior to your March 1993 paper. There are no letters from clinicians in the early years complaining that post mortem histology had been suspended, still less complaining that management had made the decision. Clinicians interviewed appear not to have realised that there was any formal suspension of post mortem histology. If the evidence as to the numbers of complaints, informally initially coming into your department and in particular through Margery Clark is accepted in 1990, it is argued that it is surprising that you did not give such an excuse of 'management decision' to the clinicians, which would almost certainly have generated documentation.

d)   …

4.   1991

a)   Your contribution to the Second Alder Hey Business Plan, undated but clearly in the early part of 1991, for the first time sets out unequivocal evidence to management that 'post mortem histology was still not possible ....' You identified resource difficulties in general terms. It is said that, crucially, you still did not identify the decision to suspend post mortem histology with a management decision. You did not make any specific case as to a failure of resource in that regard, or previous complaints as to resource in relation to post mortem histology.

b)   Following your Business Plan contribution in early 1991 it appears that Mr Birrell and Mr Tallantire became involved and there was a series of meetings in which they tried to get an impression of the work of the Unit. It may be alleged that you failed to help them understand the department or even misled them.

c)   In the second half of 1991 there were substantial dealings with the Unit III contracts as to which you made no complaint in relation to resources, other than seeking MLA assistance, which you were given. Nevertheless, there was a poor start to the Unit III work with immediate backlogs.

5.   1992

a)   In mid summer 1992 Mr Butler and Mr Birrell visited Myrtle Street and it is said that they were staggered at the numbers of people working there on the research side. The decision to relocate the laboratory from Myrtle Street to Alder Hey appears to have taken a hold, if not a complete hold, following this visit.

b)   You were asked to produce a paper on the Department which you did, and it is said to be inaccurate in the way in which it portrays huge numbers of people all carrying out substantial clinical work. It is said that your representation that the Department was biased towards the clinical side, by a substantial percentage, essentially reversed the reality in which research overwhelmed the clinical work. Numerous people were working within the department of whom the Trust and University were unaware.

c)   While perhaps half hearted attempts were made to audit your Department by Mr Highcock and Mr Harris in the autumn of 1992, it is alleged that you continued to put up a 'smoke screen' on the amount of time that the technicians really spent on clinical as opposed to research work.

d)   In or about November 1992 when you had a confidential review of your performance with Professor Orme, it is alleged that you told Professor Orme that you were essentially carrying out none of your clinical sessions.

e)   Towards the end of 1992 the number of complaints began to rise, putting you, Trust Management and University under increased pressure.

6.   1993 – end of University Review in June 1993

a)   The reorganisation of the main Department of Pathology coupled with the review of your own department appeared to put things in limbo in the early part of 1993, while complaints, especially from Dr Choonara, continued. It is said that under increasing pressure you decided to go to the press with your SIDS research and general 'scare mongering' in relation to the future of the Department.

b) The March 1993 Paper can be seen as part of your reaction to events. It is said that Karen England made no substantial contribution to the drafting of the history and views in that paper, and disagrees with them.

c) You have already given detailed evidence to Mr Jones in relation to the University Review, and why you did not bring out in front of the Review the shortcomings in your own service. It is said that you misled the Committee in representing that you were carrying out your clinical duties, namely six sessions, when you were contributing virtually nothing in terms of clinical work at that time. Such work was being carried out by Dr June Khine, who was essentially unqualified, and lacking much in the way of supervision from you. The paper(s) you prepared for the University Review contradicted the stance taken in your March 1993 Paper.

7. July – December 1993

a) While the Trust pressed for the appointment of the Senior Lecturer and Mr Butler continued negotiations in relation to the Unit III work, attempts to audit your department through Mr Lewis, in a formal external report, and Mr Harris internally met with the same 'smoke screen'.

b) It is alleged that in late 1993 you proposed that the mortuary technicians processed material, when in fact you had no such intention and were simply buying time or attempting to make a case for a new Microtome machine. A suggestion that material be processed in the mortuary was also made by Dr Khine,but you responded that it was necessary to fix the organs before blocking them. In those circumstances it is said that you can have had no genuine intention that the mortuary technicians prepare material.

8. 1994

a) Just before the New Year (1994) began Hilary Rowland arrived. It is said that you deliberately misrepresented your state of knowledge as to the relocation of the Myrtle Street Department up to Alder Hey in a letter dated 23rd December 1993. You continued with the 'smoke screen' that the department was a fully integrated NHS and Academic department. You wrote to Hilary Rowland, and had Mrs Waring write to Hilary Rowland in January 1994, misrepresenting the clinical output of the Department, attaching a misleading specimen rota showing the clinical work of the department, and making a misleading case for the conversion of Paul Eccles' employment from 'soft' money to Trust status.

b) In 1994 your clinical input is said to have been virtually none, as Dr Kaschula and Dr Khine carried the clinical workload.

c) In the rest of 1994 there is little said against you. Dr Kaschula was working as a locum and the clinical service improved. Some further attempts were made to convert Paul

Eccles' status. The events of 1994 are largely those behind the scenes between the Trust and University, and they are not allegations that are for you to answer.

9.   1995

a)   It is said that while you purported to catch up some of the Unit III backlog in March 1995 you effectively ceased to carry out any real work even on the University/Unit III side. Again, there is little to be said by way of allegation against you during this year other than a failure to fulfil your contract with the University.

10.   Additional points

There are a number of important points that you should consider which do not fit neatly into a chronological analysis. You should consider the following which, again, I stress are allegations only, at this stage, but they require your assistance to answer.

a)   You are asked to explain in detail the circumstances leading up to your acceptance of a reprimand, ostensibly for failings similar to those at Alder Hey, when working in Nova Scotia.

b)   It is alleged that there has been apparent falsification in some of your Reports. The following are by way of specimen case studies and not an exhaustive list:-

   i)   Cases in which you have purported to report including specific organ weights, when there has been total removal of viscera en-bloc and where the individual organs cannot conceivably have been weighed – [5 cases]. The post mortem reports are available for your inspection at the Inquiry as are detailed photographs of the current state of the organs.

   ii)   Cases in which you went beyond a limited consent to hospital post mortem, e.g. for thoracic organs only, taking all organs in line with your usual practice – [2 cases] below. Again, the consent form and your post mortem preliminary report are available for inspection at the Inquiry.

   iii)   In the above category of going beyond permission for limited post mortem is to be included the case of …. Permission was only granted for a biopsy in the form of a specimen from the lung through a small incision. You took all the organs as was your usual practice at post mortem. When the fact that a full post mortem examination became clear in early 1994 and the parents would not let matters lie, you wrote a letter to the parents on 21st July 1994 in which you said that you were able to assess many of the organs by gently touching them and feeling for abnormalities and that included the general assessment of size. You claimed that no post mortem had been carried out in the classic sense, and you did not interfere with the skull or damage the body. You continued with a number of statements which are said to be fantastic including that you were able to assess by hand the weight of an organ…. You concluded that consent to the post mortem examination had been signed and was indeed limited to a chest incision and lung biopsy. The Panel invite your detailed evidence on how you could come to write such a letter, as well as dealing with this case as a specimen where you went beyond the limited permission.

c) It is said that your method of working in which you took few or no notes, coupled with the delay in writing reports, led to inevitable inaccuracy, no matter how good your memory. In the case of … who was a SIDS case on the death certificate and died on 9th September 1990 you had a meeting with the family at which Mr Butler was present. It is said that you attended the meeting without notes, were of no help, and your attitude is criticised. You changed the death certificate to read 'Sudden Death, choking episode, airway obstruction'. It is said that no histology had been done prior to the alteration of the death certificate.

d) The Inquiry seeks from you greater detail as to why it is that collections of fetus from Professor Harris and Professor Gosden were delivered to, and remain at, Myrtle Street. In addition you are asked to explain why it is substantial numbers of fetus remain from prior to the establishment of the formal contract with Unit III when it was part of the agreement that they should have been disposed of respectfully by way of burial.

e) It is said that you advised the ICH, and Audrey Smith in particular, as to the requirements of Polkinghorne in 1990. The Inquiry asks you to reconsider the terms and requirements of Polkinghorne, and in particular as to the forms that were agreed between you and Audrey Smith. What steps did you take to satisfy yourself, and advise others to take, that proper informed consent was being obtained?

f) As can be seen from the chronology above, it is said that you told lies to the Trust and University, playing one off against the other.

g) It is said that you failed to provide your contractual clinical sessions to Alder Hey and that you repeatedly falsified the real throughput of clinical work in the Department in your case for resources. You persuaded Karen England and Jackie Waring to go along with you and implicated them. The Panel are well aware of what you said at interview with Mr Jones in relation to the logging of specimens in the Laboratory Day Book. However, you are invited to view the Day Book before giving evidence so as to refresh your memory on the detail of double accounting, booking in fetus and placentae as separate specimens, including post mortem histology in the routine Day Book, and in particular the channeling of large numbers of research specimens through the standard Laboratory Day Book. It is said that, however easy it may have been to identify which was which through looking at the book, whenever cases were made to management in relation to resources the total number as against the purely clinical number of requests each year was given.

h) The Panel wishes to ask you further as to your motive in slowing down and preventing the flow of hearts to the ICH, and your failure to take part in the UKCCSG scheme.

i)   The Panel asks you to develop, if you can, your allegation as to the Coroner's knowledge of wholesale organ retention. At the moment it appears to depend upon the Coroner having a knowledge of what you allege to be a protocol in terms of the removal of all whole organs at the time of autopsy. The Coroner and indeed nearly everyone involved has denied such knowledge.

j)   …

k)   It is suggested that while the Royal College of Pathologists' Report in 1990 suggested greater resources than you had available for a Regional Centre, the work that you actually provided fell well short of that envisaged in the Report, and hence you should have been able to cope, albeit with some difficulty.

l)   Above all, it is alleged that you sacrificed the mental well being of parents in delay and whole organ retention, and sometimes the clinical welfare of them and children yet to be born, in your desire for research.

I know that you have been liaising with Mr Jones and he will sort out with you an opportunity for you to see the documents in the possession of the Inquiry. From having read your interview, it seems to me that you are well aware of the main documents in any event. While I can find in our files many documents that you refer to in your interview the Inquiry is reliant upon you to provide us with any documents that you consider to be relevant on any of the above points. For obvious reasons and in order to ensure that when you give your evidence it all goes smoothly, the Inquiry needs to see your documents in Liverpool by the end of this week i.e. Friday, 16th June 2000. Mr Jones will be able to make arrangements with you to provide you with a room and the Inquiry's documents at any time to suit you, and that will include the coming weekend if you can give us some notice.

Finally, I am obliged to write to you in these specific terms so that everyone can do their best and everything is above board. I cannot emphasise enough to you that the contents of this letter do not constitute the view of the Inquiry Panel at this stage nor even a provisional view. Everything said in this letter still requires to be proved, and in weighing up whether any individual point is proved your evidence will be invaluable and attended to with the utmost care.

I anticipate that you will speak to Mr Jones, whom you have met, but if you would like to speak to me to clarify anything at all, you are free to telephone me at the Inquiry directly.

Yours sincerely

J JAMES ROWLEY
Counsel to the Inquiry

Appendix 6. Human Tissue Act, 1961

(9 & 10 ELIZ. 2, c. 54)

An Act to make provision with respect to the use of parts of bodies of deceased persons for therapeutic purposes and purposes of medical education and research and with respect to the circumstances in which post-mortem examinations may be carried out; and to permit the cremation of bodies removed for anatomical examination.   [27th July, 1961]

General Note

This Act permits the removal of parts of the body of a deceased person for medical purposes if the person has in writing requested that his body or any part of it should be used for therapeutic purposes or for the purposes of medical education or research, or the person has made such a request orally during his last illness in the presence of two or more witnesses (s. 1 (1)); the persons lawfully in possession of the body (other than persons merely in possession for the purpose of burial or cremation) may authorise the removal of any part of the body for medical purposes if, after making all reasonable enquiries which are practicable, they have no reason to believe that the deceased had expressed an objection to the body being so dealt with, and had not withdrawn this objection, or that the surviving spouse or any surviving relative of the deceased object (s. 1 (2)); removal of part of the body must be done by a fully registered medical practitioner, who must satisfy himself that life is extinct (s. 1 (4)); the Act does not apply to post-mortem examinations carried out to discover the cause of death or to investigate abnormal conditions (s. 2); bodies may be cremated (as an alternative to burial) after an anatomical examination under s. 13 of the Anatomy Act, 1832 (2 & 3 Will. 4, c. 75) (s. 3); s. 4, short title, etc.

The Corneal Grafting Act, 1952 (15 & 16 Geo. 6 and 1 Eliz. 2, c. 28), is repealed (s. 4).

The Act came into force on September 27, 1961, two months after it received the Royal Assent.

For parliamentary debates, see H.L. Vol. 233, cols. 54, 1051; H.C. Vol. 632, col. 1231; Vol. 643, col. 819.

Scotland

The Act applies to Scotland with the modifications contained in s. 1 (9).

Northern Ireland

The Act does not apply to Northern Ireland (s. 4 (4)).

Removal of parts of bodies for medical purposes

1.—(1) If any person, either in writing at any time or orally in the presence of two or more witnesses during his last illness, has expressed a request that his body or any specified part of his body be used after his death for therapeutic purposes or for purposes of medical education or research, the person lawfully in possession of his body after his death may, unless he has reason to believe that the request was subsequently withdrawn, authorise the removal from the body of any part or, as the case may be, the specified part, for use in accordance with the request.

(2) Without prejudice to the foregoing subsection, the person lawfully in possession of the body of a deceased person may authorise the removal of any part from the body for use for the said purposes if, having made such reasonable enquiry as may be practicable, he has no reason to believe—

(a) that the deceased had expressed an objection to his body being so dealt with after his death, and had not withdrawn it; or

(b) that the surviving spouse or any surviving relative of the deceased objects to the body being so dealt with.

(3) Subject to subsections (4) and (5) of this section, the removal and use of any part of a body in accordance with an authority given in pursuance of this section shall be lawful.

(4) No such removal shall be effected except by a fully registered medical practitioner, who must have satisfied himself by personal examination of the body that life is extinct.

(5) Where a person has reason to believe that an inquest may be required to be held on any body or that a post-mortem examination of any body may be required by the coroner, he shall not, except with the consent of the coroner,—

(a) give an authority under this section in respect of the body; or

(b) act on such an authority given by any other person.

(6) No authority shall be given under this section in respect of any body by a person entrusted with the body for the purpose only of its interment or cremation.

(7) In the case of a body lying in a hospital, nursing home or other institution, any authority under this section may be given on behalf of the person having the control and management thereof by any officer or person designated for that purpose by the first-mentioned person.

(8) Nothing in this section shall be construed as rendering unlawful any dealing with, or with any part of, the body of a deceased person which is lawful apart from this Act.

(9) In the application of this section to Scotland, for subsection (5) there shall be substituted the following subsection:—

"(5) Nothing in this section shall authorise the removal of any part from a body in any case where the procurator fiscal has objected to such removal."

As to post-mortem examinations, see s. 2.

Post-mortem examinations

2.—(1) Without prejudice to section fifteen of the Anatomy Act, 1832 (which prevents that Act from being construed as applying to post-mortem examinations directed to be made by a competent legal authority), that Act shall not be construed as applying to any post-mortem examination carried out for the purpose of establishing or confirming the causes of death or of investigating the existence or nature of abnormal conditions.

(2) No post-mortem examination shall be carried out otherwise than by or in accordance with the instructions of a fully registered medical practitioner, and no post-mortem examination which is not directed or requested by the coroner or any other competent legal authority shall be carried

out without the authority of the person lawfully in possession of the body; and subsections (2), (5), (6) and (7) of section one of this Act shall, with the necessary modifications, apply with respect to the giving of that authority.

Cremation of bodies after anatomical examination

3. The provision to be made and the certificate to be transmitted under section thirteen of the Anatomy Act, 1832, in respect of a body removed for anatomical examination may, instead of being provision for and a certificate of burial, as mentioned in that section, be provision for the cremation of the body in accordance with the Cremation Acts, 1902 and 1952, and a certificate of the cremation.

Short title, etc.

4.—(1) This Act may be cited as the Human Tissue Act, 1961.

(2) The Corneal Grafting Act, 1952, is hereby repealed.

(3) This Act shall come into operation at the expiration of a period of two months beginning with the day on which it is passed.

(4) This Act does not extend to Northern Ireland.

Glossary

Alder Centre – based at Alder Hey and which was formed in 1989 by a small group of health care professionals in partnership with bereaved parents. This unique centre was established as a blueprint for bereavement support.

Antenatal – before birth.

Autopsy – dissection and examination of a body after death in order to determine the cause of death or presence of disease processes (also post mortem examination and **necropsy**).

Bacteriology – the science concerned with the study of bacteria and the effects of bacteria.

Biopsy – the removal of a small piece of tissue from an organ or part of the body for microscopic examination to discover the presence, cause, or extent of a disease.

CNS – central nervous system.

Cerebellum – the largest part of the brain located at the back of the skull.

Cerebral hemisphere – one of the two paired halves of the cerebrum (the largest and most highly developed part of the brain).

CESDI – Confidential Enquiries of Stillbirths and Deaths in Infancy.

CESDI Protocols – Protocols recommended by the Royal College of Pathologists when dealing with Sudden Infant Death Syndrome (SIDS).

CHC – Community Health Council.

Clinician – a doctor having direct contact with and responsibility for treating patients, rather than one involved with theoretical or laboratory studies.

CMO (Chief Medical Officer) – the Government's most senior medical adviser, who is responsible to the Secretary of State for Health for all of the Department of Health's medical matters.

Congenital – describing a condition that is recognised at birth or that is believed to have been present since birth. Congenital malformations include all disorders present at birth whether they are inherited or caused by an environmental factor.

Consultant – a fully trained specialist in a branch of medicine who accepts total responsibility for patient care. In Britain consultants are usually responsible for the care of patients in hospital wards but they are allowed to opt for some sessions in private practice in addition to any National Health Service commitments. After registration, doctors continuing in hospital service are appointed as 'senior house officers' and then obtain 'specialist registrar post' (which replaces the old registrar and senior registrar posts) in their chosen speciality.

Coroner – the official who presides at an Inquest. He must be either a medical practitioner or a lawyer of at least five years' experience.

Coroner's post mortem (CPM) – not dependent upon parental consent but demanded by law in certain circumstances in particular when the cause of death appears unknown. The Coroner is appointed and paid by the Local Authority and is accountable to the courts for his judicial decisions and, via the Home Office, to the Lord Chancellor's Department for his conduct and administration. After notification of the death the Coroner is empowered to request a post mortem examination and he may also decide to hold an inquest in certain circumstances.

Cot death – the death of a baby, often occurring overnight while it is in its cot, from an unidentifiable cause, also known as Sudden Infant Death Syndrome **(SIDS)**.

DHA – District Health Authority (see Chapter 6 Accountability Structure: Simplified NHS (England) Organisation Chart 1982).

DoFIP – 'Department of Fetal and Infant Pathology'. Terminology sometimes used by Professor van Velzen to describe the Unit of Fetal and Infant Pathology, which in fact was part of the Department of Pathology.

Dyson Report – name given to the audit carried out on pathology services across Merseyside in 1994 by Professor Dyson and his team from Keele University. Various criticisms were made of histopathology at Alder Hey: '*The organisation, funding and cross-charging arrangements within the histopathology department are so labyrinthine as to make it impossible within the scope of this exercise to reach firm conclusions about productivity and efficiency.*' The Report concluded that the Trust should establish an internal review of the Department with a view to identifying the total workload and the proportion which was clinical as opposed to University workload.

Epidemiology – the study of epidemic disease and communicable diseases with a view to finding means of control and future prevention.

Ethics Committee – (in Britain) a group including lay people, medical practitioners, and other experts set up (especially in a hospital) to monitor investigations, concerned with teaching or research, that involve the use of human subjects. It is responsible for ensuring that patients are adequately informed of the procedures involved in a research project (including the use of dummy or placebo treatments as controls), that the tests and/or therapies are safe, and that no one is pressurised into participating.

Evisceration – the removal of organs after death from the human body.

Fetus – an unborn child from its eighth week of development.

Formalin – a water solution containing 40% formaldehyde. In pathological laboratories it is used to preserve human organs and tissue.

FSID – the Foundation for the Study of Infant Deaths.

Gestation – the period during which a fertilized egg cell develops into a baby that is ready to be delivered. In humans gestation averages 266 days.

Gould Report – an internal inquiry report commissioned by Alder Hey in October 1999 and produced in December 1999 by Dr Stephen Gould, Consultant Paediatric Pathologist, John Radcliffe Hospital, Oxford.

GRP – the Grant Review Panel of the Foundation for the Study of Infant Deaths.

Griffiths Report – NHS Management Inquiry Report, DHSS, London published in October 1983.

Gynaecology – the study of diseases of women and girls, particularly those affecting the female reproductive system.

HA – Health Authority.

HEFCE – Higher Education Funding Council for England.

Histology – the study of the structure of tissues by means of special staining techniques combined with light and electron microscopy.

Histopathology – the branch of medicine concerned with the changes in tissues caused by disease.

Hospital post mortem (HPM) – under the terms of the Human Tissue Act 1961 a clinician who wishes to have a hospital post mortem examination performed following the death of child must satisfy himself, 'having made such reasonable enquiry as may be practicable', that the surviving relatives have no objection to the post mortem examination. The purpose of the hospital post mortem examination is to enable clinicians to tell surviving relatives more about the likely cause of death, counsel them appropriately and also learn generally for the future in relation to the treatment of other children with similar problems.

ICH – Institute of Child Health which is based at the Alder Hey site.

IUGR – Intrauterine growth retardation.

Inquest – an official judicial enquiry into the cause of a person's death: carried out when the death is sudden or takes place under suspicious circumstances.

Lewis Audit – District Audit of Pathology Services prepared in September 1993 by Mr Lewis. The audit failed to form any firm conclusions in relation to the financial position of the Pathology Department at Alder Hey but did note that all clinicians felt the histology service had deteriorated over previous two years.

LHA – Liverpool Health Authority.

LREC – Local Research Ethics Committee. The purpose of a local research ethics committee is to consider the ethics of proposed research projects which will involve human subjects, and which will take place broadly within the NHS. The LREC's task is to advise the NHS body under the auspices of which the research is intended to take place. It is that NHS body which has the responsibility to decide whether or not the project should go ahead, taking account of the ethical advice of the LREC.

Locum – a doctor or clinician who stands in temporarily for a colleague who is absent or ill.

Macroscopy – naked eye examination of the human body and organs.

MIAA – Mersey Internal Audit Agency, commissioned to provide internal audit services for a number of local north west NHS Health Authorities and Trusts.

Microscopy – the use of a microscope to greatly magnify an image of an organ, tissue, etc, which may be so small as to be invisible to the naked eye. The use of optical microscopes, electron microscopes, operating microscopes and ultramicroscopes are all different forms of microscopy.

MLA – Medical Laboratory Assistant.

MLSO – Medical Laboratory Scientific Officer.

Morphology – a medical term used as a comparative in conjunction with anatomy (the study of the form and gross structure of the various parts of the human body).

MREC – Multi-Centre Research Ethics Committee – established in 1997 in each of the eight Regions across England. (See Chapter 6 – Accountability Structure, paragraph 10.6 for a more detailed explanation.)

Necropsy – another word for **autopsy**.

Neonate – an infant at any time during the first four weeks of life. This word is particularly applied to infants just born or in the first week of life.

Neurologist – a doctor who studies the structure, functioning and diseases of the nervous system including the brain, spinal cord and all the peripheral nerves.

Neuropsychologist – a doctor who studies the relationship between behaviour and brain function.

NICE – National Institute for Clinical Excellence.

Obstetrics – the branch of medical science concerned with the care of women during pregnancy, childbirth, and the period of about six weeks following the birth, when the reproductive organs are recovering.

Ophthalmology – the branch of medicine that is devoted to the study and treatment of eye diseases.

Organ (Oxford Concise English Dictionary) – a usually self-contained part of an organism having a special vital function (example, vocal organs; digestive organs).

Organ (Oxford Concise Medical Dictionary) – a part of the body, composed of more than one tissue, that forms a structural unit responsible for a particular function (or functions). Examples are the heart, lungs and liver.

Paediatrics – the branch of medicine dealing with children and their diseases.

Palpation – the process of examining part of the body by careful feeling with the hands and fingertips.

Paternalism – the policy of restricting the freedom and responsibilities of one's subordinates or dependants in their supposed best interest.

Pathology – the study of disease processes with the aim of understanding their nature and causes. This is achieved by observing samples of blood, urine, faeces, and diseased tissue obtained from the living patient or at **autopsy**, by the use of X-rays and many other techniques.

Pathologist – a doctor qualified in the study of **pathology**.

Perinatal – relating to the period starting a few weeks before birth and including the birth and a few weeks after birth.

PITY II – Parents who Inter Their Young Twice (Parent Support Group set up as a result of the revelation of organ retention at Alder Hey).

Placenta – an **organ** within the uterus (womb) by means of which the embryo is attached to the wall of the uterus. Its primary function is to provide the embryo with nourishment, eliminate its wastes and exchange respiratory gases. It also functions as a gland secreting hormones, which regulate the maintenance of pregnancy.

Polkinghorne Report – name commonly given to the 'Review of the Guidance on Research Use of Fetuses and Fetal Material' which was published in 1989. The Department of Health subsequently accepted this report as proper practice. Effectively it stated that explicit written consent of the mother was required for fetal research after July 1989, even though strictly the pre-viable fetus and the mother had no rights in law.

Post Mortem report – the report compiled from information obtained as a result of post mortem examination.

Post natal – following birth.

Pulmonary – relating to, associated with, or affecting the lungs.

Radiologist – a doctor specialised in the interpretation of X-rays and other scanning techniques for the diagnosis of disorders.

RHA – Regional Health Authority. (See Chapter 6 Accountability Structure: Simplified NHS (England) Organisation Chart 1991.)

RLC(NHS)Trust – Royal Liverpool Children's NHS Trust (Alder Hey Hospital).

RLUH – Royal Liverpool University Hospital.

SAC – Scientific Advisory Committee of the **FSID**.

SANDS – Society for Stillbirth And Neonatal Death.

Section – in **microscopy** a section is a thin slice of the specimen to be examined under a microscope. In surgery it is the act of cutting.

Scott-Grant Report – in May 1991 Scott-Grant Management Services Limited produced a preliminary report for Mr Butler into the organisation and staffing levels of Pathology. The aim of the report was 'to provide an estimate of potential efficiency and cost improvement measures, organisational changes and quality enhancements, together with a time-scale for the implementation of any recommendations'.

SIDS – Sudden Infant Death Syndrome (see **Cot death**).

SIPB – Special Incident Project Board set up in March 2000 at Alder Hey to manage organ retention issues.

Stereology – method of **microscopy** using mathematical and statistical theory based on unbiased random sub-samples leading to accurate three-dimensional conclusions for the whole sample.

Stillbirth – birth of a **fetus** that shows no evidence of life (heartbeat, respiration or independent movement) at any time later than 24 weeks after conception. *Under the Stillbirth Definition Act 1992 there is a legal obligation to notify all stillbirths to the appropriate authority.*

SUDI – Sudden Unexpected Death in Infancy.

Tissue – A collection of cells specialised to perform a particular function.

Unit III – encompassed Mill Road Hospital, which subsequently closed in 1993, Liverpool Maternity Hospital, which closed in 1995, and the Women's Hospital in Catherine Street, which also closed in 1995. The three hospitals were incorporated into the new Liverpool Women's Hospital. The Liverpool Obstetric and Gynaecology Services NHS Trust (later renamed Liverpool Women's Hospital NHS Trust) was established in April 1992 to manage the hospitals.

Viable fetus – a **fetus** capable of living a separate existence after birth. The legal age of viability of a fetus is 24 weeks – 'Still-Birth (Definition) Act 1992 – An Act to amend the law in respect of the definition of still-birth; to make certain consequential amendments of the law; and for connected purposes. 16th March 1992'. The Act says:

1.   *– (1) In section 12 of the Births and Deaths Registration Act 1926 (definitions) and section 41 of the Births and Deaths Registration Act 1953 (interpretation), in the provisions which relate to the meaning of 'still-born child' for the words 'twenty-eighth week', in both places where they occur, there shall be substituted 'twenty-fourth week'.*

However, some fetus survive birth at an even earlier stage of **gestation**.

Virology – the science of viruses.

Viscera – the organs within the body cavities, especially the organs of the abdominal cavities (stomach, intestines, etc), hence **evisceration**.

Index